Scientific Computing in Modern C++

SOFTWARE • ENVIRONMENTS • TOOLS

The SIAM series on Software, Environments, and Tools focuses on the practical implementation of computational methods and the high performance aspects of scientific computation by emphasizing in-demand software, computing environments, and tools for computing. Software technology development issues such as current status, applications and algorithms, mathematical software, software tools, languages and compilers, computing environments, and visualization are presented.

Software, Environments, and Tools

Victor Eijkhout, *Scientific Computing in Modern C++*
Walter Gautschi, *A Software Repository for Gaussian Quadratures and Christoffel Functions*
Ed Bueler, *PETSc for Partial Differential Equations: Numerical Solutions in C and Python*
D. L. Chopp, *Introduction to High Performance Scientific Computing*
Thomas Huckle and Tobias Neckel, *Bits and Bugs: A Scientific and Historical Review of Software Failures in Computational Science*
Thomas F. Coleman and Wei Xu, *Automatic Differentiation in MATLAB Using ADMAT with Applications*
Walter Gautschi, *Orthogonal Polynomials in MATLAB: Exercises and Solutions*
Daniel J. Bates, Jonathan D. Hauenstein, Andrew J. Sommese, and Charles W. Wampler, *Numerically Solving Polynomial Systems with Bertini*
Uwe Naumann, *The Art of Differentiating Computer Programs: An Introduction to Algorithmic Differentiation*
C. T. Kelley, *Implicit Filtering*
Jeremy Kepner and John Gilbert, editors, *Graph Algorithms in the Language of Linear Algebra*
Jeremy Kepner, *Parallel MATLAB for Multicore and Multinode Computers*
Michael A. Heroux, Padma Raghavan, and Horst D. Simon, editors, *Parallel Processing for Scientific Computing*
Gérard Meurant, *The Lanczos and Conjugate Gradient Algorithms: From Theory to Finite Precision Computations*
Bo Einarsson, editor, *Accuracy and Reliability in Scientific Computing*
Michael W. Berry and Murray Browne, *Understanding Search Engines: Mathematical Modeling and Text Retrieval, Second Edition*
Craig C. Douglas, Gundolf Haase, and Ulrich Langer, *A Tutorial on Elliptic PDE Solvers and Their Parallelization*
Louis Komzsik, *The Lanczos Method: Evolution and Application*
Bard Ermentrout, *Simulating, Analyzing, and Animating Dynamical Systems: A Guide to XPPAUT for Researchers and Students*
V. A. Barker, L. S. Blackford, J. Dongarra, J. Du Croz, S. Hammarling, M. Marinova, J. Wasniewski, and P. Yalamov, *LAPACK95 Users' Guide*
Stefan Goedecker and Adolfy Hoisie, *Performance Optimization of Numerically Intensive Codes*
Zhaojun Bai, James Demmel, Jack Dongarra, Axel Ruhe, and Henk van der Vorst, *Templates for the Solution of Algebraic Eigenvalue Problems: A Practical Guide*
Lloyd N. Trefethen, *Spectral Methods in MATLAB*
E. Anderson, Z. Bai, C. Bischof, S. Blackford, J. Demmel, J. Dongarra, J. Du Croz, A. Greenbaum, S. Hammarling, A. McKenney, and D. Sorensen, *LAPACK Users' Guide, Third Edition*
Michael W. Berry and Murray Browne, *Understanding Search Engines: Mathematical Modeling and Text Retrieval*
Jack J. Dongarra, Iain S. Duff, Danny C. Sorensen, and Henk A. van der Vorst, *Numerical Linear Algebra for High-Performance Computers*
R. B. Lehoucq, D. C. Sorensen, and C. Yang, *ARPACK Users' Guide: Solution of Large-Scale Eigenvalue Problems with Implicitly Restarted Arnoldi Methods*
Randolph E. Bank, *PLTMG: A Software Package for Solving Elliptic Partial Differential Equations, Users' Guide 8.0*
L. S. Blackford, J. Choi, A. Cleary, E. D'Azevedo, J. Demmel, I. Dhillon, J. Dongarra, S. Hammarling, G. Henry, A. Petitet, K. Stanley, D. Walker, and R. C. Whaley, *ScaLAPACK Users' Guide*
Greg Astfalk, editor, *Applications on Advanced Architecture Computers*
Roger W. Hockney, *The Science of Computer Benchmarking*
Françoise Chaitin-Chatelin and Valérie Frayssé, *Lectures on Finite Precision Computations*

Scientific Computing in Modern C++

Victor Eijkhout
The University of Texas at Austin
Austin, Texas

Society for Industrial and Applied Mathematics
Philadelphia

10 9 8 7 6 5 4 3 2 1

Publications Director	Kivmars H. Bowling
Executive Editor	Elizabeth Greenspan
Acquisitions Editor	Elizabeth Greenspan
Developmental Editor	Rose Kolassiba
Managing Editor	Kelly Thomas
Production Editor	Louis Primus
Copy Editor	Louis Primus
Production Manager	Rachel Ginder
Production Coordinator	Cally A. Shrader
Compositor	Lumina Datamatics
Graphic Designer	Doug Smock

Library of Congress Control Number: 2025037860

Contents

Chapter 1

Preface

Scientific computing can be defined as the collection of techniques employed to solve through computer modeling those problems that allow for a mathematical formulation. Such problems traditionally arise in the physical sciences, but they may also appear in data science, life sciences, etc.

This book is aimed at programmers with a basic knowledge of C++ who want to deepen their understanding, specifically for the purpose of using C++ in scientific computing. For this it covers a broad range of topics: finer points of C++, specific idioms of C++ in scientific computing, a discussion of parallelism, an introduction to hardware and performance, and "carpentry" topics that fall outside of programming as such, but make a programmer more productive.

1.1 ▪ How to use this book

This book is primarily for aspiring scientific programmers, using C++ as their primary language. It aims to take students with a basic knowledge of C++, say a single semester course, and lift them up to a level where they can be productive in a scientific computing project.

Thus, it focuses on computing "idioms" and applications, rather than a complete treatment of the C++ language, as well as peripheral "carpentry" topics that make students more productive as programmers.

The C++ topics discussed are chosen for their relevance to computing, and other topics are willfully excluded. Conversely, a number of topics relevant to scientific computing are included that are not intimately tied to C++ as a language. This includes chapters on computer arithmetic and code performance.

Other uses of this book include self-study by intermediate C++ programmers looking to specialize in scientific computing. Such readers will likely skip the chapters on C++ and focus on the idioms that are not likely to be found in standard C++ textbooks.

It can also be used as a textbook in a specialized course on C++ for computational scientists with prior exposure to C or Fortran, teaching them how to express scientific computing idioms in the language of modern C++.

If this book is used in a classroom context, there are various exercises to be assigned, and projects that can serve as a substitute for end-of-term exams.

The material in this book cannot be presented in a linear fashion, so there will be frequent forward and backward references from introductory sections to more applied sections where this material is used. Italicized text indicates a term that appears in the index.

The code examples in this book can be found at https://bookstore.siam.org/se33/bonus, which redirects to https://github.com/VictorEijkhout/scientific-computing-in-modern-cpp; they have been tested with the Intel 2025 and GCC 15 compilers.

We now give a short rundown of the parts of this book.

1.2 ▪ C++ techniques

We assume certain basic knowledge of C++ and build on that in Part I. Because of our focus on scientific computing certain topics in C++ will not be covered at all. Sometimes this will be remarked upon, other times it goes without saying.

- Chapter 2 goes into detail on scalar types, since control of these is important for numerical accuracy.
- Certain topics in object-oriented programming are covered in Chapter 3.
- Containers such as `vector` are covered in Chapter 4. We discuss C++20 `span` and C++23 `mdspan`, foreshadowing their use in linear algebra codes.
- I/O, most notably the "format" library, is discussed in Chapter 5.
- Lambda expressions, motivated by some particular use cases, are discussed in Chapter 6.
- Iterators, ranges, and algorithms, which allow for elegant and efficient expression of algorithms, are introduced in Chapter 7.
- Timing is discussed in Chapter 8.
- Chapter 9 is devoted to random numbers.
- Smart pointers are covered in Chapter 10.
- We discuss various "union-like" constructs in Chapter 11.
- Chapter 12 has a brief discussion of templating.
- Some remaining topics are in Chapter 13.

1.3 ▪ Idioms

In Part II we discuss some idioms in scientific computing, showing their implementation in C++.

- Chapter 14 shows various approaches to writing custom containers.
- Chapter 15 discusses matrices, in particular sparse ones.
- Other aspects of efficient linear algebra are discussed in Chapter 16 on "expression templates."
- Chapter 17 uses the design of a numerical library for zero-finding as a case study in the use of lambda expressions.

1.4 ▪ Parallelism

The important topic of parallel computing is the subject of Part III. We consider parallelism to be distinct from concurrency, so threading will be one of the topics not treated here.

- We start with a preliminary discussion of types of parallelism in Chapter 18.
- Then we outline a paradigmatic example application in Chapter 19.

- We discuss various approaches to shared memory parallelism, in particular presenting OpenMP, in Chapter 20.
- We briefly touch on accelerator programming in Chapter 21.
- Finally, distributed memory parallelism through MPI is found in Chapter 22.

1.5 ▪ Program development

We discuss a number of topics directly pertaining to code development in Part IV.

- We start with some general programming guidelines in Chapter 23.
- Mechanisms for program structuring are discussed in Chapter 24.
- The subject of code correctness leads us to discuss mathematical approaches to program development in Chapter 25.
- Code correctness by testing through the Catch2 testing framework is discussed in Chapter 26.
- Error handling is the topic of Chapter 27.
- Chapter 28 is a brief introduction to debugging.
- Dealing with memory errors through memory tools will be discussed in Chapter 29.
- Finally, we discuss some software libraries in Chapter 30.

1.6 ▪ Hardware and performance

We discuss computer architecture and how it influences program performance in Part V.

- Chapter 31 gives a brief introduction to processor architecture.
- Chapter 32 analyzes the structure of algorithms for how much room they have for optimization.
- Building on this, Chapter 33 then discusses how to write high performance code.
- Profiling and tracing is briefly discussed in Chapter 34.
- The topic of computer arithmetic is the subject of Chapter 35.

1.7 ▪ Software tools

We discuss a number of "software carpentry" topics in Part VI.

- Compiling, linking, and libraries are the topic of Chapter 36.
- We discuss project management in CMake ecosystem in Chapter 37.
- Code management with `git` is introduced in Chapter 38.

1.8 ▪ Projects

The book concludes with a number of suggestions for programming projects in Part VII. These are small scientific simulations that exercise skills acquired in this book.

1.9 ▪ Acknowledgments

Readings of this book by Daniel Hanson, Susan Lindsey, and Devin Matthews are gratefully acknowledged.

Part I

C++

We start this book with some chapters on C++ language features. It is assumed here that the reader has already gone through a C++ course that covers the basics of control structures and object-oriented programming. Here we cover some topics in more detail, or topics that are not likely to be found in a first course. Throughout, our focus and our choice of topics will be on scientific computing: many topics are chosen for their appearance in later chapters.

We start with a brief discussion of the fine points of scalar datatypes in Chapter 2: both integral types and floating point types. We discuss issues relating to short and long integers and the precision of the floating point types. (The semantics of floating point operations is the topic of Chapter 35.) Next we devote the relatively short Chapter 3 to object-oriented programming.

Chapter 4 on array-like containers mostly serves to prepare for later chapters on linear algebra. In Chapter 5 we briefly discuss the new "format" library. Lambda expressions will appear in many places in this book, so Chapter 6 goes over the basics. Next, Chapter 7 discusses ranges, one of the places where lambdas are used.

Next we discuss a couple of simpler topics: timing (Chapter 8), random numbers (Chapter 9), smart pointers (Chapter 10), and "union-like" constructs—for want of a better description—in Chapter 11.

Templates are briefly discussed in Chapter 12. These are nowhere near as prevalent in scientific computing as in other areas, but this discussion foreshadows the application topic of "expression templates" in Chapter 16. Chapter 13 contains some remaining topics.

Chapter 2
Elementary datatypes

We start by discussing some topics in elementary numerical datatypes.

2.1 ▪ Integers

There are several integer types, differing by the number of bytes they are stored in, and by whether they are signed or not.

Historically, short integers, defined as `short` or `short int`, were used as a way to save space when large values were not needed. These days, that argument is largely irrelevant. The argument for short integers now derives from the limited *bandwidth* of processors: "streaming" type applications have a performance that is determined by the available bandwidth (see section 33.3 for a discussion). Using short integers effectively doubles that bandwidth.

The need for long integers, defined as `long` or `long int`, arises from the current abundance of memory and disc space. Modern applications have large amounts of memory available to them, more than can be addressed with a 32-bit integer. This phenomenon is exacerbated by the existence of *multicore* processors, which can handle many times the memory of earlier processors in the same time. In scientific computing 64-bit integers are getting increasingly common.

2.1.1 ▪ The long and short of it

In addition to `int`, there are also `short`, `long`, and `long long` integers. These names give some imperfect indication as to their size, and therefore range. The actual sizes and ranges of these types are implementation defined. The next section will discuss types with a more precise definition.

- A `short int` is at least 16 bits (if you need an 8-bit integral datatype, use `char`).
- An `int` is at least 16 bits, which was the case in the old days of the *DEC PDP-11*, but nowadays they are commonly 32 bits.
- A `long int` is at least 32 bits, but often 64; the big exception being the *Windows* OS, where a `long` is 32 bits.
- A `long long int` is at least 64 bits.

All these types are signed integers: a k-bit integer accommodates a range $-2^{k-1}\ldots 0\ldots 2^{k-1}-1$. Prefixing these types with the keyword `unsigned` gives nonnegative types with a range $0\ldots 2^k-1$.

If you want to determine precisely the range of integers (or real numbers, which we discuss later) that is stored in an integral (or floating point, respectively) variable you can use the `limits` header; see section 2.2.1.

2.1.2 ▪ Data models

There are a number of conventions, called *data models*, for the actual sizes of the various integer types.

- *LP32* (or "2/4/4") has 16-bit `int`s, and 32 bits for `long int` and pointers. This is used in the *Win16* API.
- *ILP32* (or "4/4/4") has 32 bits for `int`, `long`, and pointers. Only `long long` is 64 bits. This is used in the *Win32* API and on most 32-bit Unix or Unix-like systems.
- *LLP64* (or "4/4/8") has 32 bits for `int` and `long` (!!!); 64 bits are used for `long long`, `size_t` and pointers. This is used in the *Win64* API.
- *LP64* (or "4/8/8") has 32-bit `int`s, and 64 bits for `long`, `long long`, `size_t`, and pointers.
- *SILP64* (or "8/8/8") uses 64 bits for all of `short`, `int`, `long`, `long long`, `size_t`, and pointers. This only existed on some early Unix systems such as *Cray UNICOS*. The related *ILP64* used 16 bits for `short`.

2.1.3 ▪ Specifying the number width

If you want to specify the number of bits that an integer variable should have, there is the `cstdint` header containing *fixed width integer types*. It defines such types as `int16_t` and `uint16_t`.

```
std::int8_t   // 8 bits
std::uint8_t  // 8 bits, unsigned
std::int16_t  // 16 bits
std::uint16_t // 16 bits, unsigned
std::int32_t  // 32 bits
std::uint32_t // 32 bits, unsigned
std::int64_t  // 64 bits
std::uint64_t // 64 bits, unsigned
```

(These can usually also be used without the `std::` prefix.) Additionally there are corresponding macros `INT16_C`, `UINT16_C` that evaluate to a constant expression of the appropriate type:

```
std::int16_t i16 = INT16_C(1);
std::uint16_t u16 = UINT16_C(1);
// et cetera
```

The following example confirms these sizes by using the `sizeof` function:

Code:

```
// int/sizeof.cpp
int8_t i8;
uint8_t u8;
int16_t i16;
uint16_t u16;
println("{}, {}, {}, {}",
        sizeof(i8),
        sizeof(u8),
        sizeof(i16),
        sizeof(u16)
        );
```

Output:

```
1, 1, 2, 2
```

Since C++20, integers are guaranteed to be stored as “2’s complement”; see section 35.4.

The use of unsigned values is fraught with danger since they are often first converted to signed quantities. For instance, comparing them to signed integers gives counterintuitive results:

Code:

```
// int/unsigned.cpp
unsigned int one{1};
int minusone{-1};
println("less: {}",(minusone<one));
```

Output:

```
less: false
```

For this reason, C++20 has introduced utility functions `cmp_equal`, `cmp_not_equal`, `cmp_greater`, etc., that do these comparisons correctly.

2.1.4 ▪ Suffixes

Often, if you need a constant such as the number zero, you can just write `0`: the compiler will cast this for you to a `short int`, a `long int`, a `float` as needed. Sometimes, however, you need to specify precisely which zero you mean. Suppose a routine has multiple overloads:

```
void f(int, int);
void f(long,long)
```

Now if you call

```
long i;
f(0,i);
```

the compiler gives an error that the statement is ambiguous between the two overloads, since the literal zero is of type `int` while `i` is of type `long`.

For this purpose, you can indicate with an *integer suffix* the exact type of the integer numeral. For the number zero that would be

```
0L // long int
0UL // unsigned long
0LL // long long
0Z // signed size_t
0UZ // unsigned size_t
```

All uppercase letters can also be used in their lowercase form. The *z* suffix is added in C++23.

2.1.5 ▪ Integer overflow

Adding integers where the result would not fit the range of the type is called *integer overflow*. For instance, a 4-byte `int` has a maximum value of about 2.14 billion, so the result of adding 1,234,567,890 to itself is no longer representable.

Overflow of unsigned quantities is performed modulo a power of 2. Example:

Code:

```
// int/overflow.cpp
using inttype = uint32_t;
inttype fourG
  {static_cast<inttype>(4000'000'000)};
auto imax = numeric_limits<inttype>::max();
println("size of int: {}",sizeof(fourG));
println(" .. with max {}",imax);
println("fourG+fourG = {}",fourG+fourG);
```

Output:

```
size of int: 4
 .. with max 4294967295
fourG+fourG = 3705032704
```

(Here `using` introduces a *type alias*: an identifier that stands for an existing type.)

Overflow of signed quantities is strictly speaking undefined behavior (UB), but in practice you'll mostly see negative numbers appear:

Code:

```
// int/overflow.cpp
using inttype = int32_t;
inttype twoG
  {static_cast<inttype>(2000'000'000)};
auto imax = numeric_limits<inttype>::max();
println("size of int: {}",sizeof(twoG));
println(" .. with max: {}",imax);
println("twoG+twoG = {}",twoG+twoG);
```

Output:

```
size of int: 4
 .. with max: 2147483647
twoG+twoG = -294967296
```

Instead of wrapping an overflowed result, you could imagine "clamping" an infinite precision result. For this, C++26 will have *saturating math* operations. The result of an overflowing operation is then represented as the limit value of that operation. For instance, the saturated sum of $200 + 200$ (computed with `std::add_sat`) as `uint8_t` is 255. With integer overflow the result would likely be $200 + 200 - 256$.

2.1.6 ▪ The loop index

In indexed loops you may be used to using `int` as the type of the loop variable:

```
for ( int i=0; i<some_array.size(); ++i ) { /* stuff */ }
```

The problem with this is that integers typically have a maximum value of about 2 billion (see section 2.2.1 for details), and containers such as `vector` can store more elements than that.

First of all, in cases where you strictly operate on array elements you can dispense with the loop variable by using *range-based loops*:

```
for ( auto &x : my_vector )
  x *= 2;
```

or standard algorithms:

```
for_each( my_vector,[] ( auto &x ) { x*= 2; } );
```

If you absolutely need that index variable, give it a type of `size_t`:

```
for ( size_t i=0; i<some_array.size(); ++i ) { /* stuff */ }
```

Remark. *Some compilers will indeed issue a warning on the first loop type, but that is not related to the choice of integer type. Instead, the warning will relate to the fact that in the stopping test you are comparing a signed quantity (the loop index) to an unsigned one (the* `size`*). Doing so is considered an unsafe practice. For this and other reasons, the* `ssize` *function returns the size as a signed quantity.*

2.1.7 ▪ Integer denotations

Integer constants can be represented in several *bases*.

Integers are normally written in decimal, and stored in 32 bits. If you need something else:

```
int d = 42;        // decimal
int o = 052;       // octal: start with zero
int x = 0x2a;      // hex
int X = 0X2A;      // also hex
int b = 0b101010; // binary
long ell = 42L;
```

Binary numbers are new to C++17.

Did you know that, as of C++23, you can write large integers more readably as `31'536'000`? The compiler ignores these optional single quotes.

2.2 ▪ Floating point numbers

C++ floating point datatypes correspond to certain formats defined in the *IEEE 754* standard (section 35.2). The most common floating point types are

- `float`, the IEEE 32-bit single precision type;
- `double`, the IEEE 64-bit double precision type;
- `long double`, a compiler / architecture dependent type that is at least as precise as double precision.

The C++23 standard declares that implementations can support *fixed width floating point types* in the `stdfloat` header:

```
float16_t // 16-bit half precision
float32_t // 32-bit single precision
float64_t // 64-bit double precision
float128_t // 128-bit double precision

bfloat16_t // 'bfloat' half precision
```

Remark. *The* `long double` *is a historical oddity. Its implementation depends on the compiler and processor architecture, but the common Linux/x86 combination implements it as an 80-bit type, stored in 128 bits. Here we query its makeup:*

`long double`: *64 bits for the mantissa, 15-bit exponent, 1 sign bit ⇒ 80 bits.*

Code:

```
// basic/double.cpp
println("Bytes: {}",sizeof(T));
println("Bits in mantissa: {}",
        limit<T>::digits);
println("Min exp: {}",
        limit<T>::min_exponent);
println("Max exp: {}",
        limit<T>::max_exponent);
```

Output:

```
Bytes: 16
Bits in mantissa: 64
Min exp: -16381
Max exp: 16384
```

There are two 16-bit floating point types. The `float16_t` is the type originally defined in the IEEE 754 standard; the `bfloat16_t` has the layout that you get from the IEEE 32-bit type by omitting the last two bytes (see section 35.2.2). This makes sense in machine learning (ML) applications, both from a precision point of view and for increased bandwidth over using 32-bit floats.

Remark. *The half precision type makes sense when less accuracy is required; conversely, the quadruple precision type is needed in some numerical applications. However, while these types may be available in a language implementation, this can be without hardware support, which would make their use very slow.*

Discussion of the computational aspects of floating point numbers can be found in Chapter 35.

2.2.1 ▪ Limits

Numeric limits can be queried with the `std::numeric_limits` function of the `limit` header. Inherited from C, there is a header file `limits.h` / `climits` containing macros such as `MAX_INT` and `MIN_INT`, but this should not be used.

Use header file `limits`:

```
#include <limits>
using std::numeric_limits;
```

Limits for signed and unsigned integers:

Code:

```
// int/unsigned.cpp
println("max int      : {}",
    std::numeric_limits<int>::max());
println("min int      : {}",
    std::numeric_limits<int>::min());
println("max unsigned: {}",
    std::numeric_limits<unsigned int>::max());
println("min unsigned: {}",
    std::numeric_limits<unsigned int>::min());
```

Output:

```
max int      : 2147483647
min int      : -2147483648
max unsigned: 4294967295
min unsigned: 0
```

For floating point numbers more limit quantities are defined.

- The largest number is given by `max`.
- `min` is the smallest positive number that is not a denormal (section 35.2.4.3); use `lowest` for "most negative."
- The smallest denormal number is given by `denorm_min`.
- There is an `epsilon` function for machine precision (section 35.2.3):

Limits of floating point numbers:

Code:

```
// stl/limits.cpp
println("Single lowest {}",
    numeric_limits<float>::lowest());
println(" .. and epsilon {}",
    numeric_limits<float>::epsilon());
println("Double lowest {}",
    numeric_limits<double>::lowest());
println(" .. and epsilon {}",
    numeric_limits<double>::epsilon());
```

Output:

```
Single lowest -3.4028235e+38
 .. and epsilon 1.1920929e-07
Double lowest
    ↪-1.7976931348623157e+308
 .. and epsilon
    ↪2.220446049250313e-16
```

Exercise 2.1. Write a program to discover what the maximal n is so that $n!$, that is, n-factorial, can be represented in an `int`, `long`, or `long long`. Can you write this as a templated function?

2.2.2 ▪ Unrepresentable numbers: `NaN` and `Inf`

Operations such as dividing by zero lead to floating point numbers that do not have a valid value. For efficiency of computation, the processor will compute with these as if they are any other floating point number. We will now discuss these quantities.

2.2.2.1 ▪ Infinity: `Inf`

Computing a number outside the range of representable numbers, such as by causing "overflow" or by dividing by zero, gives a bit pattern that is represented in plain text output as *inf*. Here we illustrate an overflowing computation; see section 2.2.2.2 for the test:

Code:

```
// limits/overflow.cpp
float bignum = 1.e40;
float product = bignum*bignum;
println("product: {}",product);
println("overflow: {}",
    std::isinf(product));
```

Output:

```
product: inf
overflow: true
```

For more detail, see section 35.2.4.

2.2.2.2 ▪ Not a number: NaN

The *IEEE 754* standard for floating point numbers states that certain bit patterns correspond to the value *NaN*: "not a number." This is the result of such computations as the square root of a negative number, or zero divided by zero; you can also explicitly generate it with `quiet_NaN` or `signaling_NaN`. These are methods of the `numeric_limits` type in the `limits` header; see the example below.

- *NaN* is only defined for floating point types; the test `has_quiet_NaN` is false for other types such as `bool` or `int`.
- Even though `complex` is built on top of floating point types, there is no *NaN* for it.

Code:

```
// limits/nan.cpp
println("Double NaNs: {} {}",
    std::numeric_limits<double>
        ::quiet_NaN(),
    std::numeric_limits<double>
        ::signaling_NaN());
println("zero divided by zero: {}",
    0 / 0.0);
println("Int has NaN: {}",
    std::numeric_limits<int>
        ::has_quiet_NaN);
```

Output:

```
Double NaNs: nan nan
zero divided by zero: nan
Int has NaN: false
```

2.2.2.3 ▪ Tests

There are tests for detecting whether a number is *Inf*, *NaN*, etc. However, using these may slow a computation down.

The functions `isinf`, `isnan`, `isfinite`, `isnormal` are defined for the floating point types (`float`, `double`, `long double`), returning a `bool`.

```
#include <math.h>
isnan(-1.0/0.0);    // false
isnan(sqrt(-1.0)); // true
isinf(-1.0/0.0);    // true
isinf(sqrt(-1.0)); // false
```

2.3 ▪ Bits and booleans

2.3.1 ▪ Conversion to bool

Objects can sometimes be "contextually converted" to a boolean value. Such implicit conversion to boolean is performed

- if an object appears in a context where a boolean is expected; and
- the `operator bool` (see section 3.2.1) is defined on it.

As an example, here is a *FuzzyBit* class, where a `float` is `true` if $\geq .5$, and `false` otherwise.

Constructor and data:

```
// object/logic.cpp
class FuzzyBit {
private:
  float value_; // between 0 and 1
public:
  FuzzyBit( float value) : value_(value) {};
  /* ... */
```

Overloaded logical operators and conversion to `bool`:

Operators

```
// object/logic.cpp
FuzzyBit operator&&( FuzzyBit other ) {
  return FuzzyBit
    ( std::min(value_,other.value_) );
};
FuzzyBit operator||( FuzzyBit other ) {
  return FuzzyBit
    ( std::max(value_,other.value_) );
};
operator bool() const {
  return value_>=.5f; };
```

Main

```
// object/logic.cpp
FuzzyBit yes{1},no{0};
FuzzyBit confirm = (yes or no );

if ( confirm )
  println("Yes");
else
  println("No");
```

2.3.2 ▪ Vector of `bool` versus bit sets

Watch out for `vector<bool>`: this uses a compact scheme storing multiple values per byte. This has the unfortunate side effect that you cannot get a reference to a vector element. Thus, while you can write

```
for ( auto b : my_vector_of_bool ) /* something */
```

writing the following is not grammatically correct:

```
// DOES NOT COMPILE
for ( auto& b : my_vector_of_bool ) /* something */
```

Also, multiple threads may not be able to set elements independently because of *false sharing*; see section 31.5.3.

Bit *operations* can be done with a dedicated `bitset` class. Bit sets are constructed from integer quantities, after which they provide the usual logic operations:

Code:

```
// bit/bitset.cpp
bitset<8> xb(6);
bitset<8> yb(3);
cout << "6|3 = " << (xb|yb)
     << " = " << xory << '\n';
auto xandy = (xb&yb).to_ulong();
cout << "6&3 = " << (xb&yb)
     << " = " << xandy << '\n';
```

Output:

```
6|3 = 00000111 = 7
6&3 = 00000010 = 2
```

As a practical example, consider encoding two digits, each stored in four bits, into one byte:

Code:

```
// bit/bcd.cpp
uint8_t five{5}, seven{7};
bitset<8> low_byte{seven};
bitset<8> high_byte = ( bitset<8>{five} )<<4;
bitset<8> fiftyseven_bits =
  high_byte | low_byte;
uint8_t fiftyseven_bcd =
  static_cast<uint8_t>(
    fiftyseven_bits.to_ulong() );
cout << "fiftyseven bits:\n  "
     << fiftyseven_bits << " = "
     << fiftyseven_bcd << '\n';
```

Output:

```
fiftyseven bits:
  01010111 = W
```

This encoding of decimal digits is known as binary coded decimal (BCD). Can you imagine applications where this is useful?

Exercise 2.2. Write the converse, the decode operation, which takes a byte and splits it into two 4-bit quantities.

Remark. *Some obvious operations such as rotating bits by* `std::rotr` *(in the C++20* `bit` *header) cannot be done on a* `bitset`*; they are only defined on unsigned integer types.*

2.4 ▪ Complex numbers

Complex numbers require the `complex` header. The `complex` type uses templating to set the precision, and the real/imaginary parts of a number are available through the `.re` and `.im` members.

```
#include <complex>
std::complex<float> f;
f.re = 1.; f.im = 2.;

complex<double> d(1.,3.);
```

Math operators such as `+,*` are defined between complex numbers. Numerical expressions involving a complex number and a simple scalar are well-defined if the scalar is of the underlying type of the complex number:

```
complex<float> x;
x + 1.f; // Yes
x + 1.;  // No, because '1.' is double
```

You can use the imaginary unit number i through the literals `i`, `if` (float), `il` (long):

```
using namespace std::complex_literals;
  std::complex<double> c = 1.0 + 1i;
```

Beware: `1+1i` does not compile; you need to write `1.+1i` for the compiler to deduce the types.

Operations on complex scalars:

Code:

```
// complex/basicprint.cpp
using namespace std::complex_literals;
auto e = d*2.;
println("{}",e);
auto g = e + 2.5i + 3.; // note 3dot
println("{}",g);
```

Output:

```
(2,6)
(5,8.5)
```

Operations on vector of complex:

Code:

```
// complex/veccomplex.cpp
vector<complex<double>>
  vec1( N, 1.+2.5i );
auto vec2( vec1 );
  /* ... */
for ( int i=0; i<vec1.size(); ++i ) {
  vec2[i] = vec1[i] * ( 1.+1.i );
}
  /* ... */
auto sum = accumulate
  ( vec2.begin(),vec2.end(),
    complex<double>(0.) );
println( "result: {}",sum );
```

Output:

```
result: (-1500000,3500000)
```

There are support functions for such things as exponentiation (`exp`) and complex conjugation (`conj`), as well as `abs`, `norm`, `polar`.

Exercise 2.3. Let $x = .5 + i$ and compute

$$x + \bar{x} - e^{2\pi i},$$

which should be one. Is it actually one? How close do you get in `float` and `double` complex?

2.4.1 ▪ Formatting complex numbers

The C++20 `format` library can deal with basic datatypes, but notably not with complex numbers. The following snippet fixes that (see section 5.2.2 for details) and has been used in this book.

```
// complex/basicprint.cpp
template<>
class std::formatter<complex<float>>{
public:
  constexpr auto parse( std::format_parse_context& ctx ) {
    return ctx.begin(); };
  auto format( const complex<float>& z,std::format_context& ctx ) const {
    return std::format_to
      ( ctx.out(),"({},{})",z.real(),z.imag());
  };
};
```

2.5 ▪ Enums and enum classes

The C-style enum keyword defines global names, so it's easy to have name collisions. For example:

```
// enum/enumnot.cpp
enum trafficlight { red,yellow,green };
cout << red << "," << yellow << "," << green << '\n';
enum flag { red,white,blue }; // Collision!
```

In C++ the enum class (or enum struct) is introduced, which makes the names into class members. For instance, you can make a vector of such enum class objects and fill it:

```
// enum/enumclass.cpp
enum class flowers { grass, poppy, bluebonnet };
vector<flowers> field(10,flowers::grass);
field[1] = flowers::poppy;
field[5] = flowers::bluebonnet;
```

With the enum class mechanism you can now have multiple identical names for an enum, since they are scoped to a class (C++ Core Guidelines [12, Enum.3]).

By default, a variable of an enum type is allocated as an int. You can change this by letting the type inherit from another type:

```
// enum/enumclass.cpp
enum class flag : unsigned short { red,white,blue };
```

If such a class inherits from an integral type, this does not mean it behaves like an integer; for instance, you cannot immediately ask if one is less than another. Instead, this form of inheritance only determines the amount of space taken for an enum item.

To let enum objects behave like the underlying integral type, you need to cast them:

```
// enum/enumclass.cpp
cout << static_cast<unsigned short>( flag::red ) << ","
     << static_cast<unsigned short>( flag::white ) << ","
     << static_cast<unsigned short>( flag::blue ) << '\n';
```

In C++23 this can be done more concisely with to_underlying:

```
// enum/enumclass.cpp
enum class flag : unsigned int { red,white,blue };
// but we still need to cast them
cout << std::to_underlying( flag::red ) << ","
     << std::to_underlying( flag::white ) << ","
     << std::to_underlying( flag::blue ) << '\n';
```

Instead of an enum class you can often also enclose your enum in the namespace of a class:

```
// enum/spaced.cpp
class Field {
public:
  enum color { invalid=-1,white=0,red=1,blue=2,green=3 };
private:
  color mycolor;
public:
  void set_color( color c ) { mycolor = c; };
   /* ... */
```

```
Field onefield;
onefield.set_color( Field::color::blue );
```

2.6 ▪ Math functions

Some *math functions*, such as `abs`, can be included through `cmath`:

```
#include <cmath>
using std::abs;
```

The function `std::abs` is overloaded for different numeric types. Calling `abs` without that namespace prefix invokes an integer function `abs`, and the compiler may suggest that you use `fabs` for floating point arguments.

Others math functions, such as `max`, are in the less obvious `algorithm` header (see section 7.3):

```
#include <algorithm>
using std::max;
```

Chapter 3

Object-oriented programming

In this chapter we cover a couple of more advanced topics in object-oriented programming. It is assumed that the reader already has a basic understanding of the topic.

3.1 ▪ Pure virtual classes

It is possible for a base class to define a method, and for a derived class to override this. The base class declares a method `thevalue` as `virtual`, and the derived class redeclares it as both `virtual` and `override`.

Base and derived class share a method:

Base class:

```
// object/virtual.cpp
class Base {
protected:
  int i;
public:
  Base(int i) : i(i) {};
  virtual int thevalue() { return i; };
};
```

Derived class:

```
// object/virtual.cpp
class Deriv : public Base {
public:
  Deriv(int i) : Base(i) {};
  virtual int thevalue() override {
    int ivalue = Base::thevalue();
    return ivalue*ivalue;
  };
};
```

Now we can call the `thevalue` method on the base class and the derived class:

Calling base and derived method:

Code:

```
// object/virtual.cpp
Base fiveb(5);
println("{}",fiveb.thevalue());
Deriv fived(5);
println("{}",fived.thevalue());
```

Output:

```
5
25
```

In library design, a more useful mechanism is that of *pure virtual* methods. Here the base method is not defined, but its name and signature are given, with a special syntax indicating that any derived class needs to define this method.

Pure virtual base classes are used in section 19.2 to implement several variants of a basic benchmark code.

Here is an example of a base class and a derived class; the base class has a virtual function `thevalue`, recognized by the `= 0` declaration. The derived class then defines that function. Note the qualifiers on the methods.

Syntax for pure virtual method:

// object/purevirtual.cpp

```
class Base {
protected:
  int i;
public:
  Base(int i) : i(i) {};
  virtual ~Base() {};
  virtual int thevalue() = 0;
};
```

```
class Deriv : public Base {
public:
  Deriv(int i) : Base(i) {};
  virtual int thevalue() override {
    return 25;
  };
};
```

Because of the virtual function you cannot create objects of the base class, only of the derived class.

The next example is of a *pure virtual* class: all methods are virtual. (Other programming languages may call this an *interface*.) This is a way of enforcing an application programmer interface (API) on derived classes.

Use case:

// object/virtualvec.hpp

```
class VirtualVector {
private:
public:
  virtual ~VirtualVector() {};
  virtual void setlinear(float) = 0;
  virtual float operator[](int) = 0;
};
```

Suppose `DenseVector` derives from `VirtualVector`:

// object/densevec.cpp

```
DenseVector v(5);
v.setlinear(7.2);
println("{:.3}",v[3]);
```

In the above codes, classes that have virtual methods have a virtual destructor. Otherwise, the derived class's destructor will not be called if the object is deleted through a pointer to the base class.

For completeness we give the implementation of the derived class of this pure virtual class.

Implementation:

Class:

```
// object/densevec.cpp
class DenseVector : VirtualVector {
private:
  vector<float> values;
public:
  DenseVector( int size ) {
    values = vector<float>(size,0);
  };
```

Methods:

```
// object/densevec.cpp
  void setlinear( float v ) {
    for (int i=0; i<values.size(); ++i)
      values[i] = i*v;
  };
  float operator[](int i) {
    return values[i];
  };
};
```

Exercise 3.1. Write a small "integrator" library for ordinary differential equations (ODEs). Assuming "autonomous ODEs," that is, $u' = f(t)$ with no u-dependence, there are two simple integration schemes:

- explicit: $u_{n+1} = u_n + \Delta t\, f_n$; and
- implicit: $u_{n+1} = u_n + \Delta t\, f_{n+1}$.

Write an abstract `Integrator` class where the `nextstep` method (which integrates for another Δt) is pure virtual; then write `ExplicitIntegrator` and `ImplicitIntegrator` classes deriving from this.

```
// ode/pureint.cpp
double stepsize = .01;
auto integrate_linear =
  ForwardIntegrator( [] (double x) { return x*x; }, stepsize );
double int1 = integrate_linear.to(1.);
```

You can hardcode the function to be integrated, or try to pass a lambda expression or functor.

3.2 ▪ Operator overloading

Instead of writing

```
myobject.add(anotherobject)
```

you can actually redefine the + operator so that

```
myobject + anotherobject
```

is legal. This is known as *operator overloading*: you give your own definition of common arithmetic operators. There will be several examples of operator overloading in this book, notably with "expression templates" (Chapter 16).

Syntax:

```
<returntype> operator<op>( <argument> ) { <definition> }
```

For instance:

Code:

```
// geom/pointscale.cpp
Point Point::operator*(float f) {
    return Point(f*x,f*y);
};
    /* ... */
  println("p1 to origin {:.5}",
          p1.dist_to_origin());
  Point scale2r = p1*2.;
  println("scaled right: {}",
          scale2r.dist_to_origin());
  // ILLEGAL Point scale2l = 2.*p1;
```

Output:

```
p1 to origin 2.2361
scaled right: 4.472136
```

Exercise 3.2. Write a `Fraction` class, and define the arithmetic operators on it.

Define both the + and += operators. Can you use one of them in defining the other?

3.2.1 ▪ List of overloadable operators

Arithmetic `+ - * / %`

Example:

```
// class method:
T U::operator+( const V& other );
// free function:
T operator+( const U& one, const V& two );
```

Note that this is limited to existing operators: new ones such as `**` cannot be created.

The unary *dereference operator* `operator*` is often used when writing iterators; see section 14.4.

Increment / decrement The operators `++ --` can be overloaded. This is, for instance, useful if you write a container that you want to iterate over; see section 14.4.

There is a subtlety here, because these operators can be applied as *pre-increment* and *post-increment* (or decrement, of course).

```
// pre-increment
operator ++() { ++seek; return *this; };
// post-increment
operator ++(int) { auto tmp(*this); ++seek; return tmp; };
```

Note the dummy `int` argument for the post-increment function; this only serves to distinguish the two versions of the unary operator.

Boolean operators The operators `^ & | ~ && ||` can be redefined. If `&&` is overloaded, the `and` operator is too; likewise `||` and `or`.

The negation operator `!` need not be overloaded if `operator bool` is defined. Note: the `bool` operator is defined without return type. See the example in section 2.3.1.

Comparison `== < > <= >=`

The spaceship operator (since C++20) `<=>` is discussed in section 3.2.3.

Assignment The overloadable assignment operators are `+= -= *= /= %= ^= &= |=`. For a creative use of the assignment operator, see Chapter 16.

Stream extraction and insertion `<< >> >>= <<= == != <= >=`

The most common example of this is inserting your own objects into an output stream; see section 5.2.

Function call Overloading `operator()` makes an object resemble a function, except that it has internal state in its data members; see section 3.2.2 below. For a practical example see section 15.4.1.2.

Array indexing The notation `x[i]` can be defined by the method

```
float& operator[]( size_t i } { /* ... */ };
```

Multidimensional indexing (since C++23) is similarly defined. For instance, emulating a three-dimensional array:

```
class vector3d {
private:
  std::vector<float> data;
  int n1,n2,n3;
public:
  float& operator[] int i,int j,int ,k ] {
    return data[ ( ( i*n1 + j )*n2 + k ) ]; };
```

This type of indexing is used in `mdspan`; see section 4.1.2. Note that inside the brackets the *comma operator* is no longer defined.

Sequence operator The comma (sequence) operator `,` normally has the declaration

```
T2& operator,(const T &a, T2 &b);
```

Dereference operators The operators `->* ->` can be overloaded. If you do so, you can still dereference pointers with the `get` method.

Allocation The free function `new` can be redefined:

```
void* operator new(size_t);
```

With it, you probably want to redefine

```
void operator delete(void*);
```

3.2.2 ▪ Functors

A special case of operator overloading is *overloading the parentheses*. This makes an object look like a function; we call this a *functor*.

Simple example of overloading parentheses:

Code:

```
// object/functor.cpp
class IntPrintFunctor {
public:
  void operator()(int x) {
    println("{}",x);
  }
};
  /* ... */
  IntPrintFunctor intprint;
  intprint(5);
```

Output:

```
5
```

Exercise 3.3. Extend that class as follows: instead of printing the argument directly, it should print it multiplied by a scalar. That scalar should be set in the constructor. Make the following code work:

Code:

```
// object/functor.cpp
IntPrintTimes printx2(2);
printx2(1);
for ( auto i : {5,6,7,8} )
  printx2(i);
```

Output:

```
2
10
12
14
16
```

One of the first things you learn in working with floating point numbers is that you should (almost) never test for exact equality. Even the results of simple calculations can be inexact because of roundoff and truncation behavior. (This will be covered later in Chapter 35.) Let's implement an "approximately equal" test for floating point numbers.

Exercise 3.4. Can you make this syntax work?

```
float x = // some computation
if ( x==approximately(1.0f) )
  // then something
```

If something is "approximately one," and you multiply it by a million, is it then "approximately a million" in your test?

3.2.3 ▪ The spaceship operator

It is possible to overload comparison operators <,<=,==,>=,>,!= for classes; see section 3.2. However, there is usually a lot of redundancy in doing so, even if you express one operator in terms of another:

```
bool MyClass::operator>=( const MyClass& other ) {
  return not (other<*this);
};
```

The C++20 *spaceship* `operator <=>` can make life a lot easier. This binary operator returns an ordering object, which can be one of the six relations.

Let's illustrate with a simple example. Each object of the class `Record` has a string and a unique number:

```
// stl/spaceship.cpp
class Record {
private:
  static inline int nrecords{0};
  int myrecord{-1};
  string name;
public:
  Record( string name )
    : name(name) { myrecord = nrecords++; };
```

Now you want an ordering relation purely based on the record number.

Code:

```
// stl/spaceship.cpp
Record alice("alice"), bob("bob");
println("expect  t f  t t  f f");
println( "{}", (alice==alice) );
println( "{}", (alice==bob) );
println( "{}", (alice<=bob) );
println( "{}", (alice<bob) );
println( "{}", (alice>=bob) );
println( "{}", (alice>bob) );
```

Output:

```
expect  t f  t t  f f
true
false
true
true
false
false
```

We implement this relation using the spaceship operator, using the fact that an ordering on integers exists:

```
// stl/spaceship.cpp
std::strong_ordering operator<=>( const Record& other ) const {
  return myrecord<=>other.myrecord;
};
bool operator==( const Record& other) const {
  return myrecord==other.myrecord;
};
```

The return type of this comparison is a `std::strong_ordering`, because in this case any two objects `x,y` always satisfy exactly one of

```
x<y  x==y  x>y
```

For a more complicated example, let's make a `Coordinate` class, where two coordinates compare as `<,=,>` if all components satisfy that relation. This is a partial ordering, meaning that some coordinates `x,y` do not satisfy any of

```
x<y, x==y, x>y
```

Code:

```
// stl/spaceship.cpp
Coordinate<int> p12(1,2),p24(2,4),p31(3,1);
println("expect t t f");
println("{}",(p12==p12));
println("{}",(p12<p24));
println("{}",
    (p12<p31 or p12>p31 or p12==p31));
```

Output:

```
expect t t f
true
true
false
```

In this case the spaceship operator returns a `partial_ordering` result. Equality needs to be defined separately again:

```
// stl/spaceship.cpp
std::partial_ordering operator<=>( const Coordinate& other ) const {
  std::strong_ordering c = components[0] <=> other.components[0];
  for (int i = 1; i <components.size(); ++i) {
    if ((components[i] <=> other.components[i]) != c)
      return std::partial_ordering::unordered;
  }
  return c;
};
bool operator==( const Coordinate& other ) const {
  for ( int ic=0; ic<components.size(); ++ic )
    if (components[ic]!=other.components[ic])
      return false;
  return true;
};
```

Exercise 3.5. Extend Exercise 3.2: use the “spaceship” operator to implement comparison operators between `Fraction` objects.

3.3 ▪ References to class members

Here is the naive way of returning a class member:

```
class Object {
private:
  SomeType thing;
public:
  SomeType get_thing() {
    return thing; };
};
```

Now the return statement makes a copy of `thing`, which may be the desired behavior, and it may not be. If you don't need an actual copy, but you want access to the actual data member, you can return the member by *reference*:

```
  SomeType &get_thing() {
    return thing; };
```

Now you have write access to an internal (maybe private!) data member. You may want to have that, but if you don't, use a *const reference*:

Code:

```
// const/constref.cpp
class has_int {
private:
  int mine{1};
public:
  const int& int_to_get() { return mine; };
  int& int_to_set() { return mine; };
  void inc() { ++mine; };
};
    /* ... */
  has_int an_int;
  an_int.inc(); an_int.inc();
  println("Contained int is now: {}",
          an_int.int_to_get());
  /* Compiler error: an_int.int_to_get() = 5;
  */
  an_int.int_to_set() = 17;
  println("Contained int is now: {}",
          an_int.int_to_get());
```

Output:

```
Contained int is now: 3
Contained int is now: 17
```

In the above example, the function giving a reference was used on the left-hand side of an assignment. If you would use it on the right-hand side, you would not get a reference.

Let's again make a class where we can get a reference to the internals:

```
// func/rhsref.cpp
class myclass {
private:
  int stored{0};
public:
  myclass(int i) : stored(i) {};
  int &data() { return stored; };
};
```

Now we explore various ways of using that reference on the right-hand side:

Code:

```
// func/rhsref.cpp
myclass obj(5);
println("object data: {}",obj.data());
int dcopy = obj.data();
++dcopy;
println("object data: {}",obj.data());
int &dref = obj.data();
++dref;
println("object data: {}",obj.data());
auto dauto = obj.data();
++dauto;
println("object data: {}",obj.data());
auto &aref = obj.data();
++aref;
println("object data: {}",obj.data());
```

Output:

```
object data: 5
object data: 5
object data: 6
object data: 6
object data: 7
```

You see that, despite the fact that the method `data` was defined as returning a reference, you still need to indicate whether the left-hand side is a reference.

3.4 ▪ Constructing objects in class methods

In this section we look at two aspects of constructing objects from inside class methods, including constructors.

3.4.1 ▪ Member initializer lists

First let us look at objects that contain another object, in particular ones with nontrivial construction. For example:

```
class named_field {
private:
  std::vector<double> values;
  string name;
```

How do we construct the embedded `std::vector`?

One solution would be to specify a vector without size in the class definition, create a vector in the constructor, and assign that to the vector member of the object:

```
named_field( int n ) {
  values = vector<int>(n);
};
```

However, this has the effect that

- the constructor first creates `values` as a zero size vector,
- then it creates an anonymous vector of size `n`,
- and, by assigning it, destroys the earlier created zero size vector.

This is somewhat inefficient, and the optimal solution is to create the vector as part of the *member initializer* list:

Use initializers for creating the contained vector:

```
class named_field {
private:
  string name;
  vector<double> values;
public:
  named_field( string name,int n )
    : name(name),
      values(vector<double>(n)) {
  };
};
```

Even shorter:

```
  named_field( string name,int n )
    : name(name),values(n) {
  };
```

3.4.2 ▪ Return value optimization

Suppose we construct an object inside a function:

```
auto make() {
  SomeObject thing;
  return thing;
}
// ....
auto t = make();
```

Strictly speaking, `thing` is a local variable, and the `return` copies it to the calling environment. However, in such cases *return value optimization (RVO)* is applied, and the returned object is moved into the receiving variable.

3.5 ▪ Deducing this

Object methods have access to the object itself through an implicitly defined `this` pointer. In C++23 this pointer can be made explicit:

```
class Foo {
int n;
void f( this Foo& self ) { self.n; };
};
```

The keyword `this` in first position indicates that the first parameter is the object. This has an important application: it eliminates the need for const/nonconst overloads of the same function.

```
// object/deducing.cpp
template<typename Self>
auto& x(this Self&& self) {
  return self.x_ ;
  };
```

3.6 ▪ class versus struct

The keyword `struct` indicated in C a way of bundling data:

```
struct IntAndFloat {
    int i;
    float x;
};
```

In C++, `struct` is almost synonymous with `class`: both a struct and a class can have data and function members, and all of these can be declared `private` or `public`. The only difference is that in a `struct` all members are by default public, while in a `class` they are by default private.

So when do you use either? As a recommendation, use `class` throughout, because it forces you to be explicit about which data or functions members are public. You can use `struct` as a quick way to bundle data. For instance, if a function returns three `double` variables, you could introduce a struct to name them (C++ Core Guidelines [12, F.21]):

Struct def:

```
// struct/semi.cpp
struct semiconductor {
  double p; double n; double phi;
};
```

Initialization:

```
// struct/semi.cpp
semiconductor model() {
  double p = 1.5;
  double n = 2.5;
  double phi = 3.5;
  return {.p=p, .n=n, .phi=phi};
};
```

This example uses the *designated initializer* mechanism of C++20. (Despite the unambiguous naming, the fields still need to be in declaration order.)

Another rule of thumb (C++ Core Guidelines [12, C.2]) is that you should use `class` if the class has an *invariant*; use `struct` if the members can vary independently.

Chapter 4

Arrays and other containers

C++ was not primarily designed for scientific computing, and one place where that is quite clear is that until recently it lacked support for linear algebra array operations. In this chapter we focus on the C++20 span and C++23 mdspan libraries that are essential for implementing linear algebra operations, especially involving multidimensional arrays.

We also cover the array class and make some remarks about C++ arrays versus C arrays.

4.1 ▪ Span and mdspan

Arrays in C allowed for some operations that are harder to do with C++ vectors. For instance, you could create a subset of an array, operate on it as if it were an array by itself, and have the original array be affected. Here is an illustration of this mechanism at work, using explicitly allocated data.

Form *subdata* as part of the array *data_array*, starting at the second element:

```
double *data_array = new double[N];
double *subdata = data_array+1; // pointer arithmetic: point at next element
subdata[1] = 5.;                // same as: data_array[2] = 5.;
```

Using "subarrays" would be useful, for instance, in a *quicksort* algorithm:

```
// Warning: this is pseudo-code
void qs( data ) {
  if (data.size()>1) {
    // pivoting stuff omitted
    qs( data.lefthalf() ); qs( data.lefthalf() );
  }
}
```

You cannot get this same effect with a standard vector or array since they exclusively own their data. Creating a vector from elements of another vector, for instance, with iterators, leads to a copy. The scenario of having nonowned subarrays is addressed by the span class.

4.1.1 ▪ Span

If you really want vector-like objects to share data use the span class, added in C++20. Since a span is created from a pointer and a size, it allows you to create a nonowning view into a vector;

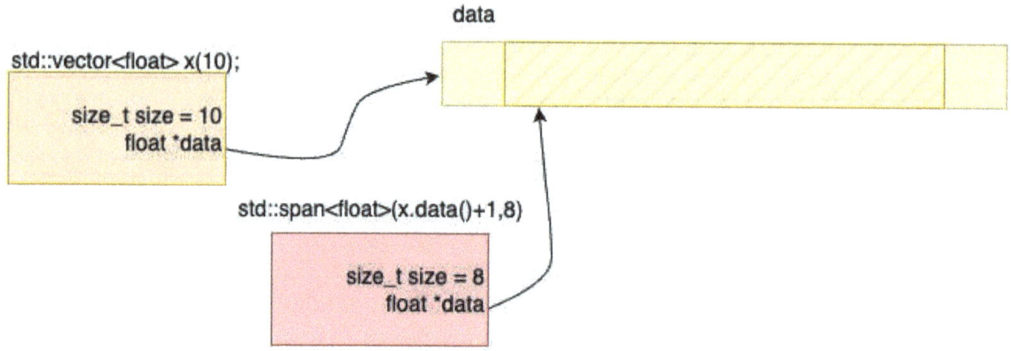

Figure 4.1. *Span using pointer into vector data*

see Figure 4.1.

Create a `span` from a `vector`, starting at its second element and ending before its last:

```
#include <span>
vector<double> v;
std::span<double> v_span( v.data()+1,v.size()-2 );
```

The `span` object has the same `data`, and `size` methods, as well as the subscript operator, as a `vector`. Also you can iterate over it, as you'll see below, but it has no dynamic methods such as `push_back`. Bound-checked indexing through the `at` method is planned for C++26.

Here is an example of `span` in use: we create a span from part of a `vector`, change an element in the span, and see that the corresponding element in the original vector is changed:

Code:

```
// span/subspan.cpp
vector v{1,2,3};
span tail( v.data()+1,2 );
tail[0] = tail[1] = 0;
println("{},{},{}",v[0],v[1],v[2]);
```

Output:

```
1,0,0
```

The previous example can be made more elegant by using `last` to create a *subspan*.

Alter a subset of a vector through a subspan:

Code:

```
// span/subspan.cpp
vector v{1,2,3};
span data( v.data(),v.size() );
span tail = data.last(2);
for ( auto& e : tail )
  e = 0;
println("{},{},{}",v[0],v[1],v[2]);
```

Output:

```
1,0,0
```

Remark. *Both* `std::vector`, `std::array`, *and* automatic arrays *can be implicitly converted to a* `std::span`, *for instance, when passing parameters.*

Code:

```
// span/spanpass.cpp
void f( span<int> s ) {
  println("{}",s[0]);
}
int main() {
  std::array<int,1> a{1};
  f( a );
  int b[2]{2,2};
  f( b );
  vector<int> c(5,3);
  f( c );
```

Output:

```
1
2
3
```

In implementation a `span` behaves like a bare pointer. That means that a `const span` is only const in that what it points to cannot be changed; its contents can still be changed. You can have a "constant span" by making a `span` of `const float`.

Constant pointer versus constant data:

Const pointer

```
// span/const.cpp
void uhoh( const span<float> vs ) {
  vs[0] = 1.;
}
```

Const data

```
// span/const.cpp
void read( const span<const float> vs ) {
  cout << vs[0];
  // NOT LEGAL:
  // vs[0] = 1.;
}
```

4.1.2 ▪ Mdspan

The C++23 standard introduced `mdspan`, a multidimensional span, which is like `span` in the sense of it being a nonowning container-like object. Its big improvement over `span` is that it offers functionality for multidimensional indexing. (A benchmark study [34] shows that this incurs no performance penalty over linearized indexing as in section 14.1.2.)

Remark. *The* `mdspan` *library is not yet implemented in all compilers. The examples in this book have been tested using the reference implementation, available from the Kokkos project. To include this, use*

```
// mdspan/index2.cpp
#include "mdspan/mdspan.hpp"
namespace md = Kokkos;
namespace KokkosEx = MDSPAN_IMPL_STANDARD_NAMESPACE::MDSPAN_IMPL_PROPOSED_NAMESPACE;
namespace mdx = KokkosEx;
```

Consequently, the examples may use `md::mdspan`*, which will read* `std::mdspan` *if your compiler supports it.*

An `mdspan` object is a multidimensional Cartesian brick, where each dimension can be specified in a number of ways. While `mdspan` can handle "dynamic extents," a common case in scientific computing has known extents in all dimensions. The definition is then fairly simple:

Create 2D `mdspan` from vector:

```
// mdspan/index2std.cpp
// matrix in row major
vector<float> A(M*N);
std::mdspan
  Amd{ A.data(),std::extents{M,N} };
```

In the following example we create a four-dimensional `mdspan` and find the coordinate at the center of this brick, illustrating the new index syntax.

Construct a multidimensional span from a vector:

```
// mdspan/midpoint.cpp
vector<float> ar10203040(10*20*30*40);
auto brick10203040 =
  md::mdspan< float,
              md::extents<size_t,10,20,30,40> >
                ( ar10203040.data() );
auto midpoint = brick10203040[5,10,15,20];
```

The `mdspan` class is templatized over the basic type, the extents, and the layout. These can be deduced by the compiler using class template argument deduction (CTAD), or have certain defaults. For instance, while the default template parameter value `LayoutPolicy = std::layout_right` corresponds to *row-major* storage (see section 14.1.2), it is also possible to have *column-major* ordering. The latter is the scheme used in *Fortran* and the Basic Linear Algebra Subprograms (BLAS) standard for linear algebra (section 15.5.1), so you may need it when interfacing across languages.

Declaration with template values specified and using column-major ordering:

```
// mdspan/index2.cpp
// matrix in column major
vector<float> B(M*N);
md::mdspan<float, md::extents<int, M,N>, md::layout_left>
  Bmd{B.data()};
```

Remark. *Introducing* `mdspan` *made it necessary to redefine the function of the comma inside square brackets (see section 3.2.1). The comma operator, denoting sequential execution, can still be used in other contexts such as loop headers. If you absolutely need the sequential comma in* *an index expression, you can write* `a[(i,j)]`. As an illustration of simple indexing, here is a rowsum calculation: given a matrix M return a vector r such that

$$r_i = \sum_j A_{ij}.$$

For this we create views (section 7.1.2) to the rows and apply the `accumulate` algorithm to it. The object has an `extent` method to query the extents.

Given `mdspan` *mat*, find its sizes, extract each row and the sum of its elements:

```
// mdspan/index2.cpp
int M = mat.extent(0); int N = mat.extent(1);
vector<float> rowsums(N);
for ( int row=0; auto& rs : rowsums ) {
  auto the_row =
    rng::iota_view(0,M)
    | rng::views::transform ( [mat,row] (int col) -> float {
        return mat[row,col]; } );
  rs = rng::accumulate( the_row, 0.f );
  row++;
}
```

Note that `the_row` is a view, not a data structure.

In the type of operations that you are likely to do on multidimensional objects, you probably need multidimensional indices. These are provided by such methods as `ranges::cartesian_product`, which can be used to construct a multidimensional version of an `iota` index set:

Two-dimensional product of `iota`s:

```
// mdspan/transpose.cpp
// (i,j) index pairs into A and B
auto Aij = rng::views::cartesian_product
  ( rng::views::iota( 0L,static_cast<long int>(Amd.extent(0)) ),
    rng::views::iota( 0L,static_cast<long int>(Amd.extent(1)) )
    );
```

These indices can now be used for matrix-like indexing in the mdspan objects. For example, here is a matrix transposition, using a parallelized range `for_each`:

Definition:

```
// mdspan/transpose.cpp
vector<float> A(N*N),B(N*N);
md::mdspan Amd{ A.data(),N,N };
md::mdspan Bmd{ B.data(),N,N };
```

Use:

```
// mdspan/transpose.cpp
std::for_each
  ( std::execution::par_unseq,
    Aij.begin(),Aij.end(),
    [&] ( auto idx ) {
      auto [i,j] = idx;
      Bmd[j,i] = Amd[i,j];
    }
    );
```

(For more examples, see section 20.12.)

A more sophisticated transpose algorithm would first transpose the quadrants of a matrix, and then transpose the quadrants themselves. This has the advantage that we now make explicit fourfold parallelism. To obtain the quadrants we use submdspan, which is proposed for C++26, and here taken from the reference implementation of the *Kokkos* library.

```
// mdspan/transpose.cpp
auto TL = md::submdspan( Amd, std::tuple{0,Nhalf},std::tuple{0,Nhalf} );
auto TR = md::submdspan( Amd, std::tuple{0,Nhalf},std::tuple{Nhalf,N} );
auto BL = md::submdspan( Amd, std::tuple{Nhalf,N},std::tuple{0,Nhalf} );
auto BR = md::submdspan( Amd, std::tuple{Nhalf,N},std::tuple{Nhalf,N} );
```

Now we write a loop over the quadrants of which the four iterations can be executed in four parallel threads:

```
// mdspan/transpose.cpp
for ( auto& [tgt,src] :
        // pairs of A/B tgt/src quadrants
        array< pair<decltype(TL),decltype(TL)>,4 >{
        pair{TL,TL}, pair{BR,BR}, pair{TR,BL}, pair{BL,TR} } ) {
  auto quadrant = rng::views::cartesian_product
    ( rng::views::iota( 0L, static_cast<long int>(tgt.extent(0)) ),
      rng::views::iota( 0L, static_cast<long int>(tgt.extent(1)) )
      );
  std::for_each
    ( quadrant.begin(),quadrant.end(),
      [&] ( auto idx ) {
        auto [i,j] = idx;
        Bmd[j,i] = Amd[i,j];
      }
      );
}
```

Of course we can apply this quadrisection recursively. First of all this allows the code to use more threads (and therefore cores), but it is also good for performance even without using parallelism. This is explored in the high performance linear algebra project in Chapter 43. For the explanation, see section 33.4.

4.2 ▪ The array class

In scientific computing applications, arrays are unlikely to be extended by push_back or shrunk by erase: they have a size that is set based on some input parameter and never changed. To express this, you could write your own storage container (see section 14.3) where such functionality is missing or disabled. For the more specialized case where the size is known at compile time, use the array class.

```
// array/stdarray.cpp
#include <array>
using std::array;
```

Array objects are declared with a static size as

```
array<float,3> coordinate;
```

```
// array/stdarray.cpp
{
  array<float,5> v5;
  cout << "size: " << v5.size() << '\n';
  // WRONG: no such function
  // v5.push_back(2);
}
```

A further important distinction between `std::vector` and `std::array` is that the former is allocated dynamically on the *heap*, while the latter is on the *stack*. Thus it may be more efficient.

Remark. *Since array bounds are known at compile time, interesting idioms involving* `constexpr` *are possible; see, for instance, section 13.1.4.*

4.2.1 ▪ Initialization

There are several ways to initialize a `std::array`.

With template parameters:

```
array<int,3> i3 = {1,2,3};
// or
array<int,3> i3 { {1,2,3} };
// or
array<int,3> i3{1,2,3};
```

With C++17 *template argument deduction*:

```
array i3 = {1,2,3};
// Note: DOES NOT COMPILE:
array not4{1.5,2,3,4};
```

4.2.2 ▪ Pass as argument

Passing an *initializer list* to a function that has a `std::array` parameter works:

```
// array/toarray.cpp
float first_of_three( array<float,3> fff ) {
  return fff[0];
};
    /* ... */
  println("{}",
          first_of_three( { 1.5 , 2.5 , 3.5 } ) );
```

However, in some cases it doesn't:

```
// array/toarray.cpp
template<unsigned long int d>
float first_of_bunch( array<float,d> fff ) {
  return fff[0];
};
    /* ... */
  // DOES NOT COMPILE:
  //  cout << first_of_bunch( { 1.5f , 2.5f , 3.5f } ) << '\n';
  // couldn't deduce template parameter 'd'
```

For this we can use `to_array` in C++20:

```
// array/toarray.cpp
// template parameter 'd' can be deduced from 'to_array':
println("{}",
        first_of_bunch( to_array( { 1.5f , 2.5f , 3.5f } ) ) );
```

4.2.3 ▪ Example: Random walks

In scientific computing, arrays are often very large. However, sometimes small arrays make sense; for instance, an array of size 2 or 3 can be used to model coordinates in two- or three-dimensional space. As an example, let's consider *random walks*, an algorithm originally used to model the spread of mosquitoes. Suppose an animal travels a unit distance every day, in a random direction. How far does it travel after N days? (The answer is proportional to $\sqrt{N}$.)

We use this to investigate the performance differences between `std::vector` and `std::array`. One basic tool is a templated routine

```
// walk/compare.cpp
template< typename VECTOR >
void random_vector( VECTOR& v );
```

that works for both vectors and arrays. Next we code the random walk three times. First the two basic implementations.

Random walk implementations

Vector:

```
// walk/compare.cpp
vector<float> random_walk_1( int steps ) {
  vector<float> result(3);
  for (int s=0; s<steps; ++s) {
    vector<float> update(3);
    random_vector<vector<float>>( update );
    for ( auto i : {0,1,2} )
      result[i] += update[i];
  }
  return result;
}
```

Array:

```
// walk/compare.cpp
array<float,3> random_walk_2( int steps ) {
  array<float,3> result = {0,0,0};
  for (int s=0; s<steps; ++s) {
    array<float,3> update{};
    random_vector<array<float,3>>
      ( update );
    for ( auto i : {0,1,2} )
      result[i] += update[i];
  }
  return result;
}
```

We can form several hypotheses why the array implementation will turn out to be more efficient:

- Arrays are statically allocated as local variables on the *stack*, while vectors are created dynamically on the *heap*, a much more complicated operation.
- Compilers can potentially perform more optimizations on array operations, since their size is known at compile time.
- Possibly stack memory is intrinsically more efficient than heap.

For the implementations above we can partly rule out the last two possibilities by considering a third implementation:

```
// walk/compare.cpp
void random_walk_3( vector<float>* result, vector<float>* update,int steps ) {
  for (int s=0; s<steps; ++s) {
    random_vector<vector<float>>( *update );
    for ( auto i : {0,1,2} )
      (*result)[i] += (*update)[i];
  }
}
```

This uses `std::vector`, but passing it as a pointer bypasses the repeated allocations.

Timing for the three algorithms:

Code:

```
// walk/compare.cpp
if (test==1) {
  vector<float> travel;
  travel = random_walk_1(steps);
  distance = norm(travel);
} else if (test==2) {
  array<float,3> travel;
  travel = random_walk_2(steps);
  distance = norm(travel);
} else if (test==3) {
  vector<float> travel(3);
  vector<float> step(3);
  random_walk_3(&travel, &step, steps);
  distance = norm(travel);
}
```

Output:

```
Test 1: distance: 2.9059e+07
run took: 7139 milliseconds
Test 2: distance: 2.9059e+07
run took: 3560 milliseconds
Test 3: distance: 2.9059e+07
run took: 2514 milliseconds
```

The array variant is clearly faster than the similar code with vectors, but for reasons unclear the third variant, passing vectors by pointer, is even marginally faster.

4.3 ▪ What not to do: C-style automatic arrays

Automatic arrays can be used as in C.

Code:

```
// array/staticinit.cpp
{
  int numbers[] = {5,4,3,2,1};
  println("{}",numbers[3]);
}
{
  int numbers[5]{5,4,3,2,1};
  numbers[3] = 21;
  println("{}",numbers[3]);
}
```

Output:

```
2
21
```

These has the (minimal) advantage of not having the overhead of a class mechanism. On the other hand, they have a number of disadvantages:

- You cannot query the size of an array by its name: you have to store that information separately in a variable.
- Passing such an array to a function is really passing the address of its first element, so it is always (sort of) by reference.

This mechanism should be avoided, per C++ Core Guidelines [12, R.14]. It is better to use `span` (section 4.1) or `array`; section 4.2.

4.3.1 ▪ Allocation

Traditionally, C arrays could only be allocated as

```
int a[5];
float b[6][7];
```

that is, with explicitly given array bounds. Some compilers supported as an extension so-called *variable length arrays*:

```
int n; scanf("%d",&n); // this reads n from the console
double x[n];
```

This mechanism was added to the C99 standard, but since support of it was not universal, the C11 standard made it optional again. The macro `__STC_NO_VLA__` is set to `1` if such support is indeed lacking.

Another thing to be aware of is that these arrays are allocated on the *stack*, so creating a too-large array may give stack overflow. This will make your code bomb with no informative error.

4.4 ▪ Sets and maps

4.4.1 ▪ Maps

Arrays use an integer-valued index. Sometimes you may wish to use an index that is not ordered, or for which the ordering is not relevant. A common example is looking up information by string, such as finding the age of a person, given their name. This is sometimes called "indexing by content," and the data structure that supports this is formally known as an *associative array*.

In C++ associative arrays are implemented through a `map` (for a practical use, see section 22.2.1),

```
#include <map>
using std::map;
map<string,int> ages;
```

which is a set of pairs where the first item (which is used for indexing) is of type `string`, and the second item (which is found) is of type `int`.

A map is made by inserting the elements one by one:

```
#include <map>
using std::make_pair;
ages.insert(make_pair("Alice",29));
ages["Bob"] = 32;
```

You can range over a map:

```
for ( auto person : ages )
  println( "{} has age {}",person.first,person.second);
```

A more elegant solution uses *structured binding* (section 11.5):

```
for ( auto [person,age] : ages )
  println("{} has age {}",person,age);
```

(It is possible to use const-references here.)

Searching for a key gives either the iterator of the key/value pair or the end iterator if not found:

```
// map/countint.cpp
for ( auto k : {4,5} ) {
  auto wherek = intcount.find(k);
  if (wherek==intcount.end())
    println("could not find key {}",k);
  else {
    auto [kk,vk] = *wherek;
    println("found key: {}; has value {}",kk,vk);
  }
}
```

Remark. *Iterating over a* map *returns results sorted by key. There is an* unordered_map *that can have speed and storage advantages but is not sorted.*

4.4.2 ▪ Sets

The set container is like a map<SomeType,bool>, that is, it only says "this element is present." Like a mathematical set, in other words.

```
#include <set>
std::set<int> my_ints;
my_ints.insert(5);
my_ints.empty(); // predicate
my_ints.size(); // obvious
```

Range iteration is defined, giving the elements in no particular order:

```
for ( auto x : my_ints )
  // do something
```

You can search through a set with find, which results in an iterator. If no match is found the end iterator is returned.

```
auto itr = my_ints.find(6);
if ( itr==my_ints.end() )
  println("not found");
```

You can search on elements that satisfy a predicate with find_if:

```
auto res = find_i(my_ints.begin(),my_ints.end(),
        [] ( auto e ) { return e>37; } );
```

Sets are useful in many computer science application such as graph algorithms; see Project Chapter 45. You often encounter idioms such as

```
while (not done) {
  for ( x in unprocessed ) {
    if (something with x) {
      processed.add(x);
      unprocessed.remove(x);
    }
  }
}
```

Chapter 5

Input/output

C++ has several mechanisms for doing ASCII output to screen or file. There is, inherited from C, printf:

```
#include <cstdio>
printf("Hello world %d\n",iworld);
```

More idiomatic is using stream formatting:

```
#include <iostream>
std::cout << "Hello world " << iworld << '\n';
```

which applies some default formatting. However, this gets cumbersome when sophisticated formatting is needed. Also, it is not atomic, so in a parallel context output from multiple threads may get tangled up.

In this chapter we look at the format header for simple I/O, which was introduced in C++20. See section 30.3 for more sophisticated scientific data file input and output. Occasionally we will use the *fmtlib* library (section 5.3) for features in C++23 that are not yet available in all compilers.

5.1 ▪ Format

We start exploring the format library. The std::format command, introduced in C++20, gives a formatted string:

```
#include <format>

std::cout << std::format( /* .... */ );
```

but we will primarily use the "print" functions from the C++23 print header:

```
#include <print> // C++23
```

The basic principle of formatting:

```
int i=2;
format("substituting {} brace expressions",i);
```

Specify format string and arguments.

The basic structure of each format call is as follows:

- The format string can have a number of placeholders indicated by braces.

- Following it are various entities to be substituted for them.

The `format` routine returns a `string`, which you can write to screen using `std::cout`.

```
cout << format( /* ... */ );
```

In C++23 routines `std::print` and `std::println` have been added in the `print` header:

```
#include <print>

std::print( /* formatting stuff*/ ); // no newline unless you insert it
std::println( /* formatting stuff*/ ); // newline added
```

so that `cout` is no longer needed.

5.1.1 ▪ Numbered arguments

The basic `format` call uses empty braces as placeholders for values to the formatted. The braces can also contain modifiers. Here we show how a single number can indicate which argument to take; arguments can be inserted into more than one placeholder.

Argument mechanism:

- Arguments indicated by curly braces in the format string.
- Braces can contain numbers (and modifiers, see next).

Code:

```
// iofmt/fmtbasic.cpp
println("{}",2);
string hello_string = format
  ("{} {}!","Hello","world");
cout << hello_string << '\n';
println
  ("{0}, {0} {1}!",
   "Hello","world");
```

Output:

```
2
Hello world!
Hello, Hello world!
```

We now proceed to discuss various modifiers on the default formatting.

5.1.2 ▪ Align and padding

The "greater-than" sign plus a number indicates right aligning and the width of the field. Numbers that don't fit that width "overflow" on the right.

Right-align with > character and width:

Code:

```
// iofmt/fmtlib.cpp
for (int i=10; i<200000000; i*=10)
  cout << format("{:>6}\n",i);
```

Output:

```
    10
   100
  1000
 10000
100000
1000000
10000000
100000000
```

By default, the space character is used for padding a right-aligned string. A different padding character can be specified immediately before the greater-than sign.

Other than space for padding:

Code:

```
// iofmt/fmtlib.cpp
for (int i=10; i<200000000; i*=10)
  cout << format("{0:.>6}\n",i);
```

Output:

```
....10
...100
..1000
.10000
100000
1000000
10000000
100000000
```

5.1.3 ▪ Number bases

You can indicate the base with which to represent an integer by specifying one of `b,o,x` for binary, octal, hex, respectively.

Code:

```
// iofmt/fmtlib.cpp
cout << format
  ("{0} = {0:b} bin\n",17);
cout << format
  ("   = {0:o} oct\n",17);
cout << format
  ("   = {0:x} hex\n",17);
```

Output:

```
17 = 10001 bin
   = 21 oct
   = 11 hex
```

5.1.4 ▪ Floating point numbers

So far we have looked at integers. Floating point numbers, `float` and `double`, can be rendered a number of ways. First we consider "scientific notation" which is forced with the `e` modifier, and a compact format that tries to avoid scientific notation if the number is not too large.

Floating point or normalized exponential with e specifier;
Fixed: use decimal point if it fits, m.n specification

Code:

```
// iofmt/fmtfloat.cpp
x = 1.234567;
for (int i=0; i<6; ++i) {
  println
    ("{0:.3e}/{0:7.4}",
     x);
  x *= 10;
}
```

Output:

```
1.235e+00/  1.235
1.235e+01/  12.35
1.235e+02/  123.5
1.235e+03/   1235
1.235e+04/1.235e+04
1.235e+05/1.235e+05
```

If you're printing out a column of numbers in scientific format, you will find that the above specifier makes the column wobble if there are both positive and negative number. An extra specifier indicates the treatment of any initial plus or minus:

- a plus sign will always print a leading plus or minus;
- a minus sign will print a minus sign for negative numbers, and nothing otherwise;
- a space will use a minus sign, or a space for nonnegative numbers.

Positive sign always, if needed, replace by blank:

Code:

```
// iofmt/fmtsci.cpp
float pi=3.14159f;
cout <<
  format("|{:+.2e}|{:+.2e}|\n",
         pi,-pi);
cout <<
  format("|{:-.2e}|{:-.2e}|\n",
         pi,-pi);
cout <<
  format("|{: .2e}|{: .2e}|\n",
         pi,-pi);
```

Output:

```
|+3.14e+00|-3.14e+00|
|3.14e+00|-3.14e+00|
| 3.14e+00|-3.14e+00|
```

For comparison of numbers that are roughly of the same order of magnitude, it is convenient to list them in "fixed point" notation, with the decimal point aligned. This is achieved by using the f modifier in the final location.

Use f modifier, give enough width, precision becomes number of decimal digits;
compare g modifier for general:

Code:

```
// iofmt/fmtfix.cpp
float pi=3.14159f;
for ( auto x : { 0.543f, 1.13f, -21.55f, 33.4f,
    156.8f } )
  println("{0:8g} : {0:-7.2f}",x);
```

Output:

```
   0.543 :    0.54
    1.13 :    1.13
  -21.55 :  -21.55
    33.4 :   33.40
   156.8 :  156.80
```

5.1.5 ▪ Truth values

Booleans are by default printed as `true` or `false`:

```
format( "{}", true ); // gives 'true'
```

To get them printed as zero or one, use the `:d` modifier:

```
format( "{:d}", true ); // gives '1'
```

5.1.6 ▪ Limitations

The format library cannot take any type to display. What it can display depends on what types the `std::formatter` is specialized for. Currently that's mostly numerical types, character/string types, and types from the `chrono` library. Notable additions in C++23 are ranges.

However, many library types, notably `complex` and `bitset`, are still missing. You can write such specializations yourself; see section 5.2.2.

5.2 ▪ Outputting objects

The standard output mechanisms of C++ can only deal with primitive types and pointers. If you want to output objects, of your own devising or otherwise, it is possible to have them rendered, after a little coding.

5.2.1 ▪ Stream formatting

You have used statements like

```
cout << "My value is: " << myvalue << "\n";
```

How does this work? The "double less" is an operator with a left operand that is a stream, and a right operand for which output is defined; the result of this operator is again a stream. Recursively, this means you can chain any number of applications of << together.

If you want to output a class that you wrote yourself, you have to define how the << operator deals with your class.

Here we solve this in two steps:

Define a function that yields a string representing the object:

```
#include <sstream>
using std::stringstream;
```

```
// geom/pointfunc.cpp
string as_string() {
  stringstream ss;
  ss << "(" << x << "," << y << ")";
  return ss.str();
};
```

```
// geom/pointfunc.cpp
string as_fmt_string() {
  auto ss = format("({},{})",x,y);
  return ss;
};
```

Redefine the less-less operator:

```
// geom/pointfunc.cpp
std::ostream& operator<<
(std::ostream &out,Point &p) {
  out << p.as_string(); return out;
};
```

Use:

```
// geom/pointfunc.cpp
Point p1(1.,2.);
cout << "p1 " << p1
     << " has length "
     << p1.length() << "\n";
```

If you don't want to write that accessor function, you can declare the less-less operator as a `friend`:

```
class container {
private: double x;
public:
  friend ostream& operator<<( ostream& s,const container& c ) {
    s << c.x; /* no accessor */
    return s; };
};
```

5.2.2 ▪ Format library

Formatting with the `format` header (or the library) is done by writing a specialization of the templated `std::formatter` class. Let's say you have a class `XYclass`; in order to be able to write

```
// iofmt/fmtclass.cpp
XYclass x(5,6.7);
println("XYclass: {}",x);
```

you need to define

```
template<>
class std::formatter<XYclass>;
```

A sophisticated implementation involves some tedium, but we can sketch a minimal solution. This involves writing a method `format` that returns an `output_iterator` object (details omitted). Here is the example formatter for the `XYclass`, which you can now use as a template:

```
// iofmt/fmtclass.cpp
template<>
class std::formatter<XYclass>{
public:
  constexpr auto parse( std::format_parse_context& ctx ) {
    return ctx.begin(); };
  auto format( const XYclass& z,std::format_context& ctx ) const {
    return std::format_to
      ( ctx.out(),"[ {}, {} ]",z.x,z.y);
  };
};
```

5.3 ▪ The `fmtlib` library

The `fmtlib` library gave rise to the `format` header in C++20. It still contains some functionality that may not have made it into the `format` header of your compiler, such as the `std::print` function.

5.3.1 ▪ CMake integration

In the following example, we use the *fmtlib* library. The main *CMake* file is

```
cmake_minimum_required( VERSION 3.13 )
project( fmtlibmod VERSION 1.0 )

add_executable( program program.cxx )
find_package( fmt )
target_link_libraries( program PUBLIC fmt::fmt )

install( TARGETS program DESTINATION . )
```

5.3.2 ▪ Example: fmtlib used in library

We continue using the *fmtlib* library, but now the generated library also has references to this library, so we use `target_link_directories` and `target_link_library`.

Main file:

```
cmake_minimum_required( VERSION 3.13 )
project( pkgconfiglib VERSION 1.0 )

find_package( PkgConfig REQUIRED )
pkg_check_modules( FMTLIB REQUIRED fmt )
message( STATUS "fmtlib includes : ${FMTLIB_INCLUDE_DIRS}" )
message( STATUS "fmtlib lib dirs : ${FMTLIB_LIBRARY_DIRS}" )
message( STATUS "fmtlib libraries: ${FMTLIB_LIBRARIES}" )

add_executable( program program.cxx )
target_include_directories(
        program PUBLIC
        ${FMTLIB_INCLUDE_DIRS})

add_subdirectory( prolib )
target_link_libraries( program PUBLIC prolib )

install( TARGETS program DESTINATION . )
```

Library file:

```
project( prolib )

add_library( prolib SHARED aux.cxx aux.h )
target_include_directories(
        prolib PUBLIC
        ${FMTLIB_INCLUDE_DIRS})
target_link_directories(
        prolib PUBLIC
        ${FMTLIB_LIBRARY_DIRS})
target_link_libraries(
        prolib PUBLIC fmt )
```

5.4 ▪ VT100 animation

Often you want some sort of graphical or animated output. However, not all programming languages generate visual output equally easily. There are very powerful video/graphics libraries in C++, but these are also nontrivial to use. There is a simpler way out.

For simple output you can make some low-budget graphics. Every *terminal emulator* under the sun supports *VT100 cursor control* codes [53], named after the 1980s *DEC VT100* terminal. With these you can send certain magic sequences to your screen to control cursor positioning, or set other terminal properties such as switch to alternate character sets.

While a large number of control codes are available, the following minimum often suffices.

- Wipe the screen clean by "printing"

  ```
  #include <cstdio>
  printf( "%c[2J",(char)27 );
  ```

- Then position the cursor at the top left coordinate:

  ```
  printf( "%c[0;0H",(char)27 );
  ```

With the `format` header you could also:

```
cout << format("\u{1b}[2J");
cout << format("\u{1b}[0;0H");
// or use std::print
```

This is used in the project of Chapter 44.

Chapter 6

Lambda expressions

In this chapter we will look at lambda expressions, which we can roughly consider as a way of writing a function definition inline. There are two important motivations for this.

Use in algorithms Many of the functions in the `algorithm` header work by applying a function to each element of a range; see Chapter 7. Being able to inline the function recipe makes it possible to write elegant "data-parallel" code.

Callbacks Numerical libraries traditionally make heavy use of the "callback" mechanism: the library calls a piece of user code. One example of this is iterative algorithms, which can have a user-defined monitoring routine, applied in each iteration. Another example concerns libraries for zero-finding or numerical quadrature; here the library algorithm intrinsically needs to call the user-supplied function. Chapter 17 has a worked out example of this.

6.1 ▪ Introduction to lambda expressions

The mechanism of *lambda expressions* makes dynamic definition of functions possible.

Traditional function usage:
Explicitly define a function and apply it:

```
float sum(float x,float y) { return x+y; }
cout << sum( 1.2f, 3.4f );
```

New:
Apply the function recipe directly:

Code:

```
// lambda/lambdaex.cpp
[] (float x,float y) -> float {
  return x+y; } ( 1.5, 2.3 )
```

Output:

```
3.8
```

This example illustrates the basic syntax of a lambda expression:

```
[capture] ( inputs ) -> outtype { definition };
```

- The square brackets—empty in this case, but not in general—are the *capture* part;
- then follows the parenthesized parameter list;
- with a stylized arrow you can indicate the return type;
- and finally the usual function body, including `return` statement for nonvoid functions.

Several of these components are optional:

- the parameter list can be omitted if there are no parameters, but this cannot be combined with qualifiers or trailing return type;
- the trailing return type is optional if the compiler can figure it out by itself;
- there can be several keywords on the lambda; below we will describe the keyword `mutable`.

Remark. *Lambda expressions are sometimes inaccurately called* closures; *this concept refers to the internal object containing the function recipe and captured environment.*

The above example can be classified as an *immediately invoked lambda* expression. While that example was somewhat pointless, there are uses for this idiom, such as being able to choose dynamically between two constructors.

Invoke different constructors based on runtime condition:

Does not work:

```
// lambda/invoke.cpp
if (foo)
  MyClass x(5,5);
else
  MyClass x("foo");
```

Solution:

```
// lambda/invoke.cpp
auto x =
  [foo] () {
    if (foo)
      return MyClass(5,5);
    else
      return MyClass("foo");
  }();
```

Note the use of `auto` and the omitted return type.

Another use of immediately invoked lambda expression can be found in section 15.4.1.

For a slightly more useful example, we can assign the lambda expression to a variable and repeatedly apply it.

Lambda expression assigned to a variable:

Code:

```
// lambda/lambdaex.cpp
auto summing =
  [] (float x,float y) -> float {
  return x+y; };
cout << summing ( 1.5, 2.3 ) << '\n';
cout << summing ( 3.7, 5.2 ) << '\n';
```

Output:

```
3.8
8.9
```

- This is a variable declaration.
- Uses `auto` for technical reasons; see later.

Return type could have been omitted:

```
auto summing =
  [] (float x,float y) { return x+y; };
```

You can now exercise this by writing a toy numerical library.

Exercise 6.1. Do Exercise 17.2 of the zero-finding project.

6.2 ▪ Lambda expressions as function argument

Above, when we assigned a lambda expression to a variable, we used `auto` for the type. The reason for this is that each lambda expression gets its own unique type that is dynamically generated. Now we have a problem if we want to pass that variable to a function.

Suppose we want to pass a lambda expression to a function:

```
int main() {
    somefun( [] (int i) { cout << i+1; } );
```

What type do we use for the function parameter?

```
void somefun( /* what type are we giving? */ f ) {
    f(5);
}
```

Since the type of the lambda expression is dynamically generated, we cannot specify that type in the function declaration.

The way out is to use the `functional` header:

```
#include <functional>
using std::function;
```

With this, you can declare parameters by their signature.

In the following example we write a function `apply_to_5` which

- takes a function `f`, and
- applies it to `5`.

We call the `apply_to_5` function with a lambda expression as argument:

Code:

```
// lambda/lambdaex.cpp
void apply_to_5
    ( function< void(int) > f ) {
  f(5);
}
    /* ... */
  apply_to_5
    ( [] (int i) {
      println("Int: {}",i);
     } );
```

Output:

```
Int: 5
```

Another possibility for passing function is to templatize the receiving function:

```
template< typename F >
void apply_to_5( F f ) { /* ... */ };
```

Thanks to *template argument deduction* such a function can actually be called without specifying the type of `F` in angle brackets, if this type is clear at the calling site.

Use these mechanisms to extend the numerical library you started before.

Exercise 6.2. Do exercise 17.3 of the zero-finding project.

6.2.1 ▪ Lambda members of classes

The fact that a lambda expression has a dynamically generated type also makes it hard to store it in an object. To do this we again use `std::function`.

In the following example we make a class `SelectedInts` which takes a boolean function in the constructor: an object will contain only those integers that satisfy the function.

A set of integers, with a test on which ones can be admitted:

Class:

```
// lambda/lambdafun.cpp
#include <functional>
using std::function;
    /* ... */
class SelectedInts {
private:
  vector<int> bag;
  function< bool(int) > selector;
public:
  SelectedInts
      ( function< bool(int) > f ) {
    selector = f; };
```

Methods:

```
// lambda/lambdafun.cpp
  void add(int i) {
    if (selector(i))
      bag.push_back(i);
  };
  int size() {
    return bag.size(); };
  std::string as_string() {
    std::string s;
    for ( int i : bag )
      s += to_string(i)+" ";
    return s;
  };
};
```

We use the above class to construct an object as follows:

- we read an integer `divisor`,
- and accept only those integers into our object that are divisible by that number.

For this we write a lambda expression `is_divisible` that

- captures the divisor, and then
- takes an integer as (its only) argument,
- returning whether that argument is divisible.

The above code in use:

Code:

```
// lambda/lambdafun.cpp
println("Give a divisor: ");
cin >> divisor;
println(".. divisor {}",divisor);
auto is_divisible =
  [divisor] (int i) -> bool {
    return i%divisor==0; };
SelectedInts multiples( is_divisible );
for (int i=1; i<50; ++i)
  multiples.add(i);
```

Output:

```
Give a divisor:
.. using 7
Multiples of 7:
7 14 21 28 35 42 49
```

6.3 ▪ Captures

A *capture* is a way to “bake variables into” a function. Let’s say we want a function that increments its input, and the increment amount is set when we define the function.

Increment function:

- scalar in, scalar out;
- the increment amount has been fixed through the capture.

Code:

```
// lambda/lambdacapture.cpp
int n;
cin >> n;
auto increment_by_n =
  [n] ( int input ) -> int {
    return input+n;
};
println("{}",increment_by_n (5));
println("{}",increment_by_n (12));
println("{}",increment_by_n (25));
```

Output:

```
(input value: 1)

6
13
26
```

The captured value is copied into the lambda expression. If you capture a variable, and change it afterwards, the lambda expression does not change. The reason is that the captured value is copied; below you will see that there is a possibility of capturing by reference.

Illustrating that the capture variable is copied once and for all:

Code:

```
// lambda/lambdacapture.cpp
int inc;
cin >> inc;
auto increment =
  [inc] ( int input ) -> int {
    return input+inc;
  };
println("increment by: {}",inc);
println("1 -> {}",increment(1));
inc = 2*inc;
println("1 -> {}",increment(1));
```

Output:

```
increment by: 2
1 -> 3
1 -> 3
```

Exercise 6.3. Write a program that

- reads a `float` factor;
- defines a function `multiply` of one argument that multiplies its input by that factor.

You can capture more than one variable. Explicitly capturing variables is done with a comma-separated list.

Example: multiply by a fraction.

```
int d=2,n=3;
times_fraction = [d,n] (int i) ->int {
    return (i*d)/n;
}
```

Exercise 6.4.

- Set two variables

  ```
  float low = .5, high = 1.5;
  ```

- Define a function `is_in_range` of one variable that tests whether that variable is between `low,high`.
  (Hint: what is the signature of that function? What is/are input parameter(s) and what is the return result?)

Use this again in the numerical library you are developing.

Exercise 6.5. Do Exercises 17.4 and 17.5 of the zero-finding project.

6.3.1 ▪ Capture by reference

Normally, captured variables are copied by value.

Attempting to change the captured variable doesn't even compile:

```
auto f = // WRONG DOES NOT COMPILE
    [x] ( float &y ) -> void {
        x *= 2; y += x; };
```

If you do want to alter the captured parameter, pass it by reference:

Code:

```
// lambda/lambdacapture.cpp
int stride = 1;
auto more_and_more =
  [&stride] ( int input ) -> void {
    println("{} => {}",input,input+stride);
    ++stride;
};
more_and_more(5);
more_and_more(6);
more_and_more(7);
more_and_more(8);
more_and_more(9);
println("stride is now: {}",stride);
```

Output:

```
(input value: 1)

5 => 6
6 => 8
7 => 10
8 => 12
9 => 14
stride is now: 6
```

Capturing by reference can, for instance, be useful if you are performing some sort of reduction. The capture is then the reduction variable, and the numbers to be reduced come in as function parameter to the lambda expression.

In this example we count how many of the input values test true under a certain function *f*:

Capture a variable by reference so that you can update it:

Code:

```
// lambda/countif.cpp
int count=0;
auto count_if_f =
  [&count] (int i) {
    if (i%2==0) count++; };
for ( int i : {1,2,3,4,5} )
  count_if_f(i);
println("We counted: {}",count);
```

Output:

```
We counted: 2
```

6.3.2 ▪ Capturing "this"

In addition to capturing specific variable, whether by reference or not, as you saw above, you can also capture the whole environment of a lambda. For this the following shorthand exists:

```
[=] () {} // capture everything by value
[&] () {} // capture everything by reference
```

As of C++20, implicit *capture* of `this` by value is deprecated: writing

```
[=] (params) { /* ... */ }
```

would capture `this` by value, but noting that `this` is a pointer, its members are actually captured by reference. Therefore, one should write either

```
[=,*this] (params} { /* ... */ );
[=,this] (params} { /* ... */ );
```

which capture members by value and reference, respectively.

It is worth noting that capturing by value involves calling the copy constructor and destructor. To illustrate this we need a class that traces its constructor/destructor:

```
// lambda/capturethis.cpp
class trace {
private:
  int i{314};
public:
  trace()  {
    println("construct"); };
  trace( trace& t ) {
    println("copy"); };
  ~trace() {
    println("destruct"); };
```

Capturing by value:

Code:

```
// lambda/capturethis.cpp
void testv() {
  println(" .. testing");
  [*this] () {
    println(" .. lambda {}",i);
  }();
  println(" .. done");
};
```

Output:

```
 .. testing
copy
 .. lambda 314
destruct
 .. done
```

Capturing by reference:

Code:

```
// lambda/capturethis.cpp
void testr() {
  println(" .. testing");
  [this] () {
    println(" .. lambda {}",i);
  }();
  println(" .. done");
};
```

Output:

```
 .. testing
 .. lambda 314
 .. done
```

6.3.2.1 ▪ Void pointers and callback functions

Lambda expression can always be used to get rid of the traditional use of *void pointer*s in libraries written in C.

A typical use of void pointers appears in the PETSc [4, 5] library. Normally when you call a library routine, you have no further access to what happens inside that routine. However, PETSc has the functionality for you to specify a monitor so that you can print out internal quantities.

```
int KSPSetMonitor(KSP ksp,
  int (*monitor)(KSP,int,PetscReal,void*),
  void *context,
  // one parameter omitted
  );
```

Here you can declare your own monitor routine that will be called internally: the library makes a *callback* to your code. Since the library cannot predict whether your monitor routine may need further information in order to function, there is the `context` argument, where you can pass a structure as void pointer.

This mechanism is no longer needed in C++, where you would use a *lambda*:

```
KSPSetMonitor( ksp,
  [mycontext] (KSP k,int iter,PetscReal r) -> int {
    my_monitor_function(k,iter,r,mycontext); } );
```

6.4 ▪ More

6.4.1 ▪ Making lambda stateful

Let's consider the issue of lambda expressions and mutable state, by which we mean no more than that a variable internal to the lambda expression can get updated. Above you have already seen how you can capture a variable from the calling environment by reference.

Lambda expressions are normally stateless, meaning that the capture is captured by value, and is in fact `const`:

Code:

```
// lambda/mutable.cpp
float x = 2, y = 3;
auto f = [x] ( float &y ) -> void {
  int xx = x*2; y += xx; };
f(y);
cout << y << '\n';
f(y);
cout << y << '\n';
```

Output:

```
7
11
```

You can make the capture non-`const`, and thereby make the lambda expression stateful, with the `mutable` keyword:

Code:

```
// lambda/mutable.cpp
float x = 2, y = 3;
auto f = [x] ( float &y ) mutable -> void {
  x *= 2; y += x; };
f(y);
cout << y << '\n';
f(y);
cout << y << '\n';
```

Output:

```
7
15
```

How about if that capture is not really needed in the calling environment of the lambda expression; can we somehow make it internal? Indeed, we can initialize local variables with a *capture-default*, which in this case doesn't really capture anything.

```
[count=0] ( /* arguments */ ) mutable {
  count++; /* other statements */
}
```

Here is a nifty application: printing a list of numbers, separated by commas, but without trailing comma:

Code:

```
// lambda/lambdaexch.cpp
  vector x{1,2,3,4,5};
  auto printdigit =
    [start=true] (auto xx) mutable -> string{
      if (start) {
        start = false;
        return to_string(xx);
      } else
        return ","+to_string(xx);
    };
  for ( auto xx : x )
    cout << printdigit(xx);
  cout << '\n';
```

Output:

```
1,2,3,4,5
```

For another example see section 19.2.

6.4.2 ▪ Generic lambdas

The `auto` keyword can be used for *generic lambdas*:

```
auto compare = [] (auto a,auto b) { return a<b; };
```

Here the return type is clear, but the input types are generic. This is much like using a templated function: the compiler instantiates the expression with whatever types are needed from the context.

6.4.3 ▪ Algorithms

The `algorithm` header contains a number of functions that naturally use lambdas. For instance, `any_of` can test whether any element of a `vector` satisfies a condition. You can then use a lambda to specify the `bool` function that tests the condition.

This uses mechanisms we haven't discussed yet, so we postpone this until section 7.3.

6.4.4 ▪ C-style function pointers

The C language had a—somewhat confusing—notation for function pointers. If you need to interface with code that uses them, it is possible to use lambda functions to an extent: lambdas without captures can be converted to a function pointer.

Lambda expression with empty capture are compatible with C-style function pointers:

Code:

```
// lambda/lambdacptr.cpp
int cfun_add1( int i ) {
  return i+1; };
int apply_to_5( int(*f)(int) ) {
  return f(5); };
    /* ... */
  auto lambda_add1 =
    [] (int i) { return i+1; };
  cout << "C ptr: "
       << apply_to_5(&cfun_add1)
       << '\n';
  cout << "Lambda: "
       << apply_to_5(lambda_add1)
       << '\n';
```

Output:

```
C ptr: 6
Lambda: 6
```

Chapter 7

Range algorithms

There are many ways to loop over the elements of a container. You may know that

```
for ( int i=0; i<v.size(); ++i )
   f( v[i] )
```

is better written with a *range-based loop* as

```
for ( auto e : v )
   f( e )
```

The "range" mechanism of C++20 goes even further. Now you write

```
some_range_method( v, ..lambda expression with f.. )
```

where examples of the range method are `for_each`, for applying a function to each element in place; `filter`, for giving only the elements satisfying some condition; or `all_of`, to test whether all elements satisfying some condition.

In this chapter we will look at the range mechanism, and we consider its underlying "iterator" mechanism. This knowledge is then used in Chapter 14 to write your own iteratable and range-able containers. Lambda expressions were introduced in Chapter 6.

7.1 ▪ Ranges

The C++20 standard contains a `ranges` header, which generalizes iteratable objects into as-it-were streams. This allows you to express algorithms in terms of operations on whole ranges, rather than on individual elements.

We need to introduce two new concepts: ranges and views. First of all, a range is something you can iterate over. The containers of the pre-17 standard library such as `std::vector` are ranges and you can iterate over them in range-based loops, but in this chapter you'll learn other ways of ranging.

In the examples to follow we will abbreviate

```
#include <ranges>
namespace rng = std::ranges;
```

so that you can write

```
rng::transform
```

and such.

The `ranges` header contains a number of algorithms. Here are two examples, sorting and summing a vector. In both cases no iteration is explicitly mentioned:

Sorting:

```
// rangestd/sort.cpp
vector<int> v{3,1,2};
rng::sort(v);
for ( auto e : v )
  cout << e << '\n';
```

Summing:

```
// range/sumsquare.cpp
vector<float> elements{.5f,1.f,1.5f};
auto sum_of_elts =
  rng::accumulate( elements, 0.f );
cout << "Sum of elements: "
     << sum_of_elts << '\n';
```

7.1.1 ▪ Introduction

Let's consider some simple examples in which we combine a rangeable container, a lambda expression to apply to each element, and an algorithm that combines these. At first we use `for_each` to output each element of a vector.

With

```
// rangestd/range.cpp
vector<int> v{2,3,4,5,6,7};
```

Code:

```
// rangestd/range.cpp
#include <ranges>
namespace rng = std::ranges;
#include <algorithm>
    /* ... */
  vector<int> v{2,3,4,5,6,7};
  rng::for_each
    ( v, [] (int i) { cout << i << " "; } );
```

Output:

```
2 3 4 5 6 7
```

Often we use a *capture by reference*, for instance, to let a variable act as an accumulator. In the following example, the lambda expression is applied to each data element, and updates a global variable that was captured by reference.

Capture a global accumulator by reference:

Code:

```
// rangestd/range.cpp
count = 0;
rng::for_each
  ( v,
    [&count] (int i) {
      count += (i<5); }
    );
cout << "Under five: "
     << count << '\n';
```

Output:

```
Under five: 3
```

Let's use ranges to reformulate some loop-based code.

Exercise 7.1. Write a `norm` function that computes the Euclidean norm of a `std::vector`. Instead of iterating, use a `for_each` algorithm.

Also write a `scale` function using a `for_each` algorithm.

7.1.2 ▪ Views

A *view* is somewhat similar to a range, in the sense that you can iterate over it. The difference is that unlike, for instance, a `vector`, a view is not a completely formed object: its elements are formed as needed, often by applying a *range adapter* to a range. You would typically write something like

```
yourcontainer | someview
```

and the result of this is just as iteratable as the original container. The "view" is often a *range adaptor*, taken from the `views` namespace. For instance:

```
myvector | views::drop(5)
```

which acts as if you omitted the first 5 elements from your vector.

Views act like ranges, for instance in the sense that you can iterate over them.

Filter a range by some condition:

Code:

```
// rangestd/filter.cpp
vector<float> numbers
  {1,-2.2,3.3,-5,7.7,-10};
for ( auto n :
        numbers
        | std::ranges::views::filter
          ( [] (float f) -> bool {
              return f>0; } )
    )
  cout << n << " ";
cout << '\n';
```

Output:

```
1 3.3 7.7
```

A view doesn't own any data, and any elements you view in it get formed as you iterate over it. This is sometimes called *lazy evaluation* or *lazy execution*. Stated differently, its elements are constructed as they are being requested by the iteration over the view. This even makes it possible to have infinite ranges, for example, with `iota_view` (see section 7.1.4): everything works as long as you don't ask for the last element.

Views are composable: you can take one view, and pipe it into another one. Because of the lazy evaluation, no temporary objects corresponding to the intermediate ranges and views are formed. If you need the resulting object, rather than the elements as a stream, you can call (in C++23) `ranges::to`:

```
auto newvector = myvector | views::drop(5) | to<vector<int>>();
```

Let's look at some examples of views.

We start with a `transform` view, which applies a function to each element of the range or view in sequence. In this particular example we multiply each element by two.

Code:

```
// range/filtertransform.cpp
vector<int> v{ 1,2,3,4,5,6 };
cout
  << "Original data:\n  "
  << vector_as_string(v)
  << '\n';
auto times_two = v
  | rng::views::transform
      ( [] (int i) {
        return 2*i; } );
cout << "Times two:\n  ";
for ( auto c : times_two )
  cout << c << " "; cout << '\n';
```

Output:

```
Original vector:
  1, 2, 3, 4, 5, 6,
Times two:
  2 4 6 8 10 12
```

Next we use `filter` on the transform results, which only yields those elements that satisfy some boolean test.

Code:

```
// range/filtertransform.cpp
auto over_five = times_two
  | rng::views::filter
      ( [] (int i) {
        return i>5; } );
cout << "Over five: ";
for ( auto c : over_five )
  cout << c << " "; cout << '\n';
```

Output:

```
Over five: 6 8 10 12
```

In the above examples `times_two` and `over_five` are views, and explicitly formed and stored objects. The required elements in the loops are generated from the initial range object as the iteration requires. In particular, no temporary object of size comparable to the initial range is created.

We can collapse the two above snippets into one by composition of views:

Code:

```
// range/filtertransform.cpp
vector<int> v{ 1,2,3,4,5,6 };
/* ... */
auto times_two_over_five = v
   | rng::views::transform
       ( [] (int i) {
         return 2*i; } )
   | rng::views::filter
       ( [] (int i) {
         return i>5; } );
```

Output:

```
Original vector:
  1, 2, 3, 4, 5, 6,
Times two over five:
  6 8 10 12
```

Let's exercise this piping of containers and views.

Exercise 7.2. Make a vector that contains both positive and negative numbers. Use ranges to compute the minimum square root of the positive numbers.

1. Start with a vector of numbers.
2. Make an iteratable view containing just the square roots of the positive numbers.
3. Find the minimum of these roots.

Other available operations:

- dropping initial elements: `std::views::drop`;
- reversing a vector: `std::views::reverse`.

In C++23 some more views have been added. For instance, if you have to iterate simultaneously over two containers, you can use the `zip` view. Here each iteration gives a tuple of elements from the zipped containers.

Zip ranges together with `ranges::views::zip`, giving a tuple:

Code:

```
// rangestd/zip.cpp
vector a { 10, 20, 30, 40, 50 };
vector<string> b
  { "one", "two", "three", "four" };

for (const auto& [num, name] :
       rng::views::zip(a, b))
  cout << name << " -> " << num << '\n';
```

Output:

```
one -> 10
two -> 20
three -> 30
four -> 40
```

If you need both the elements of the range and their index, it is not necessary to fall back on the old indexed `for` loop. The C++23 standard added the `enumerate` adapter.

Enumerating a range gives a pair of a `long int` and the corresponding range element:

Code:

```
// range/enumerate.cpp
vector<int> values{2,4,5,7,10};
for ( auto [i,v] : values
        | rng::views::enumerate )
  cout << "Element " << i
       << ": " << v << '\n';
```

Output:

```
Element 0: 2
Element 1: 4
Element 2: 5
Element 3: 7
Element 4: 10
```

So far we have only seen range adapters that apply a function to a single element of the range. It is also possible to combine successive elements.

Return adjacent elements with `ranges::adjacent` as a tuple:

```
// range/adjacent.cpp
  for ( auto [ lt,md,rt ] : values | views::adjacent<3> )
    cout << fixed
         << setw(3) << lt << ","
         << setw(3) << md << ","
         << setw(3) << rt << '\n';
```

7.1.3 ▪ Example: Sum of squares

For computing the sum of squares of the elements of a vector, we can use the range `transform` method for constructing a "lazy container" of the squares. We use the `accumulate` adapter from C++23.

```
// range/sumsquare.cpp
vector<float> elements{.5f,1.f,1.5f};
auto squares =
  rng::views::transform(elements, [] (auto e) { return e*e; } );
auto sumsq =
  rng::accumulate( squares, 0.f );
cout << "Sum of squares: " << sumsq << '\n';
```

7.1.4 ▪ Infinite sequences

Since views are lazily constructed, it is possible to have an infinite object—as long as you don't ask for its last element.

In the following example we make a view `even_numbers` that "contains" all even numbers, and then we print only the first ten of them:

Code:

```
// range/infinite.cpp
auto even_numbers =
  rng::views::iota(0)
  | rng::views::filter
      ( [] ( auto n ) { return n%2==0; } );
for ( auto n : even_numbers
        | rng::views::take(10) )
  cout << n << '\n';
```

Output:

```
0
2
4
6
8
10
12
14
16
18
```

Here we used the range version of `iota` in the variant where only the lower bound is specified, and we use `ranges::views::take` to take only the head of this list.

7.2 ▪ Iterators

Next we look at the "iterator" mechanism that underlies ranges. You will not often use iterators explicitly in high level programming, but you need to know about them if you make your own iteratable classes. We will explore this in section 14.4.2.

Equivalence of range and iterator code:

The range code

```
vector<int> myvector(20);
for ( auto copy_of_int : myvector )
  s += copy_of_int;
```

is actually short for:

```
for
  ( std::vector<int>::iterator
      it=myvector.begin() ;
      it!=myvector.end() ; ++it ) {
        int copy_of_int = *it;
        s += copy_of_int ;
        }
```

Range iterators can be used with anything that is iteratable: vector, map, your own classes! For that last point, see section 14.4.

7.2.1 ▪ Iterator arithmetic

The `begin` / `end` functions give *iterators*, which are objects that act a little like pointers to the start and end of the container. For instance, you can increment and decrement them:

Code:

```
// iter/iter.cpp
vector<int> counts{1,2,3,4};
auto second = counts.begin(); ++second;
cout << "Second element: " << *second << '\n';
auto last = counts.end(); last--;
cout << "Last element: " << *last << '\n';
```

Output:

```
Second element: 2
Last element: 4
```

There are also library functions (in the `iterator` library) for this:

Code:

```
// iter/iternext.cpp
vector<int> counts{1,2,3,4};
auto second = counts.begin();
second = std::next(second);
cout << "Second element: " << *second << '\n';
auto last = counts.end();
last = std::prev(last);
cout << "Last element: " << *last << '\n';
```

Output:

```
Second element: 2
Last element: 4
```

In addition to `std::next` and `std::prev` there is a more general function `std::advance`.

7.2.2 ▪ Iterating with iterators

The container class has a subclass *iterator* that can be used to iterate through all elements of a container.

An `iterator` can be used outside of strictly iterating. You can consider an iterator as a sort of "pointer into a container," and you can move it about.

Let's look at some examples of using the `begin` and `end` iterators. In the following example:

- We first assign the `begin` and `end` iterators to variables; the begin iterator points at the first element, but the end iterator points just beyond the last element.
- Given an iterator, you get the value of the corresponding element by applying the "star" operator to it.
- A sort of "pointer arithmetic" can be applied to iterators.

Use independent of looping:

Code:

```
// stl/iter.cpp
vector<int> v{1,3,5,7};
auto pointer = v.begin();
cout << "we start at "
     << *pointer << '\n';
++pointer;
cout << "after increment: "
     << *pointer << '\n';

pointer = v.end();
cout << "end is not a valid element: "
     << *pointer << '\n';
pointer--;
cout << "last element: "
     << *pointer << '\n';
```

Output:

```
we start at 1
after increment: 3
end is not a valid element: 0
last element: 7
```

Note that the star notation is a *unary star operator* on the iterator object, not a *pointer dereference*:

```
// iter/iter.cpp
vector<int> vec{11,22,33,44,55,66};
auto second = vec.begin(); ++second;
cout << "Dereference second: "
     << *second << '\n';
// DOES NOT COMPILE
// the iterator is not a type-star:
// int *subarray = second;
```

Another illustration of iterators is getting the last element of a vector: We start by getting the value through the `back` method.

Use `back` to get the value of the last element:

Code:

```
// array/vectorend.cpp
vector<int> mydata(5,2);
// last element:
cout << mydata.back()
     << '\n';
mydata.push_back(35);
cout << mydata.size()
     << '\n';
// last element:
cout << mydata.back()
     << '\n';
```

Output:

```
2
6
35
```

Next we use the iterator mechanism. The `end` iterator points just "beyond' the data, so we shift it left and get its value.

Set an iterator to the last element and "dereference" it:

Code:

```
// array/vectorend.cpp
vector<int> mydata(5,2);
mydata.push_back(35);
cout << mydata.size() << '\n';
cout << *( --mydata.end() ) << '\n';
```

Output:

```
6
35
```

7.3 ▪ Algorithms on ranges

Many simple algorithms on arrays, such as testing "there is" or "for all," no longer have to be coded out in C++. They can now be done with a single function from the `std::algorithm` library. This contains components that C++ programs may use to perform algorithmic operations on containers and other sequences.

So, even if you have learned to code a specific algorithm yourself in the foregoing, you should study the following algorithms, or at least know that such algorithms exist. It's what distinguishes a novice programmer from an industrial-grade (for want of a better term) programmer.

7.3.1 ▪ Test any/all

First we look at some algorithms that apply a predicate to the elements.

- Test if any element satisfies a condition: `any_of`. Note that both `std::any_of` and `std::ranges::any_of` exist. The former uses explicit iterators; we are mostly interested in the latter, which takes a rangeable object. The same distinction holds for the next two algorithms.
- Test if all elements satisfy a condition: `all_of`.
- Test if no elements satisfy a condition: `none_of`.
- Apply an operation to all elements: `for_each`.

Remark. *These tests correspond to mathematical* quantors *and can be helpful in writing provably correct code. See section 25.1.*

The object to which the function applies is not specified directly; rather, you have to specify a start and end iterator.

As an example of applying a predicate we look at a couple of examples using `any_of`. This returns true or false depending on whether the predicate is true for any element of the container. Such boolean range algorithms use *short-circuit evaluation*: they stop evaluating range elements at the first true (for "there is") or false (for "for all").

Reduction with boolean result:
See if any element satisfies a test:

Code:

```
// iter/eachr.cpp
#include <ranges>
#include <algorithm>
    /* ... */
    vector<int> ints{1,2,3,4,5,7,8,13,14};
    std::ranges::for_each
      ( ints,
        [] ( int i ) -> void {
          cout << i << '\n';
        }
        );
```

Output:

```
1
2
3
4
5
7
8
13
14
```

(Why wouldn't you use an `accumulate` reduction?)

Here is an example using `any_of` to find whether a certain element appears in a vector:

Code:

```
// iter/eachr.cpp
vector<int> ints{1,2,3,4,5,7,8,13,14};
bool there_was_an_8 =
  std::ranges::any_of
  ( ints,
    [] ( int i ) -> bool {
      return i==8;
    }
    );
println( "There was an 8: {}",there_was_an_8 );
```

Output:

```
There was an 8: true
```

Capturing the value to be tested gives the following:

Code:

```
// iter/eachr.cpp
vector<int> ints{1,2,3,4,5,7,8,13,14};
int tofind = 8;
bool there_was_an_8 =
  std::ranges::any_of
  ( ints,
    [tofind] ( int i ) -> bool {
      return i==tofind;
    }
    );
println( "There was an 8: {}",there_was_an_8 );
```

Output:

```
There was an 8: true
```

Remark. *The previous examples rely on C++20 ranges. With iterators they look like this:*

Code:

```
// iter/each.cpp
vector<int> ints{2,3,4,5,7,8,13,14,15};
bool there_was_an_8 =
  any_of( ints.begin(),ints.end(),
          [] ( int i ) -> bool {
            return i==8;
          }
          );
cout << "There was an 8: " << boolalpha <<
     there_was_an_8 << '\n';
```

Output:

```
There was an 8: true
```

Code:

```
// iter/each.cpp
#include <algorithm>
     /* ... */
     vector<int> ints{2,3,4,5,7,8,13,14,15};
     for_each( ints.begin(),ints.end(),
               [] ( int i ) -> void {
                 cout << i << '\n';
               }
               );
```

Output:

```
2
3
4
5
7
8
13
14
15
```

7.3.2 ▪ Apply to each

The `for_each` algorithm applies a function to every element of a container. Unlike the previous algorithms, this can alter the elements.

To introduce the syntax, we look at the pointless example of outputting each element:

Apply `cout` to each array element:

Code:

```
// iter/eachr.cpp
#include <ranges>
#include <algorithm>
  /* ... */
  vector<int> ints{1,2,3,4,5,7,8,13,14};
  std::ranges::for_each
    ( ints,
      [] ( int i ) -> void {
        cout << i << '\n';
      }
      );
```

Output:

```
1
2
3
4
5
7
8
13
14
```

Exercise 7.3. Use `for_each` to sum the elements of a vector.

Hint: the problem is how to treat the sum variable. Do not use a global variable!

7.3.3 ▪ Iterator result

Some algorithms do not result in a value, but rather in an iterator that points to the location of that value. Examples: `min_element` takes a begin and end iterator and returns the iterator in between where the minimum element is found. To find the actual value, we need to "dereference" the iterator:

```
// range/minelt.cpp
vector<float> elements{.5f,1.f,1.5f};
auto min_iter = std::min_element
  (elements.begin(),elements.end());
cout << "Min: " << *min_iter << '\n';
```

Similarly `max_element`.

7.3.4 ▪ Mapping

The `transform` algorithm applies a function to each container element and returns the result. There are two variants. Using `std::transform` and iterators, you can write the result into a second container:

Code:

```
// rangestd/range.cpp
vector<float> in{1,2,3,4},out(4);
std::transform
  ( in.begin(),in.end(), out.begin(),
    [] (float x ) { return std::sqrt(x); } );
for ( auto x : out ) cout << x << '\n';
```

Output:

```
1
1.41421
1.73205
2
```

Using `ranges::transform` you obtain another range view:

Code:

```
// rangestd/range.cpp
  vector<float> in{1,2,3,4},out(4);
  for ( auto x : in
        | rng::views::transform
          ( [] (float x ) { return std::sqrt(x); } ) )
    cout << x << '\n';
```

Output:

```
1
1.41421
1.73205
2
```

7.3.5 ▪ Reduction

Numerical *reductions* can be computed by `accumulate` (using iterators) or `ranges::accumulate` (using ranges), both requiring the `numeric` header. If no reduction operator is specified, a *sum reduction* is performed.

Default is sum reduction:

```
// range/sumsquare.cpp
vector<float> elements{.5f,1.f,1.5f};
auto sumsq =
  rng::accumulate
  ( elements
    | rng::views::transform( [] (auto e) { return e*e; } ),
    0.f );
cout << "Sum of squares: " << sumsq << '\n';
```

Other binary *arithmetic operators* that can be used as *reduction operators* are found in `functional`:

- `plus`, `minus`, `multiplies`, `divides`;
- integers only: `modulus`;
- boolean: `logical_and`, `logical_or`.

This header also contains the unary `negate` operator, which of course cannot be used for reductions.

As an example of an explicitly specified reduction operator:

```
auto p = std::accumulate
  ( x.begin(),x.end(),1.f,
    std::multiplies<float>()
  );
```

Note:

- the operator is templated, and it is followed by parentheses to become a functor, rather than a class;
- the accumulate function is templated, and it takes its type from the init value. Thus, in the above example, a value of `1` would have turned this into an integer operation.

Supply multiply operator:

Code:

```
// range/reduce.cpp
vector<int> v{1,3,5,7};
auto product =
  rng::accumulate
    (v,2,multiplies<>());
cout << "multiplied: " << product << '\n';
```

Output:

```
multiplied: 210
```

Specific for the max reduction is `max_element`. This can be called without a comparator (for numerical max), or with a comparator for general maximum operations. The maximum and minimum algorithms return an iterator, rather than only the max/min value.

Example: maximum relative deviation from a quantity:

```
max_element(myvalue.begin(),myvalue.end(),
    [my_sum_of_squares] (double x,double y) -> bool {
      return std::abs( (my_sum_of_squares-x)/x ) < std::abs( (my_sum_of_squares-y)/y );
    }
);
```

For more complicated lambdas used in `accumulate`,

- the first argument should be the reduce type;
- the second argument should be the iterated type

In the following example we accumulate one member of a class:

Two-component class and accumulate just one:

Class with `i,j`:

```
// stl/reduce.cpp
class x {
public:
  int i,j;
  x() {};
  x(int i,int j) : i(i),j(j) {};
};
```

Accumulate one component:

```
// stl/reduce.cpp
std::vector<x> xs(5);
auto xxx =
  std::accumulate
  ( xs.begin(),xs.end(),0,
    [] ( int init,x x1 ) -> int {
      return x1.i+init; }
    );
```

Remark. *The* `accumulate` *algorithm does not have a parallel version with an execution policy. For that, see* `std::reduce` *in the* `numeric` *header.*

7.3.6 ▪ Sorting

The `algorithm` header also has a function `sort`.

With iterators you can easily apply this to things such as vectors:

```
sort( myvec.begin(),myvec.end() );
```

The comparison used by default is ascending. You can specify other compare functions:

```
sort( myvec.begin(),myvec.end(),
      [] (int i,int) { return i>j; }
    );
```

or

```
sort( people.begin(),people.end(),
      [] ( const Person& lhs,const Person& rhs ) {
         return lhs.name < rhs.name; }
    )
```

With iterators you can also do things like sorting a part of the vector:

Code:

```
// rangestd/sort.cpp
vector<int> v{3,1,2,4,5,7,9,11,12,8,10};
cout << "Original vector: "
     << vector_as_string(v) << '\n';

auto v_std(v);
std::sort( v_std.begin(),v_std.begin()+5 );
cout << "Five elements sorts: "
     << vector_as_string(v_std) << '\n';
```

Output:

```
Original vector: 3, 1, 2, 4,
    ↪5, 7, 9, 11, 12, 8, 10,
Five elements sorts: 1, 2, 3,
    ↪4, 5, 7, 9, 11, 12, 8,
    ↪10,
```

7.4 ▪ Parallel execution policies

The C++17 standard added the `ExecutionPolicy` concept to standard algorithms, describing how an element of the `algorithm` library may be executed in parallel.

There are three choices for the *execution policy*, defined in the `execution` header:

- `std::execution::seq`: iterations may not be parallelized, but are indeterminately sequenced in the evaluation thread;
- `std::execution::par`: iterations may be executed in parallel, but are indeterminately sequenced;
- `std::execution::par_unseq`: iterations may be parallelized, vectorized, migrated over threads;
- `std::execution::unseq` (since C++20): iterations are allowed to be vectorized over.

To accommodate the indeterminate evaluation order, new "unordered" algorithms are introduced based on existing "ordered" algorithms:

- `reduce`: similar to `accumulate`, but unordered and therefore parallelizable through an `ExecutionPolicy`;
- `inclusive_scan`: similar to `partial_sum`;
- `exclusive_scan`: no ordered equivalent;
- `transform_reduce`, `transform_inclusive_scan`, `transform_exclusive_scan`. Example usage:

```
transform_reduce( execpol, first,final, init, reduce_op,transform_op );
```

As an alternative to execution policies, iteratable containers can be parallelized with OpenMP; see section 20.7.

Chapter 8

Time

The C++ standard library has a header chrono with timers that are good enough for many purposes. For more on timing and profiling, see Chapter 34.

We will mostly devote attention to measurement of time intervals, since this is most relevant to scientific computing.

Header:

```
#include <chrono>
```

As a simple example how you would time a function f:

```
// chrono/simple.cpp
using clock = std::chrono::steady_clock;
clock::time_point  before = clock::now();
f();
auto after = clock::now();
cout << "Duration: "
     << std::chrono::duration_cast<std::chrono::milliseconds>(after-before).count()
     << "ms\n";
```

8.1 ▪ Time durations

You can define durations with seconds:

```
// chrono/second.cpp
seconds s{3};
auto t = 4s;
```

You can do arithmetic and comparisons on this type:

Code:

```
// chrono/second.cpp
cout << "This lasts "
     << s.count() << "s" << '\n';
cout << "This lasts ";
print_seconds( s+5s );
auto nine = 3.14*3s;
cout << nine.count()
     << "s is under 10 sec: "
     << boolalpha << (nine<10s)
     << '\n';
```

Output:

```
This lasts 3s
This lasts 8s
9.42s is under 10 sec: true
```

While `seconds` takes an integer argument, you can then multiply or divide it to get fractional values.

The `milliseconds` function gives a duration, and you can convert seconds implicitly to milliseconds, but the other way around you need `duration_count`:

```
// chrono/second.cpp
print_milliseconds( 5s );
// DOES NOT COMPILE print_seconds( 6ms );
print_seconds( duration_cast<seconds>(6ms) );
```

The full list of durations (with suffixes) is: `hours` (`1h`), `minutes` (`1min`), `seconds` (`1s`), `milliseconds` (`1ms`), `microseconds` (`1us`), `nanoseconds` (`1ns`).

8.2 ▪ Time points

A *time point* can be considered as a duration from some starting point, such as the start of the Unix *epoch*: the start of the year 1970

```
time_point<system_clock,seconds> tp{10'000s};
```

is `2h+46min+40s` into 1970.

You make this explicit by calling the `time_since_epoch` method on a time point, giving a duration.

8.3 ▪ Clocks

There are several clocks. The common supplied clocks are

- `system_clock` for time points that have a relation to the calendar; and
- `steady_clock` for precise measurements.
- C++20 added some more clocks such as `utc_clock`, which are like `system_clock` but with a different offset.

Usually, `high_resolution_clock` is a synonym for either of these, but because of this lack of precise definition you should probably not use it.

A clock has methods:

- *duration* indicates a time duration; it consists of *rep*, the repetition count, and a *period* which is usually 1.
- time_point representing a point in time. This is usually obtained from the now method of a clock:

```
const std::chrono::time_point<std::chrono::system_clock> now =
        std::chrono::system_clock::now();
```

- Some clocks obey leap years and leap seconds; the property *is_steady* indicates whether a clock makes the time progress at one second per second, that is, without leaps.

As shown above, a time_point is associated with a clock, and time points of different clocks cannot be compared or converted to each other.

8.3.1 ▪ Duration measurement

To time a segment of execution, use the now method of the clock, before and after the segment. Subtracting the time points gives a duration in nanoseconds, which you can cast to anything else by *duration_cast*:

Code:

```
// chrono/clock.cpp
using myclock = system_clock;
myclock::time_point before =
  myclock::now();
// do something that takes time
std::this_thread::sleep_for( 1.5s );//
        snippetexclude
auto after = myclock::now();
cout << "Action took: "
     << duration_cast<milliseconds>
          (after-before).count()
     << "ms\n";
```

Output:

```
Action took: 1505ms
```

8.3.2 ▪ Clock resolution

The *clock resolution* can be found from the *period* property:

```
auto
  num = myclock::period::num,
  den = myclock::period::den;
auto tick = static_cast<double>(num)/static_cast<double>(den);
```

Timing:

```
auto start_time = myclock::now();
auto duration = myclock::now()-start_time;
auto microsec_duration =
    std::chrono::duration_cast<std::chrono::microseconds>(duration);
cout << "This took " << microsec_duration.count() << "usec" << endl;
```

Computing new time points:

```
auto deadline = myclock.now() + std::chrono::seconds(10);
```

Chapter 9

Random numbers

The standard library has a *random number generator* that is based on a two- (or three-)step process, which decouples randomness from the distribution of the random numbers.

Use header:

```
#include <random>
```

Steps:

1. First there is the random engine which contains the mathematical random number generator.
2. The random numbers used in your code then come from applying a distribution to this engine.
3. Optionally, you can use a random seed, so that each program run generates a different sequence.

There are several choices of engines and distributions, some of which we will discuss.

9.1 ▪ Generator

There is an implementation-defined generator `default_random_engine`:

```
std::default_random_engine generator;
```

Used this way, the generator will start at the same value every time. To seed it, use `random_device`:

```
std::random_device r;
std::default_random_engine generator{ r() };
```

This typically relies on an operating system (OS) function to find a random seed.

To get reproducible random numbers, you can seed (certain) generators with a `seed` function:

```
std::default_random_engine generator;
generator.seed(5);
```

(This is especially useful in parallel, where you can seed with a process or thread number.)

Other generators include the *Mersenne twister* `mt19937`, `knuth_b`, and several others. They differ in how much space they need to maintain their internal state, and the length of their period.

9.2 ▪ Distributions

The most common mode of generating random numbers is to pick them from a distribution. For instance, a uniform distribution between given bounds:

```
std::uniform_real_distribution<float> distribution(0.,1.);
```

Code:

```
// rand/xrand.cpp
// seed the generator
std::random_device r;
// set the default random number generator
std::default_random_engine generator{r()};
// distribution: real between 0 and 1
std::uniform_real_distribution<float>
     distribution(0.,1.);

for ( int i=0; i<5; i++)
  cout << "random: "
       << distribution(generator)
       << '\n';
```

Output:

```
random: 0.38229
random: 0.140263
random: 0.400579
random: 0.535661
random: 0.847095
```

A roll of the dice would result from

```
std::uniform_int_distribution<int> distribution(1,6);
```

```
// set the default generator
std::default_random_engine generator;

// distribution: ints 1..6
std::uniform_int_distribution<int> distribution(1,6);

// apply distribution to generator:
int dice_roll = distribution(generator);
  // generates number in the range 1..6
```

Other distributions are Poisson, Bernoulli, Normal, Chi-squared, and several more.

Poisson distributed integers:
chance of k occurrences, if m is the average number
(or $1/m$ the probability)

```
std::default_random_engine generator;
float mean = 3.5;
std::poisson_distribution<int> distribution(mean);
int number = distribution(generator);
```

9.3 ▪ Usage scenarios

In some scenarios you want, as it were, a bunch of random number generators. For example, in a simulation you could have multiple objects that each take random actions.

```
class Thing {
public:
```

```
  void do_something_random() {
    rnd = some_distribution( some_generator );
    f(rnd);
  };
};
int main() {
  for ( many iterations ) {
    Thing t;
    t.something_random();
  }
};
```

You might be tempted to include not only the invocation of a random number generator (RNG) in a routine that needs it, but also the definition.

Wrong approach: random generator local in the function.

Code:

```
// rand/static.cpp
int nonrandom_int(int maxval) {
  std::default_random_engine engine;
  std::uniform_int_distribution<>
    ints(1,maxval);
  return ints(engine);
};
    /* ... */
  // call 'nonrandom_int' three times
```

Output:

```
Three ints: 1, 1, 1.
```

Generator gets recreated in every function call.

This is not going to work, because the generator will be initialized every time you call the function, leading to a sequence of identical numbers.

Exercise 9.1. What is wrong with the following code?

```
int somewhat_random_int(int maxval) {
  random_device r;
  default_random_engine generator{ r() };
  std::uniform_int_distribution<> ints(1,maxval);
  return ints(generator);
};
```

You can fix this by making the generator variable `static`, so that there is only one generator, shared by all function invocations.

Wrong approach:

Code:

```
// rand/static.cpp
int nonrandom_int(int maxval) {
  std::default_random_engine engine;
  std::uniform_int_distribution<>
    ints(1,maxval);
  return ints(engine);
};
    /* ... */
  // call 'nonrandom_int' three times
```

Output:

```
Three ints: 1, 1, 1.
```

Good approach:

Code:

```
// rand/static.cpp
int realrandom_int(int maxval) {
  static std::default_random_engine static_engine;
  std::uniform_int_distribution<>
    ints(1,maxval);
  return ints(static_engine);
};
```

Output:

```
Three ints: 15, 98, 70.
```

Remark. *A similar diagnosis and solution hold for objects:*

```
class Thing {
private:
  random_device r;
  default_random_engine generator{ r() };
public:
  void do_something_random() {
    rnd = some_distribution( generator );
    f(rnd);
  };
};
```

The solution is that the device and generator should be static.

What if you have multiple routines that use random numbers? To keep it all statistically justified you could move the RNG into a separate routine:

```
// rand/static.cpp
int realrandom_int(int maxval) {
  static std::default_random_engine static_engine;
  std::uniform_int_distribution<>
    ints(1,maxval);
  return ints(static_engine);
};
```

To clean up this design, you could then even put this in an object with inline static class methods:

Note the use of `static`:

```
// rand/randname.cpp
class generate {
private:
  static inline std::default_random_engine engine;
public:
  static int random_int(int max) {
    std::uniform_int_distribution<> ints(1,max);
    return ints(generate::engine);
  };
};
```

Usage:

```
auto nonzero_percentage = generate::random_int(100)
```

9.4 ▪ Permutations

The function `shuffle` shuffles an array. Coupled with the `iota` function (from the `numeric` header) this easily gives a permutation:

Code:

```
// rand/shuffle.cpp
std::vector<int> idxs(20);
iota(idxs.begin(),idxs.end(),0);
/* ... */
std::shuffle
   (idxs.begin(), idxs.end(), g);
```

Output:

```
Iota:
 0  1  2  3  4  5  6  7  8  9
10 11 12 13 14 15 16 17 18 19
Permute:
18 11  5  1  2 16 12 17  6 19
10  3  9  7 13  8 15  4  0 14
```

(where g is a random generator).

9.5 ▪ Seeding and reproducibility

Without seeding, the random number generator (RNG) routine generates the same sequence every time your program runs. However, there is no guarantee that that same sequence appears if you run your program on a different computer, or with a different compiler on the same.

Therefore it is a good idea to seed your program with an explicitly specified seed, if reproducibility is an issue. If on the other hand you run your program multiple times to get an average result or an "ensemble," you want your seed to be different each time. You could use the `random_device`, or a readout of the time of day.

If your program is parallel, random number generation is even trickier. The C++ RNGs can safely be used in threaded code, but now you need to prevent the case where each thread gets the same sequence of random numbers: in scientific applications you want the interleaving of all threads' actions to be equivalent to some single-threaded program run. The solution usually taken is to seed the RNGs either from the `random_device`, or some explicit seed, but incorporating the thread of process number.

9.6 ▪ C language random generators

There are several *random number generator*s available in the standard library of the C language. These should no longer be used for C++ code.

The function `rand` yields an `int`—a different one every time you call it—in the range from zero to `RAND_MAX`. Using scaling and casting you can then produce a fraction between zero and one with the above code.

```
#include <random>
using std::rand;
float random_fraction =
    (float)rand()/(float)RAND_MAX;
```

This generator has some problems.

- The C random number generator has a period that can be as small as 2^{15}.
- There is only one generator algorithm, which is implementation-dependent and has no guarantees on its quality.
- There are no mechanisms for transforming the sequence to a range. The common idiom

  ```
  int under100 = rand() % 100
  ```

  is biased to small numbers.

Chapter 10
Pointers

Pointers are an indirect way of associating an entity with a variable name. Consider, for instance, the circular-sounding definition of a list:

> A list consists of nodes, where a node contains some information in its "head," and the node has a "tail" that is a list.

Naive code:

```
class Node {
private:
  int value;
  Node tail; // This does not work!
  /* ... */
};
```

This would take infinite memory.

Indirect inclusion: only "point" to the tail:

```
class Node {
private:
  int value;
  PointToNode tail;
  /* ... */
};
```

This chapter will explain C++ *smart pointers* and give some uses for them.

10.1 ▪ Pointer usage

Initially, we will focus on pointers to objects of some class. We use the following example class.

Simple class that stores one number:

Definition:

```
// pointer/pointx.cpp
class HasX {
private:
  double x;
public:
  HasX( double x) : x(x) {};
  auto value() { return x; };
  void set(double xx) {
    x = xx; };
};
```

Example usage:

```
// pointer/pointx.cpp
HasX xobj(5);
println("{}",xobj.value());
xobj.set(6);
println("{}",xobj.value());
```

With class objects, the "dot" notation for class members becomes an "arrow" notation when you use a pointer. If you have an object `Obj X` with a member *y*, you access that with `X.y`; if you have a pointer `X` to such an object, you write `X->y`.

- If *x* is an object with member *y*:
  `x.y`
- If *xx* is a pointer to an object with member *y*:
  `xx->y`
- Arrow notation works with C-style pointers and new shared/unique pointers.

Instead of creating an object, you now create an object with a pointer to it, in a single call. We use the following example class:

```
make_shared< ClassName >( constructor arguments );
```

The resulting object is of type `shared_ptr<ClassName>`, but you can save yourself spelling that out and use `auto` instead.

Note that you don't first create an object and then set a pointer to it, the way it happens in many other languages. Smart pointers work differently: you create the object and the pointer to it in one call.

Object vs. pointed-object:

Code:

```
// pointer/pointx.cpp
#include <memory>
using std::make_shared;

  /* ... */
  HasX xobj(5);
  println("{}",xobj.value());
  xobj.set(6);
  println("{}",xobj.value());

  auto xptr = make_shared<HasX>(5);
  println("{}",xptr->value());
  xptr->set(6);
  println("{}",xptr->value());
```

Output:

```
5
6
5
6
```

Using smart pointers requires at the top of your file:

```
#include <memory>
using std::shared_ptr;
using std::make_shared;

using std::unique_ptr;
using std::make_unique;
```

Why do we use pointers? Pointers are generally said to pertain to "ownership," and with pointers we can let one object be "owned" equally by two variables.

Set two pointers to the same object:

Code:

```
// pointer/pointx.cpp
auto xptr = make_shared<HasX>(5);
auto yptr = xptr;
println("{}",xptr->value());
yptr->set(6);
println("{}",xptr->value());
```

Output:

```
5
6
```

Sometimes you want to get hold of the actual object being pointed to. For this you can use the `operator*` which dereferences the pointer.

Example: function:

```
float distance_to_origin( Point p );
```

How do you apply that to a `shared_ptr<Point>`?

```
shared_ptr<Point> p;
distance_to_origin( *p );
```

So far, you have created a smart pointer variable by immediately initializing it. This is good C++ practice. However, sometimes you need to declare such a variable and you cannot immediately initialize it. In that case the pointer is in a null state, which you can test by comparing it to `nullptr`.

Initialize smart pointer to null pointer; test on null value:

```
shared_ptr<Foo> foo_ptr; // is nullptr by default initialization;
// stuff
if (foo_ptr!=nullptr)
  foo_ptr->do_something();
```

10.2 ▪ How smart pointers prevent memory problems

Smart pointers (and the way C++ deals with containers) help prevent some memory problems that are common in C code. We discuss the major types here.

10.2.1 ▪ Memory leaks

One problem with C-style pointers is the chance of a *memory leak*. If a pointer to a block of memory goes out of scope, the block is not returned to the OS, but it is no longer accessible.

```
// attach memory to 'array':
double *array = new double[25];
// do something with array
// overwrite the pointer
array = new double[26];
// the first allocated memory is still reserved.
```

Shared and unique pointers do not have this problem: if they go out of scope, or are overwritten, the destructor on the object is called, thereby releasing any allocated memory.

An example.

We need a class with constructor and destructor tracing:

```
// pointer/ptr1.cpp
class thing {
public:
  thing()  { cout << ".. calling constructor\n"; };
  ~thing() { cout << ".. calling destructor\n"; };
};
```

Just to illustrate that the destructor gets called when the object goes out of scope we show an example without any pointers for now:

Code:

```
// pointer/ptr0.cpp
cout << "Outside\n";
{
  thing x;
  cout << "create done\n";
}
cout << "back outside\n";
```

Output:

```
Outside
.. calling constructor
create done
.. calling destructor
back outside
```

Now we do the same with a pointer, to illustrate that the destructor of the object is called when the pointer no longer points to the object. We do this by assigning `nullptr` to the pointer. (This is very different from *NULL* in C: the null pointer is actually an object with a type; see section 10.3.5.)

Let's create a pointer and overwrite it:

Code:

```
// pointer/ptr1.cpp
cout << "set pointer1"
     << '\n';
auto thing_ptr1 =
  make_shared<thing>();
cout << "overwrite pointer"
     << '\n';
thing_ptr1 = nullptr;
```

Output:

```
set pointer1
.. calling constructor
overwrite pointer
.. calling destructor
```

However, if a pointer is copied, there are two pointers to the same block of memory, and only when both disappear, or point elsewhere, is the object deallocated.

Code:

```
// pointer/ptr2.cpp
cout << "set pointer2" << '\n';
auto thing_ptr2 =
  make_shared<thing>();
cout << "set pointer3 by copy"
     << '\n';
auto thing_ptr3 = thing_ptr2;
cout << "overwrite pointer2"
     << '\n';
thing_ptr2 = nullptr;
cout << "overwrite pointer3"
     << '\n';
thing_ptr3 = nullptr;
```

Output:

```
set pointer2
.. calling constructor
set pointer3 by copy
overwrite pointer2
overwrite pointer3
.. calling destructor
```

- The object counts how many pointers there are.
- This is called "reference counting."
- A pointed-to object is deallocated if no one points to it.

10.2.2 ▪ Memory leaks and exceptions

A more obscure source of memory leaks has to do with exceptions:

```
void f() {
  double *x = new double[50];
  throw("something");
  delete x;
  }
```

Because of the exception (which can of course come from a nested function call) the `delete` statement is never reached, and the allocated memory is leaked. Smart pointers solve this problem: throwing the exception leaves the scope and therefore the destructor is called.

10.2.3 ▪ Use after free

A serious memory problem arises from using a pointer after it has been freed, the *use-after-free* condition:

```
double *x = new double[N];
/* operations on x */
delete[] x;
... x[500] ... // use of free'd memory
```

By the time you access the freed memory, that memory may have been allocated to, and used by, another array. Your program, in other words, may continue to run, but with unintended values. On the other hand, a smart pointer will have been set to `nullptr`, and dereferencing that will likely crash your code. However, it will not throw an exception.

10.3 ▪ Advanced topics

10.3.1 ▪ Get the pointed data

Most of the time, accessing the target of the pointer through the arrow notation is enough. However, if you actually want the object, you can get it with `get`.

```
X->y;
// is the same as
X.get()->y;
// is the same as
( *X.get() ).y;
```

Note that `get` does not give you the pointed object, but a traditional pointer.

Demonstrate the `get` function:

Code:

```
// pointer/pointy.cpp
auto Y = make_shared<HasY>(5);
cout << Y->y << '\n';
Y.get()->y = 6;
cout << ( *Y.get() ).y << '\n';
```

Output:

```
5
6
```

Remark. *Using the* `get` *method has the (small) advantage that it still works if the* `->` *operator is overloaded.*

10.3.2 ▪ Unique pointers

Shared pointers are fairly easy to program, and they come with lots of advantages, such as the automatic memory management. However, they have more overhead than strictly necessary because they have a *reference count* mechanism to support the memory management. Therefore, there exists a *unique pointer*, `unique_ptr`, for cases where an object will only ever be "owned" by one pointer.

While unique pointers may have lower overhead, they are more tricky to use, for instance, because you cannot copy them. It is possible to transfer the pointed-to object from one unique pointer to another with `std::move`, but we will not go into that here. In scientific computing this does not actually seem to occur often; consider an iterative process:

```
auto X = make_unique< VectorField >();
for ( /* many time steps */ ) {
  X->update();
```

The unique pointer has a long life, and its object never needs to be transferred.

10.3.3 ▪ Base and derived pointers

Suppose you have base and derived classes:

```
class A {};
class B : public A {};
```

Just like you could assign a `B` object to an `A` variable,

```
B b_object;
A a_object = b_object;
```

is it possible to assign a `B` pointer to an `A` pointer?

The following construct makes this possible:

```
auto a_ptr = shared_ptr<A>( make_shared<B>() );
```

See also section 13.3.2 about casting between base and derived pointers and references.

10.3.4 ▪ Shared pointer to "this"

Inside an object method, the object is accessible as `this`. This is a pointer in the classical sense. So what if you want to refer to "this" but you need a shared pointer?

For instance, suppose you're writing a linked list code, and your `node` class has a method `prepend_or_append` that gives a shared pointer to the new head of the list.

Your code would start something like this, handling the case where the new node is appended to the current:

```
shared_ptr<node> node::prepend_or_append
    ( shared_ptr<node> other ) {
  if (other->value>this->value) {
    this->tail = other;
    return *this; // ALMOST BUT NOT QUITE
  } else {
    other->tail = this; // ALSO A LITTLE OFF
    return other;
  }
```

Now you need to return this node, as a shared pointer. However, `this` is a `node*`, not a `shared_ptr<node>`.

The solution here is that you can return

```
return this->shared_from_this();
```

if you have defined your node class to inherit from what probably looks like magic:

```
class node : public enable_shared_from_this<node>
```

Note that you can only return a `shared_from_this` if already a valid shared pointer to that object exists.

10.3.5 ■ Null pointer

In C there was a macro `NULL` that, only by convention, was used to indicate *null pointers*: pointers that do not point to anything. C++ has the `nullptr`, which is an object of type `std::nullptr_t`.

There is also the abstract concept of "the null pointer value of a type." Both zero and `NULL` can be converted to that, but use of `nullptr` is preferred.

There are some scenarios where this is useful, for instance, with polymorphic functions:

```
void f(int);
void f(int*);
```

Calling `f(ptr)` where the pointer is `NULL`, the first function is called, whereas with `nullptr` the second is called.

Note: *dereferencing a nullptr* does not give an exception, so you need to test explicitly on null pointers.

10.3.6 ■ Pointers to nonobjects

So far we have made smart pointers to objects. You can make shared pointers to scalar data, for instance, to an array of scalars. You then get the advantage of the memory management, but you do not get the `size` function and such that you would have if you'd used a `vector` object.

Here is an example of a pointer to a solitary double:

Code:

```
// pointer/ptrdouble.cpp
// shared pointer to allocated double
auto array = shared_ptr<double>( new double );
double *ptr = array.get();
array.get()[0] = 2.;
cout << ptr[0] << '\n';
```

Output:

```
2
```

You can also have pointers to arrays:

Code:

```
// pointer/ptrdouble.cpp
auto array = std::make_unique<double[]>(50);
double *ptr = array.get();
array[1] = 2.81;
cout << ptr[1] << '\n';
```

Output:

```
2.81
```

10.4 ■ Bare pointers

The C-style pointer

```
int *pi;
float *py;
```

has the following uses in C:

- to pass data "by reference":

  ```
  void inc( int *i ) { *i += 1; };
  int main() {
    int i=6;
    inc(&i);
    // i now 7
  };
  ```

  (This is actually passing an address by value, rather than passing a variable by reference.) This use is no longer needed in C++ because of references, although you will often see this in the interface to C libraries.
- For pointer arithmetic:

  ```
  float ar[5];
  float *first = &ar[0];
  float *second = first+1;
  ```

  This is (mostly) replaced by using iterators into containers; see section 7.2.
- Dynamic allocation of array:

  ```
  int n = // something
  float *ar = (float*) malloc( n*sizeof(float) ); // C
  float *ar = new float[n]; // C++
  ```

  This last usage is no longer needed on the user level, being replaced by `std::vector` and other containers. However, as a library writer you may still employ this idiom for writing your own containers. See, for instance, section 14.3.

10.4.1 ▪ Nonowning bare pointers

One legitimate use of bare pointers is in cases where the pointer is nonowning. Consider a linked list, and

```
unique_ptr<Node> head
```

We can then count the list length iteratively:

```
// tree/linkunique.cpp
int listlength_iterative() {
  int count = 0;
  Node *current_node = head.get();
  while (current_node!=nullptr) {
    current_node = current_node->next.get(); count += 1;
  }
  return count;
};
```

10.5 ▪ Implementation

In case you're curious how smart pointers work behind the scenes, here is a toy implementation of shared pointers. This is only to illustrate the basic mechanism: a real implementation is much more sophisticated; for instance, it has to make sure not to leak memory if exceptions occur; also the implementation here is not thread-safe.

Just for the sake of the discussion we create a simple class to which we'll make smart pointers:

```
// pointer/implementation.cpp
class HasY {
private:
```

```
  double y;
public:
  HasY() = delete;
  HasY( double y) : y(y) {};
  auto& value() { return y; }
};
```

A smart pointer is a structure comprising a pointer to the class object and a pointer to a reference count object. Here are the data members, class constructor, and use case:

```
// pointer/implementation.cpp
template<typename T>
class SmartPointer {
private:
  T* _data;
  ReferenceCounter *count_;
    /* ... */
template<typename T>
SmartPointer<T>::SmartPointer( T* data)
  : _data(data),count_( new ReferenceCounter ) {};
    /* ... */
  auto y = SmartPointer<HasY>( new HasY(3.7) );
```

If we copy a smart pointer, we make a new structure, with the same data and counter pointers, and we increase the counter:

```
// pointer/implementation.cpp
template<typename T>
SmartPointer<T>::SmartPointer( const SmartPointer<T>& sp )
  : _data(sp._data),count_(sp.count_) {
  cout << "calling copy constructor\n";
  count_->count()++;
};
    /* ... */
  SmartPointer<HasY> z = y;
```

The destructor lowers the count, and frees the data if the count is zero:

```
// pointer/implementation.cpp
template<typename T>
SmartPointer<T>::~SmartPointer() {
  count_->count()--;
  if (count_->count()==0) {
    cout << "final delete\n";
    delete _data; delete count_;
  } else cout << "ref count lower only\n";
};
```

In order to get data from a smart pointer we overload the arrow:

```
// pointer/implementation.cpp
template<typename T>
T* SmartPointer<T>::operator->() {
  return _data;
};
```

Chapter 11

Union-like constructs

In this chapter we will look at the phenomenon that sometimes the type of a variable can be dynamically determined at runtime. For want of a better term we will call these "union-like" constructs. They can be motivated from a variety of circumstances.

There are cases where you need a value that is one type or another, for instance, a number if a computation succeeded, and an error indicator if not.

Let us consider the example of a square root function that returns an error if you call it with a negative number. The simplest solution is to have a function that returns both a boolean and a number:

Function:

```
// union/optroot.cpp
bool RootOrError(float &x) {
  if (x<0)
    return false;
  else
    x = std::sqrt(x);
  return true;
};
```

Use:

```
// union/optroot.cpp
for ( auto x : {2.f,-2.f} )
  if (RootOrError(x))
    cout << "Root is "
         << x << '\n';
  else
    cout
      << "could not take root of "
      << x << '\n';
```

There are various inelegancies with this solution. For one, you're using two different mechanisms for returning the two values. Furthermore, you don't actually need two values: if there is an error, the returned value is irrelevant.

We will now consider some more idiomatically C++17 solutions to this.

11.1 ▪ Optional

The most elegant solution to "a number or an error" is to have a single quantity that you can query whether it's valid. For this, the C++17 standard introduced the concept of a *nullable type*: a type that can somehow convey that it's empty.

In this section we discuss `std::optional`, which uses the `optional` header:

```
#include <optional>
using std::optional;
```

11.1.1 ▪ Creating an optional

The function we are writing has a return type of `optional<float>`. This is realized by returning either an actual `float`, or `{}`, which is a synonym for `std::nullopt`.

```
// union/optroot.cpp
optional<float> MaybeRoot(float x) {
  if (x<0)
    return {};
  else
    return std::sqrt(x);
};
```

11.1.2 ▪ Getting the optional value, if any

You can test whether the optional quantity actually has a quantity with the method `has_value`, in which case you can extract the quantity with the method `value`. Alternatively, you can use the fact that the `optional` object can be implicitly cast to `bool`, and dereferenced:

Two ways:

```
// union/optroot.cpp
for ( auto x : {2.f,-2.f} )
  if ( auto root = MaybeRoot(x);
       root.has_value() )
    cout << "Root is "
         << root.value()
         << '\n';
  else
    cout
      << "could not take root of "
      << x << '\n';
```

```
// union/optroot.cpp
for ( auto x : {2.f,-2.f} )
  if ( auto root = MaybeRoot(x) ; root )
    cout << "Root is "
         << *root << '\n';
  else
    cout
      << "could not take root of "
      << x << '\n';
```

Trying to take the `value` for something that doesn't have one leads to a `bad_optional_access` exception:

Code:

```
// union/optional.cpp
optional<float> maybe_number = {};
try {
  cout << maybe_number.value() << '\n';
} catch (std::bad_optional_access) {
  cout << "failed to get value\n";
}
```

Output:

```
failed to get value
```

There is a function `value_or` that gives the value, or a default if the optional did not have a value:

```
optional<int> some_int;
some_int.value_or(-1);
```

Exercise 11.1. Write a function `first_factor` that optionally returns the smallest factor of a given input.

```
// primes/optfactor.cpp
```

```
auto factor = first_factor(number);
if (factor.has_value())
  cout << "Found factor: " << factor.value() << '\n';
else
  cout << "Prime number\n";
```

Remark. *If you have an optional class object, you can assign that object with the* `emplace` *method:*

Class definition:

```
// union/optional.cpp
class WithInt {
public:
  WithInt( int i ) {};
  void foo() {};
};
```

Emplacing into optional:

```
// union/optional.cpp
optional<WithInt> maybe;
{ maybe.emplace(5); }
cout << maybe.has_value() << '\n';
maybe.value().foo();
```

11.1.3 ▪ Monadic extensions

In C++23, `std::optional` and `std::expected` received *monadic extensions*: ways of further processing the optional result, but only if it has a value.

```
// union/optroot.cpp
optional<float> MaybeRoot(float x);
for ( auto x : {2.f,-2.f} )
  MaybeRoot(x)
    .transform( [] ( float x ) { return x*x; } )
    .and_then( [] (float x ) -> optional<float> {
        cout << "checkin" << x << '\n'; return x; } );
```

11.2 ▪ Expected

The `std::optional` of the previous section is great for cases such as the square root, where it is clear what it means if the value does not exist. However, if the nonexistence comes from some sort of error, you may want to ask what the reason for it is.

The C++23 addition of `std::expected` (in the `expected` header) allows you to return a value, or provide more information on why that error is not there, with `std::unexpected`.

Expect double, return info string if not:

Function returning expected:

```
// union/expected.cpp
std::expected<double,string>
square_root( double x ) {
  if (x<0)
    return std::unexpected("negative");
  else if (x<limits<double>::min())
    return std::unexpected("underflow");
  else {
    auto result = sqrt(x);
    return result;
  }
}
```

In Use:

```
// union/expected.cpp
auto root = square_root(x);
if (x)
  cout << "Root=" << root.value() << '\n';
else if (root.error()==/* et cetera */ )
  /* handle the problem */
```

11.3 ▪ Variant

In C/C++, a `union` is an entity that can be one of a number of types. Similarly to how C arrays do not know their size, a `union` does not know what type it is. The C++ `variant` (C++17) does not suffer from this limitation.

In the above `optional` solution we have a `value` function. Since a `variant` can have multiple types, we cannot directly have such a function. Instead, we need to test on what type is being returned, and use `get` or `get_if` to retrieve a value by type.

It is safer to use `get_if`, which takes a pointer to a variant, and returns a pointer if successful, and a *null pointer* if not:

```
// union/intdoublestring.cpp
union_ids = "Hello world";
if ( auto union_int = get_if<int>(&union_ids) ; union_int )
  cout << "Int: " << *union_int << '\n';
else if ( auto union_string = get_if<string>(&union_ids) ; union_string )
  cout << "String: " << *union_string << '\n';
```

For a first example we consider the square root example that we started this chapter with, although this example is actually better done with an `optional`.

Return square root or false result:

```
// union/optroot.cpp
#include <variant>
using std::variant, std::get_if;
   /* ... */
variant<bool,float> RootVariant(float x) {
  if (x<0)
    return false;
  else
    return std::sqrt(x);
};
```

```
// union/optroot.cpp
for ( auto x : {2.f,-2.f} ) {
  auto okroot = RootVariant(x);
  auto root = get_if<float>(&okroot);
  if ( root )
    cout << "Root is "
         << *root << '\n';
  auto nope = get_if<bool>(&okroot);
  if (nope)
    cout
      << "could not take root of "
      << x << '\n';
}
```

If we have more than two possibilities, `get_if` may get cumbersome. With `index` it is possible to query directly which of the variants is used.

Illustrating the usage:

```
// union/intdoublestring.cpp
variant<int,double,string> union_ids;
```

The `index` returns $0, 1, 2$, and we `get` the value accordingly:

```
// union/intdoublestring.cpp
union_ids = 3.5;
switch ( union_ids.index() ) {
case 1 :
  cout << "Double case: " << std::get<double>(union_ids) << '\n';
}
```

Getting the wrong variant leads to a `bad_variant_access` exception:

```
// union/intdoublestring.cpp
union_ids = 17;
cout << "Using option " << union_ids.index()
     << ": " << get<int>(union_ids) << '\n';
try {
  cout << "Get as double: " << get<double>(union_ids) << '\n';
} catch ( bad_variant_access b ) {
  cout << "Exception getting as double while index="
       << union_ids.index() << '\n';
}
```

Exercise 11.2. Write a routine that computes the roots of the quadratic equation

$$ax^2 + bx + c = 0.$$

The routine should return two roots, or one root, or an indication that the equation has no solutions.

```
// union/abctuple.cpp
auto root_cases = abc_cases( sunk );
switch (root_cases.index()) {
case 0 : cout << "No roots\n"; break;
case 1 : cout << "Single root: " << get<1>(root_cases); break;
case 2 : {
  auto xs = get<2>(root_cases);
  auto [xp,xm] = xs;
  cout << "Roots: " << xp << "," << xm << '\n';
} ; break;
}
```

In this exercise you can return a boolean to indicate "no roots," but a boolean can have two values, and only one has meaning. For such cases there is the `monostate` class, also from the `variant` header. You would then return an object of that class as

```
return std::monostate{};
```

11.3.1 ▪ Calling the same function on all variants

Suppose you have a variant of some classes, which all support a method with identical signature:

```
class x_type {
public: r_type method() { ... };
};
class y_type {
public: r_type method() { ... };
};
```

It is not directly possible to call this method on a variant:

```
variant< x_type,y_type> xy;
// WRONG xy.method();
```

For a specific example we define classes `double_object`, `string_object` containing a string and a double, respectively, and both classes have methods `stringer`, which gives a string representation, and `sizer`, which gives the "size" of the object. Next we define two variant objects, one of each type. We also define *functors*

String object class:

```
// union/visit.cpp
class string_object {
private:
  string s;
public:
  string_object( string s );
  string value();
};
```

Variant objects:

```
// union/visit.cpp
variant<double_object,string_object>
  union_is_double{ double_object(2.5) },
  union_is_string{
      string_object{"two-point-five"} };
```

In order to apply the method `stringer` to a variant of the two types, we need `visit` from the `variant` header. We make a functor: a class with an overloaded `operator()`. This is used to apply an object (defined below) to the variant object:

Code:

```
// union/visit.cpp
cout << "Size of <<"
     << visit( stringer{},union_is_double )
     << ">> is "
     << visit( sizer{},union_is_double )
     << '\n';
cout << "Size of <<"
     << visit( stringer{},union_is_string )
     << ">> is "
     << visit( sizer{},union_is_string )
     << '\n';
```

Output:

```
Size of <<2.5>> is 2
Size of <<two-point-five>> is
    ↪14
```

The implementations of the functors are as follows:

Stringer class:

```
// union/visit.cpp
class stringer {
public:
  string operator()
      ( double_object d ) {
    stringstream ss;
    ss << d.value();
    return ss.str(); };
  string operator()
      ( string_object s ) {
    return s.value(); };
};
```

Sizer class:

```
// union/visit.cpp
class sizer {
public:
  int operator()
      ( double_object d ) {
    return static_cast<int>( d.value() ); };
  int operator()
      ( string_object s ) {
    return s.value().size(); };
};
```

Remark. *There is a further visit idiom:*

```
template <typename... Ts>
struct overload : Ts... { using Ts:operator... };
f = overload {
  [] ( int i ) { /* int stuff */ };
  [] ( float f ) { /* float stuff */ };
};
```

This uses variadic templates, a topic not covered here.

11.4 ▪ Any

While `variant` can be any of a number of prespecified types, `std::any` can contain really any type. Thus it is the equivalent of `void*` in C.

An `any` object can be cast with `any_cast`:

```
std::any a{12};
std::any_cast<int>(a); // succeeds
std::any_cast<string>(a); // fails
```

11.5 ▪ Tuples and structured binding

A tuple is a way to pack together variables, possibly of different types. An object of the class `tuple` is parametrized by its constituent types:

```
tuple<int,char,double> icd;
```

Such an object is created with the `make_tuple` function:

```
auto icd = make_tuple(5,'d',3.14);
```

Note that the function is templated, but usually it's easier to leave out the types and have them deduced.

Conversely, a tuple can be unpacked into its components, using a method called *structured binding*:

```
auto [i,c,d] = icd;
// or by reference:
auto& [i,c,d] = icd;
```

Unpacking by reference is a little tricky: the variables `i,c,d` behave largely as if they are of type `int,char,double`, but they are actually components in a reference to the tuple. You may notice this if you pass them as function argument.

For pairs, there the class `pair` with the function `make_pair`. This is equivalent to a tuple with two elements, except that there are now data members `first` and `second`.

11.5.1 ▪ Example: Roots of a quadratic equation

As an illustration of the above, we consider computing the roots x_+, x_- of the quadratic equation $ax^2 + bx + c = 0$. We could define a `quadratic` class, but it suffices to use a `using` statement:

```
// union/abctuple.cpp
using quadratic = tuple<double,double,double>;
    /* ... */
  // polynomial: x^2 - 2
  auto sunk = quadratic(1.,0.,-2);
```

You can now use structured bindings to unpack the tuple:

Discriminant of the quadratic polynomial

Definition:

```
// union/abctuple.cpp
double discriminant
    ( quadratic q ) {
  auto [a,b,c] = q;
  return b*b-4*a*c;
}
```

Use:

```
// union/abctuple.cpp
auto d = discriminant( sunk );
cout << "discriminant: "
     << d << '\n';
```

Now use structured bindings to return the two roots:

Exercise 11.3. Write the function `abc_roots` that makes this code work:

```
// union/abctuple.cpp
auto roots = abc_roots( sunk );
auto [xplus,xminus] = roots;
cout << xplus << "," << xminus << '\n';
```

11.5.2 ▪ Example: Square root

For results returned from a function, it is preferable to have a `return` result, rather than a parameter passed by reference (C++ Core Guidelines [12, F.20]). But what if you want to return multiple results? One possibility is the `tuple` class from the standard library.

You can make a *tuple* with `tuple`: an entity that comprises several components, possibly of different type, and which unlike a `struct` you do not need to define beforehand. (For tuples with exactly two elements, use `pair`.)

In C++11 you would use the `get` method to extract elements from a pair or tuple.

Use `get` to unpack a tuple:

```
#include <tuple>

std::tuple<int,double,char> id = \
    std::make_tuple<int,double,char>( 3, 5.12, 'f' );
    // or:
    std::make_tuple( 3, 5.12, 'f' );
double result = std::get<1>(id);
std::get<0>(id) += 1;
```

```
// also:
std::pair<int,char> ic = make_pair( 24, 'd' );
```

Annoyance: all that "get"ting.

This does not look terribly elegant. Fortunately, C++17 can use denotations and the `auto` keyword to make this considerably shorter.

Consider the case of a function that returns a tuple. You could use `auto` to deduce the return type:

```
// stl/tuple.cpp
auto maybe_root1(float x) {
  if (x<0)
    return make_tuple
      <bool,float>(false,-1);
  else
    return make_tuple
      <bool,float>
        (true,sqrt(x));
};
```

but more interestingly, you can use a *tuple denotation*:

```
// stl/tuple.cpp
tuple<bool,float>
    maybe_root2(float x) {
  if (x<0)
    return {false,-1};
  else
    return {true,sqrt(x)};
};
```

Here the return type of the function is indicated, but the `return` statements do not construct this type explicitly.

The calling code is particularly elegant:

Code:

```
// stl/tuple.cpp
auto [succeed,y] = maybe_root2(x);
if (succeed)
  cout << "Root of " << x
       << " is " << y << '\n';
else
  cout << "Sorry, " << x
       << " is negative" << '\n';
```

Output:

```
Root of 2 is 1.41421
Sorry, -2 is negative
```

This is known as *structured binding*.

Structured bindings will be used in section 20.12 to unpack the elements of a `cartesian_product` view.

Chapter 12

Templates

You have seen how objects of type `vector<string>` and `vector<float>` are very similar: both have methods with the same names, and these methods behave largely the same. This angle-bracket notation is called "templating" and the `string` or `float` is called the *template parameter*.

If you go digging into the source of the C++ library, you will find that, somewhere, there is just a single definition of the `vector` class, but with a new notation it gets the type `string` or `float` as template parameter.

It is as if (and reality is of course more complicated) the templated class (or function) is preceded by a line

```
template< typename T >
class vector {
  ...
};
```

This mechanism is available for your own functions and classes too.

Remark. *Historically* `typename` *was* `class`*, but that's confusing. However, you may still come across this in older code.*

12.1 ▪ Templated functions

We will start by taking a brief look at templated functions.

For this example observe that $\sqrt{3.14} = 1.77200451467$.

Definition:

```
// template/func.cpp
template <typename Real>
void sqrt_diff( Real x ) {
  cout << std::sqrt(x)-1.772 << '\n';
};
```

We use this with a templated function:

Code:

```
// template/func.cpp
sqrt_diff<float>( 3.14f );
sqrt_diff<double>( 3.14 );
```

Output:

```
4.48513e-06
4.51467e-06
```

If the value of the template parameter is clear from the function argument, the template argument deduction (TAD) mechanism allows you to dispense with specifying the template parameter.

The compiler can deduce the template:

```
// template/func.cpp
sqrt_diff( 3.14f );
sqrt_diff( 3.14 );
```

In this example we took a square root of the argument, but we didn't specify that the template parameter was numeric at all. What happens if you call `sqrt_diff("abc")`? In that case the compiler will complain.

The explanation is that templated code is not compiled as such; only when the templated function is called will the compiler (try to) generate code for that particular type. At that point it will detect that you are, in effect, trying to take the square root of a string. A compiler error will ensue.

Exercise 12.1. Machine precision, or "machine epsilon," is sometimes defined as the smallest number ϵ so that $1 + \epsilon > 1$ in computer arithmetic.

Write a templated function `machine_eps` so that the following code prints out the values of the machine precision for the `float` and `double` type, respectively:

Code:

```
// template/eps.cpp
float float_eps =
  machine_eps<float>();
cout << "Epsilon float: "
     << setw(10) << setprecision(4)
     << float_eps << '\n';

double double_eps =
  machine_eps<double>();
cout << "Epsilon double: "
     << setw(10) << setprecision(4)
     << double_eps << '\n';
```

Output:

```
Epsilon float: 1.1921e-07
Epsilon double: 2.2204e-16
```

Hint: you may need to cast scalars to the appropriate type.

Exercise 12.2. If you're doing the zero-finding project, you can now do the exercises in section 17.1.3.

12.2 ▪ Templated classes

The most common use of templates is probably to define templated classes. You have in fact seen this mechanism in action with the `std::vector` class, which is templated over the type of element contained in the vector.

The templated vector class looks roughly like

```
template<typename T>
class vector {
private:
  T *vectordata; // internal data
public:
  T at(int i) { return vectordata[i]  };
  int size() { /* return size of data */ };
  // much more
}
```

Let's consider a worked out example. We write a class `Store` that stored a single element of the type of the template parameter.

Intended behavior:

Code:

```
// template/example1.cpp
Store<int> i5(5);
cout << i5.stored_value() << '\n';
```

Output:

```
5
```

The class definition is preceded by a `template` line and uses the template parameter throughout.

Template parameter is used for private data, return type, etc.

```
// template/example1.cpp
template< typename T >
class Store {
private:
  T stored;
public:
  Store(T v) : stored(v) {};
  T stored_value() { return stored;};
```

Exercise 12.3. Take your `Point` class from a previous exercise and templatize the class definition.

Write the `distance` function for the templated class. Write a main program that tests this.

If we write methods that refer to the templated type, things get a little more complicated. Let's say we want two methods `copy` and `negative` that return objects of the same templated type:

Given:

```
// template/example1.cpp
Store<float> f314(3.14);
```

Methods that return a templated object:

Code:

```
// template/example1.cpp
Store<float> also314 = f314.copy();
cout << also314.stored_value() << '\n';
Store<float> min314 = f314.negative();
cout << min314.stored_value() << '\n';
```

Output:

```
3.14
-3.14
```

Exercise: can you write this with `auto`?

The method definitions are fairly straightforward; if you leave out the template parameter, the *class name injection* mechanism uses the same template value as for the class being defined. In the following example the template parameter can be specified or left out, and the CTAD mechanism will deduce the missing template parameter.

Template parameter can often be left out in methods:

```
// template/example1.cpp
// spell out the template parameter
Store<T> copy() const { return Store<T>(stored); };
// using CTAD:
Store negative() const { return Store(-stored); };
```

12.2.1 ▪ Out-of-class method definitions

If we separate the class declaration and the method definitions (for instance, for separate compilation; see section 24.1.4) things get trickier. The class declaration is basically the class definition minus method bodies.

Declaration of a templated class:

```
// template/example2.cpp
template< typename T >
class Store {
private:
  T stored;
public:
  Store(T v);
  T value() const;
  Store copy() const;
  Store<T> negative() const;
};
```

The method definitions are more tricky. Now the template parameter needs to be specified every time you mention the templated class:

Each method needs the `template` line:

```
// template/example2.cpp
template< typename T >
Store<T>::Store(T v) : stored(v) {};
```

```
template< typename T >
T Store<T>::value() const { return stored;};

template< typename T >
Store<T>  Store<T>::copy() const { return Store<T>(stored); };

template< typename T >
Store<T> Store<T>::negative() const { return Store<T>(-stored); };
```

If your declaration and definitions are in separate files, there is a further complication; see section 12.2.3.

12.2.2 ▪ Specific implementations: Template specializations

Sometimes the template code works for a number of types (or values), but not for all. In that case you can specify the instantiation for specific types with empty angle brackets:

```
template <typename T>
void f(T);
template <>
void f(char c) { /* code with c */ };
template <>
void f(double d) { /* code with d */ };
```

12.2.3 ▪ Templates and separate compilation

The use of templates often makes *separate compilation* hard: in order to compile the templated definitions the compiler needs to know with what types they will be used. For this reason, many libraries are set up as *header-only library*: they have to be included in each file where they are used, rather than compiled separately and linked.

In the case where you can foresee which types a templated class will be instantiated with, there is a way to have separate compilation of the library routines. Suppose you have a templated class and it will only be used (instantiated) with certain types:

Class definition:

```
// namespace/instantlib.h
template< typename T >
class instant {
 public:
  instant() = default;
  void out();
};
```

Only instantiations:

```
// namespace/instant.cpp
instant<char> ic;
ic.out();
instant<int> ii;
ii.out();
```

We can then add, for each type, a line to the implementation file, stating that the class will be instantiated with that type.

Lines added to implementation file:

```
// namespace/instantlib.cpp
template class instant<char>;
template class instant<int>;
```

The implementation file will now have code that compiles the class for these types. This makes it possible to compile this file separately, and subsequently link it into your program.

If the file using the class is recompiled, this saved you the recompilation time of the code for the class. That makes this scheme much faster than a header-only setup.

12.3 ▪ Example: Polynomials over fields

It makes sense for numerical applications to be templated to allow for computation in *single precision* `float`s, *double precision* `double`s, and perhaps `std::complex` numbers. However, we can often also generalize the computation to other *fields*. Consider as an example polynomials, in both scalars and (square) matrices.

Let's start with a simple class for polynomials:

```
// polynomial/poly_eval.cpp
class polynomial {
private:
  vector<double> coefficients;
public:
  polynomial( vector<double> c )
    : coefficients(c) {};
  // 5 x^2 + 4 x + 3 = 5 x + 4 x + 3
  double eval( double x ) const {
    double y{0.};
    for_each(coefficients.rbegin(),coefficients.rend(),
             [x,&y] (double c) { y *= x; y += c; } );
    return y;
  };
  double operator()(double x) const { return eval(x); };
```

We store the polynomial coefficients, with the zeroth-degree coefficient in location zero, etc. The routine for evaluating a polynomial for a given input x is an implementation of *Horner's rule*:

$$5x^2 + 4x + 3 \equiv ((5) \cdot x + 4) \cdot x + 3.$$

(Note that the `eval` method above uses `rbegin`, `rend` to traverse the coefficients in the correct order from last to first.)

For instance, the coefficients `2,0,1` correspond in increasing order of x to the polynomial $2 + 0 \cdot x + 1 \cdot x^2$:

```
// polynomial/poly_eval.cpp
polynomial x2p2( {2., 0., 1.} );
for ( auto x : {1., 2., 3.} ) {
  auto y = x2p2(x);
  cout << "Second power of x=" << x << " plus 2 gives y=" << y << '\n';
}
```

We can generalize the above to the case of matrices, where both the x input and y output are matrices. For now we let the polynomial coefficients be scalars.

The above code for evaluating a polynomial for a certain input works just as well for matrices, as long as the multiplication and addition operators are defined. So let's say we have a class `mat` and have member functions:

```
// polynomial/poly_mat.cpp
mat operator+( const mat& other ) const;
void operator+=( const mat& other );
mat operator*( const mat& other ) const;
mat operator*( double other ) const;
void operator*=( const mat& other );
void operator*=( double other );
```

Now we redefine the `polynomial` class, templated over the scalar type:

```
// polynomial/poly_mat.cpp
template< typename Scalar >
class polynomial {
private:
  vector<double> coefficients;
public:
  polynomial( vector<double> c )
    : coefficients(c) {};
  int degree() const { return coefficients.size()-1; };
  Scalar eval( Scalar x ) const {
    Scalar y{0.};
    for_each(coefficients.rbegin(),coefficients.rend(),
             [x,&y] (double c) { y *= x; y += c; } );
    return y;
  };
```

The code using polynomials stays the same, except that we have to supply the scalar type as template parameter whenever we create a polynomial object. The above example of $p(x) = x^2 + 2$ becomes for scalars

```
// polynomial/poly_mat.cpp
polynomial<double> x2p2( {2., 0., 1.} );
for ( auto x : {1., 2., 3.} ) {
  auto y = x2p2(x);
  cout << "Second power of x=" << x << " plus 2 gives y=" << y << '\n';
}
```

and for matrices

```
// polynomial/poly_mat.cpp
polynomial<mat> x2p2( {2., 0., 1.} );
for ( auto x : {1., 2., 3.} ) {
  auto y = x2p2(x);
  cout << "Second power of x=" << x << " plus 2 gives y=" << y << '\n';
}
```

Exercise 12.4. Can you extend the matrix class to allow for matrix-valued coefficients?

12.4 ▪ Nontype template parameters

Imagine you write a physics simulation library, and you code everything to accommodate either 2D or 3D space. At any given time, you will run either a 2D or a 3D simulation, but not a mix. For such cases you can use the integer dimensionality as a template parameter:

```
Simulation<2> mysimulation;
mysimulation.run();
```

This is known as a nontype template parameter (NTTP).

The template quantity is an integer value, not a type:

Code:

```
// template/cl3.cpp
template<int val>
class initvector
  : public vector<int> {
public:
  initvector( int n )
    : vector<int>(n,val) {};
};
    /* ... */
  initvector<5> v(20);
  cout << v.size() << ":"
       << v.front() << ","
       << v.back() << '\n';
```

Output:

```
20:5,5
```

Exercise 12.5. Write a class that contains an array. The length of the array should be templated.

12.5 ▪ Concepts

The C++20 standard added the notion of *concept*.

Templates can be too generic. For instance, one could write a templated *gcd* function

```
template <typename T>
T gcd( T a, T b ) {
  if (b==0) return a;
  else return gcd(b,a%b);
}
```

which will work for various integral types. To prevent it being applied to nonintegral types, you can specify a *concept* to the type

```
// template/concept.cpp
#include <type_traits>
template<typename T>
concept Integral = std::is_integral_v<T>;
```

used as

```
// template/concept.cpp
template <typename T>
requires Integral<T>
T gcd0( T a, T b ) {
  if (b==0) return a;
  else return gcd0(b,a%b);
}
```

or

```
// template/concept.cpp
template <Integral T>
T gcd1( T a, T b ) {
```

```
    if (b==0) return a;
    else return gcd1(b,a%b);
}
```

We can even dispense with the `template` keyword altogether:

```
// template/concept.cpp
Integral auto gcd
      ( Integral auto a, Integral auto b ) {
    if (b==0) return a;
    else return gcd(b,a%b);
}
```

Now we use this:

Code:

```
// template/concept.cpp
int i=27,j=30;
cout << "gcd(27,30)="
      << gcd(i,j) << '\n';
long ii=27'000'000'000,
    jj=30'000'000'000;
cout << "gcd(27G,30G)="
      << gcd(ii,jj) << '\n';
// WRONG: DOES NOT COMPILE
// gcd(27.1,30.2);
```

Output:

```
gcd(27,30)=3
gcd(27G,30G)=3000000000
```

You can now do the exercises in section 17.1.4 in the Newton method chapter.

Chapter 13
Other language features

We discuss a couple of features of C++ that do not fit in other chapters.

13.1 ▪ Const

The keyword `const` can be used to indicate that various quantities cannot be changed. This is not an issue of program performance; it mostly serves programming safety: if you declare that a method will not change any members, and it does so (indirectly) anyway, the compiler will warn you about this.

Another way of looking at this is that using const expresses the intent of code: if something does not change, it should be marked as such. In fact, some recent programming languages have this const behavior as default, and things that can change have to be marked as such.

13.1.1 ▪ Const arguments

The use of const arguments is one way of protecting you against yourself. If an argument is conceptually supposed to stay constant, the compiler will catch it if you mistakenly try to change it.

Function arguments marked `const` cannot be altered by the function code. The following segment gives a compilation error:

```
// const/constchange.cpp
void f(const int i) {
  ++i; // COMPILER ERROR!
}
```

13.1.2 ▪ Const references

A more sophisticated use of const is the *const reference*:

```
void f( const int &i ) { .... }
```

This may look strange. After all, references, and the pass-by-reference mechanism, were introduced to return changed values to the calling environment. The `const` keyword negates that possibility of changing the parameter.

But there is a second reason for using references. Parameters are passed by value, which means that they are copied, and that includes big objects such as `std::vector`. Using a reference to pass a vector is much less costly in both time and space, but then there is the possibility of changes to the vector propagating back to the calling environment.

Consider a class that has methods that return an internal member by reference, once as const reference and once not:

Code:

```
// const/constref.cpp
class has_int {
private:
  int mine{1};
public:
  const int& int_to_get() { return mine; };
  int& int_to_set() { return mine; };
  void inc() { ++mine; };
};
    /* ... */
  has_int an_int;
  an_int.inc(); an_int.inc();
  println("Contained int is now: {}",
          an_int.int_to_get());
  /* Compiler error: an_int.int_to_get() = 5;
  */
  an_int.int_to_set() = 17;
  println("Contained int is now: {}",
          an_int.int_to_get());
```

Output:

```
Contained int is now: 3
Contained int is now: 17
```

We can make visible the difference between pass-by-value and pass-by-const-reference if we define a class where the *copy constructor* explicitly reports itself:

```
// object/copyscalar.cpp
class has_int {
private:
  int mine{1};
public:
  has_int(int v) {
    cout << "set: " << v
         << '\n';
    mine = v; };
  has_int( has_int &h ) {
    auto v = h.mine;
    cout << "copy: " << v
         << '\n';
    mine = v; };
  void printme() {
    cout << "I have: " << mine
         << '\n'; };
};
```

Now if we define two functions, with the two parameter passing mechanisms, we see that passing by value invokes the copy constructor, and passing by const reference does not:

Code:

```
// const/constcopy.cpp
void f_with_copy(has_int other) {
  cout << "function with copy"
       << '\n'; };
void f_with_ref(const has_int &other) {
  cout << "function with ref"
       << '\n'; };
  /* ... */
  cout << "Calling f with copy..."
       << '\n';
  f_with_copy(an_int);

  cout << "Calling f with ref..."
       << '\n';
  f_with_ref(an_int);
```

Output:

```
Calling f with copy...
(calling copy constructor)
function with copy
Calling f with ref...
function with ref
... done
```

13.1.2.1 ▪ Const references in range-based loops

The same pass-by-value/reference issue comes up in range-based for loops. The syntax

```
for ( auto v : some_vector )
```

copies the vector elements to the *v* variable, whereas

```
for ( auto& v : some_vector )
```

makes a reference. To get the benefits of references (no copy cost) while avoiding the pitfalls (inadvertent changes), you can also use a const reference here:

```
for ( const auto& v : some_vector )
```

13.1.3 ▪ Const methods

We can distinguish two types of methods: those that alter internal data members of the object, and those that don't. The ones that don't can be marked `const`. While this is in no way required, it contributes to a clean programming style:

Using `const` will catch mismatches between the declaration and definition of the method. For instance,

```
class Things {
  private:
  int var;
  public:
  f(int &ivar,int c) const {
    var += c; // typo: should be 'ivar'
  }
}
```

Here, the use of `var` was a typo, and should have been `ivar`. Since the method is marked `const`, the compiler will generate an error because the function makes changes outside of its local scope.

It encourages a functional style, in the sense that it makes *side effects* impossible:

```
class Things {
private:
  int i;
public:
  int getval() const { return i; }
  int inc() { return i++; } // side effect!
  void addto(int &thru) const { // effect through parameter
    thru += i; }
}
```

Note that a method being const does not mean you cannot call nonconst functions in it: it means that the `this` object cannot be affected.

13.1.4 ▪ Const expr

Recent versions of C++ have been getting increasingly sophisticated in what expressions can be evaluated at compile time. Such expressions are marked with `constexpr`:

```
constexpr int i = 5*6;
```

and they will be evaluated by the compiler rather than at runtime.

Using `constexpr` in a conditional causes the compiler to eliminate all but the true branch from the generated code:

```
operator()( int a, int b ) {
  if constexpr (sym == TensorSymm::NONE) {
    return data_[b + ndim*a];
  } else if (sym == TensorSymm::SYM2) {
    if (b < a) {
      return data_[b*(2*ndim - b - 1)/2+a];
    } else {
      return data_[a*(2*ndim - a - 1)/2+b];
    }
  }
}
```

Since this indexing operator will likely be executed many times, eliminating branches will greatly improve performance.

Another example, this time in combination with templates:

```
template<int ndim> // rank 2
constexpr int TensorDOF<ndim, 2> = ndim*ndim;
template<int ndim> // rank 3
constexpr int TensorDOF<ndim, 3> = ndim*ndim*ndim;
```

13.1.5 ▪ Const design

If you try to make an existing code-base "const correct," you'll find that you have to start at the bottom. In the following snippet the const method `multiply` calls a nonconst method `get`:

```
// const/constproblem.cpp
class has {
private:
  float x;
public:
  void setv( float v ) {
```

```
    x = v; };
  void getv( float v ) {
    return x;};
  void multiply( float &v ) const {
    v *= getv(); };
};
```

The compiler will complain about this, probably stating that it could not find a const variant of `getv`. This illustrates that you have to introduce const-correctness from the bottom up.

13.1.6 ▪ Const overloads

A const method and its nonconst variant are different enough that you can use this for overloading and have them both.

Const and nonconst versions of `at`:

Code:

```
// const/constat.cpp
class has_array {
private:
  vector<float> values;;
public:
  has_array(int l,float v)
    : values(vector<float>(l,v)) {};
  auto& at(int i) {
    cout << "var at" << '\n';
    return values.at(i); };
  const auto& at (int i) const {
    cout << "const at" << '\n';
    return values.at(i); };
  auto sum() const {
    float p;
    for ( int i=0; i<values.size(); ++i)
      p += at(i);
    return p;
  };
};

int main() {

  int l; float v;
  cin >> l; cin >> v;
  has_array fives(l,v);
  cout << fives.sum() << '\n';
  fives.at(0) = 2;
  cout << fives.sum() << '\n';
```

Output:

```
const at
const at
const at
1.5
var at
const at
const at
const at
4.5
```

Exercise 13.1. Explore variations on this example, and see which ones work and which ones do not.

1. Remove the second definition of `at`. Can you explain the error?

2. Remove either of the `const` keywords from the second `at` method. What errors do you get?

This mechanism can be made more elegant with the C++23 mechanism of *deducing this*; see section 3.5.

13.1.7 ▪ Mutable

Sometimes you may want methods that are marked `const`, but that still affect data outside of their scope. To illustrate this, consider a typical class with nonconst update methods, and const readout of some computed quantity:

```
class Stuff {
private:
  int i,j;
public:
  Stuff(int i,int j) : i(i),j(j) {};
  void seti(int inew) { i = inew; };
  void setj(int jnew) { j = jnew; };
  int result () const { return i+j; };
```

Now suppose that the `i+j` computation in the `result` function stands for something expensive. You can solve that by doing the following:

1. Cache the computed value.
2. The `result` function returns the cached value without further computation.
3. Let the `seti/setj` methods recompute the cached value.

```
class Stuff {
private:
  int i,j;
  int cache;
  void compute_cache() { cache = i+j; };
public:
  Stuff(int i,int j) : i(i),j(j) { compute_cache(); };
  void seti(int inew) { i = inew; compute_cache(); };
  void setj(int jnew) { j = jnew; compute_cache(); };
  int result () const { return cache; };
```

For the next complication, assume that setting `i,j` happens far more often than requesting the computed value through the `result` method. The previous solution is then inefficient, and instead we do the following:

1. Maintain a boolean flag that records whether the cached value is valid.
2. The `seti/j` function sets this flag to `false`.
3. The `result` function recomputes the cache, but only if necessary.

```
class Stuff {
private:
  int i,j;
  int cache;
  bool cache_valid{false};
  void update_cache() {
    if (!cache_valid) {
      cache = i+j; cache_valid = true;
  };
public:
  Stuff(int i,int j) : i(i),j(j) {};
  void seti(int inew) { i = inew; cache_valid = false; };
  void setj(int jnew) { j = jnew; cache_valid = false; }
  int result () const {
    update_cache(); return cache; };
```

This does not compile, because `result` is const, but it calls a nonconst function.

We can solve this by declaring the cache variables to be `mutable`. Then the methods that conceptually don't change the object can still stay `const`, even while altering the state of the object. (It is better not to use `const_cast`.)

```
class Stuff {
private:
  int i,j;
  mutable int cache;
  mutable bool cache_valid{false};
  void update_cache() const {
    if (!cache_valid) {
      cache = i+j; cache_valid = true;
  };
public:
  Stuff(int i,int j) : i(i),j(j) {};
  void seti(int inew) { i = inew; cache_valid = false; };
  void setj(int jnew) { j = jnew; cache_valid = false; }
  int result () const {
    update_cache(); return cache; };
```

13.2 ▪ Auto

The `auto` keyword can be used in circumstances where the compiler can deduce the type of a variable, saving you from having to spell it out.

13.2.1 ▪ Declarations

A first use of `auto` is in declarations. Sometimes the type of a variable being declared is obvious from the initial value it is assigned:

```
std::vector< std::shared_ptr< myclass >>*
  myvar = new std::vector< std::shared_ptr< myclass >>
              ( 20, new myclass(1.3) );
```

(Pointer to vector of 20 shared pointers to `myclass`, initialized with unique instances.) You can write this as

```
auto myvar =
  new std::vector< std::shared_ptr< myclass >>
          ( 20, new myclass(1.3) );
```

13.2.2 ▪ Return type deduction

In many functions, the type of the return type can be deduced from the return statement. Since C++17 it is therefore allowed to declare the return type as `auto`. This is known as *return type deduction*.

Function return type deduction:

```
// auto/autofun.cpp
auto equal(int i,int j) {
  return i==j;
};
```

Similar to functions, the return type of class methods can also be declared `auto`.

Return type of methods can be deduced:

```
// auto/plainget.cpp
class A {
private: float data;
public:
  A(float i) : data(i) {};
  auto &access() {
    return data; };
  void print() {
    cout << "data: " << data << '\n'; };
};
```

If you declare a variable with `auto`, and you assign a reference to it, the variable does not automatically become a reference:

With this class definition:

```
class X {
private:
 int _x;
public:
  int &x () { return _x};
}
```

This is not a reference:

```
X x;
auto ix = x.x();
```

but this is:

```
auto& ix = x.x();
```

13.2.3 ▪ decltype: Declared type

There are places where you want the compiler to deduce the type of a variable, but where this is not immediately possible. Suppose that in

```
auto v = some_object.get_stuff();
f(v);
```

you want to put a `try ... catch` block around just the creation of *v*:

```
try { auto v = some_object.get_stuff();
} catch (...) {}
f(v);
```

This does not work, because the `try` block is a scope. It also doesn't work to write

```
auto v;
try { v = some_object.get_stuff();
} catch (...) {}
f(v);
```

because there is no indication what type *v* is created with. Also, this presumes the existence of a default constructor.

Instead, it is possible to query the type of the expression that creates *v* with `decltype`:

```
decltype(some_object.get_stuff()) v;
try { auto v = some_object.get_stuff();
} catch (...) {}
f(v);
```

13.3 ▪ Casts

In C++, constants and variables have clear types. For cases where you want to force the type to be something else, there is the *cast* mechanism. With a cast you tell the compiler, treat this thing as such-and-such a type, no matter how it was defined.

Remark. *The C cast has a syntax of*

```
sometype x;
othertype y = (othertype)x;
```

One practical problem with this syntax is that it is hard to spot, for instance, by searching in an editor. Because C++ casts have a unique keyword, they are easier to recognize in a text editor.

We will now discuss some casting mechanisms. See section 11.4 for `any_cast`.

13.3.1 ▪ Static cast

One use of casting is to convert to constants to a "larger" type. For instance, allocation does not use integers but `size_t`.

Code:

```
// cast/longint.cpp
int hundredk = 100000;
int overflow =
  hundredk*hundredk;
cout << "overflow: "
     << overflow << '\n';
size_t bignumber =
  static_cast<size_t>(hundredk)*hundredk;
cout << "bignumber: "
     << bignumber << '\n';
```

Output:

```
overflow: 1410065408
bignumber: 10000000000
```

However, if the conversion is possible, the result may still not be "correct."

Code:

```
// cast/intlong.cpp
long int hundredg = 100000000000;
cout << "long number:       "
     << hundredg << '\n';
int overflow;
overflow = static_cast<int>(hundredg);
cout << "assigned to int: "
     << overflow << '\n';
```

Output:

```
long number:       100000000000
assigned to int: 1215752192
```

There are no runtime tests on static casting.

In templated code, a static cast can be used to ensure that constants are of the right type. Suppose we have

```
g(int,int);
g(long,long);
```

then

```
long x;
g(x,0);
```

is ambiguous. Instead, use a cast to ensure a zero of the right type:

```
template< typename scalar >
void f (scalar x) {
```

```
  g( x, static_cast<scalar>(0) );
}
```

Static casts are a good way of casting back void pointers to what they were originally. This mechanism is used extensively in C codes, where void pointers are also called *opaque handles*.

Main:

```
// cast/opaque.cpp
int i=5;
f( (void*)(&i),1 );
float f=.5;
f( (void*)(&f),2 );
```

Function:

```
// cast/opaque.cpp
void f( void *p,int type ) {
  if (type==1) {
    int *i = static_cast<int*>(p);
    cout << i << '\n';
  } // other cases omitted
}
```

13.3.2 ▪ Dynamic cast

The `dynamic_cast` can be used to cast up and down a class hierarchy. In particular, it can cast pointers and references from a base to a derived class. Note that this involves a runtime check, so this type of cast is more expensive than others that fulfill a more syntactic function.

Consider the case where we have a base class and derived classes.

```
// cast/toderived.cpp
class Base {
public:
  virtual void print() = 0;
};
class Derived : public Base {
public:
  virtual void print() {
    cout << "Call Derived function!"
         << '\n'; };
};
class Erived : public Base {
public:
  virtual void print() {
    cout << "Call Erived function!"
         << '\n'; };
};
```

Also suppose that we have a function that takes a pointer or reference to the base class:

```
void f( Base& obj );
```

The function can discover what derived class the base pointer refers to:

```
// cast/toderived.cpp
void f( Base& obj ) {
  try {
    Derived &der =
      dynamic_cast<Derived&>(obj);
    der.print();
  } catch (...) {
    cout << "Could not be cast to Derived"
         << '\n';
  }
};
```

If the dynamic cast is unsuccessful:

- on a pointer, it gives a *null pointer*;
- on a reference, it throws a `bad_cast` exception.

If we have a pointer to a derived object, stored in a pointer to a base class object, it's possible to turn it safely into a derived pointer again:

Code:

```
// cast/toderived.cpp
cout << "Dynamic cast to Derived\n";
Derived object1;
f(object1);
Erived object2;
f(object2);
```

Output:

```
Dynamic cast to Derived
Call Derived function!
Could not be cast to Derived
```

On the other hand, a `static_cast` would not do the job:

Code:

```
// cast/toderivedp.cpp
Base *object = new Derived();
g(object);
Base *nobject = new Erived();
g(nobject);
```

Output:

```
Static cast to Derived
Call Derived function!
Call Erived function!
```

Note: the base class needs to be polymorphic, meaning that a pure virtual method is needed. This is not the case with a static cast, but, as said, this does not work correctly in this case.

This mechanism is used in section 19.2.

13.3.3 ▪ Const cast

With `const_cast` you can add or remove const from a variable. This is the only cast that can do this.

This cast can go two ways, and one is considered a bad idea: if something is marked const and you want to alter it, there is something wrong with your design (C++ Core Guidelines [12, ES.50]). You probably need to use `mutable`; see section 13.1.7.

However, there is a use case for the other direction. Suppose you are interfacing to a library that is not strict about its use of `const`, as is, for instance, the case with many old C libraries. Then you may need to cast some arguments to const when you call this function from a const method of your own.

In this example, both the input and output arguments of a C routine are not const. To pass a `const` array to this routine, you need to `const_cast` the `const` away.

```
// const/constcast.cpp
void old_c_routine( float*in,float*out );
void new_cpp_routine( const vector<float>&in, vector<float>&out ) {
  old_c_routine
    ( const_cast<float*>( in.data() ), out.data() );
};
```

As a less verbose alternative to const_cast, you can use the (C++17) templated function as_const.

13.3.4 ▪ Reinterpret cast and bit cast

The reinterpret_cast and std::bit_cast perform the functions corresponding to the C mechanism of "take this byte and pretend that it is of type whatever." The former is mostly intended for conversions to and from pointers:

```
int i = 7;
char* p2 = reinterpret_cast<char*>(&i);
    std::cout << (p2[0] == '\x7' ? "This system is little-endian\n"
                                 : "This system is big-endian\n");
```

The library function bit_cast (in the bit header; C++20) has additional uses, including in constexpr contexts.

Part II

Scientific Programming Idioms

Chapter 14

Writing your own containers

Scientific applications often feature large data objects: matrices, graphs, fields and vector fields in physics, etc. In this chapter we will see some issues in designing containers for these entities.

14.1 ▪ Multidimensional arrays

C++ traditionally had little native support for multidimensional arrays, which are essential for linear algebra operations and many other physics algorithms. In section 30.2 we will look at the *Eigen* library, which provides linear algebra objects and operations, but for now we take a look at some of the modern mechanisms that can be used to handle multidimensional objects natively in C++.

14.1.1 ▪ Matrix as vector-of-vectors

A first and—spoiler—inferior way of emulating a multidimensional structure is to create a vector-of-vectors:

```
vector<float> row(20);
vector<vector<float>> matrix(10,row);
/* you can now write: */
  ... matrix[i][j] ...
```

Here you first create a vector that stands for a matrix row, then fill a second vector with a number of copies of that.

To understand the problem with this, we need to go into a little detail on how vectors are realized. You can think of a `std::vector` as consisting of two parts: a small block (allocated on the *stack*) with the size and capacity of the vector, and a block (on the *heap*) with the actual data; see Figure 14.1. This is in contrast to C and Fortran, where a vector is only the data array.

Now if you make a vector-of-vectors (Figure 14.2) you get a bunch of vectors, potentially spread throughout memory. While this implementation acts like a matrix in that it allows you to write `matrix[i][j]`, there are various arguments against it.

- You cannot interface this to software (such as C and Fortran libraries) that expect a matrix to be contiguous; and
- for performance reasons you want the data to be contiguous, too; see section 31.2.3.

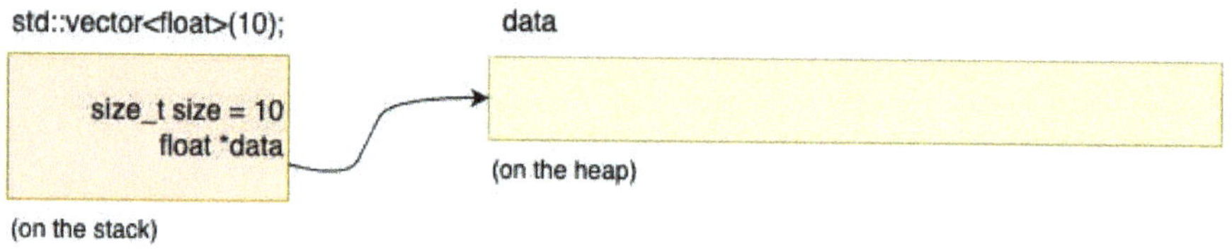

Figure 14.1. *Implementation of a standard vector*

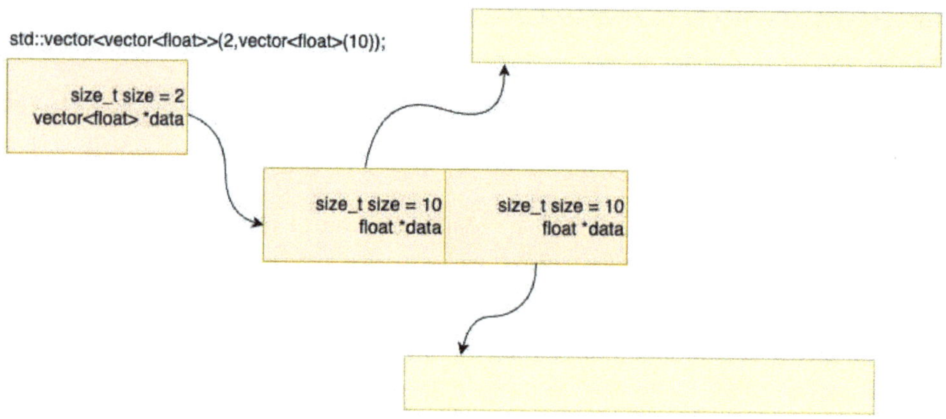

Figure 14.2. *A vector of vectors*

We will develop a better implementation in the next section.

Remark. *You could also have written the above fragment as*

```
vector<vector<float>> matrix(10);
for ( auto &row : matrix ) {
  row = vector<float>(20);
}
```

This loop formulation makes some special effects possible. For instance, can you think how to create a triangular array?

14.1.2 ▪ A better matrix class

The problem of the noncontiguous matrix rows can be solved by making a matrix class where the objects store a long enough `vector`. You then need a translation from two-dimensional `i,j` indexing to a linear scheme.

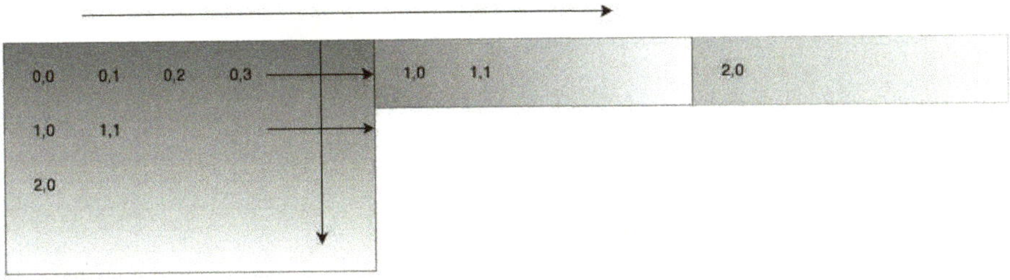

Figure 14.3. *Matrix storage by rows*

Linearized indexing:

Class:

```
// array/matrixclass.cpp
class matrix {
private:
  vector<double> matrix_data;
  int m,n;
public:
  matrix(int m,int n)
    : m(m),n(n),matrix_data(m*n) {};
```

Methods:

```
void setij(int i,int j,double v) {
  matrix_data.at( i*n +j ) = v;
};
double getij(int i,int j) {
  return matrix_data.at( i*n +j );
};
```

Under the particular index translation used here, the matrix is said to be "stored by rows," also known as in "*row-major* storage" since the rows are contiguous in memory; see Figure 14.3. Column-major storage, with columns stored contiguously, is possible too; this scheme is used in the *Fortran* language.

Exercise 14.1. In the matrix class of the previous slide, why are `m,n` stored explicitly, while that would not be needed in the scheme of section 14.1.1?

One big advantage of having the matrix storage be contiguous is that it is compatible with the storage traditionally used in many libraries and codes. It is also likely to be more efficient in execution because of increased spatial locality; see section 31.2.3.

The syntax for `setij` / `getij` can be improved.

Exercise 14.2. Overload the `operator[]` so that you can write

```
A[2,3] = 7.24;
```

(See section 3.2.1.)

14.2 ▪ Inheriting from existing containers

Sometimes an existing container is almost, but not quite, good enough. How would you write a container with extended functionality, while using as much as possible the functionality of the original one?

14.2.1 ▪ Composition

We start by *composing* two classes. As a simple example, consider a "named vector," which is a `std::vector`, except that it has a `string` as name. We could realize this as a class that contains both a vector and a string:

```
// array/arrayprint.cpp
class namedvector {
private:
  string name;
  vector<int> values;
public:
  namedvector(int n,string name="unnamed")
    : name(name),values(n) {
  };
  string rendered() {
    stringstream render;
    render << name << ":";
    for (auto v : values )
      render << " " << v << ",";
    return render.str();
  }
    /* ... */
};
```

A problem with this approach is that you may have to recreate some methods to access the vector. For instance, you need to define the `at` method on the object to access elements of the vector:

```
// array/arrayprint.cpp
int &namedvector::at(int i) {
  return values.at(i);
};
```

14.2.2 ▪ Public inheritance

One way out of the need for redefinitions is to let the new class inherit from a container class. Let's explore a class `witharray` that inherits from `std::vector`; we will ignore other components it may have. At first we make this class with *public inheritance*:

```
// object/isavector.cpp
class witharray : public vector<float> {
```

Now the constructor calls the constructor of the vector:

```
// object/isavector.cpp
witharray::witharray( float n )
  : vector<float>(n) {
};
```

but after that the object has all the methods of the vector:

Code:

```
// object/isavector.cpp
witharray x(5);
x[ x.size()-1 ] = 3.14;
println( "{}",x.back() );
```

Output:

```
3.14
```

Remark. *With the inheritance mechanism you could create a "named vector" by inheriting from both* `std::vector` *and* `std::string`*. Do you see a problem with that? This so-called* multiple inheritance *mechanism should only be used with great caution.*

14.2.3 ▪ Private inheritance

If you object to all methods from the base container now being available, the more cautious approach uses *private inheritance*:

```
// object/usingvector.cpp
class witharray : private vector<float> {
  using BaseVector = vector<float>;
public:
  using BaseVector::back;
  using BaseVector::size;
  using BaseVector::operator[];
```

Now the base container is private, meaning that its methods can only be used internally to the derived class. The first `using` statement allows us to refer to the base class by name; the remaining ones explicitly state which methods of the base class are to be public methods of the derived class.

As an illustration, we made the `back` method public, but not the `front` method. Therefore, while this compiles:

```
// object/usingvector.cpp
witharray x(5);
x[ x.size()-1 ] = 3.14;
println( "{}",x.back() );
```

we get a compilation error on trying to use `front`:

```
// object/usingvector.cpp
// This does not compile:
println( "{}",x.front() );

/*
  error: constexpr std::vector< ... >::front() is inaccessible within this context
 40 |  println( "{}",x.front() );
    |                ~~~~~~~^~
*/
```

There is a further technical point for preferring private over public inheritance from standard containers. With public inheritance it becomes possible to obtain a pointer to the base class; the derived object may then not be properly deallocated in the destructor. We dispense with giving detailed examples and discussion of this.

14.3 ▪ Managing your own storage

Inheriting from existing containers is one way of writing containers, but sometimes you want to manage your own storage. For this you use the commands `new` and `delete`, for allocating and deallocating, respectively.

```
// alloc/newdelete.cpp
template< typename scalar>
class container {
private:
  int n;
  scalar *allocated = nullptr;
public:
  container( int n )
    : n(n), allocated( new scalar[n] ) {
    println( "Allocating {}",n );
  };
```

```
  ~container() {
    println( " .. freeing {}",n);
    delete[] allocated;
  };
```

The copy constructor also allocates, and copies data over:

// alloc/newdelete.cpp

```
  container( const container& other )
    : n(other.n),allocated( new scalar[n] ) {
    println( "Copying {}",n );
    memcpy( allocated,other.allocated,n*sizeof(scalar) );
  };
```

On the other hand, there may be reasons why you want objects to not be copyable. For instance, in physics simulations there should only be one instance of the object to be modeled. In that case you can disable the copy constructor:

```
container( const container& other ) = delete;
```

Another option for an uncopyable class would be to base your container on a *unique pointer* to an array allocated with `new`:

// alloc/uniquearray.cpp

```
template< typename scalar >
class container : private unique_ptr<scalar[]> {
  using allocated = unique_ptr<scalar[]>;
public:
  using allocated::operator[];
private:
  int n;
public:
  container( int n )
    : n(n), unique_ptr<scalar[]>( new scalar[n] ) {
    println("Allocating {}",n);
  };
  scalar& at( int i ) {
    if (i<0 or i>=n ) throw( std::out_of_range("") );
    return (*this)[i];
  };
};
```

This has the advantages that

- deallocation is now done automatically in the destructor of the unique pointer; and
- objects of this class cannot be copied (though they can be moved) because unique pointers cannot; also
- the `operator[]` is available for unique pointers.

On the other hand, the unique pointer does not track the size of the array, so this needs to be stored separately.

14.3.1 ▪ Aligned storage

Often it is advantageous for performance if variables or arrays are created at an address that is a multiple of 64 bytes. We say that such an address is “64-byte *aligned*.” This alignment puts it at the beginning of a cacheline (section 31.2.5), and among others it facilitates the use of *vector instructions*. For arrays and large objects it can be advantageous to use an even larger alignment: typically 4096 bytes, the size of a *small page* (section 31.4).

C++ has various tools for making sure that a variable, whether of primitive type or of object type, is aligned. For simple cases, you can prefix a declaration with an alignas specification:

```
alignas(64) int i;
alignas(256) myobject( /* constructor arguments */ );
```

The alignment of a variable can be tested with alignof.

For dynamic storage a different mechanism is needed. Here we use aligned_alloc, which is a variant of malloc, the traditional byte-specified allocation mechanism in C. (This is the reason we need the reinterpret_cast on the resulting pointer.) Here we create an array that is 4096-byte aligned:

```
// hardware/allocation.cpp
allocation_ = reinterpret_cast<R*>
  ( std::aligned_alloc( 4096,allocated_size_in_words*sizeof(R) ) );
```

Since this is formulated entirely in terms of bytes, we need to get the sizeof of the scalar type and cast it to the appropriate array type.

Remark. *The routine* aligned_storage *is deprecated as of C++23.*

14.4 ▪ Iterate over your own containers

You know that you can iterate over vector objects, in range-based syntax or with explicit iterators. Here we use range-based syntax to normalize the elements of a vector:

```
vector<float> myvector(20);
float s{0.f};
for ( auto copy_of_float : myvector )
  s += copy_of_float;
for ( auto &ref_to_float : myvector )
  ref_to_float /= s;
```

(Many other standard library classes are iteratable like this.)

This range-based syntax was introduced in C++11; prior to that, looping over a vector looked like

```
for (auto elt_ptr=vec.begin(); elt_ptr!=vec.end(); ++elt_ptr)
  element = *elt_ptr;
```

The more modern syntax is translated into this, and from this we see that the requirements for a class to be *iteratable* are the existence of

- begin and end methods; these give an *iterator* object in the initial and final states, respectively;
- a test on whether the iterator has reached the final state;
- an *increment operator*; and
- a "star" operator (that is sort of, but not quite, like a *dereference*) that gives the value that the iterator points at.

Some remarks:

- This is one of the few places where you need the asterisk in C++. However, you're applying it to an iterator, not a pointer, and this is an operator you are applying (see section 3.2).
- As with a normal loop, the end iterator points just beyond the end of the vector.

- You can do "pointer arithmetic" on iterators (section 7.2.1), as you can see in the `++elt_ptr` update part of the loop header.

14.4.1 ▪ Example: Iterator class

Recall that range-based syntax is shorthand for a more elaborate syntax, involving an iterator subclass. This means that if we want to write a range-based iteration over a user-defined class

```
for ( auto e : my_object )
    ... e ...
```

we need an iterator class with methods such as `begin`, `end`, `*`, and `++`.

Ranging over a class with iterator subclass:

Class:

```
// iterator.cpp
template<typename T>
class NewVector {
protected:
  T *storage;
  int s;
public:
// iterator stuff
  class iter;
  iter begin();
  iter end();
};
```

Main:

```
NewVector<float> v(s);
for ( auto e : v )
  cout << e << " ";
```

In order to have a random-access iterator, strictly speaking we need quite a number of functions. However, in practice the following set is often enough. (The minus operator is not necessary for ranged iteration, but it is necessary to let OpenMP parallelize that iteration; see section 20.2.)

The following operators are needed:

```
NewVector<T>::iter& operator++();
T& operator*();
bool operator==( const NewVector::iter &other ) const;
bool operator!=( const NewVector::iter &other ) const;
// needed for OpenMP
int operator-
    ( const NewVector::iter& other ) const;
NewVector<T>::iter& operator+=( int add );
```

Exercise 14.3. Write the missing iterator methods. Here's something to get you started.

```
template<typename T>
class NewVector<T>::iter {
private: T *searcher;
};
template<typename T>
NewVector<T>::iter::iter( T* searcher )
  : searcher(searcher) {};
template<typename T>
NewVector<T>::iter NewVector<T>::begin() {
  return NewVector<T>::iter(storage); };
```

```
template<typename T>
NewVector<T>::iter NewVector<T>::end() {
  return NewVector<T>::iter(storage+NewVector<T>::s); };
```

14.4.2 ▪ Range over your own containers

With the mechanisms in the previous section you can iterate over your class:

```
MyClass myobject;
for ( auto x : myobject )
  f(x);
```

However, this is not enough to apply range algorithms:

```
std::ranges::for_each( myobject, []( auto x ) { f(x); } );
```

For this, the `iter` member class needs to satisfy some more conditions.

We start with the basic design:

```
// range/foreach.cpp
class iter {
private:
  R* seek{0};
public:
  iter(R* s) : seek(s) {};
  iter& operator++() { seek++; return *this; };
  iter operator++(int i) { return std::exchange( *this,operator++() ); };
```

Note that both the *pre-* and *post-*increment operators need to be defined.

A number of types need to be defined:

```
// range/foreach.cpp
using iterator_category = std::forward_iterator_tag; // for completeness
using value_type = R; // std::iter_value_t required by std::indirectly_readable <= std::input_iterator <= std::
    input_range
using difference_type = std::ptrdiff_t; // for completeness
using pointer = R*; // for completeness
using reference = R&; // for completeness
```

We need the default constructor:

```
// range/foreach.cpp
iter() = default; // std::default_initializable required by std::semiregular <= std::sentinel_for
```

A number of operators need to be constant:

```
// range/foreach.cpp
R& operator*() const { return *seek; }; // const, required by std::indirectly_readable <= std::input_iterator
    <= std::input_range
bool operator==( const iter& other ) const { return seek==other.seek; }; // const, required by std
    ::equality_comparable <= std::sentinel_for
ptrdiff_t operator-( const iter& other ) const { return seek-other.seek; }; // const also added,
    not required for an std::input_iterator, but needed for OpenMP
```

The iterator class now satisfies a number of assertions:

```
static_assert(std::ranges::input_range<MyClass<R>>);
static_assert(std::input_iterator<MyClass<R>::iter>);
static_assert(std::sentinel_for<iter, MyClass<R>::iter>);
```

Chapter 15
Linear algebra, mostly sparse

If you have taken a basic linear algebra class, you know about square and rectangular matrices and things such as inverses and factorizations. In scientific computing inverting a matrix or computing a factorization is still important (actually, usually when you need to invert a matrix, it is for the purpose of solving a linear system, and there are better methods for that than inverting the matrix), but the nature of the matrices is often different.

Outwardly, the matrices are still square or rectangular, but we no longer store them that way. Matrices in scientific computing are often *sparse*, meaning that so many of their elements are zero that a storage scheme other than as a two-dimensional array is called for.

We will look at two classes of sparse matrices. First we discuss matrices associated with computational stencils, which come from graphics transformations or certain partial differential equation (PDE) problems; after that we will consider general sparse matrices, which come from PDE simulations and graph computations.

We conclude with a brief look at linear algebra library software.

15.1 ▪ Stencil matrices

Suppose you have an image of $m \times n$ pixels, and you want to apply a "blur" operation on it. (In graphics terms this is known as a *convolution*.) Mathematically that means each pixel gets a new value that's a combination of its old value and that of the pixels around it. An example of a *Gaussian blur* is

$$q_{i,j} \leftarrow \begin{bmatrix} +1{\cdot}p_{i-1,j-1} & +2{\cdot}p_{i-1,j} & +1{\cdot}p_{i-1,j+1} \\ +2{\cdot}p_{i,j-1} & +4{\cdot}p_{i,j} & +2{\cdot}p_{i,j+1} \\ +1{\cdot}p_{i+1,j-1} & +2{\cdot}p_{i+1,j} & +1{\cdot}p_{i+1,j+1} \end{bmatrix} \cdot \frac{1}{16}. \tag{15.1}$$

We render this compactly by writing down only the *stencil*:

$$\begin{bmatrix} 1 & 2 & 1 \\ 2 & 4 & 2 \\ 1 & 2 & 1 \end{bmatrix} /16.$$

Such a stencil can also be considered a compact way of describing a large matrix-vector multiplication as follows. First we observe that the $m \times n$ square of pixels corresponds to a vector of size $m \times n$. The update of equation (15.1) then corresponds to a matrix-vector multiplication $q \leftarrow Ap$ where

$$A = \begin{bmatrix} \ddots & \ddots & \ddots & & \ddots & \ddots & \ddots & & \ddots & \ddots & \ddots & & \\ \emptyset & 1 & 2 & 1 & \emptyset & 2 & 4 & 2 & \emptyset & 1 & 2 & 1 & \emptyset \\ & & \ddots & \ddots & \ddots & & \ddots & \ddots & \ddots & & \ddots & \ddots & \ddots \end{bmatrix} /16, \quad (15.2)$$

where the diagonal dots indicate constant values on each diagonal. However, the stencil formulation of the operator is often more insightful than the matrix one, so we use that. Note that the stencil, while usually rendered as a small 2D array, is not itself a matrix.

Remark. *The matrix structure of Figure 15.2 is known mathematically as a* Toeplitz matrix, *or more precisely, a "block Toeplitz matrix." We have simplified the matrix picture somewhat: corresponding to edge variables, some matrix elements can be zero.*

Stencils also occur frequently in physical sciences. The PDE

$$-\Delta u(x, y) = f(x, y) \quad (15.3)$$

can be solved approximately as a linear algebra problem,

$$Au = f,$$

where the matrix A is based on the stencil

$$\begin{bmatrix} \cdot & -1 & \cdot \\ -1 & 4 & -1 \\ \cdot & -1 & \cdot \end{bmatrix}. \quad (15.4)$$

Designating the size of this matrix $N = mn$, we see that only $9N$ elements are nonzero for the blur operator, and $5N$ for the PDE operator, as opposed to N^2 for a full matrix. Thus, rather than storing an $N \times N$ square array, it is enough to store an $N \times 9$ or $N \times 5$ two-dimensional array of nonzero coefficients. This array corresponds to compressing the diagonals of equation (15.2) to a contiguous block. In the current case we can cut down storage even further.

Both the above examples can be further optimized by recognizing that each row has the same coefficients, so we need to store them only once. In fact, we don't even need a data structure for the matrix, and we only write a routine that codes the matrix-vector product; this idea is used in section 20.12.1. In case the stencil coefficients can vary, which is often the case with PDEs, and only the structure of the stencil is constant, we do need to store all nonzero coefficients.

15.1.1 ▪ Note on scalar types

Before we start, there are two design choices to be made: what integer type to use for indexing, and what scalar type to use for the field (mathematical term) over which we operate. To start with the integers: in scientific computing, problems are regularly large enough that *64-bit integers* are increasingly commonly used. However, we want to leave our options open, so we define a type alias with `using`,

```
// sparse/crs_mat.hpp
using idxint = std::int64_t;
```

and use the type `idxint` throughout.

The scalars are trickier. In the same application you may want to combine single and double precision objects, or real and complex. Hence we use a template parameter:

```
// sparse/crs_mat.cpp
template< typename scalar >
scalar Vector<scalar>::norm2() const {
  scalar s=static_cast<scalar>(0);
  for ( auto e : elements )
    s += e*e;
  return std::sqrt(s);
};
```

15.1.2 ▪ Implementation

Sticking with the two-dimensional case for now (which makes sense for convolutions on images; in PDEs dimensions higher than two are common), we first define a vector class.

```
// sparse/stencil.cpp
template< typename F >
class Vector : private std::vector<F> {
public:
  using std::vector<F>::begin;
  using std::vector<F>::end;
  using std::vector<F>::vector;
private:
  idxint m,n;
public:
  Vector( idxint m,idxint n )
    : m(m),n(n),std::vector<F>::vector<F>(m*n) {};
```

(Here we use *private inheritance* to let `Vector` inherit from a `std::vector`; see section 14.2.)

We need to index in this vector with two indices i, j:

```
// sparse/stencil.cpp
template< typename F >
F Vector<F>::operator[]( idxint i,idxint j ) const {
  return std::vector<F>::operator[](i*n+j);
};
template< typename F >
F& Vector<F>::operator[]( idxint i,idxint j ) {
  return std::vector<F>::operator[](i*n+j);
};
```

Exercise 15.1. Can you implement the vector class using `mdspan` (see section 4.1.2) so that you get the two-dimensional indexing for free?

As observed above, for the matrix we only need to store the "legs" of the stencil of equation (15.4).

Stencil matrix from "legs":

Constructor:

```
// sparse/stencil.cpp
template< typename F >
using Leg = tuple<int,int,F>;

template< typename F >
class StencilMatrix {
private:
  std::vector<Leg<F>> legs;
public:
  StencilMatrix
      ( const std::vector<Leg<F>>& legs )
    : legs(legs) {};
```

Use:

```
// sparse/stencil.cpp
StencilMatrix<FloatType> A
  ( { {0,0,4.},
      {1,0,-1.},{-1,0,-1.},
      {0,1,-1.},{0,-1,-1.} } );
```

The matrix-vector product routine `StencilMatrix::times` is then

```
// sparse/stencil.cpp
void times( const Vector<F>& rhs,Vector<F>& lhs ) const {
  // vector dimensions; enforce agreement
  auto [m,n] = rhs.dimensions();
  auto [mm,nn] = lhs.dimensions();
  assert( m==mm and n==nn );


  for ( auto [ishift,jshift,v] : legs )
    for ( idxint i=max<idxint>(0,0-ishift);
              i<min<idxint>(m,m-ishift); ++i )
      for ( idxint j=max<idxint>(0,0-jshift);
                j<min<idxint>(n,n-jshift); ++j )
        lhs[i,j] += v * rhs[i+ishift,j+jshift];
};
```

Exercise 15.2. The three loops in this product routine are independent, so they can be arbitrarily permuted.

- Why would you not want to exchange the `i` and `j` loops?
- Experiment with moving the loop over the stencil "legs" to inside the `i,j` loops. (You will need to add a condition to handle the case where $i+1$ and such are not valid coordinates.) Do you see a difference in performance? What can you attribute this to? (Hint: branch prediction and bandwidth are two of the possibly involved factors.)

Stencil matrices will be used in the section on parallelism of this book.

15.2 ▪ General sparse matrices

Stencil matrices are a special case of sparse matrices. In the previous section there was a clear structure to the location of the nonzeros, but in contexts such as Partial Diffential Equation (PDE) calculations there need not be such a structure. In this section we develop the tools to implement a *power method* (for more on this, see the intro to Chapter 19), where the matrix is a more general sparse matrix.

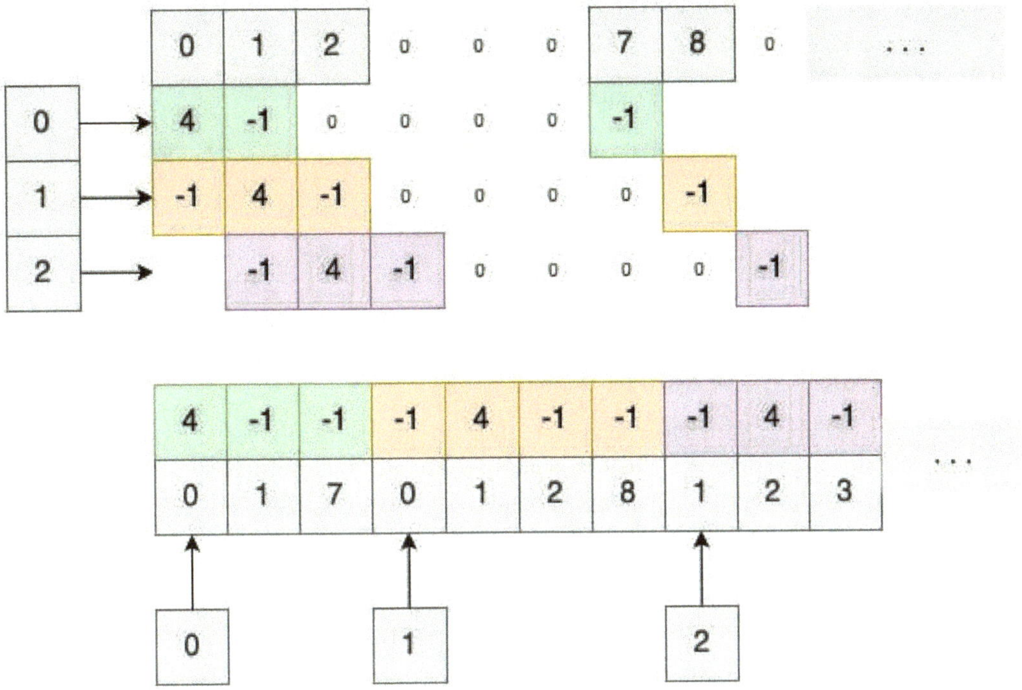

Figure 15.1. *Compressed row storage matrix of the PDE stencil*

15.2.1 ▪ Compressed row storage

In the case of the numerical solution of PDEs you often have to deal with matrices where

- the number of nonzeros per row is not constant;
- the location of the nonzeros is not simply predictable.

In such cases, the compressed row storage (CRS) scheme is often used, which we illustrate in Figure 15.1 for the PDE stencil (15.4) above.

The name derives from the fact that each row is stored compressed to only the nonzeros. Thus we allocate a one-dimensional array to store the nonzero matrix elements:

```
idxint number_of_nonzeros;
vector<double> nonzeros( number_of_nonzeros );
```

Since the nonzero elements could have come from any location, we need to store an array of column indices:

```
idxint number_of_nonzeros;
vector<idxint> column_indices( number_of_nonzeros );
```

Finally, since rows can have any number of nonzeros, we need a pointer (in an informal sense) array to indicate where each row starts:

```
idxint nrows;
vector<idxint> row_pointer(nrows+1);
```

The matrix-vector product is then computed as

```
// compute each component of the output:
for ( idxint row=0; row<number_of_rows; ++row ) {
  // sum a(i,j) * x(j) for all nonzero components:
  double s{0.};
  for ( idxint icolumn=row_pointer[row]; icolumn<row_pointer[row+1]; ++icolumn ) {
    // we find j by looking the column index array:
    auto column = column_indices[icolumn];
    s += nonzeros[icolumn] * input[column];
  }
  output[row] = s;
}
```

15.2.2 ▪ Building the sparse matrix

So far we have only indicated how to use a CRS matrix for the matrix-vector product. However, the matter of constructing such a matrix is not trivial at all. As a possible strategy, do you start with an empty matrix, with all the row pointers at zero, and every time you insert an element you shift a bunch of data and pointers?

Inserting elements is fairly easy to code since C++ makes it so easy to insert elements in containers like `std::vector`. Let's explore this idea, and then explore a better one immediately after.

Approach 1: Fully dynamic insertion In the constructor we set up data structures as described above. We also track the length of the rows explicitly:

```
// sparse/crs_mat0.cpp
colidx.at(0) = 0; rowptr.at(0) = 0;
for ( idxint row=0; row<m_; ++row ) {
  rowlen.at(row) = 0;
  rowptr.at(row+1) = rowptr.at(row) + rowlen.at(row);
  if (row<m_-1)
    colidx.at( rowptr.at(row+1) ) =
      colidx.at( rowptr.at(row) ) + nonzeros_per_row;
}
```

Inserting an element (i, j) by

```
// sparse/crs_mat0.cpp
template< typename F >
void CRSMatrix<F>::set( idxint i,idxint j,F v ) {
```

is then a matter of incrementing the row pointers for later rows, and inserting a nonzero value and its column index:

```
// sparse/crs_mat0.cpp
auto insertloc = rowptr.at(i)+rowlen.at(i); //rowptr.at(i+1);
colidx   .insert( colidx   .begin()+insertloc, j );
elements.insert( elements.begin()+insertloc, v );
rowlen.at(i) += 1;
for ( int row=i+1; row<=m_; ++row )
  rowptr.at(row)++;
```

However, this dynamic insertion comes at the expense of doing many memory allocations for the expanding arrays of the nonzero and column indices, and copying data each time these arrays are reallocated. If something is known about the structure of the matrix beforehand, it is more efficient to preallocate data, and fill in elements as they are declared.

Approach 2: Preallocation For simplicity, let's assume that we know an upper bound on the number of nonzeros in each row, and that reserving that much space for each row is not too wasteful. For instance, in the stencil matrix above most rows had five nonzero elements. We now have a use for the extra array `row_length` we introduced above; this keeps track of how many elements in a row have actually been filled.

The matrix construction now becomes

```
// sparse/crs_mat1.cpp
colidx.at(0) = 0; rowptr.at(0) = 0;
for ( idxint row=0; row<m_; ++row ) {
  // no elements stored, but space for nonzeros_per_row
  rowlen.at(row) = 0;
  rowptr.at(row+1) = rowptr.at(row) + nonzeros_per_row;
  if (row<m_-1)
    colidx.at( rowptr.at(row+1) ) =
      colidx.at( rowptr.at(row) ) + nonzeros_per_row;
}
```

and inserting an element:

```
// sparse/crs_mat1.cpp
  auto insertloc = rowptr.at(i);
  auto newloc    = rowptr.at(i)+rowlen.at(i);
  for ( ; insertloc<newloc; ++insertloc )
    if ( colidx.at(insertloc)==j ) /* existing column */ break;
  if ( insertloc==newloc )
    /* need to create new column: */ rowlen.at(i)++;
  if ( insertloc>=rowptr.at(i+1) )
    throw(std::format("Insertloc {} past next rowptr {}",
                      insertloc,rowptr.at(i+1)));
  colidx.at(insertloc) = j; elements.at(insertloc) = v;
```

15.2.3 ▪ Matrix-vector product

The main mathematical operation we focus on is the matrix-vector product. The code is the same for both approaches, since in both cases we have the `rowlen` array telling us the number of nonzeros in each row:

```
// sparse/crs_mat.cpp
template< typename scalar >
void CRSMatrix<scalar>::times( const Vector<scalar>& in,Vector<scalar>& out ) const {
  for ( idxint row=0; row<out.size(); ++row ) {
    scalar s{0};
    for ( idxint icol=rowptr[row]; icol<rowptr[row]+rowlen[row]; ++icol ) {
      auto col = colidx[icol];
      auto aij = elements[icol];
      auto x   = in[col];
      s += aij * x;
    }
    out[row] = s;
  }
};
```

Remark. *In sparse matrix operations, the matrix-vector product is far more common than the matrix-matrix product, so we don't discuss the latter.*

The LU factorization of a sparse matrix would be a useful operation to discuss, but the complications of storage management put it beyond the scope of this book. See the HPC book [23, section 5.4.3] for details.

15.2.4 ▪ Test problem

We test our sparse matrix code on a power method applied to a tridiagonal matrix:

```
// sparse/crs.cpp
real nrm;
for ( int iteration=0; iteration<1000; ++iteration ) {
  mat.times(x,y);
  nrm = y.norm2();
  x.scale( 1./nrm,y );
}
```

Timing the two approaches shows that the preallocation strategy is much faster than the dynamic strategy. In the following table we compare the Intel 2024 and GCC 13 compilers on an Intel Cascade Lake processor. Some observations:

- With Approach 1, the setup time is much larger than the iteration time.
- With Approach 2, the setup time is less than the iteration time.
- Both compilers give essentially the same iteration time and setup for Approach 2.
- For Approach 1, GCC is roughly 15% faster than the Intel compiler.

Problem size	Approach 1 (Intel/GCC)	Approach 2 (both equal)	Iteration (both equal)
10k	0.173 / 0.146	0.000	0.057
30k	1.556 / 1.312	0.001	0.171
100k	19.72 / 16.48	0.005	0.586

The main takeaway from this experiment is that, with the right strategy, we can dismiss the matrix creation as a one-time setup. Conversely, this means that we are now mostly interested in the performance of the matrix-vector product. For this, see section 33.8.

15.3 ▪ Sparse matrices and graphs

In the traditional computer science literature, graph algorithms are often described in terms of sets or queues of nodes: during the algorithm, nodes are added to or taken from one of these until some termination condition.

However, in large scale computing it is often more fruitful to consider graphs as sparse matrices, often in CRS format. You are invited to explore this connection for yourself; Chapter 45, in particular section 45.2, gives a guided set of exercises.

15.4 ▪ More topics in linear algebra

15.4.1 ▪ A polymorphism conundrum

Many examples of object-oriented programming have a structure where there are derived classes and we create instances of them:

```
class Animal {
public:
virtual void utter() = 0;
}
class Dog : public Animal {
public:
```

```
void utter() override { cout << "Woof\n"; };
};
class Dolphin : public Animal {
public:
void utter() override { cout << "Blub\n"; };
};
int main() {
  Dog lassie; lassie.utter();
  Dolphin flipper; flipper.utter();
  }
```

In mathematical software we have a similar situation. We have a base class for matrices with at least a *virtual method* for the matrix-vector product, and derived classes for diagonal, banded, sparse, ... matrices that implement a specific type of product.

```
class Matrix {
public:
  Vector multiply(Vector) = 0;
};

class DiagonalMatrix : public Matrix {
private:
  Vector diagonal;
public:
  Vector multiply(Vector in) {
    return pointwisemult(diagonal,in); };
};
class SparseMatrix : public Matrix {
/* details omitted */
};
```

However, in the main program we would like to manipulate the matrices through variables of the base type:

```
int main() {
  vector invec,outvec;
  Matrix mat = // create matrix with dynamically determined type
    [] () {
      if (something) return DiagonalMatrix( /* stuff */ );
      else           return SparseMatrix  ( /* stuff */ );
    }();
  // THIS DOES NOT WORK
  outvec = mat.multiply(invec);
};
```

That is, we want to manipulate the basic class, but we want it to have the functionality of some derived class.

Remark. *The above snippet uses an* immediately invoked lambda expression; *see section 6.1.*

There are several solutions possible to this polymorphism problem.

15.4.1.1 ▪ Pointer approach

One solution would be to create a pointer to the object of the derived class, cast that to a pointer of the base class, and then access methods through the regular pointer syntax:

```
auto dmat = unique_ptr<Matrix>
    ( make_unique<DiagonalMatrix>( /* constructor */ ) );
auto smat = unique_ptr<Matrix>
    ( make_unique<SparseMatrix>( /* constructor */ ) );
outvec = dmat->multiply(invec);
outvec = smat->multiply(invec);
```

See section 10.3.2 for more on unique pointers.

15.4.1.2 ▪ Variant approach

Another approach is to capture the different matrix types in a `std::variant` and use `std::visit` to treat them uniformly. Let's say we have two matrix types, both with a matrix-vector multiply method:

```
// union/matvisit.cpp
class sparse_matrix {
public:
  vector multiply( const vector& in ) const;
```

```
// union/matvisit.cpp
class lowrank_matrix {
public:
  vector multiply( const vector& in ) const;
```

Next we make a *function object* (sometimes called a "functor") for the multiplication operation. The *function-call operator* of this functor has several overloads based on the type of matrix object it is applied to:

```
// union/matvisit.cpp
class multiply_by {
private:
  const vector& in;
public:
  multiply_by( const vector& in ) : in(in) {};
  vector operator()( sparse_matrix m ) {
    return m.multiply(in); };
  vector operator()( lowrank_matrix m ) {
    return m.multiply(in); };
};
```

Finally, we now use `std::visit` to have a uniform way of invoking this function object on the variant:

```
// union/matvisit.cpp
variant<sparse_matrix,lowrank_matrix>
  this_is_sparse{ sparse_matrix{} },
  this_is_lowrank{ lowrank_matrix{} };

vector invec;
visit( multiply_by{invec},this_is_sparse );
visit( multiply_by{invec},this_is_lowrank );
```

Alternatively, there is an idiom (using mechanisms not covered in this book) that dispenses with defining the function object:

```
// union/matvisit.cpp
template<class... Ts> struct overload
  : Ts... { using Ts::operator()...; };
template<class... Ts> overload(Ts...)
  -> overload<Ts...>;
```

```
// union/matvisit.cpp
visit
  ( overload{
    [invec] ( const sparse_matrix& m ) {
      return m.multiply(invec); },
    [invec] ( const lowrank_matrix& m ) {
      return m.multiply(invec); }
    },
    this_is_sparse );
```

15.4.1.3 ▪ Function approach

A final approach uses only the base class and stores a function pointer for the "derived class" functions:

```
// object/funcinherit.cpp
class Matrix {
public:
  Matrix();
  std::function< void(const Vector&,Vector&) > multiply;
};

class DiagonalMatrix : public Matrix {
private:
  Vector diagonal;
public:
  DiagonalMatrix( const Vector& d )
    : Matrix::Matrix(), diagonal(d) {
    multiply = [*this] (const Vector& in,Vector& out) {
      pointwisemult( diagonal,in,out ); };
  };
};

int main() {
  Vector diag(100);
  Matrix m = DiagonalMatrix(diag);
  Vector invector(100),outvector(100);
  m.multiply(invector,outvector);
  return 0;
};
```

This approach has as its advantage that the specific functions such as `multiply` can be dynamically set during the program run. This allows it to change implementation, or to set as implementation a lambda expression that captures information of the runtime environment. Also, no pointer syntax is needed.

15.4.2 ▪ Algorithm choices

In the context of a linear algebra library you will probably find yourself writing a `Vector` class, which likely will have a `vecnorm` method. From your math class you may know that there are several norms, such as

$$\|x\|_1 = \sum_i |x_i|, \quad \|x\|_2 = \sqrt{\sum_i x_i^2}, \quad \|x\|_\infty = \max_i |x_i|.$$

Do you now write three different `vecnorm` methods?

One solution is to use an `enum` parameter to the norm method:

```
enum norm_type { Norm_1, Norm_2, Norm_inf };
auto Vector::vecnorm( /* norm type */ ) {
  switch (type) { /* ... */ }
};
```

The problem here is that the norm types are ordinary integers, and there are no safeguards so that you don't use an out-of-bound value. The solution is to define the `enum` scoped to the `Vector` class; see section 2.5.

Scoped definition of enum:

Definition:

```
// enum/vnorm.cpp
class vector
  : public std::vector<double> {
public:
  vector( int n )
    : std::vector<double>(n) {};
  enum norm_type {
    Norm_1, Norm_2, Norm_inf };
  double vecnorm( norm_type typ ) {
    switch (typ) {
    case Norm_1 :
```

Use:

```
// enum/vnorm.cpp
cout << values.vecnorm
  ( vector::Norm_1 ) << '\n';
cout << values.vecnorm
  ( vector::Norm_2 ) << '\n';
cout << values.vecnorm
  ( vector::Norm_inf ) << '\n';
```

15.5 ▪ Linear algebra software

15.5.1 ▪ The BLAS standard

Linear algebra operations are common in scientific computing, and are often the determining factor in the performance of scientific codes. For this reason, many *linear algebra operations* have been standardized, both formally and in library software.

Linear algebra standardization probably started with the *Basic Linear Algebra Subprograms (BLAS)* standard for dense linear algebra. BLAS Level 1 [40] contains vector operations, Level 2 [19] has matrix-vector operations, and Level 3 [18] concerns itself with matrix-matrix operations. The Level 3 routines have long been recognized as the key to high performance; see, for instance, [14, 26]. In this book, you can find this discussed in sections 32.2 and 33.7.2.

Building on the BLAS routines, the *Lapack* library [1] offers routines for linear system solving and eigenvalue calculations, largely for dense matrices. While a Fortran reference implementation of Lapack exists, optimized versions of Lapack exist in libraries such as *MKL*.

15.5.1.1 ▪ Sparse BLAS

Most BLAS operations have a direct counterpart in sparse matrices, but sparse operations are far less standardized. While proposals exist [21], in practice there are only *de facto* standards in libraries such as Eigen (below) and *PETSc* [4].

15.5.1.2 ▪ Parallel linear algebra

Likewise, parallelization is also a mixed bag: shared memory parallelization is easily attained preserving the sequential API, but distributed memory parallelization again only has *de facto* standards in libraries such as *Scalapack* [11].

15.5.2 ▪ Library software

Standardized linear algebra operations are available in many common libraries. While BLAS and Linear Algebra Package (LAPACK) are sometimes called "Fortran libraries" this is not accurate: their reference implementation is written in Fortran, but actual implementations, such as in Intel's *MKL*, can be written in any language. Still, such implementations often provide a Fortran or C-like API that is unidiomatic for C++.

For this reason, libraries such as Eigen (section 30.2) wrap them in a more native looking interface.

15.5.2.1 ▪ C++ standard

The C++26 standard will have a `linalg` library, which provides an interface to various BLAS Level 1, 2, or 3 routines plus other tools. Presumably, C++ implementations will use this to wrap optimized BLAS libraries in a native interface.

Chapter 16

Efficient linear algebra through expression templates

In section 3.2 you saw the basics of operator overloading. In the context of a linear algebra library you may be tempted now to define routines such as

```
Vector Vector::operator+( const Vector& other ) const;
// use as:
Vec v1,v2;
auto v3 = v1+v2;
```

For some code this makes sense. However, in numerical applications such additions may occur in a loop:

```
for ( int it=/* whole lotta times */ ) {
  // stuff
  auto v3 = v1+v2;
  // stuff
}
```

Your code will now do a large number of allocations and deallocations. Therefore, it may be better to pass input and output as parameters, by const reference and reference, respectively, so that the once-allocated data structures are then reused.

```
void add( Vector& out,const Vector& in1,const Vector& in2 );
```

This solves the allocation/deallocation problem at the cost of less elegant syntax:

```
// v4 = v1+v2+v3
v4.copyfrom(v1);
v4.add(v2);
v4.add(v3);
```

The setup where the output object was a function return,

```
Vector Vector::operator+( const Vector& other ) const;
```

has the advantage that you can write mathematical expressions such as

```
auto w = v1+v2+v3+v4;
```

which is not possible with the parameter passing approach. Can we have both the elegant mathematical syntax and efficient execution? The answer is: yes.

Let's design a `Vector` class so that we have an addition operator:

Code:

```
// template/fxpression2.cpp
Vector one(10,1),two(10,2);
Vector three(10);
three = one+two;
cout << three.front() << ","
     << three.back() << '\n';
```

Output:

```
3,3
```

but without generating temporaries.

Remark. *While the presentation in this chapter will lead to an elegant expression, its efficiency relies on compiler sophistication. Programmers would do well to test the resulting code for performance against more naive code.*

16.1 ▪ Basics

The essential trick is to let the "plus" operator not actually evaluate the sum, but only return a sum object,

```
// template/fxpression2.cpp
VectorSum operator+( const Vector& one, const Vector& other ) {
  return VectorSum( one,other );
};
```

which is defined to store the operands:

Declaration:

```
// template/fxpression2.hpp
class VectorSum {
private:
  const Vector& one,&two;
```

Constructor:

```
// template/fxpression2.cpp
VectorSum::VectorSum
    ( const Vector& one,const Vector& two )
  : one(one),two(two) {};
```

The actual mathematical addition operation is then triggered by the "equals" operator, which copies values into the left-hand side:

```
// template/fxpression2.cpp
void Vector::operator=( const VectorSum& ops ) {
  Vector sum( size() );
  for ( size_t i=0; i<size(); ++i )
    (*this)[i] = ops[i];
};
```

where the right-hand side values are computed by the sum object:

```
// template/fxpression2.cpp
float VectorSum::operator[]( size_t i ) const {
  return one[i]+two[i];
};
```

This setup, where the expression is not evaluated until it's actually assigned, is known as *lazy evaluation*.

16.2 ▪ Recursion through templates

The code developed so far only allows us to add two vectors. We will now extend the basic idea to allow for more terms:

Code:

```
// template/fxpression3.cpp
Vector one(10,1),two(10,2),three(10,3),four(10,4);
Vector five(10);
five = one+two+three+four;
cout << five.front() << "," << five.back() << '\n';
```

Output:

```
10,10
```

For this, we need to templatize the `VectorSum` class so that it can store not only `Vector` objects, but also `VectorSum` objects:

```
// template/fxpression3.cpp
template< typename ONE,typename TWO >
VectorSum<ONE,TWO>::VectorSum( const ONE& one,const TWO& two )
  : one(one),two(two) {};
```

The "plus" operator likewise gets templatized:

```
// template/fxpression3.cpp
template< typename ONE,typename TWO >
VectorSum<ONE,TWO> operator+( const ONE& one, const TWO& other ) {
  return VectorSum<ONE,TWO>(one,other);
};
```

The actual assignment is relatively unchanged,

```
// template/fxpression3.cpp
template< typename ONE,typename TWO >
void Vector::operator=( const VectorSum<ONE,TWO>& ops ) {
  for ( size_t i=0; i<size(); ++i )
    (*this)[i] = ops[i];
};
```

as is the evaluation of the right-hand side,

```
// template/fxpression3.cpp
template< typename ONE,typename TWO >
float VectorSum<ONE,TWO>::operator[]( size_t i ) const {
  return one[i]+two[i];
};
```

16.3 ▪ Other operators

So far we have only dealt with the plus operator. Let's generalize this code by allowing scalar multiplication of a vector:

```
Vector x(10),y(10),z(10);
z = x + y*2;
```

For this, we generalize the `VectorSum` class to a `VectorExpr` class which has a template parameter for the operation. The sum and product operations on vectors now create an expression object with the corresponding operator:

```
// template/fxpression4.cpp
template< typename ONE,typename TWO >
auto operator+( const ONE& one, const TWO& other ) {
  return VectorExpr< ONE,TWO,sum<ONE,TWO> >(one,other);
};

template< typename ONE,typename TWO >
auto operator*( const ONE& one, const TWO& other ) {
  return VectorExpr< ONE,TWO,mul<ONE,TWO> >(one,other);
};
```

The assignment operator stays more or less the same:

```
// template/fxpression4.cpp
template< typename ONE,typename TWO,typename EVAL >
void Vector::operator=( const VectorExpr<ONE,TWO,EVAL>& ops ) {
  for ( size_t i=0; i<size(); ++i )
    (*this)[i] = ops[i];
};
```

where the indexing operator of the `VectorExpr` invokes the evaluation

```
// template/fxpression4.cpp
template< typename ONE,typename TWO,typename EVAL >
float VectorExpr<ONE,TWO,EVAL>::operator[]( size_t i ) const {
  return EVAL()(one,two,i);
};
```

and the operators are defined as

```
// template/fxpression4.cpp
template< typename ONE,typename TWO >
class sum {
public:
  float operator()( ONE one,TWO two,size_t i ) const {
    return one[i]+two[i]; };
};
template< typename ONE,typename TWO >
class mul {
public:
  float operator()( ONE one,TWO two,size_t i ) const {
    return one[i]*two; };
};
```

Note that the addition operator is between vectors, while multiplication takes a scalar as its second operand.

Expressions with parentheses such as

```
(x+y)*3.14;
```

evaluate correctly without further programming, since the parentheses only express grouping.

Chapter 17

Zero-finding library: Lambda expressions

In this chapter we develop the basic design of a numerical library for zero-finding as a case study in the use of *lambda expressions*. The problem of zero-finding is the following: given a function f, find the value of x that satisfies

$$\underset{x}{?}: f(x) = 0.$$

In particular we do this through Newton's method. The problem we are tackling here is a separation of concerns:

1. The library needs to have the numerical sophistication of a robust Newton's method; while
2. the actual objective function needs to be specified by the user of the library, and should in no way be limited by the library design. As an example of an unnecessarily limited design, you would have a library that can only find zeros of polynomials, which you specify by passing an array of coefficients.

The focus of this chapter is on the mechanism for passing the objective function to the zero-finding library. In particular we will explore lambda expressions; see Chapter 6.

17.1 ▪ Newton's method

In this section we look at *Newton's method*. This is an iterative method for finding zeros of a function f, that is, it computes a sequence of values $\{x_n\}$, so that $f(x_n) \to 0$. The sequence is defined by

$$x_{n+1} = x_n - \frac{f(x_n)}{f'(x_n)},$$

with x_0 arbitrarily chosen. For details, see the HPC book [23, Appendix 23].

While in practice Newton's method is used for complicated functions, here we will look at a simple example, which actually has a basis in computing history. Early computers had no hardware for computing a square root. Instead, they used Newton's method.

Suppose you have a positive value y and you want to compute $x = \sqrt{y}$. This is equivalent to finding the zero of

$$f(x) = x^2 - y,$$

where y is fixed. To indicate this dependence on y, we will write $f_y(x)$. Newton's method then finds the zero by evaluating

$$x_{\text{next}} = x - f_y(x)/f'_y(x)$$

until the guess is accurate enough, that is, until $f_y(x) \approx 0$.

We will not go into the matter of how to choose a sophisticated stopping test for the iteration; that is a matter for a numerical analysis course, not a programming course.

17.1.1 ▪ Function implementation

We start with the special case of $\sqrt{2}$, that is, the function $f(x) = x^2 - 2$.

It is of course simple to code a Newton's method for such a special case: it should take you about 10 lines. Ultimately we want to have a general code that takes any two functions f, f', and then uses Newton's method to find a zero of our specific function f. We get there in steps.

Exercise 17.1. Compute $\sqrt{2}$ as the zero of $f_y(x) = x^2 - y$ for the special case of $y = 2$.

- Write functions `f(x)` and `deriv(x)`, that compute $f_y(x)$ and $f'_y(x)$ for the particular definition of f_y.
- Iterate until $|f(x, y)| < 10^{-5}$. Print x and $f(x)$ in each iteration; don't worry too much about the stopping test and accuracy attained.
- Second part: write a function `newton_root` that computes $\sqrt{y}$ again: only for $\sqrt{2}$.

17.1.2 ▪ Using lambda expressions

Above you wrote functions with a declaration,

```
// newton/newton-fun.cpp
double f(double x);
double fprime(double x);
```

and the algorithm

```
// newton/newton-fun.cpp
double x{1.};
while ( true ) {
  auto fx = f(x);
  cout << "f( " << x << " ) = " << fx << '\n';
  if (std::abs(fx)<1.e-10 ) break;
  x = x - fx/fprime(x);
}
```

We will now start introducing lambda expressions, rather than using named functions.

Exercise 17.2. Rewrite your code to use lambda functions for `f` and `fprime`.

If you use variables for the lambda expressions, put them in the main program.

Next, we make the code modular by writing a general function `newton_root` that contains the Newton method of the previous exercise. Since it has to work for any functions f, f', you have to pass the objective function and the derivative as arguments:

```
double root = newton_root( f,fprime );
```

(See section 6.2 on how to handle lambda expressions as function arguments.)

Exercise 17.3. Rewrite the Newton exercise by implementing a `newton_root` function:

```
double root = newton_root( f,fprime );
```

Call the function

1. first with the lambda variables you already created;
2. then directly with the lambda expressions as arguments, that is, without assigning them to variables.

Next we extend the functionality of our code to finding the square root of any nonnegative number, but not by changing the objective function f. Instead, we use a more general way of specifying the objective function and derivative.

Exercise 17.4. Extend the Newton exercise to compute roots in a loop:

```
// newton/newton-lambda.cpp
  for ( double n=2.; n<10; n+=.5 ) {
    cout << "sqrt(" << n << ") = "
         << newton_root(
  /* ... */
                        )
         << '\n';
```

Without lambdas, you would define a function

```
double squared_minus_n( double x,double n ) {
  return x*x-n; }
```

However, the `newton_root` function takes a function of only a real argument. Use a capture to make `f` dependent on the second parameter.

It is possible to dispense with the derivative function by using numerical differentiation: we use the limit formula for the derivative, and use a finite difference, rather than a limit. The result is an "inexact Newton's method," and mathematical theory says that this will also converge if the inexactness is not too bad, though it may converge more slowly. This is a topic for numerical analysis [38, 24], which we will not go into here. We will use this fact to simplify our Newton code.

You can approximate the derivative of a function f as

$$f'(x) = \big(f(x+h) - f(x)\big)/h,$$

where h is small.
This is called a "finite difference" approximation.

This looks like the limit equation for computing the derivative, but in code we cannot take a limit, so by taking a finite h we are computing a "numerical derivative" here. See a numerical analysis textbook for discussion.

Exercise 17.5. Write a version of the root finding function that only takes the objective function

```
double newton_root( function< double(double)> f )
```

and approximates the derivative by a finite difference. You can use a fixed value `h=1e-6`.

Do not reimplement the whole Newton method: instead create a lambda expression for the gradient and pass it to the function `newton_root` you coded earlier as the second argument.

17.1.3 ▪ Templated implementation

Newton's method works equally well for complex numbers as for real numbers.

Exercise 17.6. Rewrite your Newton code where the algorithm is in the main program so that it works for complex numbers. Here is the main; you need to write the functions:

```
// newton/newton-complex.cpp
complex<double> z{.5,.5};
while ( true ) {
  auto fz = f(z);
  cout << "f( " << z << " ) = " << fz << '\n';
  if (std::abs(fz)<1.e-10 ) break;
  z = z - fz/fprime(z);
}
```

You may run into the problem that you cannot operate immediately between a complex number and a `float` or `double`. Use `static_cast`:

```
static_cast< complex<double> >(2)
```

So do you have to write two separate implementations, one for reals, and one for complex numbers? (And maybe you need two separate ones for `float` and `double`!) This is where *templates* come in handy.

You can templatize the objective function and the derivative,

```
// newton/newton-double.cpp
template<typename T>
T f(T x) { return x*x - 2; };
template<typename T>
T fprime(T x) { return 2 * x; };
```

and then write in the main program:

```
// newton/newton-double.cpp
double x{1.};
while ( true ) {
  auto fx = f<double>(x);
  cout << "f( " << x << " ) = " << fx << '\n';
  if (std::abs(fx)<1.e-10 ) break;
  x = x - fx/fprime<double>(x);
}
```

The final step is to have a templatized Newton function that you can instantiate with any suitable type. It would, for instance, be called as

```
// newton/newton-templatefun.cpp
double two = 2.;
double sqrt2 =
  newton_root<double>
  ( [two] ( double x ) { return x*x - static_cast<double>(two); },
    []    ( double x ) { return static_cast<double>(2) * x; },
    1.
    );
```

Exercise 17.7. Update your `newton_root` function with a template parameter. Test it by having a main program that computes some roots in `float`, `double`, and `complex<double>`.

Exercise 17.8. Use your complex Newton method to compute $\sqrt{2}$. Does it work?

How about $\sqrt{-2}$? If it doesn't work, why, and can you fix this?

There is no reason to limit the template parameter to the type of the function argument. You could also use a template parameter for the functions:

```
template< typename F >
void call_on_5( F f ) {
  f(5);
};
```

Now apply this idea to the Newton function.

Exercise 17.9. Write a Newton method where the objective function is itself a template parameter, not just its arguments and return type. Hint: no changes to the main program are needed.

Then compute $\sqrt{-2}$ as

```
// newton/lambda-complex.cpp
cout << "sqrt -2 = " <<
  newton_root<complex<double>>
  ( // objective function
    [] (complex<double> x) -> complex<double> {
        return x*x + static_cast<complex<double>>(2); },
    // derivative
    [] (complex<double> x) -> complex<double> {
        return x * static_cast<complex<double>>(2); },
    // initial value
```

```
    complex<double>{.1,.1}
    )
     << '\n';
```

This may look strange: how do you enforce that the functions are of a type that fits with the scalar type? For instance, you may write mismatch the routine type and the types of the functions:

```
// newton/newton-templatetf.cpp
complex<double> sqrte2 =
  newton_root<double>
  ( // objective function
    [two] ( complex<double> x ) -> complex<double> {
        return x*x - static_cast<complex<double>>(-two); },
    // derivative
    []    ( complex<double> x ) -> complex<double> {
        return static_cast<complex<double>>(2) * x; },
    // initial value
    {1.,1.}
    );
```

And the answer is that you don't have to enforce this: you leave it up to the compiler to complain if there is a mismatch.

In the previous exercise you were told to use the main program unchanged, meaning that you still call the Newton routine as

```
newton_root<complex<double>>
```

Did you wonder that you specify only one template parameter here, while the routine is defined with three? The compiler is very good at "argument-dependent lookup," where it figures out the missing template parameters from the one you specify and the code.

17.1.4 ▪ Templating with concepts

(For concepts, see section 12.5.)

Using templated functions with types that do not "fit" (such as templatizing the Newton method over integers) can lead to long error messages. You can express what types are valid for instantiation,

```
// newton/newton-conceptreal.cpp
template<typename T>
concept RealType = std::is_floating_point_v<T>;
```

and use that for the objective function and derivative:

```
// newton/newton-conceptreal.cpp
template<RealType T>
T f(T x);
template<RealType T>
T fprime(T x);
```

Exercise 17.10. Rewrite your templated code using the above concept. Confirm that the compiler is equally happy with `float` and `double`, but does not accept an attempt to apply the Newton method to integers:

```
// newton/newton-conceptint.cpp
```

```
// WRONG: this should not compile
int i{5};
while ( true ) {
  auto fi = f<int>(i);
  cout << "f( " << i << " ) = " << fi << '\n';
  if (std::abs(fi)<1.e-10 ) break;
  i = i - fi/fprime<int>(i);
}
```

Part III

Parallelism

Chapter 18

Types of parallelism

In this part of the book we give a concise introduction to some of the many ways you can parallelize your code. C++ natively has some mechanisms that would seem to pertain to this topic, most notably threading and execution policies. However, here we will mostly focus on mechanisms that are external to the language.

We start with *OpenMP*, which primarily concerns itself with shared memory parallelism, that is, using all the cores of a single processor (or possibly two) to access a single memory space. OpenMP excels at getting very high performance on structured operations, such as looping over all elements of multidimensional arrays. OpenMP is a combination of a library and a language extension that is supported by almost every compiler these days.

OpenMP can also deal with accelerators such as graphics processing units (GPUs), but we omit that here. Instead, we discuss two heterogeneous programming models, meaning that they target both CPU and GPU programming: *SYCL* and *Kokkos*.

Finally, we give a brief introduction to the message passing interface (MPI) library, which provides distributed memory parallelism, that is, using many processors simultaneously that are connected through a network. MPI is the *de facto* standard for parallelization on supercomputer *clusters*.

For the theory of parallel computing, see the HPC book [23, Chapter 2]; for more details on OpenMP, see the MPI/OpenMP book [22, Part II], and for MPI see the MPI/OpenMP book [22, Part I].

18.1 ▪ Instruction level parallelism

Programs can have parallelism where two instructions are totally independent of each other:

```
x *= 2;
y += 3;
```

This is known as instruction level parallelism (ILP). Since we are dealing with tiny amounts of work, this is also referred to as *fine-grained parallelism*. As programmers, we don't concern ourselves with this: if the processor has two independent functional units (one for addition, one for multiplication), the compiler or the processor hardware will schedule these instructions appropriately.

18.2 ▪ Vector instructions; data parallelism

A little more sophisticated are so-called single instruction multiple data (SIMD) instructions, or vector instructions. In a loop such as

```
for ( int i=0; i<N; i++ )
  c[i] = a[i] + b[i];
```

all iterations are independent and can be executed simultaneously. This is referred to as *data parallelism*, since each data point can be evaluated independently.

Ignoring the parallelism of multicore processors for a minute, modern processors offer parallelism on a low level through *vector instructions*, operating on *vector registers*, where 4 or 8 operands—here subsequent elements of `a,b,c`—are subjected in one clock cycle to the same operation.

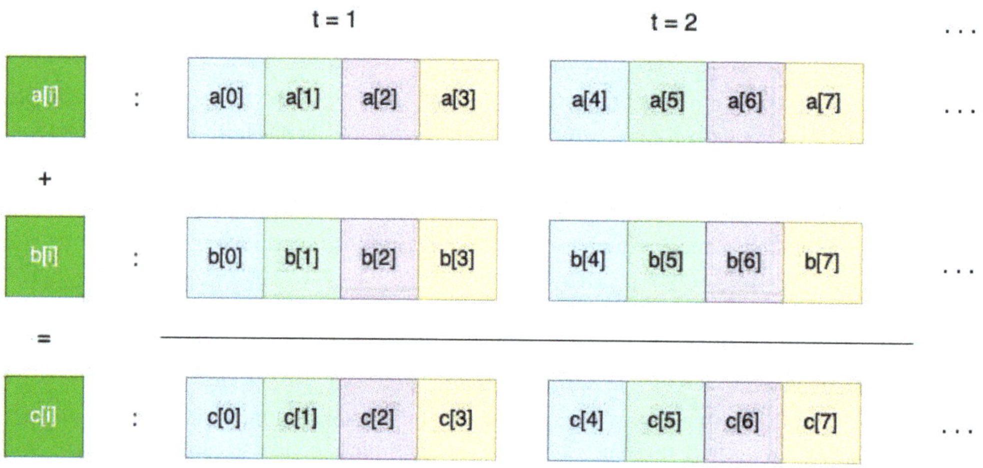

Often the compiler is clever enough to figure out this type of parallelism by itself. For nontrivial cases, OpenMP has a `simd` directive, and a `simd` library has been proposed for C++26. There is also the Open Sourced ISPC [47, 36] library. We will not devote any further discussion to this type of parallelism.

18.3 ▪ Multicore parallelism

The main type of parallelism we concern ourselves with in this book addresses the multiple cores of modern processors. Here we need to say something about processes and threads.

18.3.1 ▪ Processes and threads; task parallelism

A process is how the OS organizes the resources to run a "program": an address space, executable code, a unique identifier, handles to open files, etc. On a Unix computer you can do

```
ps guwax
```

to get a listing of all the processes on your computer: all the programs that are running simultaneously. (How many of them are owned by you?)

Each process has its own distinct area of memory that cannot be accessed by any other process. (In fact, thanks to *virtual memory*, each process thinks it has all the memory of the computer.)

In process-based parallelism you could, for instance, give each core its own process. If you manage to coordinate these processes, a single scientific application can extract all performance out of the available hardware. This is in fact the basic model of MPI; see Chapter 22.

On the other hand, you can let a process create multiple threads. A thread is a bit like a process in that it independently executes a stream of instructions, except that it can access the memory of the process that started it. This makes thread parallelism easier to program than process-based parallelism. However, this is as much a source of flexibility as of trouble.

This type of parallelism is sometimes referred to as *task parallelism*: the amount of work between synchronization points (such as thread creation/deletion) is roughly equivalent to a subroutine call, rather than a single instruction as in data parallelism.

It's important to note that threads are a software construct: they can be created by the OS or by a library layer. In scientific applications you would let the number of threads correspond to the number of available cores, but it can be either more or less. Before there were ever such things as "cores," OSs would use threads for different activities, and *time slice* between them.

It's possible to engage in *hybrid parallelism* using both processes and threads, where the product of the number of processes and threads is made to relate to the number of cores. This is beyond the scope of this book.

18.3.2 ▪ Shared memory parallelism: OpenMP

Since threads can access each other's memory, we call thread programming also *shared memory* programming. In this type of parallelism, a process is started on one core, and it dynamically creates threads to use all other available cores of that processor, or possibly multiple processors on a single *node*. The efficiency of your code now depends on how many parts of it you execute in parallel by threading.

We will look in some detail at the OpenMP system for shared memory programming, which is probably the most common system in scientific computing. OpenMP offers an abstraction of the underlying threads, making it easy to parallelize scientific codes.

18.3.3 ▪ Explicit threading

C++ has a number of constructs related to *concurrency* through threading, meaning the explicit creation of threads. In this book we mainly discuss scientific applications that are *data-parallel*, in which case explicit threading is hardly ever used, with mechanisms such as OpenMP preferred.

Explicit use of threads can still have its place, mostly in "big data" applications, such as in instrument control, or in data acquisition and processing pipelines.

18.4 ▪ Distributed memory programming: MPI

Above we noted that each process has its own data area. In the good old days before multicore processors, you could have parallelism by using multiple computers, each running one process, and then using network communication to coordinate them. This distributed mode of parallelism is still viable, and in fact it is how supercomputer clusters work, but now additionally we can have a process per core. In aggregate, a supercomputer cluster can run a program spread out over up to millions of cores.

We will look at MPI, which is in practice the only system for expressing this type of supercomputer parallelism. Rather than using its C interface, we use the third-party message passing library (MPL) that wraps MPI in a native-looking C++ interface. In distributed memory programming the processes can (obviously) not touch each other's data, so now the problem becomes to partition the data, and to coordinate data exchange through explicit network messages.

In case you think that you now need a supercomputer to program MPI, you can also run it on your multicore laptop or desktop, spawning a process per core, or even *time slice* between processes.

18.5 ▪ Accelerators

Another way to get high performance is to have an attached processor to offload certain operations to. This is called an coprocessor or accelerator. Presumably this processor is specialized in some way, and therefore faster and more energy efficient for the work assigned to it.

By far the most popular type of accelerator is the graphics processing unit (GPU), originally designed for graphics operations, but long co-opted into scientific computing. The leading vendor of GPUs is *NVidia*, which invented the *Compute-Unified Device Architecture (CUDA)* language (actually, an extension of C and Fortran) for programming their GPUs. Since CUDA is proprietary, and GPUs now exist from Intel and AMD too, we consider two portable models: Kokkos and SYCL.

In GPU programming, the challenge is to keep the accelerator(s) active all the time, since often the bulk of the processing power of the system resides in them. This may require rewriting applications to suit this programming model.

Chapter 19

Example application

In the coming chapters we will look at different ways of parallelizing a common algorithm: the *power method*. This linear algebra algorithm computes the largest eigenvalue of a matrix and its corresponding eigenvector. While this is valuable in itself—it is, for instance, the basis of Google's *PageRank*—it is also the basis for more general mathematical methods for linear systems of equations and eigenvalue calculations.

Computationally, the power method is an attractive paradigmatic example in that it exhibits the most common parallelism patterns:

- independent or "convenient" parallelism, where actions can be taken without any coordination;
- global reduction operations, where processing elements combine their data, here by summing;
- point-to-point communications, where processing elements pairwise exchange data.

To be precise, the power method is defined as follows:

Let A be a matrix of interest
Let x be a random vector
Iterate until convergence
  compute the product $y \leftarrow Ax$
  compute the norm $\gamma = \|y\|$
  normalize $x \leftarrow y/\gamma$

where in the limit γ will be the largest eigenvalue of A, and x the corresponding eigenvector.

19.1 ▪ Parallel operations

The basis to parallelizing the power method lies in the distribution of x. Formally, if x has size N we split the set $[0, \ldots N-1]$ over the processing elements:

$$[0, \ldots, N-1] = \bigcup_p I_p,$$

where processing element p, whether it be a core or processor, computes the value of x_i for $i \in I_p$. (The sets I_p are disjoint from each other.) We say that p "owns" the indices I_p or the elements $\{x_i : i \in I_p\}$.

There are now three types of parallel operations.

Independent parallelism In the normalization step of the power method each component $y_i = x_i/\gamma$ can be *independently* computed in parallel. Now processing element p can compute y_i for $i \in I_p$ without any synchronization with others.

Collectives Computing γ is a reduction, a single operation where all processing elements contribute to a single final result, in this case by summing them together. Such operations are known as *collectives*. Computing γ in parallel proceeds by letting each processing element p first compute the norm γ_p of its owned data independently:

$$\gamma_p = \sqrt{\sum_{i \in I_p} y_i^2}.$$

The global norm $\gamma = \sqrt{\sum_p \gamma_p}$ is then formed by combination. (We will discuss the mechanisms for this later.) This final result is made available to all p, which makes the computation an "all-reduce."

Point-to-point data exchange The matrix-vector product $y \leftarrow Ax$ can be written componentwise as

$$\forall_i \colon y_i = \sum_j A_{ij} x_j.$$

This means that the processing element computing y_i needs x_j components, including from other processing elements. Thus it needs to communicate. In the case of shared memory such communication is simple, since each core can access the memory from other cores. However, in distributed memory parallelism, or in the case of multiple GPUs, there may be explicit communication instructions.

In our example application, the operator A will be a sparse matrix, for instance, a finite difference (FD) stencil for a PDE, or a *convolution* kernel (see section 15.1 about stencils). Now each process needs data from only its four neighbors, as illustrated in Figure 19.1.

As was discussed in section 15.1, we assign two-dimensional indexing to the vectors and store them as two-dimensional arrays. The matrix-vector operation

$$\forall_{i,j} \colon y_{ij} = 4x_{ij} - x_{i-1,j} - x_{i+1,j} - x_{i,j-1} - x_{i,j+1}$$

can be represented by the computational stencil

$$\begin{bmatrix} \cdot & -1 & \cdot \\ -1 & 4 & -1 \\ \cdot & -1 & \cdot \end{bmatrix},$$

and we don't actually store the matrix.

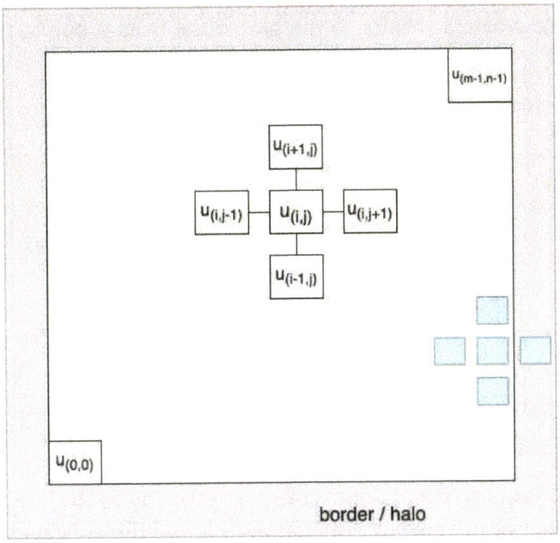

Figure 19.1. *A difference stencil applied to a two-dimensional square domain*

19.2 ▪ Main program

We use the same main program for all tests:

```
// diff2d/main.cpp
for ( int it=0; it<itcount; it++ ) {
  // Matrix-vector product
  Y->central_difference_from( *X,trace );
  // norm computation
  auto bnorm = Y->l2norm();
  // scale
  X->scale_interior( *Y,1./bnorm );
}
```

The functionality is ensured by letting each datatype inherit from a base class `bordered_array_base` in a namespace `sparsealg`,

```
// diff2d/lib/base.hpp
template< typename real >
class bordered_array_base {
```

where these functions are declared virtual (section 3.1):

```
// diff2d/lib/base.hpp
virtual void central_difference_from
  ( const sparsealg::bordered_array_base<real>&,bool=false ) = 0;
virtual void scale_interior
  ( const sparsealg::bordered_array_base<real>&, real ) = 0;
virtual real l2norm() = 0;
virtual void set_value( real value,bool trace=false ) = 0;
virtual void set_bc(bool down, bool right, bool trace=false) = 0;
```

The actual data structures are then created from a derived class:

```
// diff2d/seq/diff2d.cpp
auto X = unique_ptr<sparsealg::bordered_array_base<real>>
  ( make_unique<sparsealg::bordered_array_seq<real>>(msize,nsize,border) );
```

Note the idiom that we create a pointer to the base class from a pointer to a derived class; see further section 15.4.1.

In each specific implementation, the pointer to the base class is *up-cast* to the appropriate derived class with `dynamic_cast` (section 13.3.2):

```
// diff2d/lib/seq.cpp
template< typename real >
void bordered_array_seq<real>::scale_interior
    ( const sparsealg::bordered_array_base<real>& _other, real factor ) {
  // upcast base to derived type
  const auto& other =
    dynamic_cast<const sparsealg::bordered_array_seq<real>&>(_other);
```

19.3 ▪ Data structures

In a matrix-vector algorithm you might expect the vector to be a linear array such as a `std::vector`, and the matrix to be some realization of a two-dimensional array. In this example application the situation is a little more subtle. We recapitulate the discussion of section 15.1.2.

First of all, we don't store the matrix. The matrix is operationally defined through its action: there is a routine that takes a vector (in the application sense) as input and gives a vector as output, but there is no actual matrix data structure.

Next, the vector is based on a two-dimensional array since it models a two-dimensional image or physical object. Also, for the case where we are simulating a PDE we need some border elements around the vector data.

19.3.1 ▪ Storage

Our base class stores the actual data as a bare pointer, but data access will mostly happen through an `mdspan`:

```
// diff2d/lib/base.hpp
private:
  std::unique_ptr<real[]> data_{nullptr};
  md::mdspan<
    real,
    md::dextents<idxint,2>
            > cartesian_data;
```

The `cartesian_data` member is constructed in the base constructor:

```
// diff2d/lib/base.cpp
template< typename real >
bordered_array_base<real>::bordered_array_base
      ( idxint m,idxint n,int border )
  : m_(m),n_(n),_border(border)
  , data_( make_unique<real[]>( (m+2*border)*(n+2*border) ) )
    //, data_( new real[ (m+2*border)*(n+2*border) ] )
  , data_owned(true)
  , cartesian_data
    ( md::mdspan
      ( data_.get(),md::extents{m+2*border,n+2*border} )
      )
```

This object can now be indexed two-dimensionally,

```
cartesian_data[i,j]
```

with `i,j` indices in the range $[0 \cdots m+2b-1] \times [0 \cdots n+2b-1]$, meaning the domain including borders.

Below we will define a second `mdspan` object corresponding to the $[b \cdots m+b-1] \times [b \cdots n+b-1]$ indices of the interior.

19.3.2 ▪ Indexing

All three operations (stencil application, norm, scaling) operate on a two-dimensional data structure. Traditionally this was expressed by linearizing two-dimensional indices to a single index. For instance, the essence of the scaling operation is

```
// diff2d/lib/seq.cpp
for ( idxint i=0; i<m; i++ )
  for ( idxint j=0; j<n; j++ )
    out[ index2d(i,j,m,n,b) ] = in[ index2d(i,j,m,n,b) ] * factor;
```

where we use an index translation function:

```
// diff2d/lib/base.hpp
inline constexpr idxint index2d( idxint i,idxint j,idxint m,idxint n,idxint b ) {
  return (i+b)*(n+2*b) + j+b;
};
```

(The `b` parameter is the size of the border.)

Remark. *In C style programming the index translation would be done by a macro, in an idiom that you frequently encounter in older code bases:*

```
// diff2d/lib/seq.cpp
#define IINDEX( i,j,m,n,b ) ((i)+b)*(n+2*b) + (j)+b
```

As we contemplate how to write this in modern C++, two possibilities are immediately clear:

- We can use true two-dimensional indexing,

  ```
  out[i,j] = // ...
  ```

  since (in C++23) the `operator[]` can take a comma-separated expression list; see section 3.2.
- We can try to formulate these loops as range algorithms. This runs into various problems, such as the need to skip "border" elements, and, in the matrix-vector product, to combine widely separated array elements. Instead we will use an approach where we range over the indices. This will be used in section 20.12.

Chapter 20

OpenMP

In many scientific applications the bulk of the work takes the form of loops over large datasets, specifically multidimensional arrays. Often, the loop iterations are independent, for instance, in computing the output components of a matrix-vector product, the pixels of an image under convolution, or any operation on the points of a finite elements (FE) grid. Since the iterations are independent, they can be processed in parallel.

OpenMP offers an easy way to execute such loops in parallel: the programmer inserts a directive in front of the loop stating that the iterations can indeed be done in parallel. Note that this puts the burden of analyzing the parallelism on the programmer: stating that a loop is parallel while it is not may give incorrect results. Over time, however, the approach of leaving the parallelism analysis to the programmer has turned out to be more productive than hoping for a magical *parallelizing compiler*.

In this chapter you will see some of the mechanisms for parallelism in OpenMP. We will focus on parallelizing loops; there is also a "task" construct, briefly discussed, which gives something closer to the *fork-join parallelism* of classic threading models. Not discussed here is the OpenMP facility of offloading computations to a GPU or other accelerator.

Logistics OpenMP is realized as a language extension and library, supported by most compilers. Generally, a compile flag of `-fopenmp` (for Intel compilers, `-qopenmp`) is needed at both the compile and link stages. In CMake, you can find the OpenMP module with `find_package`; see section 20.14.

For the library routines, add

```
#include <omp.h>
```

to your sources.

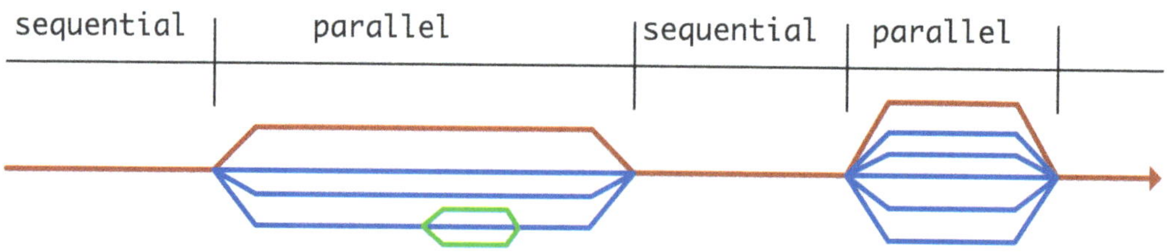

Figure 20.1. *Thread creation and deletion during parallel execution*

20.1 ▪ Thread teams and worksharing constructs

OpenMP uses *parallel regions* for a simplified type of thread programming. OpenMP constructs are indicated by a pragma followed by omp and further keywords:

```
#pragma omp construct clause ....
```

The keyword parallel indicates that the following statement or block is executed in parallel by a *team of threads*:

```
// your program starts sequentially
#pragma omp parallel
{
  // now you have a team of threads
}
// and now your program is sequential again
```

The number of threads can be dynamically determined, and teams can be created recursively; this is illustrated in Figure 20.1.

To illustrate the concept of teams of threads, consider the following segment of code:

Code:

```
// hellofmt.cpp
#pragma omp parallel
{
  int t = omp_get_thread_num();
  std::cout << std::format
    ("Hello world from {}\n",t);
}
```

Output:

```
Hello world from 3
Hello world from 1
Hello world from 0
Hello world from 5
Hello world from 4
Hello world from 2
```

You see that you get one unique number per thread; the numbers range from zero to the value returned by `omp_get_num_threads()`. (We are using `std::format` here, which is atomic: using `std::cout` with the less-less operator may have threads mingling their output.)

How does OpenMP know how much parallelism your hardware supports? It does not, as you might think, detect the core count of your processor. Instead, you need to specify the number of threads explicitly, for instance, through the *OMP_NUM_THREADS* environment variable. There are more environment variables, as well as options in your code, that you can use to fine-tune performance; we will only mention some.

The following shell script fragment demonstrates a scaling study by varying the environment variable for the number of threads:

```
for t in 1 2 4 8 12 16 ; do
  export OMP_NUM_THREADS=$t
  ./my_omp_program
done
```

The above only shows how to create a team of threads. Now you need to use those to distribute work. That's where *worksharing constructs* come in. The most common one is the parallel loop, which we'll look at next.

20.2 ▪ Loop parallelism

The most common activity in OpenMP is parallelizing loops, which are realized by using the omp pragma with the parallel and for directives. Both indexed and range-based loops are parallelized this way.

Indexed syntax:

```
#pragma omp parallel
#pragma omp for
for (int i=0; i<N; i++) {
  // do something with i
}
```

Range-based syntax:

```
#pragma omp parallel
#pragma omp for
for ( auto e : container ) {
  // do something with e
}
```

The parallel and for directives cause OpenMP to spread the loop over the available threads and execute the loop in parallel:

1. First the parallel directive creates a *team* of threads.
2. Then the for directive, which is a *worksharing construct*, divides the available work over the available threads.
3. A note on syntax: OpenMP directives are generally followed by a single statement, or a brace-delimited block. Thus the following are equivalent:

```
#pragma omp parallel
#pragma omp for
  for ( /* stuf */ ) {}
```

```
#pragma omp parallel
{
  #pragma omp for
  {
    for ( /* stuf */ ) {}
  }
}
```

You will often see the parallel/for directives combined:

```
#pragma omp parallel for
for ( /* stuff */ )
```

Exercise 20.1. Write a simple program, for instance, summing a number of vectors,

```
for ( int i=0; i<N; i++)
    s[i] = a[i] + b[i] + c[i] + d[i];
```

and do a scaling study by varying the thread count.

- For what thread counts do you get approximately linear scaling?
- At what thread count does the scaling become less than linear?
- What happens if you use a thread count larger than the core count?

You may notice that speedup can level off for high core counts. This may be due to bandwidth limitations of your hardware, but there can be other reasons. To limit interference of the runtime system, it's a good idea to always set the environment variable

```
OMP_PROC_BIND=true
```

This tells the runtime system not to migrate threads between cores. Migration might make sense in applications such as web servers or databases, where the activities of one thread and another can be very different. However, scientific applications are much more regular and the workload can be evenly divided over the threads, so migration does not help and is in fact deleterious to performance. Also, *hyperthreads* or *virtual cores* rarely improve performance, since they share the floating point units. Therefore it is normal to limit the number of threads to the physical core count.

20.2.1 ▪ Loop parallelism in our example

Let us consider the first useful instance of OpenMP parallelism in our example application. We consider loops with trivially independent iterations, which in their simplest form have the structure

```
for ( ... i ... )
  output[i] = .... input[i] ....
```

In our power method application (Chapter 19) one example of a parallel loop is scaling an array by a factor,

```
#pragma omp parallel for
for ( idxint i=0; i<m; i++ )
  for ( idxint j=0; j<n; j++ )
    out[ index2d(i,j,m,n,b) ] = in[ index2d(i,j,m,n,b) ] * factor;
```

where `m,n` are the size of the domain and `b` is the width of a halo region.

For the initial implementation, the `out,in` data are `double*` pointers, for instance, obtained as the `data` member of a `std::vector`. The loops range only over the $m \times n$ interior part of the domain, which is allocated with size $(m + 2b) \times (n + 2b)$.

The indexing function translates from two-dimensional to one-dimensional indexing, skipping the border points:

```
// diff2d/lib/base.hpp
inline constexpr idxint index2d( idxint i,idxint j,idxint m,idxint n,idxint b ) {
  return (i+b)*(n+2*b) + j+b;
};
```

Later we will explore implementing the data as an `mdspan` object so we can use the two-dimensional `[i,j]` type indexing.

20.3 ▪ Reductions

Next to fully parallel loops, as just discussed, the most common type of parallel operation is a reduction, that is, a global combination of data, for instance, through a sum operator:

```
for (int i=0; i<N; i++) {
  sum += x[i];
}
```

Simple parallelization of this with omp parallel for as above would give a *race condition*: conflicts arising from the simultaneous access to sum_of_squares by multiple threads. For details, see the HPC book [23, section 2.6.1.5].

This is easily fixed (again, by you; the compiler does not alert you to this problem) by adding a reduction clause that specifies the operator and the variable into which we are reducing:

```
float sum{0.f};
#pragma omp parallel for reduction(+:sum)
for ( const auto& e : x )
  sum += e;
```

20.3.1 ▪ Reduction in the example application

In our example application, a reduction appears in the computation of the norm, where the sum can be computed parallel over the available threads:

$$\|x\|_2 = \sqrt{\sum_i x_i^2}.$$

The sequential code for this is

```
// diff2d/lib/seq.cpp
for ( idxint i=0; i<m; i++ )
  for ( idxint j=0; j<n; j++ ) {
    auto v = in[ index2d(i,j,m,n,b) ];
    sum_of_squares += v*v;
  }
return std::sqrt(sum_of_squares);
```

The ℓ_2 reduction of our example application in simple OpenMP code looks like

```
// diff2d/lib/oned.cpp
real sum_of_squares{0};
#pragma omp parallel for reduction(+:sum_of_squares)
for ( idxint i=0; i<m; i++ )
  for ( idxint j=0; j<n; j++ ) {
    auto v = in[ index2d(i,j,m,n,b) ];
    sum_of_squares += v*v;
  }
return std::sqrt(sum_of_squares);
```

The reduction clause specifies both the reduction operator and reduction variable. The above snippet parallelizes the outer loop only; adding a directive collapse(2) parallelizes both loops simultaneously.

20.3.2 ▪ Internal realization

Using explicit threads you would solve the race condition problem of reductions by using an atomic variable. While atomic operations, and general critical regions, exist in OpenMP, the loop reduction mechanism is far more efficient.

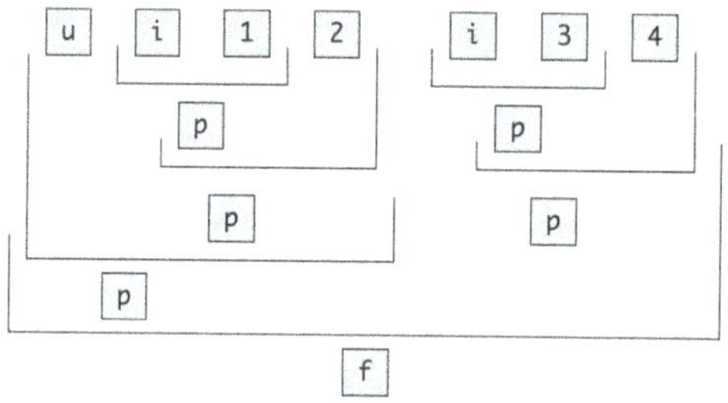

Figure 20.2. *Structure of a reduction of four items on two threads, where* u *is the user-supplied initial value, and* i *is the natural initial value for the reduction operator*

OpenMP implementations may actually implement simple reductions through atomic instructions, but in general the following mechanism is used:

1. each thread gets a local copy of the reduction variable, and
2. reduces into that without any conflicts;
3. any two threads that finish combine their local variables using the reduction operator.

In effect, reduction is done by combining partial results in a treewise structure, as illustrated in Figure 20.2. Since each thread performs a scalar operation, a sufficiently long reduction performs at the same speed as a simple traversal of the data structure.

20.3.3 ▪ Pointwise reduction on arrays

Pointwise reduction on arrays uses a notation to indicate the length of the array:

```
auto ar = new int[nelements];
#pragma omp parallel for reduction(+:ar[nelements])
```

Array reduction is of use in physics applications with multiple unknowns per point, such as elasticity or semiconductor simulation.

This mechanism can be applied to `std::vector` and other containers by extracting their `data`. There is one hitch. The code

```
vector<float> x;
#pragma omp parallel reduction(+:x.data()) // NOPE
```

does not compile because the reduction clause wants a variable, not an expression, for the array, so you need an extra bare pointer:

```
// reductarray.cpp
vector<int> data(nthreads,0);
int *datadata = data.data();
#pragma omp parallel for schedule(static,1) reduction(+:datadata[:nthreads])
```

20.4 ▪ Parallelization of random-access iterators

Above you saw examples of range-based parallel loops. This is actually a special case of a more general mechanism: any loop that iterates over a *random-access iterator* can be handled by OpenMP loop parallelism. See section 7.2 for writing your own iterators in such a way that they can be OpenMP-parallelized.

The fact that OpenMP can parallelize anything with a random-access iterator extends also to uses of the *pipe operator* to connect ranges and views. The resulting view again has a random-access iterator, so we can again parallelize it with OpenMP.

The C++20 ranges library is supported:

```
#pragma omp parallel for reduction(+:itcount)
for ( auto e : data
            | std::ranges::views::drop(1) )
      itcount += e;
#pragma omp parallel for reduction(+:itcount)
for ( auto e : data
            | std::ranges::views::transform
            ( []( auto e ) { return 2*e; } ) )
      itcount += e;
```

The reduction in the example of section 20.3.1 could have been expressed without OpenMP through the accumulate or reduce standard algorithms. Thus, OpenMP loops often are a more explicit form of C++ algorithms. We use the OpenMP formulation when parallel efficiency is an issue. C++ does have parallel execution policies for some ranges, but they are not as efficient as OpenMP explicit loops; see section 20.7. On the other hand, experiments show that using ranges and views has no measurable impact on OpenMP performance.

20.5 ▪ Advanced reductions

Above you saw an example of a simple scalar reduction. This is generalized in C++: reduction can be applied to any class for which the reduction operator is defined. In this section you will see some surprising examples of this mechanism.

Let us first consider doing a plus-reduction on objects for which operator+ or operator+= is defined.

Class with plus operator:

Definition:

```
// reductclass.cpp
class Thing {
private:
  float x{0.f};
public:
  Thing() = default;
  Thing( float x ) : x(x) {};
  Thing operator+
      ( const Thing& other ) {
    return Thing( x + other.x );
  };
};
```

Use:

```
vector< Thing >
  things(500,Thing(1.f) );
Thing res(0.f);
#pragma omp parallel for reduction( +:res )
for ( const auto& t : things )
  res = res + t;
```

A default constructor is required for the internally used init value; see the quantity i in Figure 20.2.

20.5.1 ▪ Example: Histogram

Using the `operator+` to do reductions can be used for nontrivial examples. For example, creating a histogram, or "binning," is not simply parallelizable:

```
for ( auto e : elements )
  histogram[ property(e) ]++;
```

This loop has a race condition, since many `e` values can map to the same element of `histogram`. We could solve this with an *atomic statement*, but that would essentially turn the computation into a serial one.

Instead, we use the OpenMP reduction mechanism, which solves this by creating a local `histogram` object on each thread. These are combined after the parallel part with the `histogram::operator+`, which of course we first have to define.

Reduction over a `std::map` by merging thread-local maps:

```
// charcount.cpp
template<typename key>
class histogram : public map<key,int> {
public:
  // merge other histogram into this
  void operator+=
      // some compilers want operator+
      ( const histogram<key>& other ) {
    for ( auto [k,v] : other )
      if ( map<key,int>::contains(k) )
        this->at(k) += v;
      else
        this->insert( {k,v} );
  };
  // insert one char in this map
  void inc(char k) {
    if ( map<key,int>::contains(k) )
      this->at(k) += 1;
    else
      this->insert( {k,1} );
  };
};
```

```
/*
 * Reduction loop in main program
 */
bincounter<char> charcount;
#pragma omp parallel for reduction(+ : charcount)
for ( int i=0; i<text.size(); i++ )
  charcount.inc( text[i] );
```

Other solutions are possible. For instance, the above solution is probably the best if the number of bins is much less than the size of the dataset.

Exercise 20.2. Can you come up with a solution that does not allocate a private histogram on each thread, thereby avoiding the multiplied memory demands?

20.6 ▪ Loop schedules

In the examples so far, each iteration had about the same amount of work, so by default OpenMP uses a *static loop schedule*: each thread gets a—roughly equal sized—contiguous block of iterations. There are situations where this is not optimal, such as operations where the work is some function of the iteration number.

Consider the following example:

```
for ( /* large number of iterations */ )
  if ( test_with_fairly_high_chance() )
    do_something_easy();
  else lots_of_work();
```

Giving each thread an equal block of iterations will cause some threads to take more work. Instead we want to break the iteration space into smaller blocks and assign them to whatever thread is unoccupied.

In such cases you can annotate the loop as

```
#pragma omp for schedule(dynamic)
// or
#pragma omp for schedule(guided)
```

Both involve runtime scheduling overhead; the `guided` schedule uses a heuristic, is therefore cheaper, and is often good enough.

20.7 ▪ Execution policies

The C++17/C++20 standards have introduced the notion of *execution policy* to the standard algorithms, meaning the operations on containers that are in the `algorithm` library. The policy is specified through an optional parameter to the algorithms indicating its parallel execution:

```
transform( std::execution::par,
  // the usual input iterator, output iterator, operation
  );
```

This is a C++ native mechanism for parallelism in algorithms, in practice often implemented through the use of *threading building blocks (TBBs)*.

As an example, let's consider prime number marking: create an array where `p[i]` is one if `i` is prime, zero otherwise. This example is parallel, but not load-balanced: finding that a number is prime takes longer than detecting that even numbers or those divisible by 3 are not. Thus, we expect to see a difference between OpenMP static and guided/dynamic scheduling; also this is a test of how well execution policies can deal with unbalanced loads.

OpenMP code:

```
#pragma omp parallel for \
  schedule(static)
 for ( int i=0; i<nsize; i++) {
   results[i] =
     one_if_prime( number(i) );
 }
```

C++ parallel transform:

```
// primepolicy.cpp
transform
  ( std::execution::par,
    numbers.begin(),numbers.end(),
    results.begin(),
    [] (int n ) -> int {
      return one_if_prime(n); }
    );
```

If we apply a reduction, we get a prime number counter.

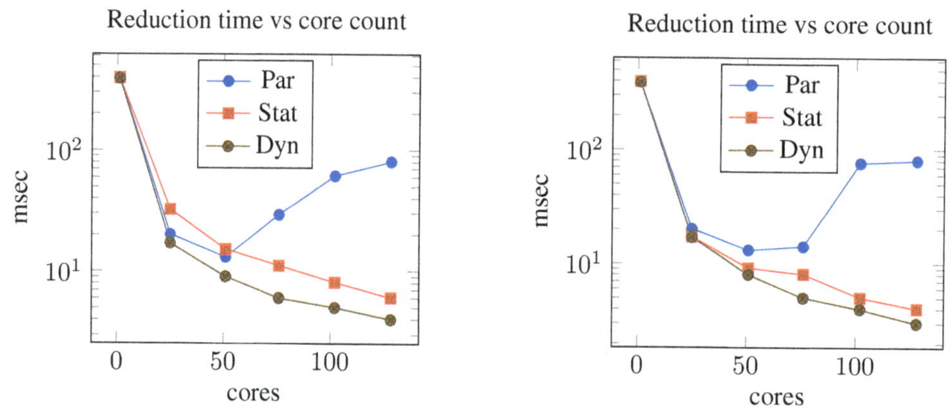

Figure 20.3. *Parallel loop timing with C++ policies and two OpenMP scheduling strategies: a transform loop (left) and a reduction loop (right)*

OpenMP:

```
#pragma omp parallel for \
  schedule(guided,8) \
  reduction(+:prime_count)
for ( auto n : numbers ) {
  prime_count += one_if_prime( n );
}
```

C++ policy:

```
// reducepolicy.cpp
prime_count = transform_reduce
  ( std::execution::par,
    numbers.begin(),numbers.end(),
    0,
    std::plus<>{},
    [] ( int n ) -> int {
        return one_if_prime(n); }
    );
```

In Figure 20.3 we list results obtained using a dual-socket *AMD Milan* node with a total of 128 cores. Legend entries are “Par” for `std::execution:par`, “Stat” for OpenMP static scheduling, “Dyn” for OpenMP dynamic scheduling. First of all we see that OpenMP dynamic scheduling has a modest advantage over static scheduling because of the load imbalance. Without load imbalance, a dynamic schedule usually performs worse, since it has runtime overhead and may negate cache-locality.

Comparing the C++ execution policies to the OpenMP schedules, we find that the parallel range algorithm is only competitive with OpenMP for low thread counts. We suspect that the execution policy, driven by TBBs, tries some load balancing, but is doing so imperfectly.

20.8 ▪ More OpenMP features

20.8.1 ▪ Shared and private data

One of the most difficult topics in shared memory programming is the handling of shared data. In the code of our example application this has not been an issue, for two reasons. First of all, local variables declared inside a parallel region are private to the threads,

```
#pragma omp parallel
{
  int i; // each thread gets its own incarnation of 'i'
```

```
  /* statements with 'i' */
}
```

so access conflicts never come into play. The same holds for loop variables: the iteration variable in a parallel `for` is always private.

Second, we have been arranging the computations in an "owner computes" fashion: each output element has an owning thread, and that thread does all of the computation for that element so that there are no conflicting writes.

One example of "owner computes" would be an array declared outside the parallel regions, which is shared by default, and each thread writes to a separate location:

```
vector<float> x(nthreads);
#pragma omp parallel
  x[ omp_get_thread_num() ] = /* ... */ ;
  // each thread writes a different index
```

Another example is the parallel loop,

```
#pragma omp parallel for
for ( int i=0; i<N; ++i )
  x[i] = /* ... */
```

where each thread is assigned a disjoint set of indices where to perform the computation.

There is a `private` clause to give each thread a private copy of a variable,

```
int t;
#pragma omp parallel private(t)
{
  t = /* ... */ ;
  /* ... */
}
```

but this is usually better solved through using a local variable. (A similar `shared` directive exists, but since that's the default, it is of less use; however see the tasking section below.)

However, in this example the initial value of `t` in the parallel region is undefined. If you need the value from before the parallel region, use the `firstprivate` clause:

```
int t=f(); // each thread gets its own incarnation of 'i'
#pragma omp parallel firstprivate(t)
{
  t *= omp_get_thread_num(); // 't' starts out initialized
```

Finally, it is possible to carry a value from the parallel region to the code after it:

```
int n;
#pragma omp parallel for lastprivate(n)
{
  for (int i=0; i<N; i++) {
    n = f(i); g(n);
  }
}
// now 'n' has the value of the last iteration.
```

20.8.2 ▪ Tasks

Parallel loops have their iterations divided in some way over the available threads. One might say that behind the scenes OpenMP makes "tasks" of these blocks of iterations, and parcels these out to the threads. The task mechanism can actually be used explicitly:

```
#pragma omp task
{ /* code */ }
```

This generates a task: a self-contained unit of computation, put on a queue to be executed later, asynchronously.

Generally, tasks are generated by a single thread, so we use the following idiom:

```
#pragma omp parallel
#pragma omp single
  {
    // code
    #pragma omp task
      { /* code of the task */ }
    #pragma omp taskwait
    // more code
  }
```

What happens here is

1. first we create a team of parallel threads;
2. then the task generation is done by only a single thread;
3. but the tasks are executed by any thread in the team;
4. those tasks are then allowed to create more tasks, no matter what thread they run on;
5. whenever the results of a task are needed, we insert a *taskwait* directive.

As an example, this code drives a Mandelbrot set drawing program:

```
// mandel_tools1.cxx
#pragma omp parallel
#pragma omp single
  {
    nt = omp_get_num_threads();
    for (;;) {
      struct coordinate xy; int res;
      workcircle->next_coordinate(xy);
      if (workcircle->is_valid_coordinate(xy)) {
        this->total_tasks += 1;
        #pragma omp task
        {
          res = belongs(xy,workcircle->infty);
          coordinate_to_image(xy,res);
        }
      }
      else break;
    }
    #pragma omp taskwait
  }
```

One subtlety with tasks concerns their data handling. Since tasks will be executed asynchronously, the following rules apply:

1. Shared data outside the task is also shared in the task. This is data from outside the parallel region, or anything explicitly declared *shared*.
2. Other data is considered *firstprivate*, meaning that it is copied into the task and becomes private there.

With that in mind, consider a Fibonacci code using tasks:

```
long fib(int n) {
  if (n<2) return n;
  else { long f1,f2;
    #pragma omp task
    f1 = fib(n-1);
    #pragma omp task
    f2 = fib(n-2);
    return f1+f2;
  }
}
```

There are two problems here:

1. The tasks are never waited on, so the program continues without waiting for the task results.
2. The variables `f1,f2` are copied into the tasks, rather than treated as results to be returned.

> **Exercise 20.3.** Fix this program and test: you need to insert a `taskwait` directive at the right place, and need the above rules about data sharing between tasks and the calling environment. Your solution only has to be correct; here we don't care about parallel speedup.

20.8.3 ▪ Atomic, critical, and such

If you have done thread programming before you may have come across atomic variables, critical sections, and locks. In the examples above these were not needed: any potential conflicts of data writing were obviated by the "owner computes" strategy, and the use of explicit reductions. That said, OpenMP has all the traditional mechanisms.

You can declare certain types of statements to be atomic:

```
#pragma omp atomic
  x += v;
```

Roughly speaking, these involve the update of a single variable. For more complicated updates there are critical sections:

```
#pragma omp critical
{
  z1 = f(x,y); // x,y possibly passed by reference
  z2 = g(x,y,z1);
}
```

Finally, there are locks, but we will not discuss those.

20.9 ▪ Thread-private random number generators

A common problem in parallel codes is how to handle random number generation. (See Chapter 9 for the C++ `random` library.) In OpenMP, the specific problem is that threads act as if they are created anew for each parallel region. Thus, to have a persistent random number generation we need thread-local data.

> The new C++ `random` header has a threadsafe generator, by virtue of the statement in the standard that no standard template library (STL) object can rely on global state. The usual idiom cannot be made threadsafe because of the initialization:

```
static random_device rd;
static mt19937 rng(rd);
```

However, the following works:

```
// privaterandom.cpp
static std::random_device rd;
#pragma omp threadprivate(rd)
static std::mt19937 rng;
#pragma omp threadprivate(rng)

int main() {

#pragma omp parallel
  rng = std::mt19937(rd());
```

20.10 ▪ Performance traps

Your OpenMP code may not achieve the expected speedup. This is quite common for the following reasons.

Not enough work OpenMP carries a certain amount of overhead in managing the threads. For instance, the barrier at the end of a parallel section can take hundreds or thousands of clock cycles to process. This means that each parallel region needs to have many thousands of operations for speedup to be apparent.

Thread team creation Strictly speaking, OpenMP creates a team of threads at the start of each parallel region. In practice, it probably creates a team once, and then suspends that outside parallel regions. In effect, the overhead from thread team creation is very small. That said, there is some overhead the very first time a team of threads is created. Be sure to exclude that from your timing.

Critical regions There are many applications that are loop-based, but not trivially parallelizable. You may be tempted to declare the loops parallel, and then turn the troublesome bits into critical sections or atomic operations: statements or code sections that can only be executed by one thread at a time. Since critical/atomic sections are effectively sequential, for such code to show any sort of speedup, the parallel work needs to be much larger than the work in the critical sections. Often you need to rethink your parallelization strategy; see section 20.5.1 for an example.

Random number generation and other thread-safety problems The old C `rand` routine is not threadsafe and it may cause considerable slowdown when used in an OpenMP code. Use the new `random` header instead. This problem of library routines with an internal, nonthreadsafe state can happen whenever you use old code. Beware.

Affinity Your OS is probably allowed to migrate OpenMP threads. This hardly ever benefits performance. Usually, it is best to forbid it by setting

```
export OMP_PROC_BIND=true
```

More subtle treatments of affinity are possible, but start with this.

We conclude this "performance traps" section with an issue that will happen on supercomputer nodes more than on desktop PCs.

20.11 ▪ Multisocket "first-touch"

The shared memory nature of OpenMP means that any core can access any data item. This does not imply that any item can be accessed at the same speed; for instance, the presence of shared and private caches plays a role here. There is another effect, which comes into play on systems with more than one socket, meaning more than one processor chip. This is known as *first-touch*, and it is another potential source of performance problems.

A little background knowledge. Memory is organized in *memory pages* (see the HPC book [23, section 1.3.9]), and what we think of as "addresses" really are *virtual addresses*, mapped to *physical addresses* through a *page table*. These data pages can be anywhere in physical memory. In particular, on a *dual socket* node, the memory can be mapped to either of the sockets.

The next thing to know is that memory allocated with `malloc` / `new` and like routines is not immediately mapped; pages are only mapped when data is written to them. Now consider the following OpenMP code:

```
double *x = new double[N];

for ( int i=0; i<N; ++i )
  x[i] = 0;

#pragma omp parallel for
for ( int i=0; i<N; ++i )
  .... something with x[i] ...
```

Since the initialization loop is not parallel it is executed by the main thread, making all the memory mapped to the socket of that thread. This is called *first-touch*: the thread that first touches a data page determines where that page will be mapped. Subsequent access by the other socket will then access data from memory not attached to that socket, which induces a considerable delay, and performance degradation.

20.11.1 ▪ Example

Let's consider an example. We make the initialization parallel subject to an option:

```
// heat.c
#pragma omp parallel if (init>0)
  {
    #pragma omp for
    for (int i=0; i<N; i++)
      y[i] = x[i] = 0.;
    x[0] = 0; x[N-1] = 1.;
  }
```

If the initialization is not parallel, the array will be mapped to the socket of the master thread; if it is parallel, it may be mapped to different sockets, depending on where the threads run.

As a simple application we run a heat equation, which is parallel, though not embarrassingly so:

```
for (int it=0; it<1000; it++) {
  #pragma omp parallel for
  for (int i=1; i<N-1; i++)
    y[i] = ( x[i-1]+x[i]+x[i+1] )/3.;
```

```
  #pragma omp parallel for
  for (int i=1; i<N-1; i++)
    x[i] = y[i];
}
```

On the *TACC Frontera* machine, with dual 28-core *Intel Cascade Lake* processors, we use the following settings:

```
export OMP_PLACES=cores
export OMP_PROC_BIND=close
# no parallel initialization
make heat && OMP_NUM_THREADS=56 ./heat
# yes parallel initialization
make heat && OMP_NUM_THREADS=56 ./heat 1
```

This gives us a remarkable difference in runtime:

- Sequential init: avg=2.089, stddev=0.1083.
- Parallel init: avg=1.006, stddev=0.0216.

This large difference will be mitigated for algorithms with higher arithmetic intensity.

Exercise 20.4. How does OpenMP dynamic scheduling relate to this issue?

20.11.2 ▪ Solution in C++

The problem with first-touch in *C++* is that `std::vector` fills its allocation with default values. This is known as "value-initialization," and it makes

```
vector<double> x(N);
```

equivalent to the nonparallel allocation and initialization above.

Here is a solution:

Uninitialized containers Default initialization is a problem. We make a template for uninitialized types:

```
// heatalloc.cpp
template<typename T>
struct uninitialized {
  uninitialized() {};
  T val;
  constexpr operator T() const {return val;};
  T operator=( const T&& v ) { val = v; return val; };
};
```

so that we can create vectors that behave normally:

```
vector<uninitialized<double>> x(N),y(N);

#pragma omp parallel for
for (int i=0; i<N; i++)
  y[i] = x[i] = 0.;
x[0] = 0; x[N-1] = 1.;
```

Running the code with the regular definition of a vector, and the above modification, reproduces the runtimes of the C variant above.

Another option is to wrap memory allocated with `new` in a `unique_ptr`:

```
// heatptr.cpp
unique_ptr<double[]> x( new double[N] );
unique_ptr<double[]> y( new double[N] );

#pragma omp parallel for
for (int i=0; i<N; i++) {
  y[i] = x[i] = 0.;
}
x[0] = 0; x[N-1] = 1.;
```

Note that this gives fairly elegant code, since square bracket indexing is overloaded for `unique_ptr`. The only disadvantage is that we cannot query the `size` of these arrays, or do bound checking with `at`, but in high performance contexts that is usually not appropriate anyway.

20.12 ▪ Example application: Discussion

There are various ways of expressing a data-parallel iteration in C++: traditional indexed iteration, range-based loops, range algorithms, etc. In this section we discuss how to make these schemes parallel with OpenMP.

20.12.1 ▪ Linear indexing

We write OpenMP with a double for loop; the 2D `i,j` indices are translated to a linear coordinate through a macro:

```
// diff2d/lib/oned.cpp
template< typename real >
void bordered_array_1d<real>::scale_interior
    ( const sparsealg::bordered_array_base<real>& _other, real factor ) {
  // upcast base to derived type
  const auto& other =
    dynamic_cast<const sparsealg::bordered_array_1d<real>&>(_other);
  auto out = this->data();
  auto in = other.data();
  auto m = this->m(), n = this->n();
  auto b = this->border();
  #pragma omp parallel for
  for ( idxint i=0; i<m; i++ )
    for ( idxint j=0; j<n; j++ )
      out[ index2d(i,j,m,n,b) ] = in[ index2d(i,j,m,n,b) ] * factor;
};
```

Here the data is a simple `double*` pointer; the `index2d` function is defined as

```
// diff2d/lib/base.hpp
inline constexpr idxint index2d( idxint i,idxint j,idxint m,idxint n,idxint b ) {
  return (i+b)*(n+2*b) + j+b;
};
```

Note how incorporating the `border` variable means that we range over the interior only.

OpenMP collapse Since we have a two-dimensional traversal, we can add a collapse(2) clause. This does not improve performance in our case, since the outer loop already has enough parallelism. Also, inspection of the assembly code shows that collapsing the loops induces a good amount of index calculation.

20.12.2 ▪ Two-dimensional indexing

Above we used fairly traditional indexing in the OpenMP parallel loops, linearizing the two-dimensional problem to a single index. We will now discuss some more sophisticated schemes.

First of all we remark that ranging with modern C++ mechanisms comes with zero performance penalty over traditional indexing. There are also "execution policies" for range algorithms, but at the high core counts common in HPC these can be dramatically worse than using OpenMP; see section 20.7. Also, in our example application ranging over the actual data can be tricky.

- In the bordered array, we need to skip the border points.
- In the stencil operation, we need to access and combine elements from disparate locations in the array.

For this reason we take a two-step approach:

1. We access data through an mdspan, so that we have multidimensional indexing:

```
// diff2d/lib/base.hpp
private:
  std::unique_ptr<real[]> data_{nullptr};
  md::mdspan<
    real,
    md::dextents<idxint,2>
          > cartesian_data;
```

```
// diff2d/lib/base.hpp
//! pointer to the data as 2D array
auto& data2d() {
  return cartesian_data; };
const auto& data2d() const {
  return cartesian_data; };
```

2. We define the iteration space as a cartesian_product range view:

```
// diff2d/lib/base.cpp
const auto& s = data2d();
int b = this->border();
idxint
  lo_m = static_cast<idxint>(b),
  hi_m = static_cast<idxint>(s.extent(0)-b),
  lo_n = static_cast<idxint>(b),
  hi_n = static_cast<idxint>(s.extent(1)-b);
range2d = rng::views::cartesian_product
  ( rng::views::iota(lo_m,hi_m),rng::views::iota(lo_n,hi_n) );
```

   This is returned by the function *inner_range*:

```
// diff2d/lib/base.hpp
auto& inner_range() const { return range2d; };
```

We can use actual two-dimensional indexing if we range over the indices of a cartesian_product view, and index into an mdspan:

```
// diff2d/lib/span.cpp
template< typename real >
void bordered_array_span<real>::scale_interior
   ( const sparsealg::bordered_array_base<real>& _other, real factor ) {
```

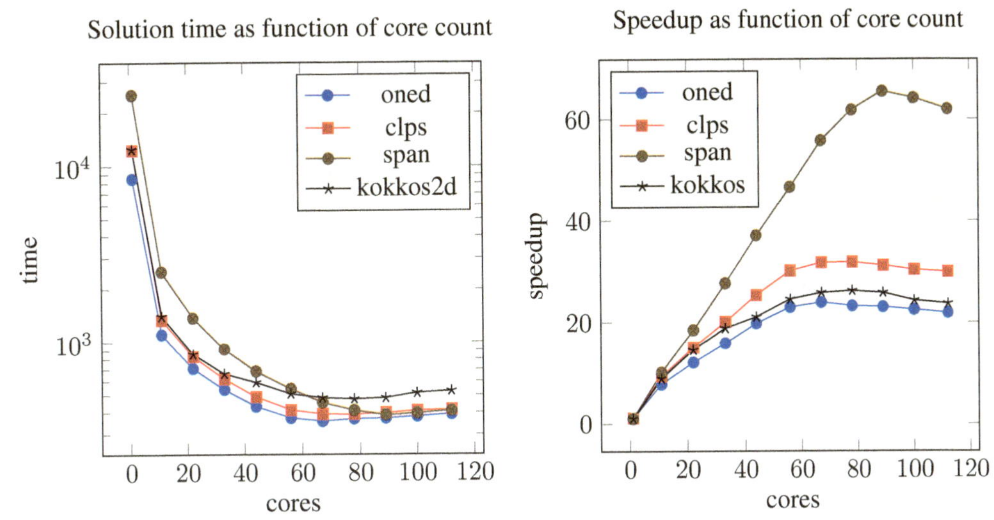

Figure 20.4. *Various implementation strategies; time and speedup as function of core count*

```
  const auto& other = dynamic_cast<const sparsealg::bordered_array_span<real>&>(_other);
  auto out = this->data2d();
  auto in = other.data2d();
  #pragma omp parallel for
  for ( auto ij : this->inner_range() ) {
    auto [i,j] = ij;
    out[ i,j ] = in[ i,j] * factor;
  }
};
```

For the trickier stencil operation this allows us to write without tests for the border points:

```
// diff2d/lib/span.cpp
auto out = this->data2d();
const auto in = other.data2d();
#pragma omp parallel for
for ( auto ij : this->inner_range() ) {
  auto [i,j] = ij;
  out[ i,j ] = 4*in[ i,j ]
    - in[ i-1,j ] - in[ i+1,j ] - in[ i,j-1 ] - in[ i,j+1 ];
}
```

20.12.3 ▪ SYCL and Kokkos

In the chapter on heterogeneous programming models we show some details of the realization of our example application in SYCL (section 21.1.6) and Kokkos (section 21.2.2).

20.12.4 ▪ Timing comparison

In Figure 20.4 we show runtime and speedup for several variants:

- *oned*: only the outer loop parallelized, using conversion of two- to one-dimensional indexing;

- *clps*: same, but with collapse(2);
- *span*: using mdspan;
- *kokkos*: using the Kokkos library.

We see for all variants that speedup levels off at some point because of bandwidth limitations. The mdspan variant is showing more speedup, but that is because it is slower on low core counts than the other variants.

20.13 ▪ OpenMP versus C++ threads

OpenMP is a thread-based programming model, but unlike the C++ thread library, the threads are largely hidden from the programmer. Here is a brief rundown of C++ threading mechanisms and their rough equivalents in OpenMP:

- threads: handled implicitly through parallel regions;
- atomics: locks, atomic operations, and critical regions;
- fork/join: task wait and task loop;
- execution policies on standard algorithms: parallel loops;
- futures: no real equivalent;
- senders and receivers (proposed for C++26): tasks.

20.14 ▪ CMake integration

OpenMP is available through a CMake module that makes available certain targets:

```
find_package(OpenMP)
if(OpenMP_C_FOUND) # or CXX
else()
        message( FATAL_ERROR "Could not find OpenMP" )
endif()
# for C:
add_executable( ${program} ${program}.c )
target_link_libraries( ${program} PUBLIC OpenMP::OpenMP_C )
# for C++:
add_executable( ${program} ${program}.cxx )
target_link_libraries( ${program} PUBLIC OpenMP::OpenMP_CXX)
# for Fortran
enable_language(Fortran)
# test: if( OpenMP_Fortran_FOUND )
add_executable( ${program} ${program}.F90 )
target_link_libraries( ${program} PUBLIC OpenMP::OpenMP_Fortran )
```

Chapter 21

Heterogeneous programming

Heterogeneous programming, using a combination of central processing units (CPUs) and GPUs or other *accelerators*, is becoming increasingly common. In this chapter we take a brief look at two systems that can execute the same code on either the "host," the CPU, or the "device," the GPU: Kokkos and SYCL. Both systems embody the spirit of range algorithms: they invoke lambda expressions in parallel over an index range. The programming system we will not consider is CUDA, which is proprietary to *NVidia* GPUs. Also, it is based on an extension to C/C++ that is not fully compliant with recent standards, and here we prefer to consider general solutions.

While on GPUs we are again faced with the issue of expressing parallelism, heterogeneity adds a further complication. The problem with heterogeneous programming is managing the coherence between host and device memory, since GPUs are often attached by mechanisms such as a *PCI bus*, rather than actually sharing memory with the CPU.

21.1 ▪ SYCL

SYCL is an open standard [51] that targets heterogeneous parallelism on CPUs, GPUs, and field programmable gate arrays (FPGAs) through strict standard C++. It is similar in spirit to other data-parallel systems such as CUDA or C++ range algorithms.

21.1.1 ▪ Devices and queues

SYCL works by submitting kernels to a queue; the queue is explicitly created on the "host" or on a "device," meaning an attached GPU or FPGA. As an example, a queue on the CPU:

```
// cpuname.cxx
sycl::queue myqueue( sycl::cpu_selector_v );
```

There are various discovery and info routines for devices that we will not mention here.

21.1.2 ▪ Memory management

SYCL has more than one mechanism of maintaining coherence between host and device. Here we limit ourselves to so-called "buffers."

Host memory is wrapped in a buffer structure:

```
std::vector<real> Mat_A(msize*nsize);
buffer<real,2> Buf_a(Mat_A.data(),range<2>(msize,nsize));
```

This buffer is then passed to the kernel, which can be executed either on the same CPU or on an attached device. Coherence between host and device is handled implicitly by the runtime system. SYCL has various other mechanisms for data synchronization that are more explicit, but they perform very similarly.

21.1.3 ▪ Queue submission

The execution mechanism in SYCL consists of queues (introduced above) that kernels are explicitly submitted to. Execution follows when the queue goes out of scope, or through an explicit `wait` call. The argument to a submit call is a lambda that takes a handle to the SYCL environment as argument.

Here we show both mechanisms of submitting and executing kernels:

Queue executed at end of scope:

```
{
  q.submit(
    [&](sycl::handler& h) { /* ... */ } );
  q.submit(
    [&](sycl::handler& h) { /* ... */ } );
} // kernels executed in either order
```

Kernels immediately executed:

```
q.submit(
    [&](sycl::handler& h) { /* ... */ }
        ).wait();
q.submit(
    [&](sycl::handler& h) { /* ... */ }
        ).wait();
```

Since SYCL purports to be a uniform way of handling heterogeneous resources, most code is the same whether it executes on a CPU or GPU (or indeed an FPGA). To distinguish between these device types you declare queue types:

```
// queue for CPU execution
auto cpu_q = queue(cpu_selector_v);
// queue for GPU execution
auto gpu_q = queue(gpu_selector_v);
```

The same kernel can now be submitted to a CPU queue for execution on the host, or to a GPU queue for execution on the attached device.

21.1.4 ▪ Kernels

In the above `submit` calls we omitted the actual parallel code. This usually comprises:

1. creating accessors to the data passed by reference; and
2. executing a parallel operation such as `parallel_for`.

Here we illustrate a kernel, submitted to a queue and immediately waited on. The kernel accesses the memory of a buffer:

```
myqueue.submit( [&] ( sycl::handler &h ) {
  sycl::accessor  deviceAccessorA(bufferA,h,sycl::read_write);
    h.parallel_for<class uniqueID>
```

```
      ( mySize,
        [=](sycl::id<1> index) {
        deviceAccessorA[index] *= 2; }
        );
  }
```

21.1.5 ▪ Buffers and accessors

SYCL has a number of mechanisms to affect the coherence of host and device memory. Here we show the buffer mechanism, using first one-dimensional ranges and buffers:

```
std::vector<float> input(N),output(N);

sycl::range<1> iteration_range(N);
sycl::buffer<float, 1> input_buf(input.data(),iteration_range);
sycl::buffer<float, 1> output_buf(output.data(),iteration_range);

q.submit([&](sycl::handler& h) {
  sycl::accessor input{ input_buf, h };
  /* parallel operation with:
   ... input[i] ...
 */ ) );
```

Next we show two-dimensional buffers. We allocate a `std::vector` of size `N*N`, but interpret this as a buffer of size `N` by `N`:

```
std::vector<float> input(N*N);
sycl::range<2> iteration_range(N,N);
sycl::buffer<float, 2> input_buf(input.data(),iteration_range);
```

By way of illustration, we show a stencil operation

$$\forall_{i\in 1\ldots N-2}\colon a[i] = (b[i-1] + b[i] + b[i+1])/3$$

Note the idioms we use to avoid the boundary points of the output array:

```
// stencil1d.cxx
sycl::range<1> stencil_range(N);
sycl::range<1> alloc_range(N + 2);
{
  sycl::buffer<float, 1> input_buf(input.data(), alloc_range);
  sycl::buffer<float, 1> output_buf(output.data(), alloc_range);

  Q.submit([&](sycl::handler& h) {
    sycl::id<1> offset{1};
    sycl::accessor input { input_buf,  h,stencil_range,offset,sycl::read_only };
    sycl::accessor output{ output_buf, h,stencil_range,offset,sycl::write_only };

// Compute the average of each cell and its immediate neighbors
    h.parallel_for(stencil_range, [=](sycl::id<1> idx) {
      int i = idx[0];

      float self = input[i];
      float right = input[i + 1];
      float left  = input[i - 1];
      output[i+1] = (self + left + right ) / 3.0f;
    });
  });
}
```

Reductions need a special accessor type:

```
q.submit([&](handler &h) {
  accessor D_a(Buf_a, h, read_only);
  auto D_Fn = reduction(Buf_n, h, std::plus<real>());
  h.parallel_for
    (range<2>(m - 2, n - 2),
     D_Fn,
     [=](item<2> index, auto &sum) { /* ... */ } ) };
```

21.1.6 ▪ Example application

We give a few relevant snippets of the SYCL implementation of our example application; see Chapter 19.

SYCL differs from other parallelism models in having an explicit task queue. This necessitates a parameter addition in the "bordered array" constructor:

```
// diff2d/lib/sycl.hpp
template< typename real >
class bordered_array_sycl : public bordered_array_base<real> {
  friend class distributed_array<real>;
public:
  sycl::queue q;
  bordered_array_sycl( idxint m,idxint n,int border,sycl::queue q );
```

The following is the ℓ_2 norm calculation. Note how the bare pointers such as `this->data()` are first turned into buffers; these are captured in the `submit` call; the parallel loop then accesses as an `accessor` and a reduction variable. Also note that we execute this code synchronously by having an immediate `wait` on the `submit` call.

```
// diff2d/lib/sycl.cpp
template < typename real >
real bordered_array_sycl<real>::l2norm() {
  real norm = 0.0;
  auto out = this->data();
  auto m = std::get<0>(this->inner_sizes());
  auto n = std::get<0>(this->inner_sizes());
  buffer<real,2> Buf_a
    (out, sycl::range<2>(m,n));
  buffer<real,1> Buf_n
    (&norm, range<1>(1));

  auto q = this->q;
  q.submit([&](handler &h) {
    accessor D_a(Buf_a, h, read_only);
    auto D_Fn = reduction
        (Buf_n, h, std::plus<real>());

    h.parallel_for
      (range<2>(m - 2, n - 2),
       D_Fn,
       [=](item<2> index, auto &sum) {
         auto row = index.get_id(0) + 1;
         auto col = index.get_id(1) + 1;
         real value = D_a[row-1][col-1];
         sum += (value*value);
    });
  }).wait();

  norm = std::sqrt(norm);
  return norm;
};
```

21.1.7 ▪ Compilation and CMake integration

The main support for SYCL is through the Intel compiler. Use the regular C++ compiler with a `-fsycl` flag during compilation and linking:

```
# compilation
icpx -fsycl -c mysyclcode.cpp
# linking
icpx -fsycl -o mysyclcode mysyclcode.o
```

However, there is an open source compiler: AdaptiveCpp.

Intel's compiler installation includes a module for finding SYCL. By default, all files are compiled with the SYCL compiler; there is a call to indicate that only certain sources are to be called with the *dpcpp* compiler:

```
find_package( IntelSYCL REQUIRED )
add_sycl_to_target(TARGET target_project SOURCES file1.cpp file2.cpp )
```

Remark. *The CMake module* `IntelDPCPP` *is deprecated.*

21.2 ▪ Kokkos

Kokkos provides data-parallel constructs in such a way that they can be executed through various backends. Among these are OpenMP and CUDA.

The structure of a Kokkos program is as follows:

```
// empty.cxx
#include "Kokkos_Core.hpp"
int main(int argc,char **argv) {
  Kokkos::initialize(argc,argv);
  /* program */
  Kokkos::finalize();
  return 0;
}
```

21.2.1 ▪ Spaces

In contrast to SYCL, but like in OpenMP, there is no explicit queue where the kernels are submitted. The difference between host and device execution is made by the declaration on which space a view is allocated:

```
Kokkos::HostSpace
Kokkos::CudaSpace // for Cuda GPUs
Kokkos::HIPSpace // for AMD GPUs
```

By default, data structures are allocated on the host:

```
// matsum.cxx
int m=10,n=100;
Kokkos::View<double**> matrix("flat",m,n);
assert( matrix.extent(0)==10 );
```

Allocation on the GPU needs specification of a `CudaSpace` parameter. The host can access the data through a mirror:

```
// matsumgpu.cu
Kokkos::View<double**,Kokkos::CudaSpace> cumatrix("flat",m,n);
Kokkos::View<double**,Kokkos::CudaSpace>::HostMirror hostmatrix
  = Kokkos::create_mirror_view(cumatrix);
/* fill in the matrix on the host */
Kokkos::deep_copy(cumatrix,hostmatrix);
```

There are further parameters on the allocation:

```
// diff2d/kokkos2d/diff2d.cpp
using MemSpace = Kokkos::HostSpace;
using Layout = Kokkos::LayoutRight;
using HostMatrixType = Kokkos::View<real**, Layout, MemSpace>;
HostMatrixType x("x", msize,nsize );
```

21.2.2 ▪ Execution

We give a few relevant snippets of the Kokkos implementation of our example application; see Chapter 19.

Kokkos kernels are executed without any reference to a queue:

```
// diff2d/kokkos2d/diff2d.cpp
Kokkos::parallel_for
  ("Update x",
   Kokkos::MDRangePolicy<Kokkos::Rank<2>>
       ({1, 1}, {msize-1, nsize-1}),
   KOKKOS_LAMBDA(int i, int j) {
     x(i, j) = Ax(i, j) / norm;
  });
```

The macro `KOKKOS_LAMBDA` stands for the capture part of a lambda expression plus a few keywords. Note the `{1,1}` offset to limit the ranging to the interior of the domain.

Reductions are handled by adding the reduction variable to the lambda expression:

```
// diff2d/kokkos2d/diff2d.cpp
real norm = 0.0;
Kokkos::parallel_reduce
  ("Compute norm squared",
   Kokkos::MDRangePolicy<Kokkos::Rank<2>>({1, 1}, {msize-1, nsize-1}),
   KOKKOS_LAMBDA(int i, int j, real& accum) {
     accum += Ax(i, j) * Ax(i, j);
  }, norm);
norm = std::sqrt(norm);
```

It is worth noting that array indexing in the Kokkos kernels uses an overloaded parentheses operator. This is to ensure that the same code uses the correct ordering for both host and device memory.

21.2.3 ▪ CMake integration

There is a CMake module for Kokkos:

```
find_package( Kokkos )
target_link_libraries( ${PROJECT_NAME} PUBLIC Kokkos::kokkos )
```

Chapter 22

MPI

With multicore processors it is tempting to think that all processing elements can access all the data, and the problem of parallelism is largely one of dividing the work. This assumption is not valid if you are dealing with a *cluster* architecture, where multiple computers (whether that's a modern multicore or a pre-2000 single-core model) are connected together through some sort of network.

With a cluster there is no longer a single unified memory space. Instead, each processor has a subset of the full problem data. We call this *distributed memory*, and in this scenario we have to worry about how one processor can access the data, and therefore the memory, of another.

In Figure 22.1 we depict the various ways of parallel programming in a cluster. A cluster consists of multiple *nodes*, each with its private memory, and hosting one or two (rarely more) processors, sometimes referred to as *sockets*, that can access all the node memory. For limited parallelism on a single node you can use OpenMP or another threading model (Chapter 20). For large scale parallelism, you can put a process on each core of the cluster and coordinate them with MPI as discussed in this chapter, or you can use some hybrid mode.

In this chapter we will see the basics of the message passing interface (MPI) library, the standard solution for programming distributed memory. We illustrate this again with the power method of Chapter 19.

The MPI standard [42] defines a C and a Fortran API. While the C API can be used directly by C++ programmers, it is decidedly unidiomatic. For this reason, in this book we use the MPL interface to MPI [43], which offers a more elegant interface to the library.

22.1 ▪ Distributed data and process parallelism

MPI is based on the single program multiple data (SPMD) model of parallelism: instead of having an executable that spawns multiple threads, you start your executable multiple times as independent processes. Figure 22.2 illustrates this for a simple "hello world" example. Each of these MPI processes has its own data space—you could also say that there are only local and no global variables—and the only way for them to collaborate is by passing explicit user-level messages.

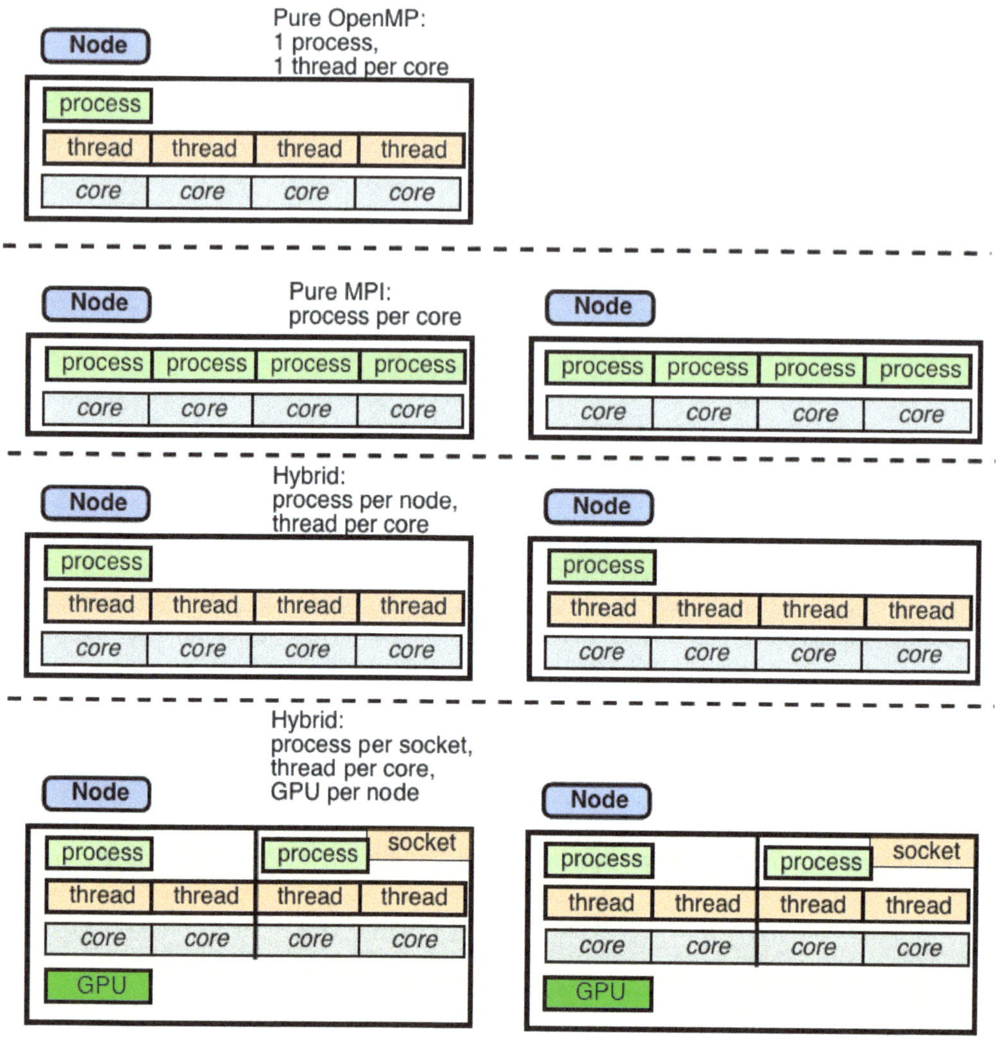

Figure 22.1. *Various parallelism modes in a cluster*

One reason for using MPI is that sometimes you need to work on a single object, say a vector or a matrix, with a size larger than can fit in the memory of a single processor. MPI provides the facility to distribute the data across all available nodes, thus dividing the work. Each processor then works on its own section of the data, and occasionally exchanges data with the other processors.

So let's say we have a large array, and we want to distribute it over the multiple processors of a supercomputer cluster. (Indeed, early applications of MPI ran on dozens of PCs connected together with Ethernet, referred to as *Beowulf* clusters [31].) By way of illustration, with `p` processes and `n` elements per processor, we have a total of $n \times p$ elements in our distributed array.

In Figure 22.3 we say that `mydata` is the local part of a *distributed array* with a total size of $\mathtt{n} \times \mathtt{p}$ elements. However, this array only exists conceptually: each processor has an array with lowest index zero, and you have to translate that yourself to an index in the global array. In other words, you have to write your code in such a way that it acts as if working with a large array distributed over the processors, while actually manipulating only the local arrays on the processors.

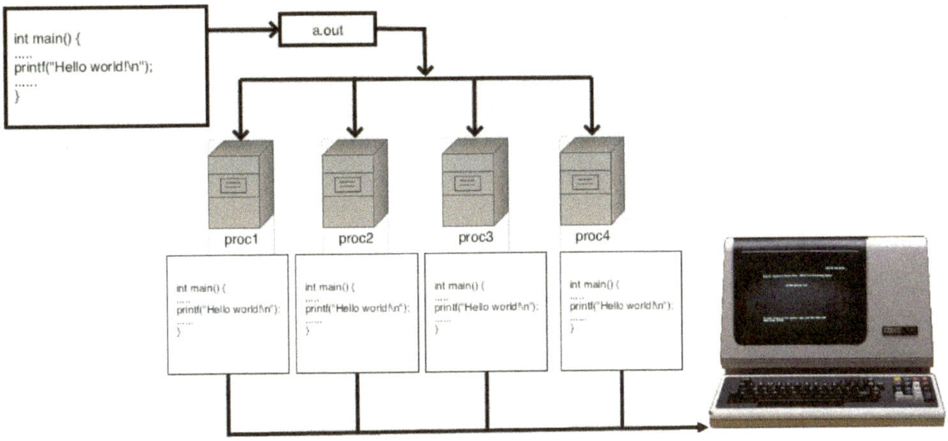

Figure 22.2. *Illustrating the SPMD model by a "hello world" program*

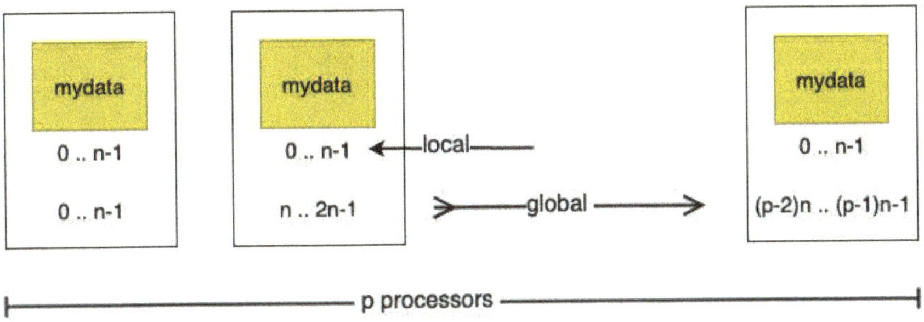

Figure 22.3. *A distributed array with local and global numbering*

The SPMD model often necessitates using conditionals in your code,

```
if ( /* I am first processor */ )
  something;
else if ( /* I am last processor */ )
  something_else;
else
  default_case;
```

since one source needs to cover all possible cases.

22.2 ▪ Parallelizing the example application

In our example application the distributed array is two-dimensional, and correspondingly we impose a two-dimensional ordering on the available processors. Naively, you could also distribute the two-dimensional domain one-dimensionally, giving each process a "block row" or "block column," but there is an important theoretical efficiency argument against this; see the HPC book [23, section 7.2.3].

In the next sections we will discuss MPI mechanisms motivated by the three operations of our example application:

- Scaling the vector is fully parallel, using no communication whatsoever.
- Computing the norm of the vector involves a global sum of all elements over all processes, or in MPI terms a "collective" routine: all processes contribute collectively to the final result.
- Evaluating the matrix-vector product requires "point-to-point" communication: processes exchange information pairwise.

We start by discussing the data structure involved. Above we called this a "distributed array," where each process stores a unique subdomain. However, the example above used a linear array of processes, while here we have a two-dimensional structure.

22.2.1 ▪ Implementation of local and distributed array

For the MPI implementation of our example application (Chapter 19) we construct a `distributed_array` object corresponding to the "distributed array" concept we just introduced. This contains a (sequential) `bordered_array_seq` on each process:

```
// diff2d/lib/dist.hpp
template< typename real >
class distributed_array {
private:
  size_t m_global,n_global;
  std::unique_ptr<bordered_array_base<real>> subdomain{nullptr};
```

(Note that this is not a distributed object as such, but rather each process has one such object, containing and coordinating its local object.)

The `distributed_array` constructor creates the local `bordered_array` and sets up the connectivity information based on a "Cartesian communicator" (about which more later) and the global grid sizes:

```
// diff2d/lib/dist.cpp
template< typename real >
distributed_array<real>::distributed_array
    ( const mpl::cartesian_communicator& comm,size_t m,size_t n,int border,
      bool trace )
      : comm(comm)
      , procrank( comm.rank() )
      , m_global(m),n_global(n)
{
  // compute local sizes...
```

Construction of the subdomain member:

```
// diff2d/lib/dist.cpp
subdomain = unique_ptr<bordered_array_base<real>>
  ( make_unique<bordered_array_seq<real>>(sm,sn,border) );
```

22.2.2 ▪ Grid and subgrid

Assume that each process can compute its number as a coordinate in a process grid (see section 22.4.1 for details). Based on this process coordinate and the size of the global grid, each process can now compute the size of its local subgrid.

The relevant data members are

```
// diff2d/lib/dist.hpp
// orthogonal sizes of processor subdomains
std::vector<idxint> proc_start_m,proc_start_n;
std::map<char,int> neighbors;
// temp array, just for the central difference routine. somewhat wasteful
std::unique_ptr<bordered_array_base<real>> tmp{nullptr};
```

(Note the use of a `map` to find the neighbors by compass direction.)

Some fairly involved calculations are needed to determine the subgrid for each process. Since we are dealing with an orthogonal grid, we compute the start and end points along the i and j dimensions:

```
// diff2d/lib/dist.cpp
// global processor grid size
dimensions = comm.get_dimensions();
auto
  pmsize = dimensions.size(0),
  pnsize = dimensions.size(1);
```

(We will get to the `dimensions` object later.)

The current process then reads out its subgrid sizes, and constructs the contained `bordered_array_seq`.

```
// diff2d/lib/dist.cpp
coord = comm.coordinates(procrank);
auto pm = coord[0], pn = coord[1];
auto
  sm = proc_start_m[pm+1]-proc_start_m[pm],
  sn = proc_start_n[pn+1]-proc_start_n[pn];
```

It also computes which processes are its neighbors; see the discussion in section 22.4.1.

Remark. *You may have noticed that we use a sequential operation inside each process, and therefore one MPI process per core. We could have used a threading model such as OpenMP, and one MPI process per socket or cluster node. This mode is called* hybrid computing, *and while it is intuitively attractive, its practical merits are far from obvious.*

22.2.3 ▪ Parallel operations

Corresponding to how each `distributed_array` contains a `bordered_array`, each operation on the distributed data structure involves doing a similar operation on the embedded structure.

The simplest type of parallel operation is applying a pointwise operation. In our example application that includes scaling the vector. The distributed implementation is straightforward: each process applies the sequential (or possible OpenMP-threaded) method to the local domain:

```
// diff2d/lib/dist.cpp
template< typename real >
void distributed_array<real>::scale_interior
    ( const sparsealg::distributed_array<real>& other, real factor ) {
  subdomain->scale_interior( *(other.subdomain),factor);
};
```

Note that each process applies the `bordered_array::scale_interior` method (section 20.2.1) to an array that is indexed $[0 \ldots n] \times [0 \ldots n]$. That is, for this operation processes have no need to know where the local domain fits into the global domain; they only need to know the local sizes.

22.3 ▪ Reductions and other collectives

Next we look at the norm calculation of our example application. This is a special case of a "collective" operation. We start with a general discussion of collectives.

22.3.1 ▪ General introduction

If all processes have individual data, for instance, the result of a local computation, you may want to bring that information together, for instance, to find the maximal computed value or the sum of all values. Conversely, sometimes one processor has information that needs to be shared with all. For this sort of operation, MPI has *collectives*.

There are various cases, illustrated in Figure 22.4, which you can (sort of) motivate by considering some classroom activities:

- The teacher tells the class when the exam will be. This is a *broadcast*: the same item of information goes to everyone.
- After the exam, the teacher performs a *gather* operation to collect the individual exams.
- On the other hand, when the teacher computes the average grade, each student has an individual number, but these are now combined to compute a single number. This is a *reduction*.
- Now the teacher has a list of grades and gives each student their grade. This is a *scatter* operation, where one process has multiple data items, and gives a different one to all the other processes.

This story, while illustrative, is an imperfect analogy to what happens with MPI processes, because these are more symmetric. There is no "main" or "master" process; the process doing the

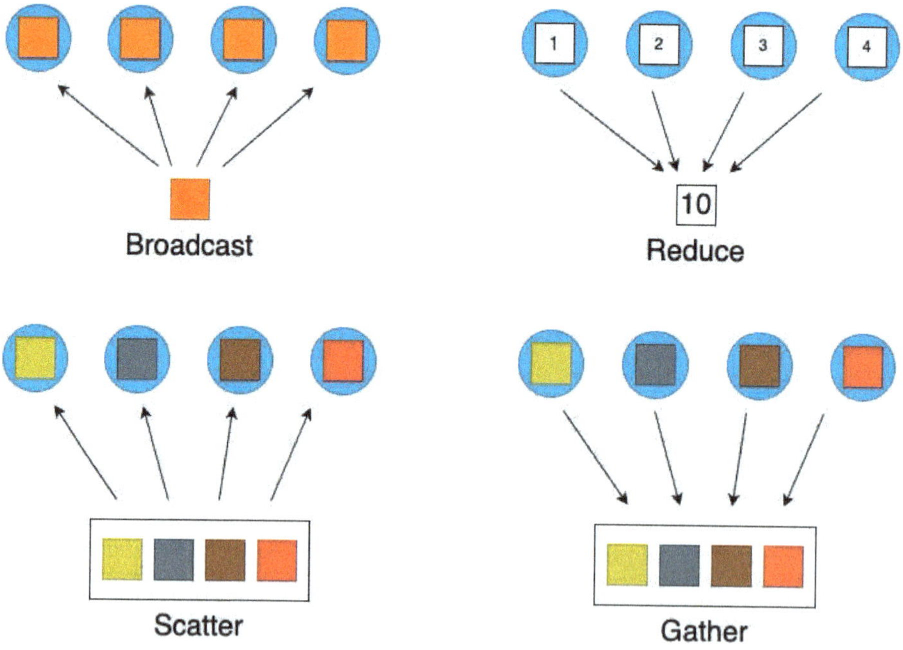

Figure 22.4. *The four most common collective structures*

reducing and broadcasting is no different from the others. Any process can function as the *root process* in a collective operation

22.3.2 ▪ Broadcast

We start by considering the *MPI broadcast* operation, where one process sends information to all others. This can occur, for instance, if that one process reads the data from file. (Why would you not let every process read that file?) In our example code a broadcast is only used to send the command-line options.

The broadcast data is sent from a "buffer." Each process provides its own buffer: the root process puts data in the send buffer and does the broadcast call. After that call the buffer on each process has been filled with the broadcast data.

The broadcast call comes in two variants, with scalar argument and general layout:

```
template<typename T >
void mpl::communicator::bcast
 ( int root_rank, T &data ) const;
void mpl::communicator::bcast
 ( int root_rank, T *data, const layout< T > &l ) const;
```

Note that the root argument comes first in a departure from the C API.

(Layouts are discussed later.)

22.3.3 ▪ Reductions

Next we consider the *MPI reduction* operation. Here each process can provide two buffers: its send buffer contains its contribution to the global result, and the reduced result is placed in the receive buffer. We start with the simple reduction operation (`MPI_Reduce` in the C API) where there is only a receive buffer on the root process.

Here is some sample code. Note that under the SPMD model we need to provide both the root and nonroot version of the call.

There are separate variants for root versus nonroot processes in rooted collectives:

```
// scangather.cxx
const int root=0;
if (procno==root) {
  comm_world.reduce
    ( mpl::plus<int>(),root,
      my_number_of_elements,total_number_of_elements );
} else {
  comm_world.reduce
    ( mpl::plus<int>(),root,my_number_of_elements );
}
```

However, in practice, as in our example application, each process needs the result of the reduction. This is known as an "all-reduce." In our example application, this operation is used in the norm calculation of $\|y\|$. We assume that each process p stores elements

$$y^{(p)} = \{y_i : i \in I_p\},$$

where $\{I_p\}_p$ are disjoints sets of elements. Process p can now compute $\|y^{(p)}\|$, and we find the global norm by summing over the processes:

$$\|y\|^2 = \sum_p \|y_p\|^2.$$

This idiom means that the *MPI allreduce* operation is more common and more useful in practice than the simple reduction.

Versions with separate send/receive buffers, and reduction in place:

```
// separate recv buffer
comm_world.allreduce(mpl::plus<float>(), proc_data,reduce_data);
// in place
comm_world.allreduce(mpl::plus<float>(), proc_data);
```

Note the parentheses after the operator. Also note that the operator comes first, not last, as in the C API.

Available: `max`, `min`, `plus`, `multiplies`, `logical_and`, `logical_or`, `logical_xor`, `bit_and`, `bit_or`, `bit_xor`.

In our code we see this structure: first the norm of the local part is computed, using the `l2norm` method on the local `bordered_array`; then this result is reduced by a single MPI call.

```
// diff2d/lib/dist.cpp
template< typename real >
real distributed_array<real>::l2norm() {
  real local_norm = subdomain->l2norm();
  local_norm *= local_norm;
  real global_norm;
  comm.allreduce( mpl::plus<real>(),local_norm,global_norm);
  return std::sqrt(global_norm);
};
```

The arguments of the `allreduce` call are the reduction operator, the send buffer, and receive buffer. Since this is a method of the `comm` object, that determines the processes involved. Other overloads of this call can deal with nonscalar buffers; see section 22.5.4.

22.3.4 ▪ Gather/scatter collectives

Gather/scatter routines are not used in our example application; we present them here only for future reference of the reader.

Gathering (by `communicator::gather`)
or scattering (by `communicator::scatter`)
a single scalar takes a scalar argument and a raw array:

```
vector<float> v;
float x;
comm_world.scatter(0, v.data(), x);
```

If more than a single scalar is gathered, or scattered into, it becomes necessary to specify a layout:

```
vector<float> vrecv(2),vsend(2*nprocs);
```

```
mpl::contiguous_layout<float> twonums(2);
comm_world.scatter
  (0, vsend.data(),twonums, vrecv.data(),twonums );
```

Logically speaking, on every nonroot process, the gather call only has a send buffer. MPL supports this by having two variants that only specify the send data.

```
if (procno==root) {
  vector<int> size_buffer(nprocs);
  comm_world.gather
    (
     root,my_number_of_elements,size_buffer.data()
     );
} else {
  /*
  * If you are not the root, do versions with only send buffers
  */
  comm_world.gather
    ( root,my_number_of_elements );
```

In the examples above we always had separate send and receive buffers. Sometimes it makes sense to put the receive data in the send buffer. For this, MPI has an "in-place" mode, which in MPL is indicated by omitting the mention of the separate receive buffer.

The in-place variant is activated by specifying only one instead of two buffer arguments:

```
// separate recv buffer
comm_world.allreduce(mpl::plus<float>(), proc_data,reduce_data);
// in place
comm_world.allreduce(mpl::plus<float>(), proc_data);
```

Reducing a buffer requires specification of a `contiguous_layout`:

```
// collectbuffer.cxx
vector<float> rank2p2p1{ 2*xrank,2*xrank+1 },reduce2p2p1{0,0};
mpl::contiguous_layout<float> two_floats(rank2p2p1.size());
comm_world.allreduce
  (mpl::plus<float>(), rank2p2p1.data(),reduce2p2p1.data(),two_floats);
if ( iprint )
  cout << "Got: " << reduce2p2p1.at(0) << ","
       << reduce2p2p1.at(1) << endl;
```

Note that the buffers are of type `T *`, so it is necessary to take the `data()` of any `std::vector` and such.

22.3.5 ▪ Reduction in the example application

The computation of the `l2norm` shows a common idiom: we compute the norm on the processor subdomain by other means, and then only use the MPI reduce call to reduce these subresults:

```
// diff2d/lib/dist.cpp
template< typename real >
real distributed_array<real>::l2norm() {
  real local_norm = subdomain->l2norm();
  local_norm *= local_norm;
  real global_norm;
  comm.allreduce( mpl::plus<real>(),local_norm,global_norm);
```

```
  return std::sqrt(global_norm);
};
```

22.4 ▪ Communicators

MPI organizes its processes in *communicators*, in which each process has a rank. When an MPI program starts, there is a "world" communicator given, which comprises all available processes.

The naive way of declaring a communicator would be

```
// commrank.cxx
mpl::communicator comm_world =
  mpl::environment::comm_world();
```

calling the predefined environment method `comm_world`.

However, if the variable will always correspond to the world communicator, it is better to make it `const` and declare it to be a reference:

```
const mpl::communicator &comm_world =
  mpl::environment::comm_world();
```

In a communicator each process has a "rank" which is purely a logical entity: it is not connected to a process ID, and it also does not imply anything about process placement on the cores of a processor or the processor nodes in a cluster.

The rank of a process and the size of a communicator are both methods of the `communicator` class:

```
const mpl::communicator &comm_world =
  mpl::environment::comm_world();
int procid = comm_world.rank();
int nprocs = comm_world.size();
```

However, in our application of a PDE on a two-dimensional domain we can actually employ two-dimensional indexing of the processes; see section 22.4.1.

22.4.1 ▪ Cartesian grid

As part of our `distributed_array` structure, we need to store communication information. The data members are

```
// diff2d/lib/dist.hpp
const mpl::cartesian_communicator& comm;
const int rank;
mpl::cartesian_communicator::dimensions dimensions;
//! coordinate of this processor
mpl::cartesian_communicator::vector coord;
```

These are constructed as follows:

First we create the Cartesian process structure. The routine `dims_create` computes a brick with minimal surface for the given number of processes. For example, 6 processes are arranged two-dimensionally as $6 = 3 \times 2$; 18 processes are arranged two-dimensionally as $18 = 6 \times 3$, or three-dimensionally as $18 = 3 \times 3 \times 2$.

The `cartesian_communicator` constructor then takes this to make a communicator where the processes have multidimensional coordinates, rather than only a linear rank:

```
// diff2d/mpl/diff2d.cpp
mpl::cartesian_communicator::dimensions brick(2);
brick = mpl::dims_create(nprocs,brick);
mpl::cartesian_communicator cart_comm( comm_world,brick );
```

In this structure we can determine the neighbors of each process by the `shift` method. For a given direction it yields the processes sending to and receiving from the calling process:

```
// diff2d/lib/dist.cpp
template< typename real >
void distributed_array<real>::set_neighbors( bool trace ) {
  mpl::shift_ranks shifted = comm.shift
    ( /* dim: */ 0,/* increasing: */ 1 );
  neighbors['S'] =
    [shifted] () { auto v = shifted.destination;
                   return (v<0 ? mpl::proc_null : v); }();
  neighbors['N'] =
    [shifted] () { auto v = shifted.source;
                   return (v<0 ? mpl::proc_null : v); }();
  shifted = comm.shift
    ( /* dim: */ 1,/* increasing: */ 1 );
  neighbors['E'] =
    [shifted] () { auto v = shifted.destination;
                   return (v<0 ? mpl::proc_null : v); }();
  neighbors['W'] =
    [shifted] () { auto v = shifted.source;
                   return (v<0 ? mpl::proc_null : v); }();
```

22.5 ▪ Point-to-point communication

The third, and most complicated, operation in our application is the stencil evaluation. As with the norm calculation this is largely based on the corresponding sequential operation on the subdomain of each process. However, Figure 22.5 shows how the combination of the "5-point stencil" and the two-dimensional processor grid means that each processor communicates with its four neighbors in NSEW directions. Organizing the processes in a grid is discussed in section 22.4.1; here we focus on the transfer of data between them. In MPI this is realized by having matched send/receive pairs.

22.5.1 ▪ Two-sided communication

In our example application, each process communicates with its four neighbors through "point-to-point" communication calls. While remote memory access (RMA) type communication exists in MPI, mostly "two-sided" communication is used, where the communicating processes issue matching send and receive calls. Both the sender and the receiver specify

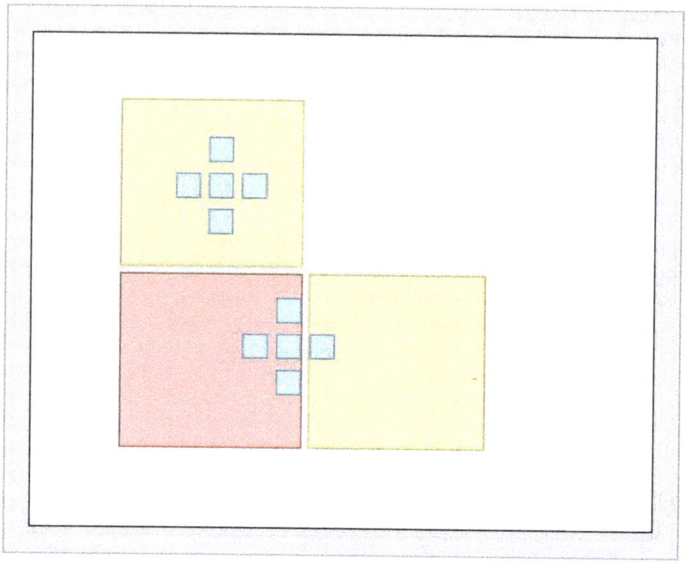

Figure 22.5. *A difference stencil applied to a two-dimensional square domain, distributed over processors. A cross-processor connection is indicated*

- a buffer for the data to be sent/received and a description of its contents. This buffer is created by ordinary C++ allocation mechanisms; we will go into the "description" aspect below. Furthermore,
- the target and source process rank, respectively; and
- an optional tag to disambiguate messages in some contexts.

We start with the case of sending a scalar, although this does not appear in our example application.

In its scalar form, send and receive calls specify the data to be communicated and the source and target processes. MPL uses a default value for the tag, and it can deduce the type of the buffer. Sending a scalar becomes

```
// sendscalar.cxx
if (comm_world.rank()==0) {
  double pi=3.14;
  comm_world.send(pi, 1);  // send to rank 1
  cout << "sent: " << pi << '\n';
} else if (comm_world.rank()==1) {
  double pi=0;
  comm_world.recv(pi, 0);  // receive from rank 0
  cout << "got : " << pi << '\n';
}
```

For sending contiguous data from a container such as `std::vector` we use the raw pointer provided by the `data` method, as well as a layout object (layouts are described in section 22.5.4) that describes what that pointer points to.

Sending vector data uses a pointer and a layout:

```
// sendbuffer.cxx
std::vector<double> v(8);
mpl::contiguous_layout<double> v_layout(v.size());
  comm_world.send(v.data(), v_layout, 1);  // send to rank 1
  comm_world.recv(v.data(), v_layout, 0);  // receive from rank 0
```

22.5.2 ▪ Example: Ping-pong

Let's look at an example of point-to-point operations.

A simple scenario for information exchange between just two processes is the *ping-pong*: process A sends data to process B, which sends data back to A. This is not an operation that is particularly relevant to applications, although it is often used as a benchmark: half the time of a ping-pong is the time for a single sent message. (Why can you generally not time a single message?) Here we discuss it to explain basic ideas.

This means that process A executes the code

```
MPI_Send( /* to: */ B ..... );
MPI_Recv( /* from: */ B ... );
```

while process B executes

```
MPI_Recv( /* from: */ A ... );
MPI_Send( /* to: */ A ..... );
```

Since we are programming in SPMD mode, this means our program looks like

```
if ( /* I am process A */ ) {
  MPI_Send( /* to: */ B ..... );
  MPI_Recv( /* from: */ B ... );
} else if ( /* I am process B */ ) {
  MPI_Recv( /* from: */ A ... );
  MPI_Send( /* to: */ A ..... );
}
```

22.5.3 ▪ Point-to-point operations in the example application

In our example application, the sends and receives are paired up: there is an exchange of data between each pair of processes. For such cases there is a "send-receive" call, which has the advantage of being deadlock-free; deadlocks are among the hazards of the send and receive calls mentioned above.

The send-recv call in MPL has the same possibilities for specifying the send and receive buffer as the separate send and receive calls: scalar, layout, iterator. However, out of the nine conceivably possible routine signatures, only the versions are available where the send and receive buffers are specified the same way. Also, the send and receive tags need to be specified; they do not have default values.

```
// sendrecv.cxx
mpl::tag_t t0(0);
comm_world.sendrecv
  ( mydata,sendto,t0,
    leftdata,recvfrom,t0 );
```

```
// sendrecvarray.cxx
mpl::tag_t t0(0);
mpl::contiguous_layout<double> twofloats(2)
    ;
comm_world.sendrecv
  ( mydata,twofloats,sendto,t0,
    leftdata,twofloats,recvfrom,t0 );
```

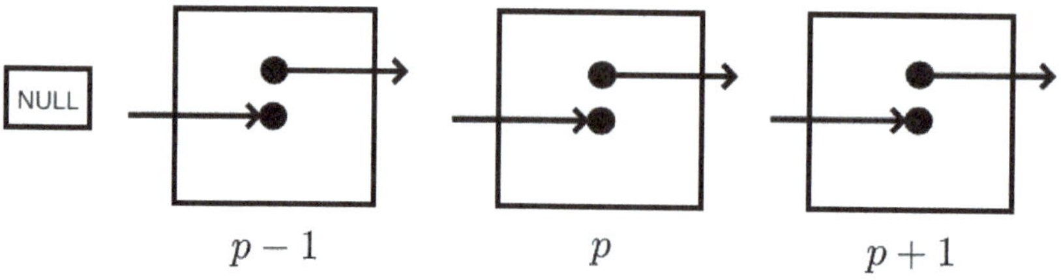

Figure 22.6. *A sendrecv operation to the right / from the left*

There are multiple ways to send messages between processes. Because of the regularity of this problem we use a sequence of four "send-recv" calls. In each of these, the processes send in one compass direction, while simultaneously receiving from the opposite direction; see Figure 22.6.

```
// diff2d/lib/dist.cpp
template< typename real >
void distributed_array<real>::halo_exchange
    ( bordered_array_base<real>& data, bool trace ) {
  for ( auto [f,t] : { make_pair('W','E'),{'E','W'},{'N','S'},{'S','N'} } ) {
    // inner edge to send in the 'to' direction
    auto [snd_ptr,snd_layout] = get_edge(data,t);
    // halo region to receive from the 'from' direction
    auto [rcv_ptr,rcv_layout] = get_halo(data,f);
    // neighbor ranks
    auto from = neighbors[f], to = neighbors[t];
    mpl::tag_t t0{0};
    comm.sendrecv
      ( snd_ptr,*snd_layout,to,  t0,
        rcv_ptr,*rcv_layout,from,t0);
  }
};
```

In this example of a 2D grid, with a 2D processor grid, it makes sense to orchestrate the sends and receives like this. On irregular grids, however, this is somewhere between difficult and impossible. For such cases you would use *nonblocking communication.*

22.5.4 ▪ Buffers and layouts

In the reduction call of section 22.3 the data was a single scalar. In the send-receive call in the previous section the data involved comprises an array. This means we now specify a pointer to the first data element, and a description of the array, called a "layout" in MPL terms.

For message in north and south directions the buffers are contiguous:

```
// diff2d/lib/dist.cpp
layout = unique_ptr<mpl::layout<real>>
  ( make_unique<mpl::contiguous_layout<real>>(n) );
```

For messages in east and west directions, the data is strided:

```
// diff2d/lib/dist.cpp
layout = unique_ptr<mpl::layout<real>>
  ( make_unique<mpl::strided_vector_layout<real>>(m,1,n+2*b) );
```

where the three parameters of the strided layout are

- `m`: how many blocks, or here: how many points in the boundary exchanged;
- `1`: blocksize, or here: how many boundary points in each line;
- `n+2*b`: displacement between blocks, or here: the length of a subdomain line, including the left and right boundaries.

There are other layout types corresponding to other MPI derived datatypes. We will not discuss those here.

22.6 ▪ Background

22.6.1 ▪ MPI software

The first thing to know is that MPI is strictly a library, and not a language extension such as OpenMP or CUDA. Thus it can be compiled with any C, C++, or Fortran compiler by adding the right include and library flags. MPI implementations typically come with scripts called `mpicc`, `mpicxx`, and `mpif90` for those three languages, respectively, that take care of all the needed commandline flags.

The MPI standard only defines interfaces to C and Fortran, so interfaces to MPI from other languages such as Julia, Java, Python are nonstandard, often developed by third parties. Using MPI from C++ can be done in two ways. One can use the C interfaces; however, these feel clumsy and unidiomatic to a C++ programmer. One can also use a third-party developed, more idiomatic, C++ interface to the C version of MPI. In this book we follow the second approach, and we use the MPL interface to MPI [43].

To compile MPL programs, add the line

```
#include <mpl/mpl.hpp>
```

to your file. You need to add a path to your compile line:

```
mpicxx -o mpiprog -I${MPL_LOCATION}/include mympiprog.cpp
```

where `MPL_LOCATION` is system-dependent.

In CMake, MPL can be found:

```
find_package( mpl )
// this defines the target: mpl::mpl
```

22.6.2 ▪ Program structure

One difference between Message Passing Library (MPL) and the C interface to MPI is that there are no explicit initialize/finalize calls. Instead, the initialization is performed implicitly at the first call that requires it. Finalization is mostly handled through the C++ RAII mechanism.

22.6.3 ▪ More about point-to-point communication

In the discussion so far we have made pointwise communication seem very deterministic. That is a distortion of the truth, but defensible in the context of the example application. In general it is possible to introduce some indeterminacy by using "wildcards" in the receive call. MPI then provides a "status" object in the receive call that can be used to query the wildcarded values.

Also, there are so-called "nonblocking" routines which can be described as deferred communication. They come with "wait" routines that can query whether the communication has taken place. In less regular applications than we have described here, nonblocking routines are the best way to prevent deadlock and optimize network utilization.

22.7 ▪ CMake integration

While many MPI implementations have a *.pc* file, it's better to use the *FindMPI* module. This package defines a number of variables that can be used to query the MPI found. Sometimes it's necessary to set the *MPI_HOME* environment variable to aid in discovery of the MPI package:

```
cmake_minimum_required( VERSION 3.13 )
project( cxxprogram VERSION 1.0 )

add_executable( ${PROJECT_NAME} ${PROJECT_NAME}.cxx )
find_package( MPI )
target_include_directories(
        ${PROJECT_NAME} PUBLIC
        ${MPI_C_INCLUDE_DIRS} ${CMAKE_CURRENT_SOURCE_DIR} )
target_link_libraries(
        ${PROJECT_NAME} PUBLIC
        ${MPI_C_LIBRARIES} )

install( TARGETS ${PROJECT_NAME} DESTINATION . )
```

The *MPL* package also uses `find_package`:

```
find_package( mpl REQUIRED )
add_executable( ${PROJECT_NAME} )
target_sources( ${PROJECT_NAME} PRIVATE ${PROJECT_NAME}.cxx )
target_include_directories(
        ${PROJECT_NAME} PUBLIC
        mpl::mpl )
target_link_libraries(
        ${PROJECT_NAME} PUBLIC
        mpl::mpl )
```

Part IV

Program Development

We all like our programs to be totally perfect: to compute the right result or display the right behavior given the inputs, and never to derail. Unfortunately this rarely happens.

Edsger Dijkstra pointed out the limitations of testing in his Turing award lecture [16]:

> Today a usual technique is to make a program and then to test it. But program testing can be a very effective way to show the presence of bugs, but is hopelessly inadequate for showing their absence. [*cue laughter*]

Instead he favored a systematic approach to program construction:

> The only effective way to raise the confidence level of a program significantly is to give a convincing proof of its correctness. But one should not first make the program and then prove its correctness, because then the requirement of providing the proof would only increase the poor programmer's burden. On the contrary: the programmer should let correctness proof and program grow hand in hand.

We will cover both sides of this issue.

- First of all you need to go about writing code in a systematic manner that most likely leads to correct code. We cover that in Chapters 23 and 24.
- Writing a program that is proved correct is briefly discussed in Chapter 25.
- Next, you can test your program before putting it in production. This will be the subject of Chapter 26.
- Your program needs to be able to deal with errors during runtime; see Chapter 27.
- External ways of debugging your program are covered in Chapter 28 about interactive debugging, and Chapter 29 about memory tools.

Chapter 23

Programming guidelines

C++ is a language with at least a 40-year history behind it, and through that history it has probably evolved more than many other languages of such vintage. This has led to the situation that you can find in books and online materials several different coding styles, some of which are frowned upon these days.

23.1 ▪ C-style constructs to leave behind

Since C++ is close to a superset of C, there are many C constructs that can, but should not, be used. Here is a short inventory:

- C-style strings are a major source of security vulnerabilities. C++, especially modern standards, has many better options. However, these are outside the scope of a scientific computing book.
- Memory allocation with `malloc` should not be used. Allocation with `new` should only be used judiciously; see section 14.3.
- Parameter passing using the ampersand *address operator* for taking addresses should be replaced by using references.
- Automatic arrays (like `int a[5]`) should be replaced by `std::array`; see section 4.3.
- Returning error codes is largely obviated by mechanisms such as `std::optional` (section 11.1). See also Chapter 27 about error handling, including exceptions.
- Opaque handles, to pass context to a callback, are replaced by the capture in lambda expressions; section 6.3.2.1.
- The C `rand.h` random functions should be replaced by the `random` library; see Chapter 9.

Here are some remarks on how you "should" code.

23.2 ▪ Attempts to leave the past behind: Core Guidelines

The C++ standards committee is loath to introduce incompatibilities, which means that you can still write code in ways you had better not. Teaching materials, including this book, deal with this by teaching the better ways, and not mentioning the bad old ways.

However, in recent years some more systematic attempts have been made to clean up the language. Foremost among these is the creation of a set of *Core Guidelines*: a set of best practice rules for how to code and how not to. These are even supported by the *GSL* library [32].

In this book we will mention specific Core Guidelines where appropriate:

- Guideline C.2, p. 34
- Guideline Enum.3, p. 20
- Guideline ES.50, p. 134
- Guideline F.20, p. 110
- Guideline F.21, p. 33
- Guideline R.14, p. 43
- Guideline SF.5, p. 234
- Guideline SF.7, p. 242
- Guideline SF.8, p. 236

23.3 ▪ Brief history of C++ standards

Starting in 2011, a new C++ standard has come out every three years. However, the fact that a standard is defined does not mean that all these features are available in every compiler. Also, compilers have a default standard that they accept, and if you use code of a newer standard, you explicitly have to tell the compiler to use that, for instance, as

```
g++ -std=c++23
```

To understand how the current state of C++ came about, you should know the bare basics of the history of C++ standards:

- The oldest viable standard is the C++98 standard.
- "Modern C++" starts with the C++11 standard, subsequently refined in C++14 and C++17.
- Sometimes referred to as "postmodern C++," C++20 and C++23 add several constructs that are useful for scientific computing—and some that are not so much. We cover these recent standards in this book, even looking forward to C++26, which, however, has not yet been ratified.

Chapter 24

Program structuring

It should be clear that it is bad style to write a program that consists of a single file with all of its code in the `main` function. While it is possible that such a program gives the correct output, it does not convince the reader that it does so. Also, the chances of it actually giving the right output are smaller than if the code were written in a structured manner.

This chapter discusses several ways of structuring your code, increasing the likelihood that it is correct, and making it more maintainable for the future.

24.1 ▪ Separate compilation and include files

As projects grow, it is common practice to split the program source over multiple files and compile them separately:

```
g++ -c file1.cpp
g++ -c file2.cpp
g++ -o myprogram file1.o file2.o
```

(For a discussion of compiling and linking, see section 36.5.) This structure inevitably leads to a situation with one file that defines a function or class, and some other one that uses it. While the file that contains the definition can be compiled by itself, the file using it needs to know about the definition to be compilable. The usual solution is to have a *header file*, containing the function or class declaration. (See section 24.2 for the more modern mechanisms of modules.)

Just to establish terminology, a *declaration* is what is also called a *signature* or *prototype* or *header*:

```
float f(char,int);
class g {private int i; public float f(char,int); };
```

that is, a description of input and return types for functions, or member data and methods for classes, including qualifiers such as `const`. On the other hand, a *definition* spells out all of this and gives the implementation code.

Using a header file with function declarations:

Header file contains only declaration:

```
// file: def.h
int tester(float);
```

The header file gets included twice:

Definitions file:

```
// compile/testerdef.cpp
#include "def.h"
int tester(float x) {
  .....
}
```

Main program:

```
// compile/testermain.cpp
#include "def.h"
int main() {
  int t = tester(...);
  return 0;
}
```

What happens in both cases if you leave out the #include "def.h"?

Having a header file is an important safety measure: it allows the compiler to check that use and definition of a class or function are compatible.

It is necessary to include the header file in the file that uses the function or class. It is not strictly necessary to include it in the definitions file, but doing so means that you catch potential errors, as argued by C++ Core Guidelines [12, SF.5].

The include file mechanism uses the C preprocessor (CPP) (section 36.3), which is external to the language definition. In section 24.2 we'll see the C++20 module mechanism, which is a native part of the C++ language.

24.1.1 ▪ The include mechanism

While you can include any kind of text file, the most common use of the preprocessor is to include a *header file* at the start of your source using a CPP #include directive; see section 36.3.1.

There are two kinds of includes:

1. The file name can be included in angle brackets,

   ```
   #include <vector>
   ```
   which is typically used for system headers that are part of the compiler infrastructure.

2. The name can also be in double quotes,

   ```
   #include "somelib.h"
   ```
   which is typically used for header files that are part of your code, or of libraries installed on your system.

24.1.2 ▪ Search paths

System headers can usually be found by the compiler because they are in some standard location. Including other files may require additional action by you. If you write

```
#include "foo.h"
```

the compiler only looks for that file in the current directory where you are compiling. So the question is how to tell the compiler to look for this file elsewhere.

If the include file is part of a library that you have downloaded and installed yourself, say it is in

```
/home/yourname/mylibrary/include/foo.h
```

then you could of course spell out the location:

```
#include "/home/yourname/mylibrary/include/foo.h"
```

However, that does not make your code very portable to other systems and other users. So how do you make

```
#include "foo.h"
```

be understood on any system?

The answer is that you can give your compiler one or more *include paths*. This is done with the `-I` flag:

```
icpc -c yourprogram.cpp -I/home/yourname/mylibrary/include
```

You can specify more than one such flag, and the compiler will try to find the `foo.h` file in all of them.

Are you now thinking that you have to type that path every time you compile? This is the time to learn about the utility *CMake*; see Chapter 37.

Remark. *Some libraries put headers in a subdirectory of the* `include` *directory. Your source would then include the header with the last level of the include path:*

```
// Eigen library:
#include "Eigen/Core"
// fmtlib
#include <fmt/format.h>
```

This mechanism is used to prevent name collisions, such as having two header files named `format.h`.

24.1.3 ▪ Include guards

It is easy to wind up including a file such as `iostream` more than once if it is included in multiple header files. This adds to your compilation time, or may lead to subtle problems. A header file may even circularly include itself. To prevent this, header files often have what is informally known as a *header guard*.

Header file tests if it has already been included:

```
// this is foo.h
#ifndef FOO_H
#define FOO_H

// the things that you want to include

#endif
```

This prevents double or recursive inclusion.

Now the file will effectively be included only once: the first time it is processed in full and the `FOO_H` macro is defined; the second time the `#ifndef` test fails and the file content after the test is skipped.

Many compilers support the pragma #pragma once that has the same effect:

```
// this is foo.h
#pragma once

// the things you want to include only once
```

However, this is not standardized, and the precise meaning is unclear (what if this is placed halfway a file?) so C++ Core Guidelines [12, SF.8] recommends the explicit guards.

24.1.4 ▪ Header files for classes

You can separate a class declaration from its definition. You can then put the declaration in a header file that you include in every file where a class is used, while the definitions get compiled only once, and linked in when the executable of your program is built, or put in a library.

Header file:

```
// proto/classheader.hpp
class something {
private:
  int i;
public:
  double dosomething( int i, char c ) const;
};
```

Implementation file:

```
// proto/classimpl.cpp
#include "classheader.hpp"
double something::dosomething(int i,char c) const {
  return 1.5d;
}
```

There are two things to remark on here:

1. The header contains not only the class name, and function member names, but also names of data members, including the private ones!
2. Function member definitions have their name prefixed with the class name and a double colon. Also, they repeat qualifiers such as `const`.

Remarks.

1. *Splitting definitions over header/implementation files can be tricky with templated classes; see section 12.2.3.*
2. *To avoid such problems, some libraries are realized as* header-only library*: all definitions are in header files that get included in their totality. This approach can give long compilation times.*

24.2 ▪ Modules

The C++20 standard is taking a different approach to header files through the introduction of *modules*. This largely dispenses with the need for header files included through the CPP. However, the CPP may still be needed for other purposes.

24.2.1 ▪ Program structure with modules

Using modules, the #include directive is no longer needed; instead, the `import` keyword indicates what module is to be used in a (sub)program:

```
// modulex/fgmain.cpp
import fg_module;
int main() {
  std::cout << "Hello world " << f(5) << '\n';
```

The module is usually in a different file. The module name does not derive from that file name; instead the `export` keyword, followed by `module`, defines the name of the module. This file can then have any number of functions; only the ones with the `export` keyword will be visible in a program that imports the module:

```
// modulex/fgmod.cpp
export module fg_module;

// internal function
int g( int i ) { return i/2; };

// exported function
export int f( int i ) {
  return g(i+1);
};
```

24.2.2 ▪ Implementation and interface units

The above naive approach to modules has a problem when building your code: if your module is edited, both it and all files that use it need to be recompiled. In cases where the interface of the module (that is, the declarations of classes, functions, etc., defined in it) is left unchanged we can do better. Now we split the module in two:

1. First, an *interface module* that declares the module name to be exported, as well as the declarations to be exported. This can be compiled separately, and this is enough to compile files that use it.

2. Second, an *implementation module* that contains the full definitions, without any statement about them being exported. If changes to this module do not involve any interfaces, only this module needs to be recompiled.

As an example, here is an interface module, which needs to be compiled first:

```
// modulex/implintface.cpp
export module module_with_intface;

// exported function
export int f( int i );
```

The actual definition of the function `f` is in the implementation module:

```
// modulex/implimpl.cpp
// implementation unit, nothing exported
module module_with_intface;
// function to be exported by the interface
int f( int i ) { return i/2; };
```

24.2.3 ▪ Partitions

A module can have a leveled structure by using names with a `modulename:partition` structure. This makes it possible to have separate

- interface partitions, which define the interface to the using program; and
- implementation partitions, which contain the code that needs to be kept from the user.

Here is an implementation partition; there is no `import` keyword because this functionality is internal:

```
// modulex/helperhelp.cpp
// implementation unit, nothing exported
module helper_module:helper;
// internal function
int g( int i ) { return i/2; };
```

Here is a file with an interface partition, which uses the internal function, and an exported function:

```
// modulex/helpermod.cpp
export module helper_module;
import :helper;

// exported function
export int f( int i ) {
  return g(i+1);
};
```

24.3 ▪ Namespaces

24.3.1 ▪ Solving name conflicts

You have probably many times used the *vector* class that implements dynamic arrays. But what if you are writing a geometry package containing a class for geometric vectors that you would like to call "vector"? Is there confusion with the vector class of the standard library? There would be if it weren't for the phenomenon *namespace*, which acts as as disambiguating prefix for classes, functions, and variables.

In a way you have already seen namespaces in action. After including the `vector` header, you write

```
std::vector<int> bunch_of_ints;
```

which gives you the `vector` class from the `std` namespace. Thus, the double colon separates a namespace and an identifier, whether that be a class, function, or variable name.

You can make your own namespaces, with the `namespace` keyword.

Introduce new namespace:

```
namespace geometry {
  // definitions
  class vector {
    // stuff
  };
```

To access a class defined in a namespace, you qualify the class name with the namespace.

Double-colon notation for namespace and type:

```
geometry::vector myobject();
```

or

```
using geometry::vector;
vector myobject();
```

or even

```
using namespace geometry;
vector myobject();
```

Some packages have a complicated namespace structure, so you may find yourself writing

```
namespace abc = space_a::space_b::space_c;
abc::func(x)
```

In the C++ standard library, having two levels is quite common.

24.3.2 ▪ Namespace header files

If your namespace is going to be used in more than one program, you want to have it in a separate source file, with an accompanying header file.

Suppose we have a `geometry` namespace containing a `vector`, in addition to the `vector` in the standard namespace:

```
// namespace/geo.cpp
#include <vector>
#include "geolib.hpp" // this contains the geometry namespace
int main() {
  // std vector of geom segments:
  std::vector<geometry::segment> segments;
  segments.push_back( geometry::segment( geometry::point(1,1),geometry::point(4,5) ) );
```

What would the implementation of this be?

The header file would contain the function and class headers, but now inside a named namespace:

```
// namespace/geolib.hpp
namespace geometry {
  class point {
  private:
    double xcoord,ycoord;
  public:
    point( double x,double y );
    double dx(point);
    double dy(point);
  };
  class segment {
  private:
    point from,to;
```

and the implementation file would have the implementations in a namespace of the same name:

```
// namespace/geolib.cpp
namespace geometry {
  point::point( double x,double y ) {
      xcoord = x; ycoord = y; };
  double point::dx( point other ) {
    return other.xcoord-xcoord; };
    /* ... */
  template< typename T >
  vector<T>::vector( std::string name,int size )
    : name_(name),std::vector<T>::vector(size) {};
}
```

Exercise 24.1. Add a `vector` class to the `geometry` namespace, which inherits from `std::vector`, and which makes the following code work:

```
// namespace/geo.cpp
  std::vector<geometry::vector<float>> vectors;
  vectors.push_back( geometry::vector<float>( "a", 5 ) );
  cout << fmt::format("First vector, \"{}\" has size {}\n",
                      vectors[0].name(),vectors[0].size());
```

24.3.3 ▪ Namespace versioning for libraries

As the introduction to this topic argued, namespaces are a good way to prevent name conflicts. This means that it's a good idea to create a namespace for all your routines. You see this design in almost all published C++ libraries.

Now consider this scenario:

1. You write a program that uses a certain library.
2. A new version of the library is released and installed on your system.
3. Your program, using shared/dynamic libraries, starts using this library, maybe even without you realizing it.

This means that the old and new libraries need to be compatible in several ways:

1. All the classes, functions, and data structures defined in the earlier version also need to be defined in the new. This is not a big problem: new library versions typically add functionality. However:
2. The data layout of the new version needs to be the same.

That second point is subtle. To illustrate, consider the library is upgraded:

First version:

```
namespace geometry {
  class vector {
    private:
    std::vector<float> data;
    std::string name;
  }
}
```

New version:

```
namespace geometry {
  class vector {
    private:
    std::vector<float> data;
    int id;
    std::string name;
  }
}
```

The problem is that your compiled program has explicit information where the class members are located in the class object. For instance, in the first version above, the `name` member may come 64 bytes from the start of the object; in the second version it will then be at 68 bytes from the start of the object.

By changing the structure of the objects, such byte offsets are no longer correct. This is called "application binary interface (ABI) breakage" and it leads to *undefined behavior*.

The library can prevent this by

```
namespace geometry {
  inline namespace v1.0 {
    class vector {
      private:
      std::vector<float> data;
      std::string name;
    }
  }
}
```

and updating the version number in future versions. A program using this library has to use explicitly the namespace version: `geometry::v1.0::vector`.

Example:

Namespace definition with versions:

```
// namespace/inline.cpp
namespace geometry {
  inline namespace v1 {
   class vector {
   public: float x,y;
   };
  }
  inline namespace v2 {
   class vector {
   public: float x,y,z;
   };
  }
}
```

Versioned use:

```
// namespace/inline.cpp
{
  using geometry::v1::vector;
  vector p; p.x = 1.f;
}
{
  using geometry::v2::vector;
  vector p; p.z = 1.f;
}
```

24.3.4 ▪ Best practices

In this book we advocated indicating the namespace of functions with a `using` statement:

```
#include <iostream>
using std::cout;
```

(The alternative being to write `std::cout` everywhere.)

It is also possible to use

```
#include <iostream>
using namespace std;
```

The problem with this is that it may make available unwanted functions. In the following example it leads to an incorrect code being compiled, and possibly executing with an erroneous result.

Illustrating the dangers of `using namespace std`:

This compiles, but should not:

```
// func/swapname.cpp
#include <iostream>
using namespace std;

def swop(int i,int j) {};

int main() {
  int i=1,j=2;
  swap(i,j);
  cout << i << '\n';
  return 0;
}
```

This gives an error:

```
// func/swapusing.cpp
#include <iostream>
using std::cout;

def swop(int i,int j) {};

int main() {
  int i=1,j=2;
  swap(i,j);
  cout << i << '\n';
  return 0;
}
```

Even if you write `using namespace`, you should only do this in a source file, never in a header file. Anyone using the header would have no idea what functions are suddenly defined; see C++ Core Guidelines [12, SF.7].

Chapter 25

Mathematical approaches to program development

It is possible to treat programs as mathematical objects and, for instance, prove their correctness. This is a big topic, and this is not the kind of book to do full justice to it. Instead, we offer two short sections.

First, we point out how codes can express mathematical statements, and therefore should be written to resemble the mathematics. We do this by considering quantors. Second, we show with a simple example how algorithms can be derived in a way to be provably correct.

25.1 ▪ Quantification

Quite often, algorithms can be expressed mathematically. In that case you should make your program look like the mathematics. Here we consider one example, pointing out the connection between for loops and mathematical *quantors*.

25.1.1 ▪ "For all" quantor

Consider a simple example: testing if a number is prime. The predicate "`isprime`" can be expressed as

$$\text{isprime}(n) \equiv \forall_{2\leq f<n}\colon \neg\,\text{divides}(f,n)$$

You see that proving the original `isprime` predicate for some value n now involves

1. a quantor over a new variable f—we call this a "bound variable";
2. a new predicate `divides` that involves the original variable n and the variable f that is bound by the quantor.

We now spell out the "for all" quantor iteratively as a loop where each iteration needs to yield true. That is, we do an "and" reduction on some iteration-dependent result:

$$\text{isprime}(n) \equiv \neg\,\text{divides}(2,n) \wedge \ldots \wedge \neg\,\text{divides}(n-1,n)$$

This sequence of "and" conjunctions can be programmed:

```
for (int f=2; f<n; f++)
  isprime = isprime && not divides(f,p)
```

You notice that the loop variable is the bound variable f that was introduced by the quantor.

Now our only worry is how to initialize *isprime*. The initial value corresponds to an "and" conjunction over an empty set, which is true, so

```
bool isprime{true};
for (int f=2; f<n; f++)
  isprime = isprime && not divides(f,p)
```

Exercise 25.1. Now that you have a loop that computes the right thing you can start worrying about performance. Can the loop be terminated prematurely in some cases? How would you program that?

25.1.2 ▪ "There is" quantor

We could also have expressed primeness as

$$\text{isprime}(n) \equiv \neg\exists_{2\le f<n} \colon \text{divides}(f,n)$$

To get a pure quantor, and not a negated one, we write

$$\text{isnotprime}(n) \equiv \exists_{2\le f<n} \colon \text{divides}(f,n)$$

Spelling out the "there is" quantor as

$$\text{isnotprime}(n) \equiv \text{divides}(2,n) \vee \ldots \vee \text{divides}(n-1,n)$$

we see that we need a loop where we test if any iteration satisfies a predicate. That is, we do an "or" reduction on the results of each iteration. As before, the loop variable is the variable introduced by the quantor:

```
for (int f=2; f<n; f++)
  isnotprime = isnotprime or divides(f,p)
bool isprime = not isnotprime;
```

Also as before, we take care to initialize the reduction variable correctly. Applying existence quantification $\exists_{s\in S} P(s)$ over an empty set S is `false`, so

```
bool isnotprime{false};
for (int f=2; f<n; f++)
  isnotprime = isnotprime or divides(f,p)
bool isprime = not isnotprime;
```

Exercise 25.2. Same question as for the "for all" quantor: can this loop be terminated prematurely? How would you code that?

25.1.3 ▪ Quantors through ranges

We have established the following correspondences to algorithms (section 7.3.1):

$\forall$ `all_of`
$\exists$ `any_of`

Instead of using loops, we are now going to express the quantors through ranges. (For ranges, see section 7.1.) Let S be a range and P a predicate; then

$$\forall_{n\in S} \colon P(n)$$

can be implemented as

```
all_of( S,[] { auto n } -> bool { return P(n); } );
```

Likewise,

$$\exists_{n\in S}\colon P(n)$$

can be implemented as

```
any_of( S,[] { auto n } -> bool { return P(n); } );
```

where the initial condition is automatically taken care of.

We now express the statement

$$\forall_n\colon \exists_m\colon m > n$$

through C++ ranges. Of course we have to limit the "all integers" clause; we use `iota(1,)` with some final value *n*.

Express quantors in code:

```
// primes/rangepred.cpp
all_of( rng::views::iota(1,20),
        [] ( auto n ) -> bool {
          return any_of( rng::views::iota(1),
                         [n] ( auto m ) -> bool {
                           if (m>n) {
```

Ranging over more complicated sets

$$\forall_{n\in S,Q(n)}\colon P(n)$$

can be implemented by piping the quantor through a `filter`:

```
all_of( S | filter( [] (auto n) -> bool { return Q(n) } ),
        [] { auto n } -> bool { return P(n); } );
```

Exercise 25.3. Write range-based code that proves

$$\forall_n\colon \exists_{m>n}\colon \text{even}(m)$$

The previous examples were very simple and served only to illustrate the principle of translating quantified statements into range algorithms. Let's now do some real math.

25.1.4 ▪ Example: Prime numbers

As an example of this mathematical approach to programming we will do a small exercise about prime numbers. As preparation you have to have a way of generating prime numbers.

Exercise 25.4.

- Write a class `primegenerator` that contains methods `number_of_primes_found` and `nextprime`.
- Also write a function `isprime` that does not need to be in the class.

Your main program should look as follows:

```
// primes/6primesbyclass.cpp
cin >> nprimes;
primegenerator sequence;
while (sequence.number_of_primes_found()<nprimes) {
  int number = sequence.nextprime();
  cout << "Number " << number << " is prime" << '\n';
}
```

Now we can start "proving" facts over prime numbers, meaning: evaluate a predicate for a number of test values. For instance, the *Goldbach conjecture* says that every even number $2n$ (starting at 4), is the sum of two primes $p+q$:

$$2n = p + q.$$

Exercise 25.5. Write a program to test the Goldbach conjecture for the even numbers up to a bound that you read in.

First formulate the quantor structure of this statement, then translate that top-down to code, using the generator you developed above:

1. Make an outer loop over the even numbers e.
2. For each e, generate all primes p.
3. From $p+q=e$, it follows that $q=e-p$ is prime; test if that q is prime.

For each even number `e` then print `e,p,q`, for instance:

```
The number 10 is 3+7
```

If multiple possibilities exist, only print the first one you find.

An interesting corollary of the Goldbach conjecture is that each prime (start at 5) is equidistant between two other primes.

Equivalently to the Goldbach statement above, every number n is equidistant from two primes:

$$n = \frac{p+q}{2} \qquad \text{or} \qquad q - n = n - p.$$

In particular this holds for each prime number:

$$\forall_{r \text{ prime}} \exists_{p,q \text{ prime}} : r = (p+q)/2 \text{ is prime.}$$

We now have the statement that each prime number is the average of two other prime numbers.

Exercise 25.6.

Write a program that tests this. You need at least one loop that tests all primes r; for each r you then need to find the primes p,q that are equidistant to it.

Use your prime generator. Do you use two generators for this, or is one enough? Do you need three, for p,q,r?

For each r value, when the program finds the p, q values, print the p, q, r triple and move on to the next r.

Exercise 25.7. Rewrite Exercise 25.6, using only range expressions, and no loops.

25.2 ▪ Programs correct by construction

We conclude with a section about how to derive algorithms to be correct by construction [9].

Many linear algebra algorithms are loop-based, and the foundation to a correctness proof is the derivation of a *loop invariant*: a predicate that is inductively shown to be true in each loop iteration, thereby guaranteeing the correctness of the whole algorithm. This is of course related to the mathematical notion of proving by induction.

However, we do not write code and subsequently prove an invariant on it; we derive the invariant mathematically, and then write code that satisfies it.

By way of illustration we derive two algorithms for the matrix-vector product. Of course you know the standard algorithm: each component of the output is the inner product of a matrix-row and the input vector. Do you know a second algorithm?

25.2.1 ▪ Derivation of the common algorithm

As a preliminary to deriving a loop invariant, we first consider the result of the computation in a partitioned form.

Original statement:

$$y = Ax.$$

Partitioned:

$$\begin{pmatrix} y_T \\ y_B \end{pmatrix} = \begin{pmatrix} A_T \\ A_B \end{pmatrix} \begin{pmatrix} x \end{pmatrix}.$$

Two equations:

$$\begin{cases} y_T = A_T x, \\ y_B = A_B x. \end{cases}$$

The key to the inductive proof is to take this partitioned form and assume that it is only partly satisfied.

In the partitioned form we now assume that only the first equation,

$$y_T = A_T x,$$

is satisfied.

Now we are getting close to an inductive proof: we consider the algorithm as aimed at increasing the size of the block for which the predicate is true. If this block equals the size of the problem, we have correctness of the full result.

Given:

$$\begin{pmatrix} y_T \\ y_B \end{pmatrix} = \begin{pmatrix} A_T \\ A_B \end{pmatrix} (x) \,.$$

The algorithm:

While T is not the whole system
  Predicate: $y_T = A_T x$ true
  Update: grow T block by one
  Predicate: $y_T = A_T x$ true for new/bigger T block

Note initial and final conditions.

Now we consider the inductive step, where the invariant holds at the start and end of an iteration. By the end of the iteration it should hold for one more row than at the start.

The steps are the following:

1. At the start of an iteration we have the state

$$\begin{pmatrix} y_T \\ y_B \end{pmatrix} = \begin{pmatrix} A_T \\ A_B \end{pmatrix} (x) \,,$$

   where only the T part is satisfied.

2. We split one row off the B part:

$$\left(\begin{array}{c} y_1 \\ \hline y_2 \\ y_3 \end{array}\right) = \left(\begin{array}{c} A_1 \\ \hline A_2 \\ A_3 \end{array}\right) (x) \,.$$

3. The update step is done, in a manner specified later.

4. We merge row 2 into the T part:

$$\left(\begin{array}{c} y_1 \\ y_2 \\ \hline y_3 \end{array}\right) = \left(\begin{array}{c} A_1 \\ A_2 \\ \hline A_3 \end{array}\right) (x) \,.$$

5. We "unsplit" this,

$$\begin{pmatrix} y_T \\ y_B \end{pmatrix} = \begin{pmatrix} A_T \\ A_B \end{pmatrix} (x) \,,$$

   so that the initial predicate holds again at the end of an iteration.

Comparing the T blocks in item 2 versus 4 gives us the extra predicate that was made to be satisfied by the iteration we consider:

Before the update:

$$\begin{pmatrix} y_1 \\ \hline \\ y_2 \\ y_3 \end{pmatrix} = \begin{pmatrix} A_1 \\ \hline \\ A_2 \\ A_3 \end{pmatrix} (x)$$

so

$$y_1 = A_1 x.$$

Then the update step, and

After:

$$\begin{pmatrix} y_1 \\ y_2 \\ \hline \\ y_3 \end{pmatrix} = \begin{pmatrix} A_1 \\ A_2 \\ \hline \\ A_3 \end{pmatrix} (x)$$

so

$$\begin{cases} y_1 = A_1 x & \text{(we had this)}, \\ y_2 = A_2 x & \text{(we need this)}. \end{cases}$$

This extra predicate can trivially be converted to an elementary computation, and so we find the full algorithm:

While T is not the whole system
  Predicate: $y_T = A_T x$ true
  Update: $y_2 = A_2 x$
  Predicate: $y_T = A_T x$ true for new/bigger T block

25.2.2 ▪ Derivation of the algorithm by columns

In the previous section we derived the matrix-vector product, expressed the usual way: each element of the output vector is the inner product of a matrix row and the input vector. You may think that this is a lot of effort for not much result.

Consider then that we can derive other algorithms for the matrix-vector product, using the same general principle. Our basic assumption was that we split the matrix horizontally into two block rows. What would happen if we split the matrix vertically into two block columns?

We divide the matrix into two block columns, and express the result of the matrix-vector product on this form.

Original equation:

$$y = Ax.$$

Partitioned:

$$(y) = \begin{pmatrix} A_L & A_R \end{pmatrix} \begin{pmatrix} x_T \\ x_B \end{pmatrix}.$$

Equation:

$$\left\{ y = A_L x_T + A_R x_B. \right.$$

Again we make a statement about a partially completed computation: we assume that

$$y = A_L x_T$$

and we gradually grow the T block.

Again we compare splitting the matrix in one iteration and the next, and comparing the partial predicates:

> Before:
>
> $$(y) = \begin{pmatrix} A_L & A_R \end{pmatrix} \begin{pmatrix} x_T \\ x_B \end{pmatrix}$$
>
> and split
>
> $$(y) = \left(A_1 \mid A_2 \quad A_3\right) \begin{pmatrix} x_1 \\ \hline x_2 \\ x_3 \end{pmatrix}.$$
>
> Then the update step, and After:
>
> $$(y) = \left(A_1 \quad A_2 \mid A_3\right) \begin{pmatrix} x_1 \\ x_2 \\ \hline x_3 \end{pmatrix}$$
>
> and unsplit
>
> $$(y) = \begin{pmatrix} A_L & A_R \end{pmatrix} \begin{pmatrix} x_T \\ x_B \end{pmatrix}.$$

This gives us by "subtracting" one predicate from the other the extra result that was derived by the single iteration, and therefore the computation that was done in that iteration.

> Before the update:
>
> $$(y) = \left(A_1 \mid A_2 \quad A_3\right) \begin{pmatrix} x_1 \\ \hline x_2 \\ x_3 \end{pmatrix}$$
>
> so
>
> $$y = A_1 x_1$$
>
> is true. Then the update step, and
>
> After:
>
> $$(y) = \left(A_1 \quad A_2 \mid A_3\right) \begin{pmatrix} x_1 \\ x_2 \\ \hline x_3 \end{pmatrix}$$
>
> so
>
> $$y = A_1 x_1 + A_2 x_2.$$
>
> In other words, we need
>
> $$y \leftarrow y + A_2 x_2.$$

As a result we obtain a second form of the matrix-vector product:

> While T is not the whole system
>
> Predicate: $y = A_L x_T$ true
>
> Update: $y \leftarrow y + A_2 x_2$
>
> Predicate: $y = A_L x_T$ true for new/bigger T block

In quasi-MATLAB notation we express both algorithms:

Two formulations:

By rows:

for $r = 1, m$
    $y_r = A_{r,*}x_*$

By columns:

$y \leftarrow 0$
for $c = 1, n$
    $y \leftarrow y + A_{*,c}x_c$

In conclusion, we have now formally derived two algorithms for the matrix-vector product. One algorithm was probably known to you, the second one may not have been.

As mathematical operations get more complicated, they allow for more splitting schemes, and consequently more—sometimes surprisingly new—algorithms.

Chapter 26

The Catch2 testing framework

In an ideal world, you would write only correct programs, but in practice that is unlikely. Most of the time programmers establish the correctness of their code by testing it.

Even though above we saw a Dijkstra quote pointing out the ultimate inadequacy of testing, we can at least gain some confidence in our code by testing it.

26.1 ▪ Types of tests

Testing code is an art, even more than writing the code to begin with. That doesn't mean you can't be systematic about it. First of all, we distinguish between some basic types of tests:

- *Unit tests* that test a small part of a program by itself. The program part should be a "unit," i.e., indivisible, and the test should demonstrate the unit's complete behavior.
- *Integration tests* demonstrate the correct interaction of multiple units.
- *System tests* test the correct behavior of the whole software system.
- *Regression tests* establish that the behavior of a program has not changed by adding or changing aspects of it.

In this section we will talk about unit testing, which is about code correctness. In scientific computing, performance can be a testable aspect; this would be a regression test, since it's not about correctness but about behavioral changes in a correctly working program.

A program that is written in a sufficiently modular way allows for its components to be tested without having to wait for a system test of the whole program. Thus, testing and program design are aligned in their interests. In fact, writing a program with the thought in mind that it needs to be testable can lead to cleaner, more modular code.

In an extreme form of this you would write your code by test-driven development (TDD), where code development and testing go hand in hand. The basic principles can be stated as follows:

- Both the whole code and its parts should always be testable.
- When extending the code, make only the smallest change that allows for testing.
- With every change, test before and after.
- Assure correctness before adding new features.

In a strict interpretation, you would even for each part of the program first write the test that it would satisfy, and then the actual code.

26.2 ▪ Unit testing frameworks

There are several "frameworks" that help you with unit testing. In the remainder of this chapter we will use *Catch2*, which is one of the most used ones in C++.

See section 26.4 for the practical matters of how to obtain, install, and compile with Catch2.

26.2.1 ▪ Test cases

A Catch2 tester file consist of `TEST_CASE` clauses. A test case is a short program that is run as an independent main. In the simplest setup, you put all your unit tests in a file without a main program. The following lines make Catch2 provide its own `main`:

```
#define CATCH_CONFIG_MAIN
#include "catch2/catch_all.hpp"
```

See further section 26.4.1.

Each test case needs to have a unique name, which is printed when a test fails. You can optionally add keys to the test case that allow you to select tests from the command line.

```
TEST_CASE( "name of this test" ) {
  // stuf
}
TEST_CASE( "name of this test","[key1][key2]" ) {
  // stuf
}
```

The body of each `TEST_CASE` section is essentially a main program, where some statements are encapsulated in test macros. You can have multiple cases in a single tester file.

The most common test is formed by enclosing a boolean condition in a `REQUIRE` clause. This is a little like an `assert` but with better reporting, and without aborting the program run.

Simple test case:

```
TEST_CASE( "test that f returns positive under 1000" ) {
  for (int n=0; n<1000; n++)
    REQUIRE( f(n)>0 );
}
```

Exercise 26.1. Write a boolean function `is_prime`, and write a test case for it. This should have both cases that succeed and that fail.

26.2.1.1 ▪ Test reporting

For failing tests, the framework will give the name of the test, the line number, and the values that were tested.

Run the tester:

Code:

```
// catch/false.cpp
#define CATCH_CONFIG_MAIN
#include "catch2/catch_all.hpp"

int five() { return 6; }

TEST_CASE( "needs to be 5" ) {
    REQUIRE( five()==5 );
}
```

Output:

```
-------------------------
needs to be 5
-------------------------
false.cpp:21
.........................

false.cpp:22: FAILED:
  REQUIRE( five()==5 )
with expansion:
  6 == 5

=========================
test cases: 1 | 1 failed
assertions: 1 | 1 failed
```

In the above case, the error message printed out the offending value of `f(n)`, not the value of n for which it occurs. To get more output, such as that value of n, insert `INFO` specifications, which are only printed if a test fails:

`INFO`: print out information at a failing test

```
TEST_CASE( "test that f always returns positive" ) {
  for (int n=0; n<1000; n++)
    INFO( "iteration: " << n ); // only printed for failed tests
    REQUIRE( f(n)>0 );
}
```

26.2.1.2 ▪ Test types

The `REQUIRE` clause takes a simple boolean expression. Most commonly, you would get this by testing some function result. Here are some examples. We start with the simplest case, testing on a boolean expression:

Test a boolean expression:

```
REQUIRE( some_test(some_input) );
REQUIRE( not some_test(other_input) );
```

Compound boolean expressions need to be parenthesized:

```
REQUIRE( ( x>0 and x<1 ) );
```

Tests on integer expressions are really also boolean tests:

Tests on integers:

```
REQUIRE( integer_function(1)==3 );
REQUIRE( integer_function(1)!=0 );
```

Tests on floating point expressions are a little more tricky. You may know that in general you shouldn't do equality tests on such numbers if they involve the outcome of a numerical calculation. In the case of unit testing that means that we need a test with some amount of leeway:

```
REQUIRE( real_function(1.5)==Catch::Approx(3.0) );
REQUIRE( real_function(1)!=Catch::Approx(1.0) );
```

Testing on a nonzero quantity computes a relative, rather than an absolute, error. This does not work when testing a quantity for being approximately zero, so in that case you can indicate the explicit (absolute) margin of error:

```
REQUIRE( zero_find()==Catch::Approx(0.).margin(1.e-8) );
```

Finally, if your code throws exceptions (section 27.2) you can test for these.

Suppose a function `g(n)` satisfies the following:

- it succeeds for input $n > 0$
- it fails for input $n \leq 0$:
  throws exception

```
TEST_CASE( "test that g only works for positive" ) {
  for (int n=-100; n<+100; n++)
    if (n<=0)
      REQUIRE_THROWS( g(n) );
    else
      REQUIRE_NOTHROW( g(n) );
}
```

Exercise 26.2. Write a square root function that throws an exception on a negative input. Write a test case that tests for proper inputs, and for correctness of the result.

26.2.2 ▪ Common code: Setup/teardown

A common occurrence in unit testing is to have multiple, similar, tests with common code before and after. In testing lingo this sometimes called "setup" and "teardown" code. Catch2 supports this through the `SECTION` mechanism:

1. All code before the first `SECTION` is setup.
2. All code after the last `SECTION` is teardown.
3. All sections are run separately, but obeying the common setup and teardown code.

Use `SECTION` if tests have intro/outro in common:

```
TEST_CASE( "commonalities" ) {
  // common setup:
  double x,y,z;
  REQUIRE_NOTHROW( y = f(x) );
  // two independent tests:
  SECTION( "g function" ) {
    REQUIRE_NOTHROW( z = g(y) );
  }
  SECTION( "h function" ) {
    REQUIRE_NOTHROW( z = h(y) );
  }
```

```
  // common followup
  REQUIRE( z>x );
}
```

26.3 ▪ Examples of TDD with Catch2

In this section you can do some exercises where you develop a code in step-by-step test-driven development. Some of these examples may seem simple, and you may think you could develop the code equally well, and probably faster, without all the tests. However, for longer and more complicated codes the test-driven approach can give you far greater confidence in your code, and find problems long before they manifest themselves.

26.3.1 ▪ Roots of a quadratic equation

We revisit Exercise 11.2, which used `std::variant` to return 0,1,2 roots of a quadratic equation. Here we use TDD to arrive at the code.

First we need a compact representation of a quadratic polynomial:

We represent the polynomial

$$ax^2 + bx + c$$

as

```
// union/quadlib.hpp
struct quadratic {
  double a,b,c;
};
```

When needed, you can unpack this again, for instance, in

```
// union/quadlib.hpp
double evaluate( quadratic coefficients, double x ) {
  auto [a,b,c] = coefficients;
  return a*x*x + b*x + c;
}
```

Exercise 26.3. Write a function

```
double discriminant( quadratic coefficients );
```

that computes $b^2 - 4ac$, and test

```
// union/quadtest.cpp
TEST_CASE( "discriminant" ) {
  quadratic one{0., 2.5, 0.};
  REQUIRE( discriminant( one ) ==Catch::Approx(6.25) );
  quadratic two{1., 0., 1.5};
  REQUIRE( discriminant( two ) ==Catch::Approx(-6.) );
  quadratic three{.1, .1, .1*.5};
  REQUIRE( discriminant( three ) ==Catch::Approx(-.01) );
}
```

It may be illustrative to see what happens if you leave out the approximate equality test:

```
REQUIRE( discriminant( make_tuple(.1, .1, .1*.5 ) ) == -.01 );
```

With this discriminant function it becomes easy to detect the case of no roots: the discriminant $D < 0$. Next we need to have the criterion for single or double roots: we have a single root if $D = 0$.

Exercise 26.4. Write a function

```
bool discriminant_zero( quadratic coefficients );
```

that passes the test

```
// union/quadtest.cpp
quadratic coefficients{a,b,c};
d = discriminant( coefficients );
z = discriminant_zero( coefficients );
INFO( a << "," << b << "," << c << " d=" << d );
REQUIRE( z );
```

Using, for instance, the values

```
a = 2; b = 4; c = 2;
a = 2; b = std::sqrt(40); c = 5; //!!!
a = 3; b = 0; c = 0.;
```

How do you handle the inexactness for the discriminant calculation?

This exercise is the first one where we run into numerical subtleties. The second set of test values has the discriminant zero in exact arithmetic, but nonzero in computer arithmetic. Therefore, we need to test whether it is small enough, compared to b.

Exercise 26.5. Be sure to also test the case where `discriminant_zero` returns false.

Now that we've detected a single root, we need the function that computes it. There are no subtleties in this one.

Exercise 26.6. Write the function `simple_root` that returns the single root. For confirmation, test

```
// union/quadtest.cpp
auto r = simple_root(coefficients);
REQUIRE( evaluate(coefficients,r)==Catch::Approx(0.).margin(1.e-14) );
```

The remaining case of two distinct roots is arrived at by elimination, and the only thing to do is write the function that returns them.

Exercise 26.7. Write a function that returns the two roots as a `std::pair`:

```
pair<double,double> double_root( quadratic coefficients );
```

Test

```
// union/quadtest.cpp
quadratic coefficients{a,b,c};
auto [r1,r2] = double_root(coefficients);
auto
```

```
  e1 = evaluate(coefficients,r1),
  e2 = evaluate(coefficients,r2);
REQUIRE( evaluate(coefficients,r1)==Catch::Approx(0.).margin(1.e-14) );
REQUIRE( evaluate(coefficients,r2)==Catch::Approx(0.).margin(1.e-14) );
```

The final bit of code is the function that tests for how many roots there are, and returns them as a `std::variant`.

Exercise 26.8. Write a function

```
variant< bool,double, pair<double,double> >
    compute_roots( quadratic coefficients);
```

Test

```
// union/quadtest.cpp
TEST_CASE( "full test" ) {
  double a,b,c; int index;
  SECTION( "no root" ) {
    a=2.0; b=1.5; c=2.5;
    index = 0;
  }
  SECTION( "single root" ) {
    a=1.0; b=4.0; c=4.0;
    index = 1;
  }
  SECTION( "double root" ) {
    a=2.2; b=5.1; c=2.5;
    index = 2;
  }
  quadratic coefficients{.a=a,.b=b,.c=c};
  auto result = compute_roots(coefficients)
    ;
  REQUIRE( result.index()==index );
}
```

The `bool` in the return type of `compute_roots` is not the most appropriate choice, since its two values do not have two distinct meanings. If you return a boolean, presumably it has the value `false` corresponding to the fact that there are no zeros. But then what does a return value of `true` mean? There is a solution to this inelegance: you can return a `monostate`, from the `variant` header.

Exercise 26.9. Instead of a `bool`, return a `monostate`. Adjust your tester code accordingly.

26.3.2 ▪ Root finding by bisection

For many functions f, finding their zeros, that is, the values x for which $f(x) = 0$, cannot be done analytically. You then have to resort to numerical *root finding* schemes. In this project you will develop gradually more complicated implementations of a simple scheme: root finding by *bisection*.

In this scheme, you start with two points where the function has opposite signs, and move either the left or right point to the midpoint, depending on what sign the function has there. See Figure 26.1.

Remark. *In section 17.1 we looked at Newton's method. This method is mathematically superior, so the current discussion of bisection should only be considered as a programming exercise.*

26.3.2.1 ▪ Simple implementation

Let's develop a first implementation step by step. To ensure correctness of our code we will use a test-driven development (TDD) approach: for each bit of functionality we write a test to ensure its correctness before we integrate it in the larger code.

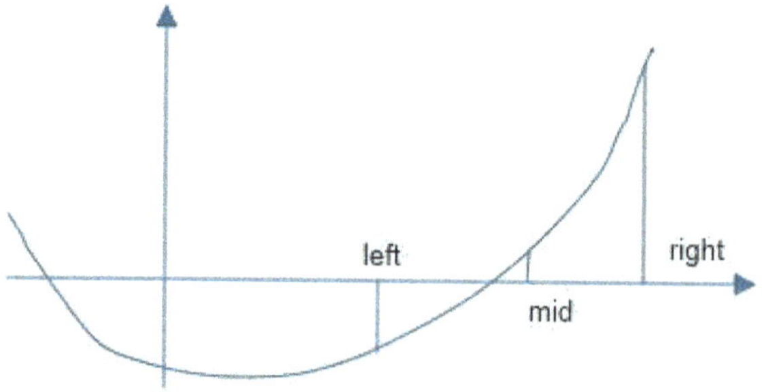

Figure 26.1. *Root finding by interval bisection*

26.3.2.2 ▪ Polynomials

First of all, we need to have a way to represent polynomials. For a polynomial of degree d we need $d+1$ coefficients:

$$f(x) = c_0 x^d + \cdots + c_{d-1} x^1 + c_d. \tag{26.1}$$

We implement this by storing the coefficients in a `vector<double>`. We make the following arbitrary decisions:

1. let the first element of this vector be the coefficient of the highest power, and
2. for the coefficients to properly define a polynomial, this leading coefficient has to be nonzero.

Let's start by having a fixed test polynomial, provided by a function `set_coefficients`. For this function to provide a proper polynomial, it has to satisfy the following test:

```
// bisect/testzeroarray.cpp
TEST_CASE( "coefficients represent polynomial" "[1]") {
  vector<double> coefficients = { 1.5, 0., -3 };
  REQUIRE( coefficients.size()>0 );
  REQUIRE( coefficients.front()!=0. );
}
```

Exercise 26.10. Write a routine `set_coefficients` that constructs a vector of coefficients,

```
// bisect/findzeroarray.cpp
vector<double> coefficients = set_coefficients();
```

and make it satisfy the above conditions.

At first write a hardcoded set of coefficients, then try reading them from the command line.

Exercise 26.11. Bonus: use the `cxxopts` library (section 30.4.2) to specify the coefficients on the command line.

Above we postulated two conditions that an array of numbers should satisfy to qualify as the coefficients of a polynomial. Your code will probably be testing for this, so let's introduce a boolean function `is_proper_polynomial`:

- this function returns `true` if the array of numbers satisfies the two conditions;

- it returns `false` if either condition is not satisfied.

In order to test your function `is_proper_polynomial` you should check that

- it recognizes correct polynomials, and
- it fails for improper coefficients that do not properly define a polynomial.

Exercise 26.12. For polynomial coefficients to give a well-defined polynomial, the zeroth coefficient needs to be nonzero:

```
// bisect/zeroclasstest.cpp
TEST_CASE( "proper test","[2]" ) {
  vector<double> coefficients{3., 2.5, 2.1};
  REQUIRE_NOTHROW( polynomial(coefficients) );

  coefficients.at(0) = 0.;
  REQUIRE_THROWS( polynomial(coefficients) );
}
```

Write a constructor that accepts the coefficients and throws an exception if the above condition is violated.

We need polynomial evaluation. We will build a function `evaluate_at` with the following definition:

```
// bisect/findzerolib.hpp
double evaluate_at( const std::vector<double>& coefficients,double x);
```

You can interpret the array of coefficients in (at least) two ways, but with equation (26.1) we prescribed one particular interpretation.

So we need a test that the coefficients are indeed interpreted with the leading coefficient first, and not with the leading coefficient last. For instance:

```
// bisect/testzeroarray.cpp
polynomial second{2,0,1};
// correct interpretation: 2x^2 + 1
REQUIRE( is_proper_polynomial(second) );
REQUIRE( evaluate_at(second,2) == Catch::Approx(9) );
// wrong interpretation: 1x^2 + 2
REQUIRE( evaluate_at(second,2) != Catch::Approx(6) );
```

(where we have left out the `TEST_CASE` header).

Now we write the function that passes these tests:

Exercise 26.13. Write a function `evaluate_at` which computes

$$y \leftarrow f(x)$$

and confirm that it passes the above tests.

```
double evaluate_at( polynomial coefficients,double x);
```

For bonus points, look up *Horner's rule* and implement it.

With the polynomial function implemented, we can start working towards the algorithm.

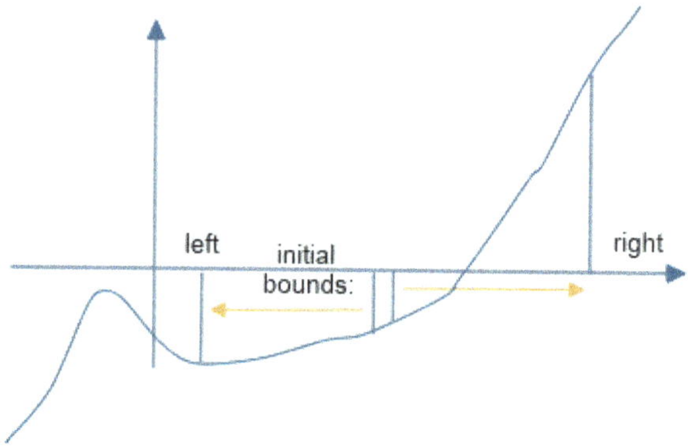

Figure 26.2. *Setting the initial search points*

26.3.2.3 ▪ Left/right search points

Suppose x_-, x_+ are such that

$$x_- < x_+ \quad \text{and} \quad f(x_-) \cdot f(x_+) < 0,$$

that is, the function values in the left and right points are of opposite sign. Then there is a zero in the interval (x_-, x_+); see Figure 26.1.

But how to find these outer bounds on the search?

If the polynomial is of odd degree you can find x_-, x_+ by going far enough to the left and right from any two starting points; see Figure 26.2. For even degree there is no such simple algorithm (indeed, there may not be a zero) so we abandon the attempt.

We start by writing a function `is_odd` that tests whether the polynomial is of odd degree.

Exercise 26.14. Write a method `is_odd` that makes the following test pass:

```
// bisect/zeroclasstest.cpp
TEST_CASE( "polynomial degree","[3]" ) {
  polynomial second( {2,0,1} ); // 2x^2 + 1
  REQUIRE( not second.is_odd() );
  polynomial third( {3,2,0,1} ); // 3x^3 + 2x^2 + 1
  REQUIRE( third.is_odd() );
}
```

Now we can find x_-, x_+: start with some interval and move the end points out until the function values have opposite sign.

Exercise 26.15. Write a function `find_initial_bounds` which computes x_-, x_+ such that

$$f(x_-) < 0 < f(x_+) \quad \text{or} \quad f(x_+) < 0 < f(x_-).$$

Address the following concerns:

1. What is a good prototype for the function?
2. How do you move the points far enough out to satisfy this condition?
3. Can you compute the above test more compactly?

Since finding left and right points with a zero in between is not always possible for polynomials of even degree, we completely reject this case. In the following test we throw an exception (see section 27.2) for polynomials of even degree:

```
// bisect/zeroclasstest.cpp
double left{10},right{11};
right = left+1;
polynomial second( {2,0,1} ); // 2x^2 + 1
REQUIRE_THROWS( find_initial_bounds(second,left,right) );
polynomial third( {3,2,0,1} ); // 3x^3 + 2x^2 + 1
REQUIRE_NOTHROW( find_initial_bounds(third,left,right) );
REQUIRE( left<right );
double
  leftval = third(left),
  rightval = third(right);
REQUIRE( leftval*rightval<=0 );
```

Make sure your code passes these tests. What test do you need to add for the function values?

26.3.2.4 ▪ Root finding

The root finding process globally looks like the following:

- You start with points x_-, x_+ where the function has opposite sign; then you know that there is a zero between them.
- The bisection method for finding this zero looks at the halfway point, and based on the function value in the midpoint
- moves one of the bounds to the midpoint, such that the function again has opposite signs in the left and right search points.

The structure of the code is as follows:

```
double find_zero( /* something */ ) {
  while ( /* left and right too far apart */ ) {
    // move bounds left and right closer together
  }
  return something;
}
```

Again, we test all the functionality separately. In this case this means that moving the bounds should be a testable step.

Exercise 26.16. Write a function `move_bounds_closer` and test it:

```
void move_bounds_closer
  ( std::vector<double> coefficients,
    double& left,double& right );
```

Implement some unit tests on this function.

Finally, we put everything together in the top level function `find_zero`.

Exercise 26.17. Make this call work:

```
// bisect/zeroclassmain.cpp
auto zero = find_zero( coefficients, 1.e-8 );
cout << "Found root " << zero
     << " with value " << evaluate_at(coefficients,zero) << '\n';
```

Design unit tests, including on the precision attained, and make sure your code passes them.

26.3.2.5 ▪ Object implementation

Revisit the exercises of section 26.3.2.2 and introduce a `polynomial` class that stores the polynomial coefficients. Several functions now become members of this class.

Also update the unit tests.

Some further suggestions:

1. Can you make your polynomial class look like a function?

   ```
   class Polynomial {
     /* ... */
   }
   main () {
     Polynomial p;
     float y = p(x);
   }
   ```

   See section 3.2.2.

2. Can you generalize the polynomial class, for instance, to the case of special forms such as $(1+x)^n$?

3. Templatize your polynomials: Make a templated version that works both with `float` and `double`. Can you see a difference in attainable precision between the two types?

26.4 ▪ Practical aspects of Catch2

In this section we cover some of the practical aspects of using Catch2: compilation, and CMake integration.

26.4.1 ▪ Two usage modes

Let's assume you have a file structure with

- a very short main program, and
- a library file that has all functions used by `main.cpp`.

In order to test the functions, you supply another main, which contains only unit tests. This is illustrated in Figure 26.3.

In fact, with Catch2 your main file doesn't actually have a `main` program: that is supplied by the framework. In the tester main file you only put the test cases:

The framework supplies its own main:

```
#define CATCH_CONFIG_MAIN
#include "catch2/catch_all.hpp"

#include "library_functions.h"
/*
  here follow the unit tests
*/
```

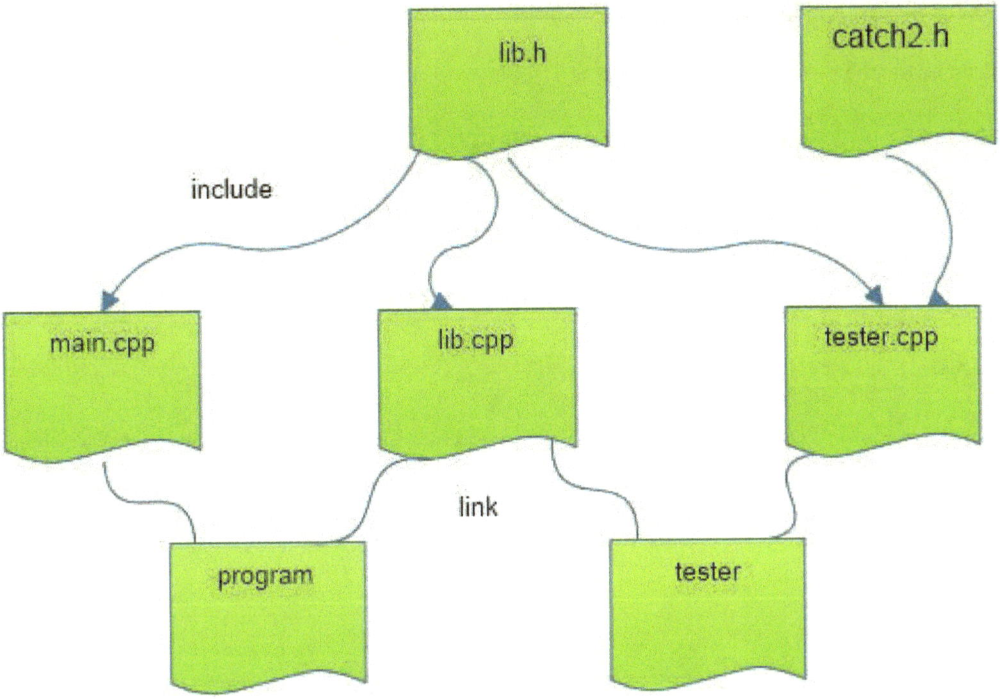

Figure 26.3. *File structure for unit tests*

Alternatively, you can invoke the tests yourself from your own `main` program:

Run all test cases:

```
// traffic/street.cpp
Catch::Session session; // there can only be one session
auto result = Catch::Session().run( argc, argv );
```

One important question is what header file to include. You can do

```
#include "catch.hpp"
```

which is the "header only" mode, but that makes compilation very slow. Therefore, we will assume you have installed Catch2 through *CMake*, and you include

```
#include "catch2/catch_all.hpp"
```

26.4.2 ▪ Compilation

The setup suggested above requires you to add compile and link flags to your setup. This is system-dependent.

Letting Catch2 supply the main:

```
icpc -o tester test_main.cpp \
    $( pkg-config --cflags catch2 )
    $( pkg-config --libs catch2-with-main )
```

If you use your own main, replace `catch2-with-main` by `catch2` for the libraries.

26.4.3 ▪ CMake integration

Catch2 can be found through *pkg-config*:

```
find_package( PkgConfig REQUIRED )
pkg_check_modules( CATCH2 REQUIRED catch2-with-main )
target_include_directories(
        ${PROGRAM_NAME} PUBLIC
        ${CATCH2_INCLUDE_DIRS}
        )
target_link_directories(
        ${PROGRAM_NAME} PUBLIC
        ${CATCH2_LIBRARY_DIRS}
        )
target_link_libraries(
        ${PROGRAM_NAME} PUBLIC
        ${CATCH2_LIBRARIES}
        )
```

Chapter 27

Error handling

When you're programming, making errors is close to inevitable. Violations of the grammar of the language, known as *syntax errors*, will be caught by the compiler. These will prevent generation of an executable. In this section we will talk about *runtime errors*: behavior at runtime that is other than intended.

Here are some sources of runtime errors:

Array indexing Using an index outside the array bounds may give a runtime error:

```
vector<float> a(10);
for (int i=0; i<=10; i++)
  a.at(i) = x; // runtime error
```

or undefined behavior:

```
vector<float> a(10);
for (int i=0; i<=10; i++)
  a[i] = x;
```

Null pointers Using an uninitialized pointer is likely to crash your program:

```
Object *x;
if (false) x = new Object;
x->method();
```

Numerical errors such as division by zero will not crash your program, so catching them takes some care.

A productive way of dealing with errors is a combination of preventing them and handling them when they occur. A block-structured code is then valuable: you can approach code block as

```
{
  // start of block: some preconditions hold
  // code of the block: deal with errors
  // end of block: some postconditions hold
}
```

Checking pre- and postconditions with assertions will be discussed in section 27.1; dealing with errors through exceptions is the topic of section 27.2.

27.1 ▪ Assertions

One way to catch errors before they happen is to sprinkle your code with assertions: statements about things that have to be true from the logic of your program. For instance, if a function should mathematically always return a positive result, such as a valid square root of a scalar, it may be a good idea to check for that anyway. You do this by using the `assert` command, which takes a boolean, and will stop your program if the boolean is false:

Check on valid input parameters:

```
#include <cassert>

// this function requires x<y
float f(x,y) {
  assert( x<y );
```

Test the result of the computation:

```
  // function computes something positive
  float positive_outcome = /* some computation */
  assert( positive_outcome>0 );
  return positive_outcome;
}
```

The `static_assert` statement checks compile-time conditions only.

Since checking an assertion is a minor computation, you may want to disable it when you run your program in production by defining the `NDEBUG` macro:

```
#define NDEBUG
```

One way of doing that is passing it as a compiler flag:

```
icpc -DNDEBUG yourprog.cpp
```

Remark. *If an assertion fails, your program will call* `std::abort`.

27.2 ▪ Exception handling

During the run of your program, an error condition may occur that requires you to take one or more steps back to deal with it. For cases where these errors are exceptional, typically caused by unforeseeable runtime conditions, we have the *exception* mechanism.

You may have already seen exceptions in action: if you access a vector element outside the bounds of that vector, your program will stop. You may see text on your screen,

```
terminating with uncaught exception
```

We say that your program has *thrown* an *exception*.

Code:

```
// except/boundthrow.cpp
vector<float> x(5);
x.at(5) = 3.14;
```

Output:

```
libc++abi.dylib: terminating
    ↪with uncaught exception
    ↪of type
    ↪std::out_of_range:
    ↪vector
```

Now you know that your program has an error, but you don't know where it occurs. You can find out by trying to *catch the exception*:

Code:

```
// except/catchbounds.cpp
vector<float> x(5);
for (int i=0; i<10; ++i) {
  try {
    x.at(i) = 3.14;
  } catch (...) {
    cout << "Exception indexing at: "
         << i << '\n';
    break;
  }
}
```

Output:

```
Exception indexing at: 5
```

The operative terms here are

- *exception throwing*, which uses the `throw` keyword to signal a problem; and
- *exception catching*, which uses the `catch` keyword to specify actions to be taken when an exception is thrown.

Illustration of exception throwing and catching:

Code with problem:

```
if ( /* some problem */ )
  throw(5);
```

Calling code:

```
try {
  /* code that can go wrong */
} catch (...) { // literally three dots!
  /* code to deal with the problem */
}
```

You can throw all sorts of exceptions; in the example just now we used an integer, but you can throw an error string, or even exception objects. More below.

27.2.1 ▪ Standard exceptions

Exceptions that the standard library throws, such as for `at` indexing out of bounds, or allocation an invalid vector size, inherit from `std::exception`. In particular they have a `what` method that returns an informative string:

Code:

```
// except/what.cpp
   switch (iexp) {
   case 1 :
     [] (int s) { vector<int> x(s); }( -3 );
     break;
   case 2 :
     [] (int s) { vector<int> x(3); x.at(s);
                  }( 4 );
     break;
   case 3 :
     [] () { throw(5); }();
     break;
 /* ... */
   }
} catch ( std::exception& e ) {
   cout << "For experiment " << iexp
        << " found standard exception: "
        << "\n  " << e.what() << '\n';
  } catch ( ... ) {
   cout << "For experiment " << iexp
        << " found unknown exception"
        << '\n';
```

Output:

```
For experiment 1 found
     ↪standard exception:
  cannot create std::vector
     ↪larger than max_size()
For experiment 2 found
     ↪standard exception:
  vector::_M_range_check: __n
     ↪(which is 4) >=
     ↪this->size() (which is
     ↪3)
For experiment 3 found unknown
     ↪exception
```

27.2.2 ▪ Exception types

In the examples above it didn't matter much what you threw, since the `catch` clause only detected that there was an exception, period. You can be much more sophisticated. For instance, you could throw an integer corresponding to some error code.

The `catch` clause now explicitly indicates that it's expecting an integer as the content of the exception.

You can actually throw any type of object as an exception. For instance, you can throw integers to indicate an error code, or a string with an actual error message. You could even make an error class:

```
class MyError {
public :
  int error_no; string error_msg;
  MyError( int i,string msg )
  : error_no(i),error_msg(msg) {};
}

throw( MyError(27,"oops");

try {
  // something
} catch ( MyError &m ) {
  cout << "My error with code=" << m.error_no
    << " msg=" << m.error_msg << endl;
}
```

You can use exception inheritance!

If different levels of your function call hierarchy throw different types of exceptions, you could have multiple `catch` clauses to deal with the different types:

You can use multiple `catch` statements to catch different types of errors:

```
try {
  // something
} catch ( int i ) {
  // handle int exception
} catch ( std::string c ) {
  // handle string exception
}
```

You can catch any exception regardless of the type by specifying three dots. This can also be used as a final case in a sequence of `catch` clauses:

Catch exceptions without specifying the type:

```
try {
  // something
} catch ( ... ) { // literally: three dots
  cout << "Something went wrong!" << endl;
}
```

Exercise 27.1. Define the function

$$f(x) = x^3 - 19x^2 + 79x + 100$$

and evaluate $\sqrt{f(i)}$ for the integers $i = 0 \ldots 20$.

- First write the program naively, and print out the root. Where is $f(i)$ negative? What does your program print?
- You see that floating point errors such as the root of a negative number do not make your program crash or something like that. Alter your program to throw an exception if $f(i)$ is negative, catch the exception, and print an error message.
- Alter your program to test the output of the `sqrt` call, rather than its input. Use the function `isnan`,

  ```
  #include <cfenv>
  using std::isnan;
  ```

  and again throw an exception.

In a somewhat rare case, imagine that you have a constructor that could throw an exception, and this constructor is used as a base case for a derived class:

```
class A{
public:
  A(int i) { /* ... */
    if (something) throw(something);
  };
};
```

```
class B : public A {
public:
  B(int i)
    : A(i) { /* something */ };
}
```

How do you now catch the exception thrown in the `A` constructor?

A *function try block* will catch exceptions, including in *member initializer* lists of constructors:

```
B::B( int i )
  try : A(i) {
    // constructor body
  }
  catch (...) { // handle exception
  }
```

Some remarks:

- Functions were able to define what exceptions they throw until C++17:
  ```
  void func() throw( MyError, std::string );
  ```
- There are many predefined exceptions: `bad_alloc`, `bad_exception`, etc.
- An exception handler can throw an exception; to rethrow the same exception use "`throw;`" without arguments.
- Exceptions delete all stack data, but not `new` data. Also:
- The main program acts as if an implicit `try/except` block is placed around it. You can replace the handler for that. See the `exception` header file.
- The keyword `noexcept` indicates that a function cannot throw an exception:
  ```
  void f() noexcept { ... };
  ```
  This can be important in some applications such as embedded systems.
- No exception is thrown when dereferencing a `nullptr`.

27.3 ▪ Remaining topics

27.3.1 ▪ "Where does this error come from?"

The CPP defines two macros, `__FILE__` and `__LINE__`, that give you the current file name and the current line number, respectively. You can use these to generate pretty error messages such as

```
Overflow occurred in line 25 of file numerics.cpp
```

The C++20 standard offers the `source_location` header as a mechanism instead:

```
// except/location.cpp
#if defined(__cpp_lib_source_location)
    std::source_location loc_info
      = std::source_location::current();
    cout << "Exception at line " << loc_info.line << '\n';
#else
    cout << "Exception at unknown source location\n";
#endif
```

In C++23 the `stacktrace` header was added. A *stack trace* is a complete list of (i) what line are we on in the current function, and (ii) what line in what calling function did we come from, and so on recursively.

We can print the whole stacktrace in one go,

```
#include <stacktrace>
[..]
auto trace = std::stacktrace::current();
std::cout << std::to_string(trace) << '\n';
```

or loop over the `stacktrace` container and analyze it line by line.

27.3.2 ▪ Numerical errors through errno

The global—but thread-local—variable *errno* is set by various numerical functions in the standard library. For instance, after

```
const double not_a_number = std::log(-1.0);
```

the variable is set to a value indicating that the argument is outside the domain of definition of the log function.

- To be precise: *errno* is a preprocessor macro that expands to a modifiable, thread-local `int`.
- Use the *cerrno* header to get this variable and symbolic names for the various error conditions. These names are system-dependent.
- This type of error handling can be a drain on performance. If you trust your computations not to generate errors, disable it by compiler options such as `-fno-math-errno` or `-ffast-math`.

27.3.3 ▪ Legacy mechanisms

The traditional approach to error checking is for each routine to return an integer parameter that indicates success or absence thereof. Problems with this approach arise if it's used inconsistently, for instance, by a user forgetting to heed the return codes of a library. Also, it requires that every level of the function calling hierarchy needs to check return codes.

The *PETSc* library uses this mechanism consistently throughout, and to great effect.

Exceptions are a better mechanism, since

- they cannot be ignored, and
- they do not require handling on the levels of the calling hierarchy between where the exception is thrown and where it is caught.

Also, thrown exceptions will automatically deallocate the memory from standard containers.

As an alternative to exceptions, consider `optional` (section 11.1) or `expected` (section 11.2).

Chapter 28

Debugging

If despite careful design and extensive unit testing your program still aborts or gives incorrect results, you need to resort to debugging. In this section you will see the *gdb* debugger in action: it allows you to step through your code, and print out variables along the way.

In this chapter we focus on using the debugger from the command line; most integrated development environments (IDEs) have a debugger built in on much the same principles, but probably a little easier to use. We will not cover this aspect.

28.1 ▪ A simple example

The following program does not have any bugs; we use it to show some of the basics of *gdb*.

```
// debug/hello.cpp
void say(int n) {
  println("hello world {}",n);
}

int main() {

  for (int i=0; i<10; ++i) {
    int ii;
    ii = i*i;
    ++ii;
    say(ii);
  }

  return 0;
}
```

28.1.1 ▪ Invoking the debugger

After you compile your program (making sure to use the `-g` flag; see section 36.4), instead of running it the normal way, you invoke *gdb*:

```
gdb myprogram
```

That puts you in an environment, recognizable by the `(gdb)` prompt:

```
GNU gdb (GDB) Red Hat Enterprise Linux 7.6.1-115.el7
```

```
[stuff]
(gdb)
```

where you can do a controlled run of your program with the *run* command:

```
(gdb) run
Starting program: /home/eijkhout/gdb/hello
hello world 1
hello world 2
hello world 5
hello world 10
hello world 17
hello world 26
hello world 37
hello world 50
hello world 65
hello world 82
[Inferior 1 (process 30981) exited normally]
```

28.2 ▪ Example: Integer overflow

The following program shows *integer overflow*. (We are using `short int` to force this to happen soon.)

Code:

```
// debug/overflow.cpp
void say(short int n) {
  println
    ("hello world {}",n);
}

int main() {

  for (short i=0; ; i+=20) {
    short ii;
    ii = i*i;
    ++i;
    say(ii);
  }

  return 0;
}
```

Output:

```
hello world 0
hello world 441
hello world 1764
hello world 3969
hello world 7056
hello world 11025
hello world 15876
hello world 21609
hello world 28224
hello world -29815
hello world -21436
hello world -12175
hello world -2032
hello world 8993
hello world 20900
hello world -31847
hello world -18176
hello world -3623
hello world 11812
hello world 28129
```

Let's do a walkthrough:

```
(gdb) list
18      void say(short n) {
19        cout << format
20          ("hello world {}\n",n);
(gdb) break 19 if n<0
Breakpoint 1 at 0x4044a5: file overflow.cpp,
     line 20.
```

We see where the erroneous output is generated, so we put a conditional break there.

```
(gdb) break 19 if n<0
Breakpoint 1 at 0x4044a5: file overflow.cpp,
     line 20.
(gdb) run
Starting program: overflow
hello world 0
[...]
hello world 28224

Breakpoint 1, say (n=-29815) at overflow.cpp
     :20
20          ("hello world {}\n",n);
```

Running the program takes us to the trouble-some spot. We use a condition break in this case.

```
(gdb) where
#0  say (n=-29815) at overflow.cpp:20
#1  0x0000000000404546 in main () at
     overflow.cpp:29
(gdb) frame 1
#1  0x0000000000404546 in main () at
     overflow.cpp:29
29          say(ii);
```

Get the call stack and the calling frame.

```
(gdb) print ii
$1 = -29815
(gdb) print i
$2 = 190
(gdb) print i * i
```

Print the offending input, see where it comes from, and compute the result, which is indeed more than 2^{15}.

28.3 ▪ More *gdb*

28.3.1 ▪ Run with command-line arguments

This program is self-contained, but if you had a program that takes *command-line arguments*,

```
./myprogram 25
```

you can supply those in *gdb*:

```
(gdb) run 25
```

28.3.2 ▪ Source listing and proper compilation

Inside *gdb*, you can get a source listing with the `list` command. You need to supply the `-g` compiler option for the *symbol table* to be included in the binary; see for yourself what happens when you leave out this option:

```
[] icpc -g -o hello hello.cpp
[] gdb hello
GNU gdb (GDB) Red Hat Enterprise Linux 7.6.1-115.el7
[stuff]
Reading symbols from /home/eijkhout/gdb/hello...done.
(gdb) list
13        using std::cout;
14        using std::endl;
[et cetera]
```

(If you hit return now, the list command is repeated and you get the next block of lines. Doing `list -` gives you the block above where you currently are.)

28.3.3 ▪ Stepping through the source

Let's now make a more controlled run of the program. In the source, we see that line 22 is the first executable one:

```
20    int main() {
21
22      for (int i=0; i<10; i++) {
23        int ii;
24        ii = i*i;
...
```

We introduce a *breakpoint* with the `break` command:

```
(gdb) break 22
Breakpoint 1 at 0x400a03: file hello.cpp, line 22.
```

(If your program is spread over multiple files, you can specify the file name: `break otherfile.cpp:34`.)

Now if we run the program, it will stop at that line:

```
(gdb) run
Starting program: /home/eijkhout/gdb/hello

Breakpoint 1, main () at hello.cpp:22
22          for (int i=0; i<10; i++) {
```

To be precise: the program is stopped in the state before it executes this line.

We can now use `cont` (for "continue") to let the program run on. Since there are no further breakpoints, the program will run to completion. This is not terribly useful, so let us change our minds about the location of the breakpoint: it would be more useful if the execution stopped at the start of every iteration.

Recall that the breakpoint had a number of 1, so we use `delete` to remove it, and we set a breakpoint inside the loop body instead, and continue until we hit it.

```
(gdb) delete 1
(gdb) break 23
Breakpoint 2 at 0x400a29: file hello.cpp, line 23.
(gdb) cont
Continuing.
Breakpoint 2, main () at hello.cpp:24
24              ii = i*i;
```

(Note that line 23 is not executable, so execution stops on the first line after that.)

Now if we continue, the program runs until the next break point:

```
(gdb) cont
Continuing.
hello world 5

Breakpoint 1, main () at hello.cpp:24
24              ii = i*i;
```

To get to the next statement, we use `next`:

```
(gdb) next
25              ii++;
(gdb)
```

Hitting return reexecutes the previous command, so we go to the next line:

```
(gdb)
26            say(ii);
(gdb)
hello world 2

Breakpoint 1, main () at hello.cpp:24
24            ii = i*i;
```

You observe that the function call

1. is executed, as is clear from the `hello world 1` output, but
2. is not displayed in detail in the debugger.

The conclusion is that `next` goes to the next executable statement in the current subprogram, not into functions and such that get called from it.

If you want to go into the function `say`, you need to use `step`:

```
(gdb) next
25            ii++;
(gdb) next
26            say(ii);
(gdb) step
say (n=10) at hello.cpp:17
17          cout << "hello world " << n << endl;
```

The debugger reports the function name, and the names and values of the arguments. Another "step" executes the current line and brings us to the end of the function, and the next "step" puts us back in the main program:

```
(gdb)
hello world 10
18        }
(gdb)
main () at hello.cpp:24
24            ii = i*i;
```

28.3.4 ▪ Inspecting values

When execution is stopped at a line (meaning right before it is executed) you can inspect any values in that subprogram:

```
24            ii = i*i;
(gdb) print i
$1 = 4
```

You can even let expressions be evaluated with local variables:

```
(gdb) print 2*i
$2 = 8
```

You can combine this looking at values with breakpoints. Say you want to know when the variable `ii` gets more than 40:

```
(gdb) break 26 if ii>40
Breakpoint 1 at 0x4009cd: file hello.cpp, line 26.
(gdb) run
Starting program: /home/eijkhout/intro-programming-private/code/gdb/hello
hello world 1
hello world 2
```

```
hello world 5
hello world 10
hello world 17
hello world 26
hello world 37

Breakpoint 1, main () at hello.cpp:26
26          say(ii);
Missing separate debuginfos, use: debuginfo-install glibc-2.17-292.el7.x86_64 libgcc
    -4.8.5-39.el7.x86_64 libstdc++-4.8.5-39.el7.x86_64
(gdb) print i
$1 = 7
```

28.3.5 ▪ A *NaN* example

The program

```
17    float root(float n)
18    {
19      float r;
20      float n1 = n-1.1;
21      r = sqrt(n1);
22      return r;
23    }
24
25    int main() {
26      float x=9,y;
27      for (int i=0; i<20; i++) {
28        y = root(x);
29        cout << "root: " << y << endl;
30        x -= 1.1;
31      }
32
33      return 0;
34    }
```

prints some numbers that are "not a number":

```
[] ./root
root: 2.81069
root: 2.60768
root: 2.38747
root: 2.14476
root: 1.87083
root: 1.54919
root: 1.14018
root: 0.447214
root: -nan
root: -nan
root: -nan
```

Suppose you want to figure out why this happens.

The line that prints the "nan" is 29, so we want to set a breakpoint there, and preferably a conditional breakpoint. But how do you test on "nan"? This requires a little trick:

```
(gdb) break 29 if y!=y
Breakpoint 1 at 0x400ea6: file root.cpp, line 28.
(gdb) run
Starting program: /home/eijkhout/intro-programming-private/code/gdb/root
root: 2.81069
root: 2.60768
root: 2.38747
root: 2.14476
root: 1.87083
root: 1.54919
root: 1.14018
root: 0.447214
```

```
Breakpoint 1, main () at root.cpp:29
29          cout << "root: " << y << endl;
```

We discover at which iteration this happens:

```
(gdb) print i
$1 = 8
```

so now we can rerun the program and investigate that particular iteration:

```
(gdb) break 28 if i==8
Breakpoint 2 at 0x400eaf: file root.cpp, line 28.
(gdb) run
The program being debugged has been started already.
Start it from the beginning? (y or n) y

Starting program: /home/eijkhout/intro-programming-private/code/gdb/root
root: 2.81069
root: 2.60768
root: 2.38747
root: 2.14476
root: 1.87083
root: 1.54919
root: 1.14018
root: 0.447214

Breakpoint 2, main () at root.cpp:28
28          y = root(x);
```

We now go into the *root* routine to see what is going wrong there:

```
(gdb) step
root (n=0.200000554) at root.cpp:20
20        float n1 = n-1.1;
(gdb)
21        r = sqrt(n1);
(gdb) print n
$2 = 0.200000554
(gdb) print n1
$3 = -0.89999944
(gdb) next
22        return r;
(gdb) print r
$4 = -nan(0x400000)
```

And there we have the problem: our input *n* is used to compute another number *n1* of which we compute the square root, and sometimes this number becomes negative. In this simple example that's the end of the story, but in a realistic example you would now probably have discovered a flaw in the program logic, and you can fix your code.

Chapter 29

Memory errors and memory tools

Some of the hardest errors to track down are the so-called *memory errors*, also known as *memory corruption*. These are errors that only appear at runtime, and that are usually hard or impossible to detect by the compiler.

In C++ it is a lot harder to have memory errors than it is in C, if you use standard containers and smart pointers. However, the possibility of memory errors cannot be ruled out completely, hence the need for various tools. In this chapter we will show the diagnostic tool valgrind; interactive debuggers (Chapter 28) can also help in locating memory errors.

Also, it deserves mention that many memory problems come from string handling, which is not a major concern in scientific computing. Programmers in scientific computing can stick with basic usage of the `string` header and not worry about performance optimization of those parts of their code.

29.1 ▪ Examples of memory errors

29.1.1 ▪ Array bound errors

Array indexing with `operator[]` does not perform bound checking for reasons of efficiency. This means that it is possible to ask for array indices that do not conform to an existing location:

```
std::vector<double> x(5);
std::cout << x[5];
```

Without bound checking, this erroneous code may run, giving some unspecified result. (Going too far outside the array bounds will typically crash your code.)

The `at` function does perform bound checking, but at some cost in performance. Range-based loops and algorithms dispense with indexing altogether, so they are a safer option for array handling.

29.1.2 ▪ Pointer errors

Like reading outside array bounds, following an uninitialized pointer may not crash your code:

```
double *x1 = NULL;
std::cout << *x1; // this will crash
double *x2;
```

```
std::cout << *x2; // not clear
std::shared_pointer<double> x3 = nullptr;
std::cout << *x3; // does not generate an exception
```

29.1.3 ▪ Uninitialized memory read

Reading from an uninitialized variable

```
int x;
std::cout << x;
int y = 2*x;
```

succeeds, but gives an unspecified result. Thus, further calculations using this variable will likely be erroneous. This problem can only be found with external tools.

29.1.4 ▪ Memory leaks

We say that a program has a *memory leak* if it allocates memory and subsequently loses track of that memory. The operating system (OS) then thinks the memory is in use, while it is not, and as a result the computer memory can get filled up with allocated memory that serves no useful purpose.

In this example data is allocated inside a lexical scope:

```
for (i=.... ) {
  float *block = malloc( /* large number of bytes */ )
  /* do something with that block of memory */
  /* and forget to call "free" on that block */
}
```

The block of memory is allocated in each iteration, but the allocation of one iteration is no longer available in the next. A similar example can be made with allocating inside a conditional.

C++ standard containers have largely made this problem go away.

Memory leaks may not be fatal to the program run, or manifest themselves in incorrect results. However, long running programs with memory leaks may abort because of an inability to allocate more memory.

29.2 ▪ Valgrind

Errors leading to memory problems are easy to make. In this section we will see how *valgrind* makes it possible to track down these errors. The use of valgrind is simplicity itself:

```
valgrind yourprogram yourargs
```

As a first example, consider out-of-bound addressing, also known as *buffer overflow*:

```
// corruption/cxx/outofbound.cpp
vector<float> x(n);
cout << x[n] << '\n';
```

This is unlikely to crash your code, but the results are unpredictable, and this is certainly a failure of your program logic.

Valgrind indicates that this is an invalid read, what line it occurs on, and where the block was allocated:

```
==9112== Invalid read of size 4
==9112==    at 0x40233B: main (outofbound.cpp:10)
==9112==  Address 0x595fde8 is 0 bytes after a block of size 40 alloc'd
==9112==    at 0x4C2A483: operator new(unsigned long) (vg_replace_malloc.c:344)
==9112==    by 0x4023CD: allocate (new_allocator.h:111)
==9112==    by 0x4023CD: allocate (alloc_traits.h:436)
==9112==    by 0x4023CD: _M_allocate (stl_vector.h:296)
==9112==    by 0x4023CD: _M_create_storage (stl_vector.h:311)
==9112==    by 0x4023CD: _Vector_base (stl_vector.h:260)
==9112==    by 0x4023CD: _Vector_base (stl_vector.h:258)
==9112==    by 0x4023CD: vector (stl_vector.h:415)
==9112==    by 0x4023CD: main (outofbound.cpp:9)
```

Remark. *Buffer overflows are a well-known security risk, typically associated with reading string input from a user source. Buffer overflows can be largely avoided by using C++ constructs such as* `cin` *and* `string` *instead of* `sscanf` *and character arrays.*

Valgrind is informative but cryptic, since it works on the bare memory, not on variables. Thus, these error messages take some exegesis. They state that line 10 reads a 4-byte object immediately after a block of 40 bytes that was allocated. In other words, the code is writing outside the bounds of an allocated array. The output also gives an indication where in the source that allocation was performed, which is usually enough to pinpoint the problem.

The next example performs a read on an array that has already been freed. In this simple case you will actually get the expected output, but if the read comes much later than the free, the output can be anything. (Do you understand how that can happen?)

```
// corruption/cxx/free.cpp
auto ar = new float[10000];
ar[n] = 3.14;
delete [] ar;
cout << ar[n] << '\n';
```

Valgrind again states that this is an invalid read; it gives both where the block was allocated and where it was freed.

```
==11431== Invalid read of size 4
==11431==    at 0x40230C: main (free.cpp:13)
==11431==  Address 0x595fdcc is 12 bytes inside a block of size 40,000 free'd
==11431==    at 0x4C2B5CF: operator delete(void*, unsigned long) (vg_replace_malloc.c:595)
==11431==    by 0x402301: main (free.cpp:12)
==11431==  Block was alloc'd at
==11431==    at 0x4C2AB28: operator new[](unsigned long) (vg_replace_malloc.c:433)
==11431==    by 0x4022E0: main (free.cpp:10)
```

On the other hand, if you forget to free memory you have a *memory leak* (just imagine allocating, and not freeing, in a loop; see section 29.1.4):

```
// corruption/cxx/leak.cpp
auto ar = new float[10000];
ar[n] = 3.14;
cout << ar[n] << '\n';
return 0;
```

which valgrind reports on:

```
==283234== LEAK SUMMARY:
==283234==    definitely lost: 40,000 bytes in 1 blocks
```

```
==283234==    indirectly lost: 0 bytes in 0 blocks
==283234==      possibly lost: 0 bytes in 0 blocks
==283234==    still reachable: 8 bytes in 1 blocks
==283234==         suppressed: 0 bytes in 0 blocks
```

Memory leaks are much more rare in C++ than in C because of containers such as `std::vector`. However, in sophisticated cases you may still do your own memory management, and you need to be aware of the danger of memory leaks.

If you do your own memory management, there is also a danger of writing to an array pointer that has not been allocated yet:

```
// corruption/cxx/init.cpp
float* ar;
ar[n] = 3.14;
cout << ar[n] << '\n';
```

The behavior of this code depends on all sorts of things: if the pointer variable is zero, the code will crash. On the other hand, if it contains some random value, the write may succeed, provided you are not writing too far from that location.

The output here shows both the valgrind diagnosis and the OS message when the program aborted:

```
==283234== LEAK SUMMARY:
==283234==    definitely lost: 40,000 bytes in 1 blocks
==283234==    indirectly lost: 0 bytes in 0 blocks
==283234==      possibly lost: 0 bytes in 0 blocks
==283234==    still reachable: 8 bytes in 1 blocks
==283234==         suppressed: 0 bytes in 0 blocks
```

Chapter 30
Software libraries

If you have a C++ compiler, you can write as much software as you want, by yourself. However, some things that you may need for your work have already been written by someone else, and with a little luck that other programmer has published the code as a library.

This chapter teaches you how to install and use libraries, and will discuss a couple of libraries that are useful in the context of scientific computing.

30.1 ▪ What are software libraries?

In this chapter you will learn about the use of *software libraries*: software that is written not as a standalone package, but in such a way that you can access its functionality in your own program.

Software libraries can be enormous, as is the case for scientific libraries, which are often multi-person multiyear projects. On the other hand, many of them are fairly simple utilities written by a single programmer. In the latter case you may have to worry about future support of that software.

30.1.1 ▪ Using an external library

Using a software library typically means that

- your program has a line

  ```
  #include "fancylib.h"
  ```

- and you compile and link as

  ```
  icpc -c yourprogram.cpp -I/usr/include/fancylib
  icpc -o yourprogram yourprogram.o \
      -L/usr/lib/fancylib -lfancy
  ```

You will see specific examples below.

Remark. *There are so-called* header-only libraries, *meaning that they consist only of files to be included, and have no library files. In that case, of course, nothing has to be added to the link line.*

If you are now worried about having to do a lot of typing every time you compile,

- if you use an IDE, you can typically add the library in the options, once and for all; or
- you can use *Make* or *CMake* for automating the build process of your program.

These include and library paths can get quite long—you certainly don't want to type them by hand. You could write a little shell script, but it's better to learn Make or CMake (see Chapter 37).

30.1.2 ▪ Obtaining and installing an external library

Sometimes a software library is available through a *package manager* (macports and homebrew on Apple; yum, dpkg, rpm, etc., on Linux), but we are going to do it the old-fashioned way: downloading and installing it ourselves.

A popular location for finding downloadable software is `github.com`, a hosting site for *Git* repositories. (For Git, see Chapter 38.) You can then choose whether to

- download everything in one file, typically with a `.tgz` or `.tar.gz` extension, which you unpack with `tar`; or
- clone the repository, which gives you access to unreleased development software, or at least makes updating your copy easier. This usually gives you a directory with a name such as

  ```
  fancylib-1.0.0
  ```

  containing the source and documentation of the library, but not any binaries or machine-specific files.

Either way, from here on we assume that you have a directory containing the downloaded package.

There are two main types of installation:

- based on *GNU autotools*, which you recognize by the presence of a `configure` program; you then install your software in the following three-step process:

  ```
  configure ## lots of options
  make
  make install
  ```

  or
- based on *CMake* (see Chapter 37), which you recognize by the presence of the `CMakeLists.txt` file:

  ```
  cmake ## lots of options
  make
  make install
  ```

Remark. *Both* `configure` *and* CMake *will by default try to install your software in a system location such as* `/usr/local/lib`. *If you don't have permission to write there, you can supply an alternative location:*

```
configure --prefix=/home/myname/mylibs
cmake -D CMAKE_INSTALL_PREFIX=/home/myname/mylibs
```

30.2 ▪ Linear algebra with Eigen

The *Eigen* library offers an idiomatic C++ implementation of common linear algebra operations, both with sparse and dense matrices. While its API is different from that of traditional linear algebra libraries, for its implementation it often relies on them, in particular for dense matrices. Consequently, it offers both programming convenience and high performance.

30.2.1 ▪ Example: Matrix operations

Matrices in Eigen can be created with compile-time determined sizes,

```
Eigen::Matrix<float,2,2> square2x2;
```

or dynamically set sizes,

```
// eigen/gemm.cpp
Eigen::MatrixXf C(size,size);
```

where `MatrixXf` is a typedef for

```
Matrix<float,Eigen::Dynamic,Eigen::Dynamic>
```

For addition and multiplication, the regular operators have been overloaded, so that you can write

```
C = A*B;
```

for matrices with conforming sizes.

Many operations in Eigen are not executed by themselves, but rather through *expression templates*; see Chapter 16. Thus

```
A+B+C*2
```

does not form any temporary matrix objects.

As an operation not part of the BLAS, we consider the *generalized inverse*:

```
// eigen/penrose.cpp
auto gen_inverse = ( A.transpose() * A ).inverse() * A.transpose();
x = gen_inverse *b;
```

30.2.2 ▪ CMake integration

The *eigen* package can use `pkgconfig`.

```
cmake_minimum_required( VERSION 3.13 )
project( eigentest )

find_package( PkgConfig REQUIRED )
pkg_check_modules( EIGEN REQUIRED eigen3 )

add_executable( eigentest eigentest.cxx )
target_include_directories(
        eigentest PUBLIC
        ${EIGEN_INCLUDE_DIRS})
```

It also has its own module:

```
find_package( Eigen3 REQUIRED  )
target_link_libraries( ${PROJECTNAME} PUBLIC Eigen3::Eigen )
```

30.3 ▪ Scientific data with HDF5

There are many ways of storing data, in particular data that comes in arrays. A surprising number of people store data in spreadsheets, then export them to ASCII files with comma or tab delimiters, and expect other people (or other programs written by themselves) to read that in again. Such a process is wasteful in several respects:

- The ASCII representation of a number takes up much more space than the internal binary representation. Ideally, you would want a file to be as compact as the representation in memory.
- Conversion to and from ASCII is slow; it may also lead to loss of precision.

For such reasons, it is desirable to have a file format that is based on binary storage. There are a few more requirements on a useful file format:

- Since binary storage can differ between platforms, a good file format is platform-independent. This will, for instance, prevent the confusion between *big-endian* and *little-endian* storage, as well as conventions of 32- versus 64-bit floating point numbers.
- Application data can be heterogeneous, comprising integer, character, and floating point data. Ideally, all this data should be stored together.
- Application data is also structured. This structure should be reflected in the stored form.
- It is desirable for a file format to be *self-documenting*. If you store a matrix and a right-hand side vector in a file, wouldn't it be nice if the file itself told you which of the stored numbers are the matrix, which the vector, and what the sizes of the objects are?

This tutorial will introduce the HDF5 library, which fulfills these requirements.

HDF5 is of a higher level than, and built on top of, file I/O and binary data storage discussed in Chapter 5. The standard application programmer interface (API) to HDF5 is very C-oriented, and far from idiomatically C++ looking. Therefore, we will use the third-party HighFive [15] library of C++ bindings. There are C++ bindings developed by the HDF group themselves, but these are old and incomplete, and not recommended.

Installing HDF5 and HighFive through CMake is covered in section 30.3.2.

30.3.1 ▪ Examples

HDF5 revolves around the two activities of writing and reading files.

For simple datasets, such as a `std::vector`, you can create the file and write it in literally two lines. Here we write an array of 10 elements, and visualize it with the utility `h5dump`:

Code:

```
// highfive/cpp/vector.cpp
File file(filename,File::Truncate);
file.createDataSet("grp/data", vectordata);
```

Output:

```
HDF5 "vector_file.h5" {
GROUP "/" {
   GROUP "grp" {
      DATASET "data" {
         DATATYPE  H5T_STD_I32LE
         DATASPACE  SIMPLE { ( 10 ) / ( 10 ) }
         DATA {
         (0): 1, 2, 3, 4, 5, 6, 7, 8, 9, 10
         }
      }
   }
}
}
```

30.3.1.1 ▪ Writing

HDF5 files behave a little like file-systems-in-a-file: you see in the second line of the example that the data is written in a "dataset," which you can compare to a subdirectory. The file dump bears out this directory structure.

Note that the behavior of the `File` class is scoped: the file is automatically flushed and closed at the end of the containing scope.

Many routines are also templated, making it unnecessary to deal with datatypes explicitly. For example, here we write both integers and strings to a file:

Code:

```
// highfive/cpp/vectors.cpp
std::vector<int>  data1 = {1,2,3,4,5};
std::vector<string> data2 = {"a","b","c","d","e
     "};
File file(filename,File::Truncate);
file.createDataSet("grp/data1", data1);
file.createDataSet("grp/data2", data2);
```

Output:

```
HDF5 "vectors_file.h5" {
GROUP "/" {
   GROUP "grp" {
      DATASET "data1" {
         DATATYPE  H5T_STD_I32LE
         DATASPACE  SIMPLE { ( 5 ) / ( 5 ) }
         DATA {
         (0): 1, 2, 3, 4, 5
         }
      }
      DATASET "data2" {
         DATATYPE  H5T_STRING {
            STRSIZE H5T_VARIABLE;
            STRPAD H5T_STR_NULLTERM;
            CSET H5T_CSET_UTF8;
            CTYPE H5T_C_S1;
         }
         DATASPACE  SIMPLE { ( 5 ) / ( 5 ) }
         DATA {
         (0): "a", "b", "c", "d", "e"
         }
      }
   }
}
}
```

You see that the dump now has information on precisely how the strings are realized.

30.3.1.2 ▪ Reading

Datasets are written by name and are retrieved similarly. In particular, we can extract them in the opposite order of the one in which they were written:

```
// highfive/cpp/vectors.cpp
File file(filename, File::ReadOnly);
auto dataset1 = file.getDataSet("grp/data1");
auto dataset2 = file.getDataSet("grp/data2");
// Read back, with allocating:
auto data2 = dataset2.read<std::vector<string>>();
auto data1 = dataset1.read<std::vector<int>>();
dataset2.read(data2);
dataset1.read(data1);
```

30.3.2 ▪ CMake integration

The basic HDF5 package can be discovered through pkgconfig:

```
find_package( PkgConfig REQUIRED )
pkg_check_modules( HDF REQUIRED hdf5 )
target_include_directories(
        ${PROJECTNAME} PUBLIC
        ${HDF_INCLUDE_DIRS}
        )
```

There is also a module:

```
find_package( HDF5 REQUIRED COMPONENTS C Fortran  )
if( ${HDF5_FOUND} )
    message( STATUS "Found hdf5: ${HDF5_INCLUDE_DIRS}" )
endif()

target_link_libraries(
        ${PROJECTNAME} PUBLIC
        hdf5::hdf5
        )
```

30.4 ▪ Command-line options processing

Suppose you have a program that does something with a large array. How are you specifying the size of the array? You can hardcode it,

```
vector<double> simulation(10000000);
```

which requires you to recompile the program if the amount of data ever changes. You can read it in from the command line,

```
size_t ndata;
cin >> ndata;
vector<double> simulation(ndata);
```

which requires you to enter this every time you run the program, and this makes it inconvenient to incorporate into a shell script.

Instead, you may want to pass this size as a command-line argument,

```
./myprogram --ndata 10000000
```

which is easier to retrieve from the shell *command history*, or to put in a shell script.

Command-line arguments enter your code through the optional `argc,argv` arguments of the `main`. We start with a brief recap of how you could parse these yourself, but then go into the `cxxopts` library that makes this easy.

30.4.1 ▪ Traditional command-line parsing

Command-line options are available to the program through the (optional) `argv` and `argc` options of the `main` program. The former is an array of strings, with the second the length of that array, noting that index 0 is the name of the program, so `argc` is always at least 1:

```
int main( int argc,char **argv ) { /* program */ };
```

For simple cases it would be feasible to parse such options yourself:

Code:

```
// args/argcv.cpp
cout << "Program name: "
     << argv[0] << '\n';
for (int iarg=1; iarg<argc; ++iarg)
  cout << "arg: " << iarg
       << argv[iarg] << " => "
       << atoi( argv[iarg] ) << '\n';
```

Output:

```
./argcv 5 12
Program name: ./argcv
arg 1: 5 => 5
arg 2: 12 => 12
./argcv abc 3.14 foo
Program name: ./argcv
arg 1: abc => 0
arg 2: 3.14 => 3
arg 3: foo => 0
```

but this gets tedious quickly and is difficult to make robust. Therefore, we will now look at a library that makes such options handling relatively easy.

30.4.2 ▪ The cxxopts library

We will now discuss the *cxxopts* "command-line argument parser." It lets you construct an options object that has the information on all possible flags, any default values, and what types they can take.

First of all you need to include the header

```
#include "cxxopts.hpp"
```

We will now discuss the workings of this library.

30.4.2.1 ▪ Simple example

The following shows how to declare two options, one for an integer value, and one getting a help message. The code tests for the help option; if it is present, it displays the help message and exits; otherwise it tests for the numeric option:

Code:

```
// args/cxxn.cpp
cxxopts::Options options
  ("cxxopts",
   "Commandline options demo");
options.add_options()
  ("n,ntimes","number of times",
   cxxopts::value<int>()
   ->default_value("37")
   )
  ("h,help","usage information")
  ;
auto result = options.parse(argc, argv);
if (result.count("help")>0) {
  cout << options.help() << '\n';
  return 0;
}
auto number_of_times = result["ntimes"].as<int
     >();
cout << "number of times: "
     << number_of_times << '\n';
```

Output:

```
./cxxn -h
Commandline options demo
Usage:
  cxxopts [OPTION...]

  -n, --ntimes arg  number of
     ↪times (default: 37)
  -h, --help        usage
     ↪information

./cxxn -n 5 foo
number of times: 5
```

30.4.2.2 ▪ Discussion

Here is a more detailed listing of the actions that are needed or possible when using `cxxoptions`.

Declare an options object:

```
cxxopts::Options options("programname", "Program description");
```

Add options:

```
// args/cxxopts.cpp
// define '-n 567' option:
options.add_options()
  ("n,ntimes","number of times",
   cxxopts::value<int>()
   ->default_value("37")
   )
  ;
  /* ... */
// read out '-n' option and use:
auto number_of_times = result["ntimes"].as<int>();
cout << "Using number of times: " << number_of_times << '\n';
```

Add array options:

```
// args/cxxopts.cpp
//define '-a 1,2,5,7' option:
options.add_options()
  ("a,array","array of values",
   cxxopts::value< vector<int> >()->default_value("1,2,3")
   )
  ;
  /* ... */
auto array = result["array"].as<vector<int>>();
cout << "Array: " ;
for ( auto a : array ) cout << a << ", ";
cout << '\n';
```

Add positional arguments:

```
// args/cxxopts.cpp
// define 'positional argument' option:
options.add_options()
  ("keyword","whatever keyword",
   cxxopts::value<string>())
  ;
options.parse_positional({"keyword"});
  /* ... */
// read out keyword option and use:
auto keyword = result["keyword"].as<string>();
cout << "Found keyword: " << keyword << '\n';
```

Parse the options:

```
auto result = options.parse(argc, argv);
```

Get help flag first:

```
// args/cxxopts.cpp
options.add_options()
  ("h,help","usage information")
  ;
```

```
/* ... */
auto result = options.parse(argc, argv);
if (result.count("help")>0) {
  cout << options.help() << '\n';
  return 0;
}
```

Options can be specified the usual ways:

```
myprogram -n 10
myprogram --nsize 100
myprogram --nsize=1000
myprogram --array 12,13,14,15
```

Options parsing can throw a `cxxopts::exceptions::option_has_no_value` exception.

30.4.3 ▪ CMake integration

The *cxxopts* package can both uses `pkgconfig` and a CMake module. Using pkgconfig,

```
find_package( PkgConfig REQUIRED )
pkg_check_modules( OPTS REQUIRED cxxopts )
target_include_directories(
     ${PROGRAM_NAME} PUBLIC
     ${OPTS_INCLUDE_DIRS}
     )
```

or using the CMake module,

```
find_package( cxxopts REQUIRED )
target_link_libraries(
        ${PROGRAM_NAME} PUBLIC
        cxxopts::cxxopts
        )
```

Part V

Performance: Measurement and Optimization

Programming and performance In this part we will look at issues in programming that are related to performance. This is an important but complicated topic: assuming you already know how to program, if there are two implementations that do the same thing, will one run faster than the other? We approach this by first looking at the hardware, then the algorithmic aspects, and finally integrating the two.

While there are many factors influencing performance, here we mostly focus on issues of how a processor interacts with memory. We do this by explaining the memory subsystem of a processor, how it influences performance, and how we can program to improve performance.

The "memory wall" problem To the programmer, a computer appears to execute a sequence of steps:

1. decode an instruction to determine the operands,
2. retrieve the operands from memory,
3. execute the operation and write the result back to memory.

This picture is unrealistic because of the so-called *memory wall* [56], also known as the *von Neumann bottleneck*: memory is too slow to load data into the processor at the rate the processor can absorb it. Specifically, a single load can have a latency of hundreds of cycles, meaning that this much time elapses between a processor requesting a memory item and it actually arriving for processing. On the other hand, a processor can perform several operations per cycle.

To circumvent this imbalance, a modern CPU has several memory levels in between the floating point unit (FPU) and the main memory: the registers and the caches, together called the *memory hierarchy*. These try to alleviate the memory wall problem by making recently used data available quicker than it would be from main memory. We analyze the memory hierarchy in Chapter 31.

Reuse as the key to performance Performance improvement by exploiting the memory hierarchy presupposes that the algorithm and its implementation allow for data to be used multiple times. Such questions of *data reuse* will be discussed in more detail in Chapter 32.

Programming for performance Since using data in register or cache is faster than getting data from main memory, a programmer obviously wants to maximize data reuse in order to get higher performance. While placing data in cache is not under explicit programmer control, even from assembly language, in most CPUs it is still possible to know what data is in cache, and to some extent to control it. We discuss this in Chapter 32.

More We conclude this part of the book with chapters on profiling and on computer arithmetic, which is related to hardware, but not really about performance.

There are other factors to high performance, such as optimizing *branch prediction*, that we will entirely not touch on, and vectorization of arithmetic instructions, which we briefly discussed in section 18.2.

Chapter 31

Processor architecture

Among the aspects of computer architecture relevant to high performance computing (HPC), probably the most important are the architectural details relating to memory and data movement inside the processor and between processor and memory. In this chapter we give a concise introduction to the memory subsystem of a computer; subsequent chapters will then apply this knowledge to coding for performance.

31.1 ▪ Registers

Every processor has a small amount of memory that is internal to the processor: the *registers*, or together the *register file*. The registers are what the processor actually operates on: an operation such as

```
a = b + c
```

can be thought of as being implemented as follows:

- load the value of `b` from memory into a register;
- load the value of `c` from memory into another register;
- compute the sum and write that into the same or yet another register; and
- write the sum value back to the memory location of `a`.

Looking at *assembly code* (for instance, the output of a compiler; see section 36.1) you see explicit load, compute, and store instructions, such as

```
addl    %eax, %edx
```

which adds the content of one register to another. As you see in this sample instruction, registers are not numbered, as opposed to memory addresses, but have distinct names that are referred to in the assembly instruction. Typically, a processor has 16 or 32 floating point registers; the *Intel Itanium* was exceptional with 128 floating point registers.

Registers are a first way of minimizing expensive data movement. For instance, a strict interpretation of these instructions,

```
a = b + c
d = a + e
```

would see a written to main memory after the first instruction, and then reloaded for the second. As an obvious optimization, the computed value of a could be left in register: we say that a stays *resident in register*. This is typically performed as a *compiler optimization*.

Keeping values in register is often done to avoid recomputing a quantity. For instance, in

```
t1 = sin(alpha) * x + cos(alpha) * y;
t2 = -cos(alpha) * x + sin(alpha) * y;
```

the sine and cosine quantity will probably be kept in register. You can help the compiler by explicitly introducing temporary quantities:

```
s = sin(alpha); c = cos(alpha);
t1 = s * x + c * y;
t2 = -c * x + s * y
```

However, compilers can often figure out such transformations by themselves, if you set the *optimization level* high enough; see section 36.4.

Of course, there is a limit to how many quantities can be kept in register; trying to keep too many quantities in register is called *register spill* and lowers the performance of a code.

31.2 ▪ Caches

To motivate the use of caches let's suppose a variable x is used twice, and that it does not stay resident in a register:

```
... = ... x .....   // instruction using x
.........           // several instructions not involving x
... = ... x .....   // instruction using x
```

The assembly code would then be

- load x from memory into register; operate on it;
- do the intervening instructions;
- load x from memory into register; operate on it.

With a cache, the assembly code stays the same, but the actual behavior of the memory system now becomes

- load x from memory into cache, and from cache into register; operate on it;
- do the intervening instructions;
- request x from memory, but since it is still in the cache, load it from the cache into register; operate on it.

Loading from cache is faster than loading from main memory in two ways. The load has a shorter *latency*, meaning the delay between the data being needed in an instruction and it actually being available. Caches also have a higher *bandwidth*, meaning the number of bytes per second transferred. Thus, if a computation can use data from cache it will be faster than if it relies on data from main memory. Caches are fairly small, so arranging a computation in this manner may take some sophisticated programming.

There is an important difference between cache memory and registers: while data is moved into register by explicit assembly instructions, the move from main memory to cache is entirely done by hardware, invisible to the programmer.

31.2.1 ▪ Cache levels

The caches are called “level 1” and “level 2” (or, for short, L1 and L2) caches. Modern processors can have an L3, and sometimes an L4 cache. The L1 and L2 caches are part of the *die*, the processor chip, although for the L2 cache that is a relatively recent development; higher level caches can be off-chip. Caches can be *private* to a core, as is typically the case for the L1 cache, or *shared* between some or all of the cores.

The L1 cache is small, typically around 16 or 32 Kbyte. Level 2 (and, when present, level 3) cache is more plentiful, up to several megabytes, but it is also slower, with longer latency and lower bandwidth. Figure 31.1 has some representative numbers. Unlike main memory, which is expandable, caches are fixed in size. If a version of a processor exists with a larger cache, it is usually considerably more expensive.

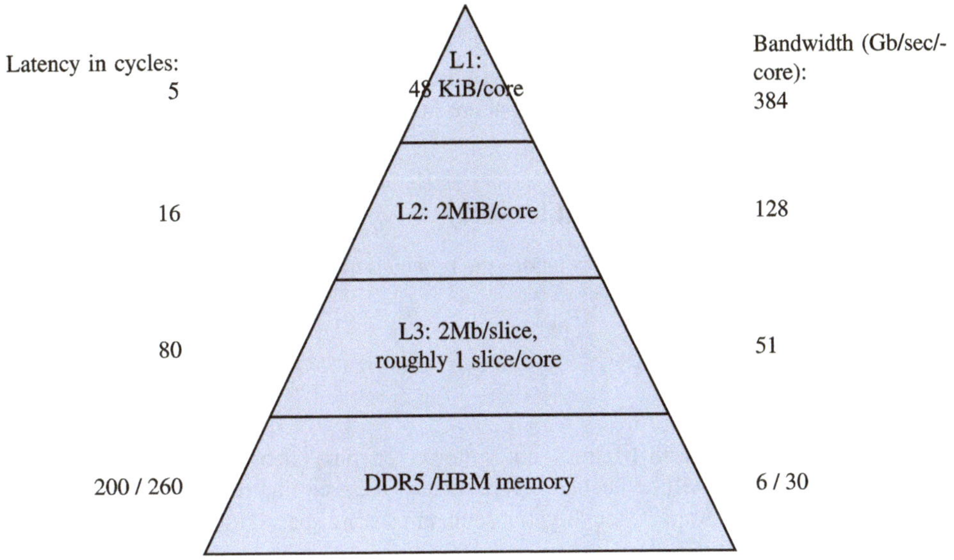

Figure 31.1. *Memory hierarchy of an Intel Sapphire Rapids processor*

31.2.2 ▪ Cache hits and misses

Data needed in some operation gets copied into the various caches on its way to the processor. If, some instructions later, a data item is needed again, it is first searched for in the L1 cache; if it is not found there, it is searched for in the L2 cache; if it is not found there, it is loaded from further cache levels or main memory. Finding data in cache is called a *cache hit*, and not finding it a *cache miss*.

The most common type of cache miss is the “capacity miss,” where more data is accessed than fits the cache. The process of cache data being overwritten by data loaded later is referred to as the earlier data being *flushed*. This is illustrated in Figure 31.2.

31.2.3 ▪ Temporal and spatial locality

In the context of performance optimization, two crucial concepts are *temporal locality* and *spatial locality*. Temporal locality is the easiest to explain: this describes the use of a data element within

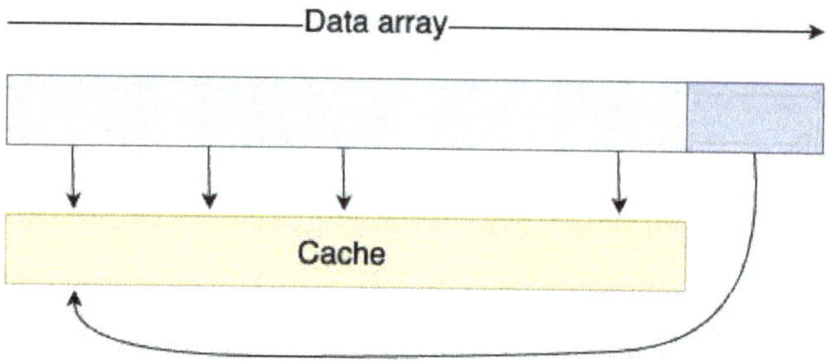

Figure 31.2. *Large vector flushes old data from cache*

a short time of its last use. If the second reference comes quickly enough after the first, data will still be in cache and is therefore more quickly accessible.

Spatial locality is harder to explain, and we will do so in detail later. The basic idea is that after one data item has been referenced, others that are in some sense "close to it" will be quicker to load.

31.2.4 ▪ Caches and temporal locality

As an example of *temporal locality*, consider the repeated traversal of a long vector:

```
for (int loop=0; loop<10; ++loop) {
  for (int i=0; i<N; ++i) {
    ... = ... x[i] ...
  }
}
```

Each element of x will be used 10 times, but if the vector (plus other data accessed) exceeds the cache size, each element will be flushed before its next use; see Figure 31.2. Therefore, the use of `x[i]` does not exhibit temporal locality: subsequent uses are spaced too far apart in time for an array element to remain in cache.

If the structure of the computation allows us to exchange the loops,

```
for (int i=0; i<N; ++i) {
  for (int loop=0; loop<10; ++loop) {
    ... = ... x[i] ...
  }
}
```

the elements of x are now repeatedly reused, and are therefore more likely to remain in the cache. This rearranged code displays better temporal locality in its use of `x[i]`. (On the other hand, the original code is more likely to use vector instructions. The loss of these counteracts the performance gain from the cache to an extent.)

31.2.5 ▪ Cache lines

Data movement between memory and cache, or between caches, is not done in single bytes, or even words. Instead, the smallest unit of data moved is called a *cacheline*, sometimes called a *cache block*. A typical cacheline is 64 or 128 bytes long, which in the context of scientific computing implies 8 or 16 double precision floating point numbers. The cacheline size for data moved into the L2 cache can be larger than for data moved into the L1 cache.

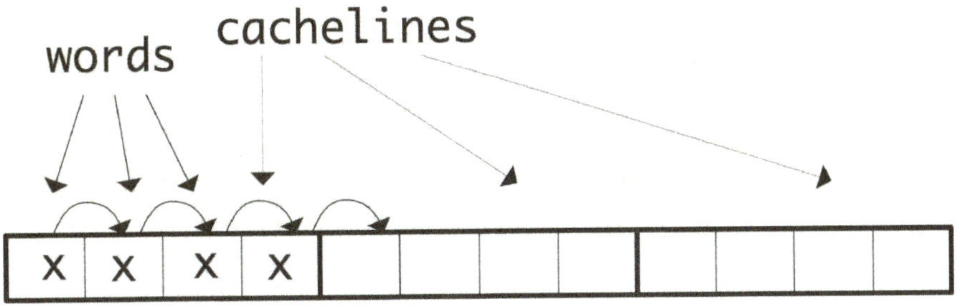

Figure 31.3. *Accessing 4 elements at stride 1*

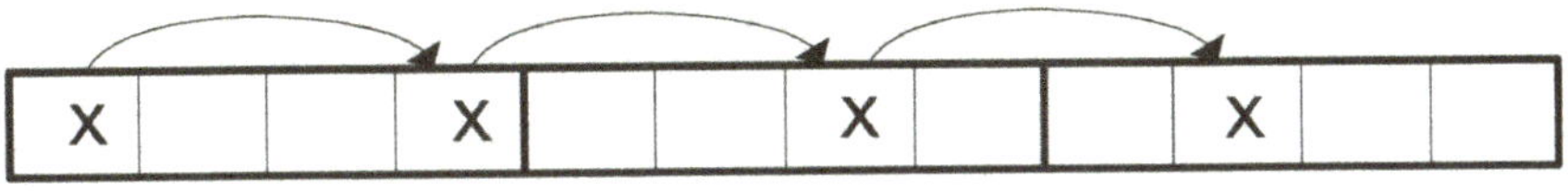

Figure 31.4. *Accessing 4 elements at stride 3*

A first motivation for cachelines is a practical one of simplification: if a cacheline is 64 bytes long, six fewer bits need to be specified to the circuitry that moves data from memory to cache. Second, cachelines make sense since many codes show *spatial locality*: if one word from memory is needed, there is a good chance that adjacent words will be needed pretty soon after.

Conversely, there is now a strong incentive to code in such a way to exploit this locality, since any memory access costs the transfer of several words. An efficient program then tries to use the other items on the cacheline, since access to them is effectively free. This phenomenon is visible in code that accesses arrays by *stride*: elements are read or written at regular intervals.

Stride 1 corresponds to sequential access of an array:

```
for (int i=0; i<N; ++i)
  ... = ... x[i] ...
```

In Figure 31.3 we have illustrated this case with 4 words per cacheline. Requesting the first element loads the whole cacheline that contains it into cache. A request for the second, third, and fourth elements can then be satisfied from cache, meaning with high bandwidth and low latency.

A larger stride, illustrated in Figure 31.4,

```
for (int i=0; i<N; i+=stride)
  ... = ... x[i] ...
```

implies that in every cacheline only certain elements are used. We illustrate that with stride 3: requesting the first element loads a cacheline, and this cacheline also contains the second element. However, the third element is on the next cacheline, so loading this incurs the latency and bandwidth of main memory. The same holds for the fourth element. Loading four elements now needs loading three cachelines instead of one, meaning that two-thirds of the available bandwidth has been wasted. (This second case would also incur three times the latency of the first, if it weren't for the hardware *prefetch* mechanism that notices the regular access patterns, and preemptively loads further cachelines; see section 31.3.)

31.2.6 ▪ Replacement policies

Data in cache is placed there by the system, outside of programmer control. Likewise, the system decides when to overwrite data in the cache if it is not referenced in a while, and as other data needs to be placed there. Below, we will go into detail on how caches do this, but as a general principle, a least recently used (LRU) cache replacement policy is used: if a cache is full and new data needs to be placed into it, the data that was least recently used is *flushed* (sometimes: *evicted*) from cache, meaning that it is overwritten with the new data, and is therefore no longer accessible. LRU is by far the most common replacement policy; other possibilities are FIFO (first in, first out) or random replacement.

31.2.7 ▪ Cache mapping and associativity

In this section we explore the idea of associativity; practical aspects of cache associativity are explored in section 33.2.

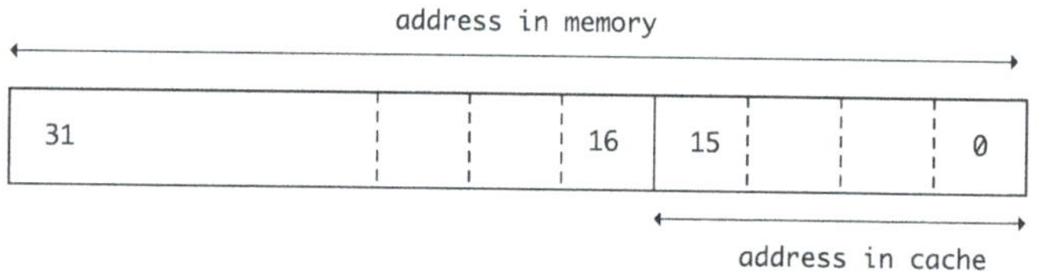

Figure 31.5. *Direct cache mapping*

We refer to the translation from memory address to cache address as *cache mapping*. If the cache size is a power of 2, either words or cachelines, a simple scheme is to take the last number of bits of the address to find the location in the cache. This scheme, called *direct mapping* makes sense: if you traverse an array, a contiguous set of addresses will be mapped to the cache without conflict. In Figure 31.5 we illustrate the direct mapping of 32-bit addresses into a 64K cache using the last 16 bits of an address.

While direct mapping is easy to realize, there are practical problems with it. The direct mapping scheme has the effect that memory addresses that are a cache size apart get mapped to the same cache location. For example, given a 64Kbyte cache, the following code maps all quantities from any given iteration to the same address:

```
double A[3][8192];
for (int i=0; i<512; ++i)
  a[2][i] = ( a[0][i]+a[1][i] )/2.;
```

Therefore, in each iteration

- the cacheline of `a[0][i]` is loaded;
- the cacheline of `a[1][i]` is loaded, flushing that of `a[0][i]`;
- the cacheline of `a[2][i]` is loaded, flushing the last loaded cacheline;
- in the next iteration `a[0][i+1]` should have been in cache because it shared a cacheline with `a[0][i]`, but that was flushed so the line needs to be reloaded.

In effect, 8 iterations should load 3 cachelines, but because of mapping conflicts they load 24. The repeated cache misses in this scenario are referred to as *conflict misses*.

The problem of cache conflicts would be solved if any data item could go to any cache location. In that case there would be no conflicts, other than the cache filling up, in which case a cache replacement policy (section 31.2.6) would flush data to make room for any incoming item. This is called a *fully associative cache*, and while this design seems optimal, it is also very costly to build, and slower in use than a direct mapped cache.

For this reason, the most common solution is to have a k-way *associative cache*, where k is at least two. In this case, a data item can go to any of k cache locations.

Code would have to have a $k+1$-way conflict before data would be flushed as in the above example. In that example, a value of $k = 3$ would suffice, but in practice higher values are often encountered. Figure 31.6 illustrates the mapping of memory addresses to cache locations for a direct mapped and a 3-way associative cache. Both caches have 12 elements, but these are used differently. The direct mapped cache (left) will have a conflict between memory addresses 0 and 12, but in the 3-way associative cache these two addresses can be mapped to any of three elements.

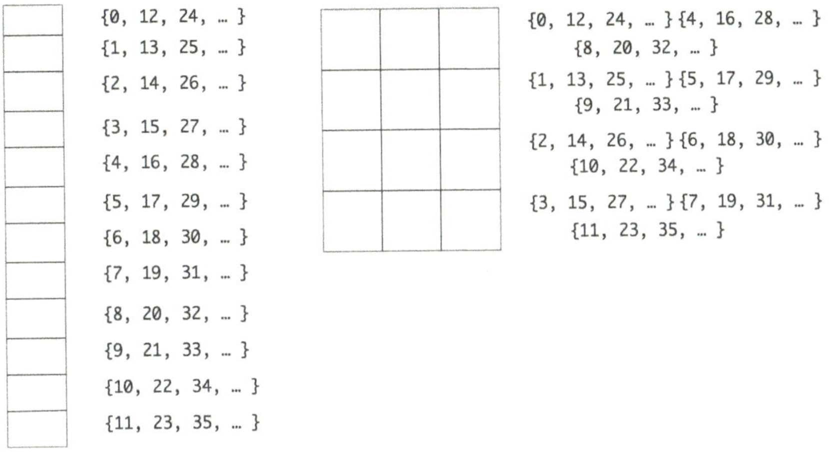

Figure 31.6. *Two caches of 12 elements: direct mapped (left) and 3-way associative (right)*

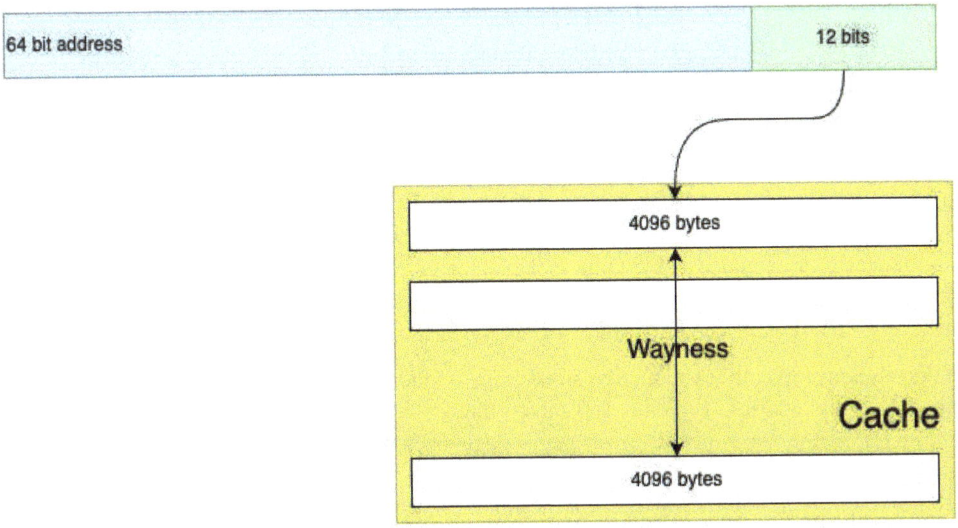

Figure 31.7. *Associative cache structure*

As a practical example, the *Intel Ice Lake* processor has an L1 cache of 48K bytes that is 12-way set associative with a 64-byte cacheline size, and an L2 cache of 1.25M bytes that is 20-way set associative with a 64-byte cacheline size. The L1 structure is depicted in Figure 31.7.

Exercise 31.1. Write a small cache simulator in your favorite language. Assume a k-way associative cache of 32 entries and an architecture with 16-bit addresses. Run the following experiment for $k = 1, 2, 4, \ldots$:

1. Let k be the associativity of the simulated cache.
2. Write the translation from 16-bit memory addresses to $32/k$ cache addresses.
3. Generate 32 random machine addresses, and simulate storing them in cache.

Since the cache has 32 entries, optimally the 32 addresses can all be stored in cache. The chance of this actually happening is small, and often the data of one address will be *evicted* from the cache (meaning that it is overwritten) when another address conflicts with it. Record how many addresses, out of 32, are actually stored in the cache at the end of the simulation. Do step 3 a hundred times and plot the results; give median and average value, and the standard deviation. Observe that increasing the associativity improves the number of addresses stored. What is the limit behavior? (For bonus points, do a formal statistical analysis.)

31.3 ▪ Prefetching

In the traditional von Neumann model each instruction contains the location of its operands, so a CPU implementing this model would make a separate request for each new operand. In practice, subsequent data requests are often adjacent or regularly spaced in memory. The memory system can try to detect such data patterns by looking at cache miss points, and request a *prefetch data stream*; see Figure 31.8.

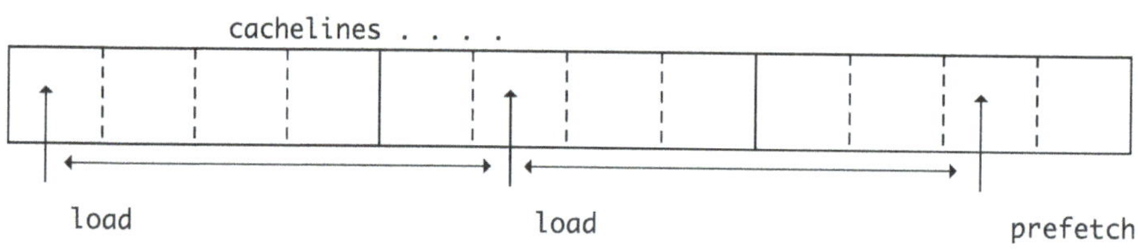

Figure 31.8. *Prefetch stream generated by equally spaced requests*

In its simplest form, the CPU will detect that consecutive loads come from two consecutive cachelines, and automatically issue a request for the next following cacheline. This process can be repeated or extended if the code makes an actual request for that third cacheline. Since these cachelines are now brought from memory well before they are needed, prefetch has the possibility of eliminating the latency for all but the first couple of data items.

Prefetch streams typically cannot cross *small page* boundaries, so it pays to have data be aligned on small page boundaries. Typically this means having a starting address at a multiple of 4K; see section 31.4. Some codes benefit from larger page sizes, for instance, of a megabyte. This can be set at the Operating System (OS) level.

We will see the performance effects of prefetching in action in section 33.1.

31.4 ▪ Paging, virtual memory, and TLB

In time-sharing OSs many programs, possibly from several users, can be active at the same time. To manage how these programs refer to the memory of the computer, *virtual memory* is used: programs refer to "virtual addresses" that are different from physical addresses. This way, each program acts as if it has access to all the memory in the computer.

For this reason, we need a translation mechanism from the memory addresses that the program uses to the actual addresses in memory. This translation has to be dynamic: if a program is run twice, the same data can be mapped to two different locations. A program has a "logical data space" (typically starting from address zero) of the addresses used in the compiled code, and this is translated during program execution to actual memory addresses. For this reason, there is a *page table* that specifies which memory pages contain which logical pages. However, address translation by lookup in this table is slow, so CPUs have a *translation look-aside buffer (TLB)*. The TLB is a cache of frequently used page table entries: it provides fast address translation for a number of pages.

If a program needs a memory location, the TLB is consulted to see whether this location is in fact on a page that is remembered in the TLB. If this is the case, the logical address is translated to a physical one; this is a very fast process. The case where the page is not remembered in the TLB is called a *TLB miss*, and the page lookup table is then searched. This is another case of *spatial locality*: accessing (many) elements that are spread far apart incurs a performance penalty from TLB misses.

While TLB misses are costly, in modern CPUs the number of entries is very large, so programmers don't have to worry about this much. Still, in "data-driven design" this is one of the factors optimized for.

31.5 ▪ Multicore processors

In recent years, the limits of performance have been reached for traditional processor chip design.

- Clock frequency cannot be increased further, since it increases energy consumption, heating the chips too much.
- It is not possible to extract more instruction level parallelism (ILP) (see section 18.1) from codes, either because of compiler limitations, because of the limited amount of intrinsically available parallelism, or because branch prediction makes it impossible.

One of the ways of getting a higher utilization out of a single processor chip is then to move from a strategy of further sophistication of the single processor to a division of the chip into multiple processing *cores*. The separate cores can work on unrelated tasks, or, by splitting a large amount of data parallelism into parallel tasks (section 18.3.1), collaborate on a common task at a higher overall performance [44].

This solves the above two problems:

- Two cores at a lower frequency can have the same throughput as a single processor at a higher frequency; hence, multiple cores are more energy efficient.
- Discovered ILP is now replaced by explicit task parallelism, managed by the programmer.

While the first multicore CPUs were in effect two processors on the same die, later generations incorporated L3 or L2 caches that were shared between the two processor cores; see Figure 31.9. This design makes it efficient for the cores to work jointly on the same problem. The cores would

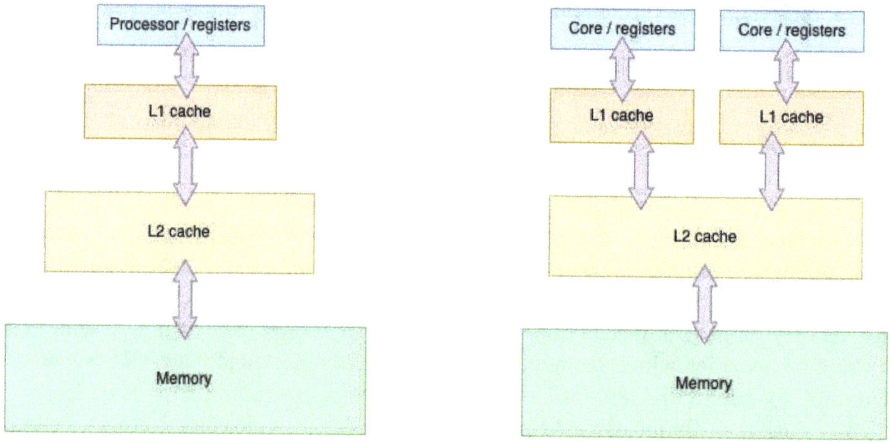

Figure 31.9. *Cache hierarchy in a single-core and dual-core chip*

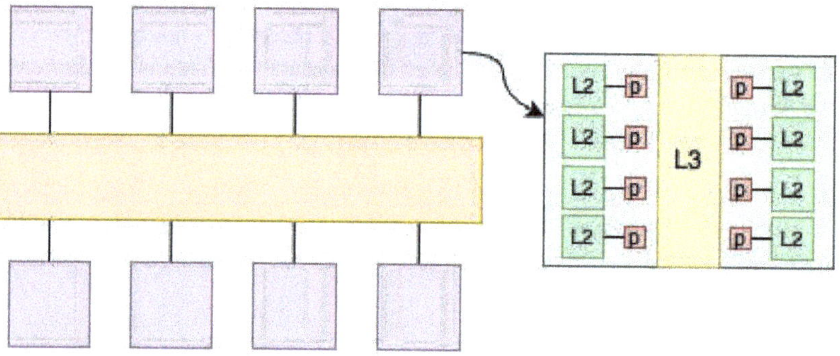

Figure 31.10. *Structure of the AMD multicore processors*

still have their own L1 cache, and these separate caches lead to a *cache coherence* problem; see section 31.5.1 below.

We note that the term "processor" is now ambiguous: it can refer to either the chip or the processor core on the chip. For this reason, we mostly talk about a *socket* for the whole chip and *core* for the part containing one arithmetic and logic unit and having its own registers. Currently, CPUs with dozens of cores are common in supercomputers. Such chips can have complicated cache structures where an L2 cache is neither private nor globally shared, but instead shared by an 8-core "chiplet"; see Figure 31.10 for an example.

With this mix of shared and private caches, the programming model for multicore processors is becoming a hybrid between shared and distributed memory:

Core The cores have their own private L1 cache, which is a sort of distributed memory.

Socket On one socket, there is often a shared L2 cache, which is shared memory between all or some of the cores.

Node There can be multiple sockets on a single "node" or motherboard, accessing the same shared memory.

Network Distributed memory programming is needed to let nodes communicate.

31.5.1 ▪ Cache coherence

With parallel processing, there is the potential for a conflict if more than one processing element has a copy of the same data item. The problem of ensuring that all cached data are an accurate copy of main memory is referred to as *cache coherence*: if the copy in one cache is altered, any other copy needs to be updated too, or at least marked as invalid.

In distributed memory architectures, a dataset is usually partitioned disjointly over the processors (see section 22.1) so conflicting copies of data can only arise with knowledge of the user, and it is up to the user to deal with the problem. The case of shared memory is more subtle: since processes access the same main memory, it would seem that conflicts are in fact impossible. However, cores typically have some private cache that contains copies of data from memory, so conflicting copies can occur.

Suppose that two cores have a copy of the same data item in their (private) L1 cache, and one modifies its copy. Now the other has cached data that is no longer an accurate copy of its counterpart: the processor will *invalidate* that copy of the item, and in fact its whole cacheline. When the process needs access to the item again, it needs to reload that cacheline.

This process of updating or invalidating cachelines is known as *maintaining cache coherence*, and it is done on a very low level of the processor, with no programmer involvement. However, it will slow down the computation, and it uses bandwidth that could otherwise be used for loading or storing operands.

The state of a cacheline with respect to a data item in main memory is usually described in terms of a protocol such as the modified-shared-invalid (MSI) coherence protocol, where a cacheline can be in the following states on a given core:

Modified: the cacheline has been modified and needs to be written to the backing store. This writing can be done when the line is evicted, or it is done immediately, depending on the write-back policy.

Shared: the line is present in at least one cache and is unmodified.

Invalid: the line is not present in the current cache, or it is present but a copy in another cache has been modified.

These states control the movement of cachelines between memory and the caches. For instance, suppose a core does a read to a cacheline that is invalid on that core. It can then load it from memory or get it from another cache which may be faster. (Finding whether a line exists in state M or S on another cache is called *snooping*; an alternative is to maintain cache directories.) If the line is Shared, it can now simply be copied; if it is in state M in the other cache, that core first needs to write it back to memory.

Exercise 31.2. Consider two processors, a data item x in memory, and cachelines x_1,x_2 in the private caches of the two processors to which x is mapped. Describe the transitions between the states of x_1 and x_2 under reads and writes of x on the two processors. Also indicate which actions cause memory bandwidth to be used.

Variants of the MSI protocol add an “Exclusive” or “Owned” state for increased efficiency.

31.5.2 ▪ Nonuniform memory access

A node in a supercomputer cluster will often have multiple sockets, meaning processor chips. While the memory of the node is accessible by any core on any socket, each memory chip is associated with a specific socket. Thus, the speed of accessing memory depends on what socket requests, and what socket hosts the memory. Requesting memory from another socket incurs a certain delay.

The phenomenon that memory is accessible from any core, but not necessarily equally fast, is called *non-uniform memory access (NUMA)*, or sometimes "cc-NUMA" for "cache-coherent" NUMA. A practical discussion of this is in section 20.11.

31.5.3 ▪ False sharing

The cache coherence problem can even appear if the cores access different items. For instance, a declaration

```
double x,y;
```

will likely allocate `x` and `y` next to each other in memory, so there is a high chance they fall on the same cacheline. Now if one core updates `x` and the other `y`, this cacheline will continuously be moved between the cores. This is called *false sharing*.

The most common case of false sharing happens when threads update consecutive locations of an array. For instance, in the following OpenMP fragment all threads update their own location in an array of partial results:

```
  local_results = new double[num_threads];
#pragma omp parallel
{
  int thread_num = omp_get_thread_num();
  for (int i=my_lo; i<my_hi; ++i)
    local_results[thread_num] = ... f(i) ...
}
// combine local results into global:
global_result = g(local_results)
```

While there is no actual *race condition* (as there would be if the threads all updated the `global_result` variable), this code may have low performance, since the cacheline(s) with the `local_result` array will continuously be invalidated.

That said, false sharing is less of a problem in modern CPUs than it used to be. We explore an example in section 33.5.

Chapter 32

Algorithm analysis

In the previous chapter you learned that processor design is unbalanced in the sense that loading data is slower than executing the actual operations. This imbalance is large for main memory and less for the various cache levels. Thus we are motivated to keep data in cache and keep the amount of *data reuse* as high as possible.

Of course, we need to determine first if the computation allows for data to be reused. For this we define the *arithmetic intensity* of an algorithm as follows:

> If n is the number of data items that an algorithm operates on, and $f(n)$ the number of operations it takes, then the arithmetic intensity is $f(n)/n$.
>
> Roughly equivalently, we define the *reuse factor* as the number of times each loaded data item is used.

(We can measure data items in either floating point numbers or bytes. The latter possibility makes it easier to relate arithmetic intensity to hardware specifications of a processor.)

32.1 ▪ Example: Vector operations

Consider, for example, the vector addition

$$\forall_i \colon x_i \leftarrow x_i + y_i.$$

This involves three memory accesses (two loads and one store) and one operation per iteration, giving an arithmetic intensity of $1/3$.

The *BLAS* (section 15.5.1) *AXPY* (for "*a* times *x* plus *y*") operation

$$\forall_i \colon x_i \leftarrow a\, x_i + y_i$$

has two operations but the same number of memory access, since the one-time load of a is amortized. It is therefore more efficient than the simple addition, with an arithmetic intensity of $2/3$.

The inner product calculation

$$\forall_i \colon s \leftarrow s + x_i \cdot y_i$$

is similar in structure to the AXPY operation, involving one multiplication and addition per iteration, on two vectors and one scalar. However, now there are only two load operations, since s can be kept in register and only written back to memory at the end of the loop. The arithmetic intensity here is 1.

32.2 ▪ Example: Matrix operations

Next, consider the *matrix-matrix product*

$$\forall_{i,j} \colon c_{ij} = \sum_k a_{ik} b_{kj},$$

which is important, for instance, in deep learning applications. This operation involves $3n^2$ data items and $2n^3$ operations, which is of a higher order. The arithmetic intensity is $O(n)$, meaning that every data item will be used $O(n)$ times. This has the implication that, with suitable programming, this operation has the potential of overcoming the bandwidth/clock speed gap by keeping data in fast cache memory.

Exercise 32.1. The matrix-matrix product, considered as mathematical operation, clearly has data reuse by the above definition. Argue that this reuse is not trivially attained by a straightforward implementation as a triple loop. What determines whether this implementation has reuse of data that is in cache?

We will devote further discussion to this algorithm in section 33.7. A relatively easy to code, high performing implementation of the matrix-matrix product is done through recursion; see Project Chapter 43.

32.3 ▪ Fourier transform

Another algorithm that has potential for data reuse is the fast Fourier transform (FFT). Here, $O(N \log N)$ operations are done on $O(N)$ data, so there is an arithmetic intensity of $\log N$. We will not go into this further.

32.4 ▪ The roofline model

Arithmetic intensity, defined above, is a statement about how the ideal algorithm, not its implementation, interacts with hardware parameters and the actual implementation to determine performance. This is known as the *roofline model* [55], and it expresses the basic fact that performance is bounded by two factors, illustrated in the first graph of Figure 32.1.

1. The *peak performance*, indicated by the horizontal line at the top of the graph, is an absolute bound on the performance, achieved only if every aspect of a central processing unit (CPU) (pipelines, multiple floating point units) are perfectly used. The calculation of this number is purely based on CPU properties and clock cycle; it is assumed that memory bandwidth is not a limiting factor.

2. The number of operations per second is also limited by the product of the bandwidth, an absolute number, and the arithmetic intensity:

$$\frac{\text{operations}}{\text{second}} = \frac{\text{operations}}{\text{data item}} \cdot \frac{\text{data items}}{\text{second}}$$

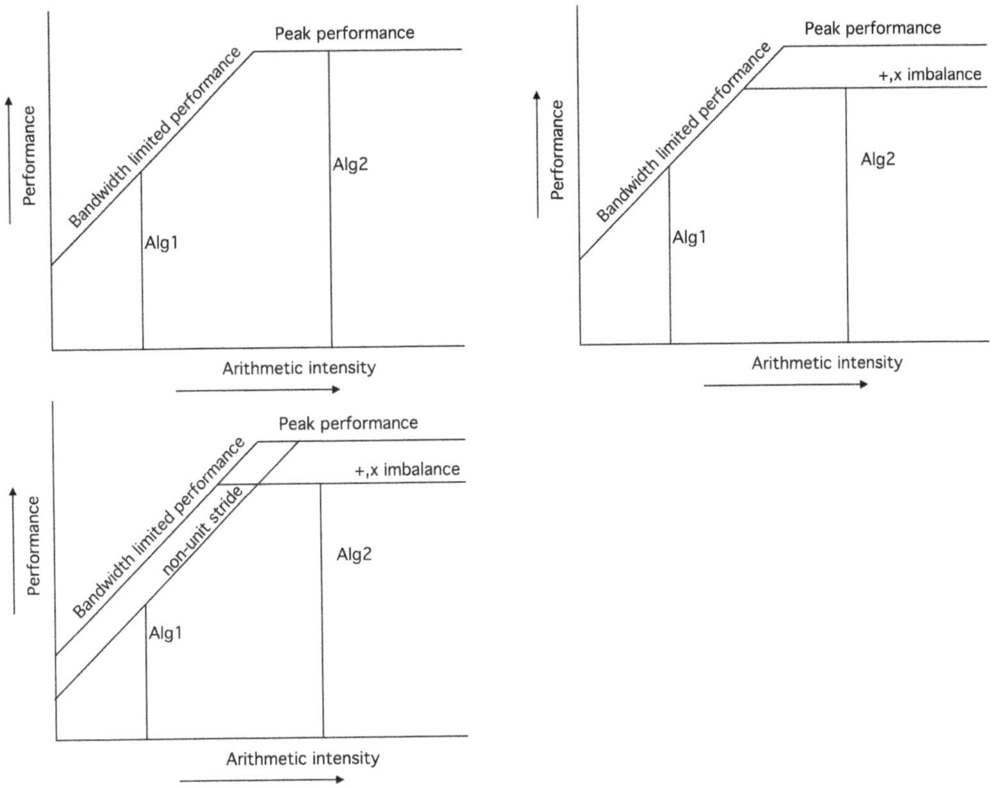

Figure 32.1. *Illustration of factors determining performance in the roofline model*

> If the first factor is 1 we have a streaming operation, and performance is limited by bandwidth. This is depicted by the linearly increasing line in the graph.

The roofline model is an elegant way of expressing that various factors lower the ceiling. For instance, if an algorithm fails to use the full *SIMD width*, this imbalance lowers the attainable peak. The second graph in Figure 32.1 indicates various factors that lower the ceiling, such as nonunit strides. There are also various factors that lower the available bandwidth, such as imperfect latency hiding. This is indicated by a lowering of the sloping roofline in the third graph.

For a given arithmetic intensity, the performance is determined by where its vertical line intersects the roof line. If this is at the horizontal part, the computation is called *compute-bound*: performance is determined by characteristics of the processor, and bandwidth is not an issue. On the other hand, if that vertical line intersects the sloping part of the roof, the computation is called *bandwidth-bound*: performance is determined by the memory subsystem, and the full capacity of the processor is not used.

32.5 ▪ Stencil matrix-vector product

In physics applications on "brick-shaped" domains such as the unit square $[0,1]^2$ we often deal with a matrix-vector product where the matrix comes from a computational stencil; see section 15.1. Regarding the performance of such code, we do not expect to get close to peak performance of the processor since this is a "streaming" operation.

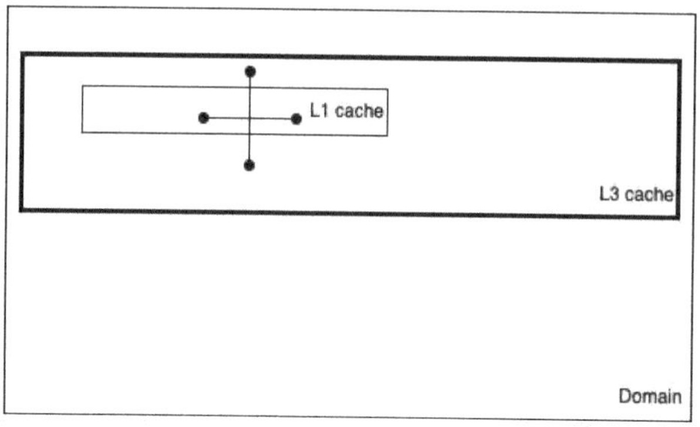

Figure 32.2. *Cache behavior of a stencil application*

The stencil application has no data reuse on the output: each element of the output is written once. However, since the output is written sequentially each cacheline is fully used and we have some spatial locality.

Treatment of the input is more subtle. As we illustrate in Figure 32.2, there is no L1 reuse, since a single line in the 2D domain is likely to exceed the L1 cache. Since we are basically streaming lines of the input vector from memory, we call this a "streaming application."

However, there is data locality (section 31.2.3), in that each cacheline is fully utilized, and we expect measured bandwidth to roughly equal the available bandwidth. Thus, while we are *bandwidth limited*, at least the data loaded is fully utilized.

Next we observe that, with the size of modern level 3 caches, likely several lines of the input will fit in the level 3 cache, so each line is read only once from memory. Thus, we conclude that

- we load one stream of data for the input;
- we load the output vector prior to it being written; and
- we write back the output vector to memory.

In other words, the bandwidth demands are N floating point reads from memory and $3N$ from cache for $5N$ operations in N stencil evaluations.

32.6 ▪ CRS sparse matrix-vector product

In section 15.2 you saw the algorithm for the matrix-vector product with a CRS matrix, which is the crucial operation in, for instance, PDE codes. The analysis of data reuse here has the following aspects:

- The elements of the output vector are each written once. This writing is also done in an inner loop, so the variable is likely to stay resident in register.
- The matrix elements are each used just once, but they are loaded from consecutive memory locations, so each cacheline loaded is fully utilized.
- Elements of the input vector are used multiple times (can you characterize the number of times in terms of the matrix?), but the spatial and temporal locality analysis is more involved. Additionally, for each $a_{ij} \cdot x_j$ product the j value is determined indirectly, so there is an extra integer load.

Purely counting scalars, we could say that for each matrix element two doubles (a_{ij} and x_j) are loaded, as well as one integer for the indirect addressing. Various attempts have been made to reduce this bandwidth by more sophisticated matrix storage, which may also help to increase locality [10, 54].

One observation we can make regarding locality is that for matrices with a random sparsity pattern there will be no spatial locality on the input vector. However, for matrices derived from PDEs there will be some locality from the physical structure of the problem. Thus, we expect the input vector to be contained in the L3 cache, and it only needs to be loaded once from memory. This is analogous to the analysis of the stencil matrix-vector product in section 32.5 above.

Chapter 33

Programming for performance

Now that we understand the basics of processor architecture, and the opportunity for high performance in some operations, let's consider how we need to code so that we actually exploit the architecture.

33.1 ▪ Blocking for cache reuse

Above you learned that data from L1 can be processed with lower latency and higher bandwidth than from L2, and L2 is again faster than L3 or memory. Therefore, if a code has the potential to reuse data, you want to write it in such a way that reused data fits in cache at some level, the higher—meaning closer to the process—the better.

As a prototypical example, consider code that repeatedly accesses the same data:

```
for (int i=0; i<NRUNS; i++)
  for (int j=0; j<datasize; j++)
    array_data[j] = 2.3*array_data[j]+1.2;
```

If the size parameter allows the array to fit in cache, the operation will be relatively fast. As the size of the dataset grows, parts of it will evict other parts from the L1 cache, so the speed of the operation will be determined by the latency and bandwidth of the L2 cache.

Exercise 33.1. Argue that with a large enough problem and an LRU replacement policy (section 31.2.6) essentially all data in the L1 will be replaced in every iteration of the outer loop. Can you write an example code that will let some of the L1 data stay resident?

It may be possible to arrange the operations to keep data in the L1 cache. For instance, in our example, we could write

```
blockstart = 0;
for (int b=0; b<datasize/l1size; b++) {
  for (int i=0; i<NRUNS; i++) {
    for (int j=0; j<l1size; j++)
      array_data[blockstart+j] = 2.3*array_data[blockstart+j]+1.2;
  }
  blockstart += l1size;
}
```

assuming that the L1 size divides evenly in the dataset size. This strategy is called *cache blocking* or *blocking for cache reuse*.

Remark. *Like unrolling, blocking code may change the order of evaluation of expressions. Since floating point arithmetic is not* associative, *blocking is not a transformation that compilers are always allowed to make. You can supply compiler options to indicate whether the language rules are to be strictly adhered to.*

33.1.1 ▪ Demonstrating the influence of cache on performance

While blocking is an essential technique in operations such as the matrix-matrix product kernel, the above example is too simple. In this section we explore blocking in more detail.

You can try to write a loop over a small array as above, and execute it many times, hoping to observe performance degradation when the array gets larger than the cache size. The number of iterations should be chosen so that the measured time is well over the resolution of your clock.

This runs into a couple of unforeseen problems. The timing for a simple loop nest

```
for (int irepeat=0; irepeat<how_many_repeats; irepeat++) {
  for (int iword=0; iword<cachesize_in_words; iword++)
    data_array[iword] += 1.1;
}
```

may seem to depend linearly on the array size, without any influence from being cache contained.

To see what the compiler does with this fragment, let your compiler generate an *optimization report*. (For the *Intel compiler* use `-qopt-report`.) In this report you see that the compiler has decided to exchange the loops: Each element of the array is then loaded only once:

```
remark #25444: Loopnest Interchanged: ( 1 2 ) --> ( 2 1 )
remark #15542: loop was not vectorized: inner loop was already vectorized
```

Now it is going over the array just once, executing an accumulation loop on each element. Here the cache size is indeed irrelevant.

In an attempt to find an example that does not show this loop exchange and observe cache influence you can try to make the inner loop too complicated for the compiler to analyze, as would be the case in applications for irregular access patterns. You could, for instance, turn the array into a sort of *linked list* that you traverse:

```
// setup
for (int iword=0; iword<cachesize_in_words; iword++)
    data_array[iword] = (iword+1) % cachesize_in_words

// use:
for ( /* several steps */ ) {
  ptr = 0;
  for (int iword=0; iword<cachesize_in_words; iword++)
      ptr = data_array[ptr];
```

Now the compiler will not exchange the loops, but you will still not observe the cache size threshold. The reason for this is that with regular access the *memory prefetcher* (section 31.3) kicks in: some component of the CPU predicts what address(es) you will be requesting next, and fetches it/them in advance.

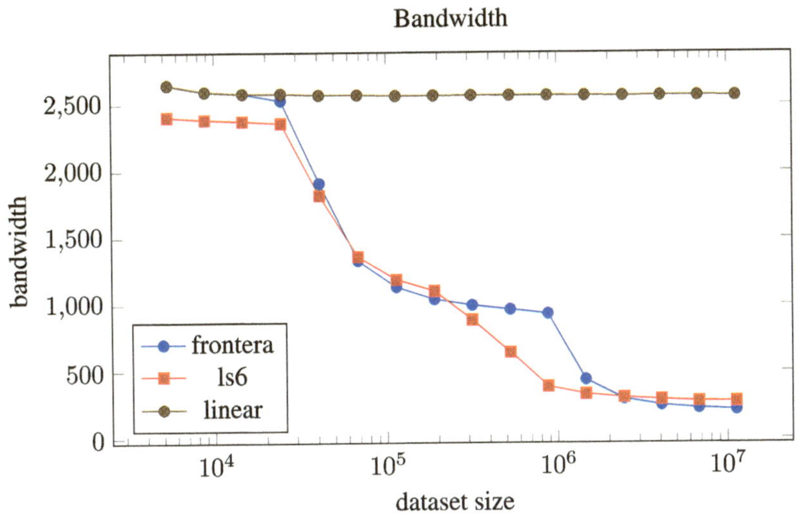

Figure 33.1. *Single-core bandwidth as function of dataset size*

To stymie this bit of cleverness you need to make the linked list more random:

```
for (int iword=0; iword<cachesize_in_words; iword++)
    data_array[iword] = random() % cachesize_in_words
```

Given a sufficiently large cache size this will be a cycle that touches all array locations, or you can explicitly ensure this by generating a permutation of all index locations.

We illustrate this in Figure 33.1. For the *TACC Frontera* machine with *Intel Cascade Lake* processors we plot the linear traversal (top line) and the random traversal. For the *TACC Lonestar6* machine with *AMD Milan* processors we plot random traversal. The dataset sizes corresponding to L1 and L2 caches are clearly visible. Exceeding the L2 cache has a drop-off in performance, but not as drastic as for the L1 cache.

Let's recap what we have learned here. First of all, cache size will a priori have an influence on code performance: the more cache contained, the better. But, secondly, if the code mostly traverses data linearly, the prefetcher makes the cache effects felt far less; only code that jumps somewhat randomly through its data is sensitive to being cache contained.

33.2 ▪ Associativity

In section 31.2.7 you saw how the operation of adding a small number of vectors

$$\forall_j : y_j = y_j + \sum_{i=1}^{m} x_{i,j}$$

is a problem for direct mapped caches or set-associative caches with associativity.

We simplify this into a code that cycles through a number of locations in the same associativity equivalence class,

```
// hardware/associativity.cpp
auto data = write_data.get_stream().data();
for ( int irepeat=0; irepeat<how_many_repeats; ++irepeat )
  for ( int loc=0; loc<data.size(); loc+=displacement_in_words )
    data[loc] += loc;
```

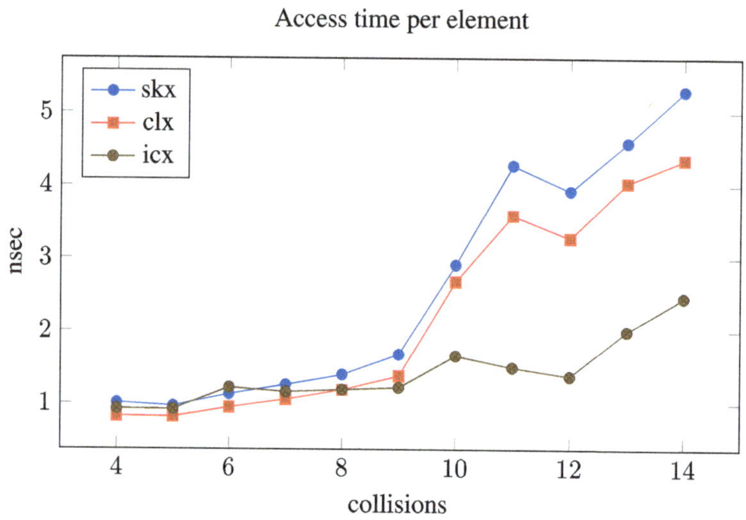

Figure 33.2. *Effects of cache associativity*

where the data size has been computed to accommodate a cycle of length `assoc`:

```
// hardware/associativity.cpp
auto datasize_in_bytes = displacement_in_bytes * assoc;
auto datasize_in_words = datasize_in_bytes / sizeof(floattype);
```

To evaluate the effects of associativity we measure the access time per element on various generations of Intel processors. Figure 33.2 shows the *Intel Sky Lake* and *Intel Cascade Lake*, both with a 32KiB L1 cache that is 8-way associative, and the *Intel Ice Lake* with a 48KiB L1 cache that is 12-way associative. In all cases we see that the access time per element goes up dramatically when cache associativity is exceeded.

33.3 ▪ Bandwidth

It has been a basic fact of processors of at least the past three decades that the processing unit is faster than the memory: the processor can operate on more numbers per second than the memory can deliver to the processor.

This means that on cache-contained datasets performance is limited by the bandwidth from that cache, and for streaming operations such as operations on long vectors by the bandwidth from main memory. If we would plot performance as a function of dataset size, you would expect a step graph, with larger datasets at a lower bandwidth and performance level.

Let's make an attempt to show such behavior. You'd think you could measure bandwidth by executing a simple *streaming kernel*:

```
// hardware/allocation.cpp
template< typename R >
R sum_stream( span<R> stream ) {
  R sum{static_cast<R>(0)};
  for ( size_t i=0; i<stream.size(); ++i )
    sum += stream[i];
  return sum;
};
```

This loads a linear stretch of memory once, and generates only one number in return. We easily compute the bandwidth as in the number of bytes loaded divided by the execution time.

However, there are several factors that complicate this story:

1. The length of the stream is relevant: if the stream is short, it may fit in a cache and a higher bandwidth will be measured than if it has to come from main memory.
2. Modern processors have multiple cores, and bandwidth to main memory is shared between them. Running the streaming kernel on only one core is likely to give a higher per-core bandwidth than when all cores are running the kernel simultaneously.

To get a realistic evaluation, we instead look at the aggregate bandwidth over all available cores. We explore the above factors by running the streaming kernel on multiple stream lengths and multiple core counts:

```
// hardware/bandwidth.cpp
vector<real> results(nthreads,0.);
float bw{0};
uint64_t data_stream_size{0};
#pragma omp parallel proc_bind(spread) reduction(+:bw)
{
  int my_thread_number = omp_get_thread_num();
  std::span<real> thread_data_stream = storage.get_stream(my_thread_number);
  for (int irepeat=0; irepeat<how_many_repeats; ++irepeat) {
    results.at(my_thread_number) += sum_stream(thread_data_stream);
  }
  bw += how_many_repeats * thread_data_stream.size()*sizeof(real);
}
```

We test this on the *TACC Stampede3* cluster, with dual-socket *Intel Ice Lake* processors, with a total of 112 cores per node. Figure 33.3 shows that for any dataset size the aggregate bandwidth grows with the core count, but the individual per-core bandwidth goes down. With the largest dataset size, aggregate bandwidth does not vary much, because the data streams from main memory. The next two small sizes probably fit in cache, so they show a higher aggregate bandwidth than from main memory. The smallest dataset size is anomalous: for all but the single-core case it is probably the thread synchronization that overwhelms the actual performance.

33.3.1 ▪ Striding

Since data is moved from memory to cache in consecutive chunks named cachelines (see section 31.2.5), code that does not utilize all data in a cacheline pays a bandwidth penalty. To explore this, we apply a strided operation

```
// hardware/allocation.cpp
template <typename R>
void Cache<R>::transform_in_place
    ( std::function< void(R&) > f,int stride,int nrepeats ) {
  for ( int irepeat=0; irepeat<nrepeats; irepeat++ ) {
    for ( size_t i=0; i<stream_cache_in_words; i+=stride )
      f( thecache[i] );
  }
};
```

for multiple stride values.

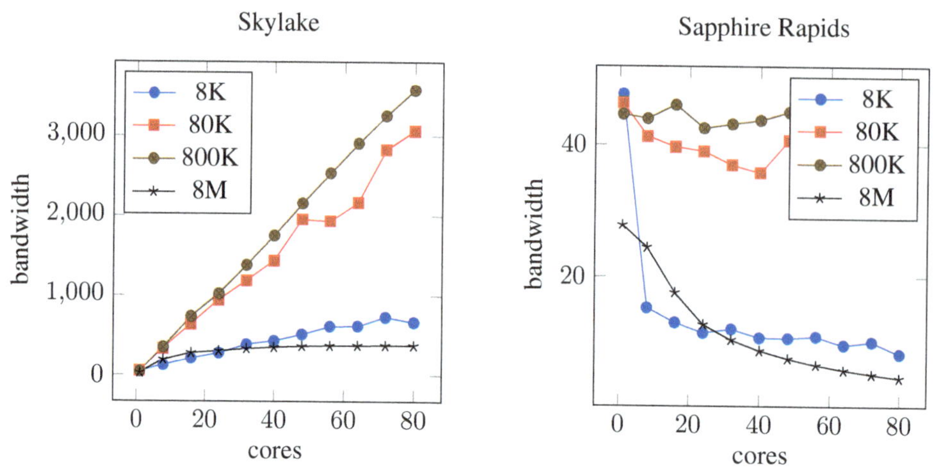

Figure 33.3. *Intel Icelake bandwidth (Gbyte/sec) as a function of core counts and dataset sizes: aggregate (left) and per-core (right)*

As above, we try multiple stream sizes and core counts:

```
// hardware/stride.cpp
#pragma omp parallel proc_bind(spread)
{
  int my_thread_number = omp_get_thread_num();
  auto my_data_stream = write_data.get_stream(my_thread_number);
  auto my_flush_stream = flush_data.get_stream(my_thread_number);
  for (int irepeat=0; irepeat<how_many_repeats; ++irepeat) {
    my_data_stream.transform_in_place( [] (floattype& x ) { x+=1.; }, stride );
  }
}
```

Here we use a constant dataset size s, and we compute the effective bandwidth from the number of elements processed: $d = s/stride$. Figure 33.4 shows that for a small dataset the access time per element is roughly constant because the data is streamed at high speed from cache. Only at large strides does the bandwidth demand increase sufficiently to become a factor.

However, for a larger dataset, data is streamed from main memory which does not have enough bandwidth for all cores. We then see the access time per word go up with the stride size.

33.3.2 ▪ Streaming operations

The worst case, performancewise speaking, of an operation is a so-called "streaming" kernel. Here, data streams from and to memory, with effectively no use of caches to increase performance. As an example, consider the vector addition:

```
for (int i=0; i<data_size; ++i)
  a[i] = b[i]+c[i]
```

Each iteration performs one floating point operation, which modern Central Processing Units (CPUs) can do in one clock cycle by using pipelines. However, each iteration needs two numbers loaded and one written, for a total of 24 bytes of memory traffic. (Actually, the cacheline of `a[i]` is loaded before it can be written, so there are 4 memory accesses with a total of 32 bytes per iteration.) Typical memory bandwidth figures (see, for instance, Figure 31.1) are nowhere near 24 (or 32) bytes per cycle. This means that, without caches, algorithm performance can be

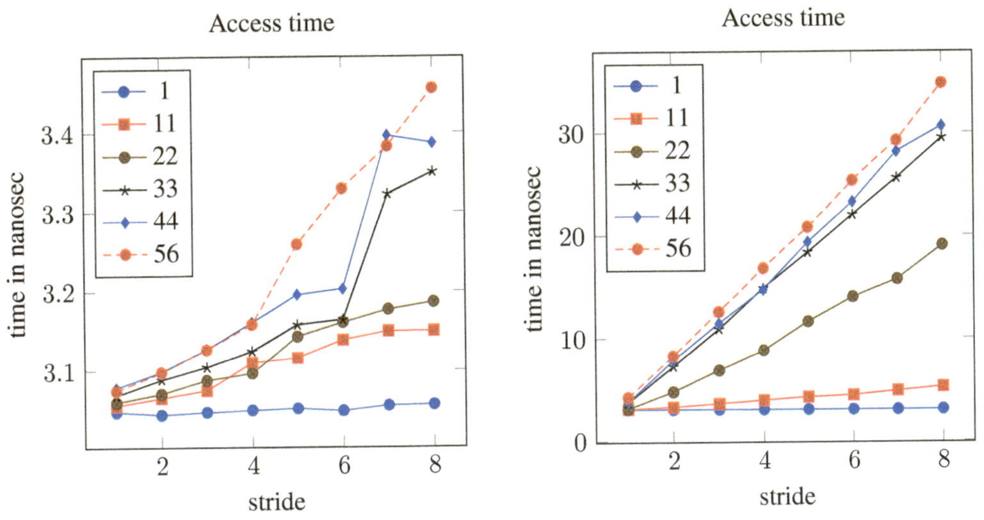

Figure 33.4. *Access time per word for different strides and core counts, Frontera; dataset size 100k (left) and 1M (right); note different y scales!*

bounded by memory performance. Of course, caches will not speed up every operation, and in fact will have no effect on the above example.

The prototypical streaming operations are the vector operations of the BLAS Level 1. However, the matrix-vector product with a stencil matrix (section 15.1.2) is also an example since it streams the input and output vectors and possibly the matrix coefficients. Likewise, we can call the matrix-vector product with a compressed row storage (CRS) matrix (section 15.2.1) a streaming kernel; see section 33.8 for an analysis.

33.4 ▪ Cache-oblivious programming

Cache-oblivious programming can be described as a way of programming that automatically uses all levels of the *cache hierarchy* without knowing the specific sizes. This is typically done by using a *divide-and-conquer* strategy, that is, recursive subdivision of a problem.

A simple example of cache-oblivious programming is the *matrix transposition* operation $B \leftarrow A^t$. First we observe that each element of either matrix is accessed once, so the only reuse is in the utilization of cachelines. If both matrices are stored by rows and we traverse B by rows, then A is traversed by columns, and for each element accessed one cacheline is loaded. If the number of rows times the number of elements per cacheline is more than the cache size, lines will be evicted before they can be reused.

In a cache-oblivious implementation we divide A and B as 2×2 block matrices, and recursively compute $B_{11} \leftarrow A^t_{11}$, $B_{12} \leftarrow A^t_{21}$, etc.; see Figure 33.5. At some point in the recursion, blocks A_{ij} will now be small enough that they fit in cache, and the cachelines of A will be fully used. Hence, this algorithm improves on the simple one by a factor approximately equal to the cacheline size.

The cache-oblivious strategy can often yield improvement, but it is not necessarily optimal. In the *matrix-matrix product* it improves on the naive algorithm, but it is not as good as an algorithm that is explicitly designed to make optimal use of caches; see section 33.7.2. You can do the “high

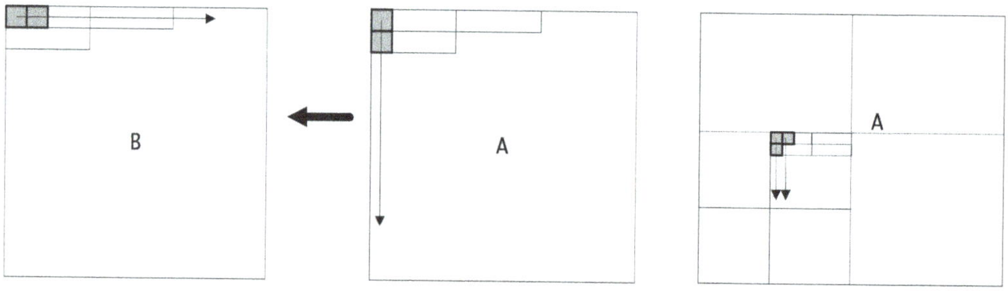

Figure 33.5. *Matrix transpose operation, with simple and recursive traversal of the source matrix*

performance linear algebra" project to explore this (Project Chapter 43).

33.5 ▪ False sharing

As an example of *false sharing* (section 31.5.3) consider a code to compute π by Riemann integration. Each core computes into its own private accumulator; the false sharing comes from these sharing a cacheline.

Parallel update:

```
// false.cxx
#pragma omp parallel
{
  int mythread = omp_get_thread_num(),
    my_nsteps=steps/nthreads,
    my_first=mythread*my_nsteps,
    my_last=(mythread+1)*my_nsteps-1;
  for (int s=my_first; s<my_last; s++) {
    double x=-1.+s*inc;
    double a=inc*sqrt(1-x*x);
    local_area[dilate*mythread] += 2*a;
  }
}
```

Followed by a summation:

```
for (int i=0; i<nthreads; i++)
  global_area += local_area[dilate*i];
```

The `dilate` parameter takes on the values `1,8`:

- with a value `1` all threads write into independent locations at a spacing of one. This means that up to 8 threads will write to the same cacheline, inducing a large amount of false sharing. On the other hand,
- with a value of `8` the locations are 8 doubles apart, meaning that each thread writes to its own cacheline and there will be no false sharing.

We now expect the second variant to run at considerably higher speed. However, running this on an Intel Skylake processor gives the following result:

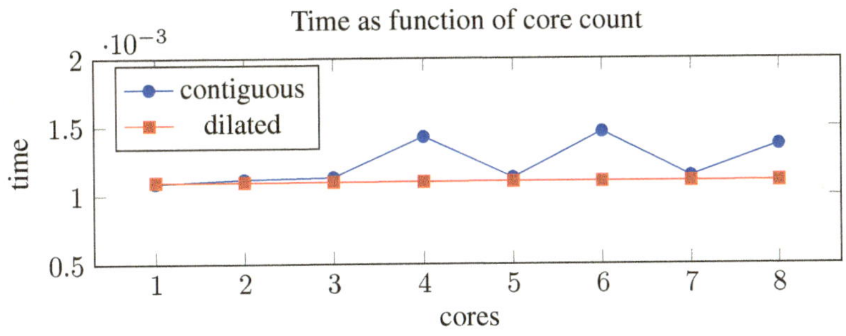

The second variant, which is supposed to "solve" the false sharing problem, is barely faster; we only see a very slight effect, probably from bandwidth limitations. We conclude that either the compiler or the processor keeps the accumulators in temporaries and only resolves them at the end.

33.6 ▪ Computing with underflow

Many processors will happily compute with denormals (see section 35.2.4.3), but they have to emulate these computations in *micro-code*. This severely depresses performance.

As an example, we compute a geometric sequence $n \mapsto r^n$ with $r < 1$. For small enough values r, this sequence underflows, and the computation becomes slow. To get macroscopic timings, in this code we actually operate on an array of identical numbers,

```
// hardware/denormal.cpp
storage.set(startvalue);
/* repeated scale the array */
for (int r=0; r<repeats; ++r) {
  storage.transform_in_place( [ratio] (floattype &x) { x *= ratio; } );
  storage.front() = storage.back();
}
```

where the transform routine is

```
// hardware/allocation.cpp
template <typename R>
void Cache<R>::transform_in_place
    ( std::function< void(R&) > f,int stride,int nrepeats ) {
  for ( int irepeat=0; irepeat<nrepeats; irepeat++ ) {
    for ( size_t i=0; i<stream_cache_in_words; i+=stride )
      f( thecache[i] );
  }
};
```

First we use the default behavior of *flush-to-zero* where any subnormal number is set to zero; this is specified by a compiler flag `-ftz`. Then we show the slowdown associated with correct handling of denormals, specified by a compiler flag `-no-ftz`. Table 33.1 reports both modes in an *Intel Cascade Lake*, an *AMD Milan*, and an *Apple M2* processor. We see that "true" handling of denormals can have severe performance penalties.

	Intel Cascade Lake	AMD Milan	MBP M2
Flush-to-zero	1.5	1.4	1.2
No Ftz	45	1.7	47

Table 33.1. *Access time per word for subnormal computing in different processors*

33.7 ▪ Dense matrix-matrix product

The dense matrix-matrix product (often known by its routine name *GEMM* in the *BLAS*) holds a strange position in computational science. Since the solution of PDEs mostly relies on sparse matrices, its use was for a long time limited to certain applications, such as *quantum chemistry*, where it is the basis for *eigenvalue* problems. One reason for its continued prominence was the *Linpack benchmark* of the TOP500 list (section 33.7.1), which is an important measure of processor peak performance.

However, in recent years it has seen a resurgence in importance with its use in the *neural nets* of deep learning. The matrix-matrix product appears there as the multiplication of a weights matrix with many simultaneous feature vectors.

Let us therefore take a brief look at this operation. We need to start by observing that the textbook algorithm for $C \leftarrow A \cdot B + C$,

```
for ( int row=0; row<m; ++row )
  for ( int col=0; col<n; ++col )
    for ( int k=0; k<inner; ++k )
      c[i,j] += a[i,k] * b[k,j];
```

has both the potential for great data reuse—there is $O(N^2)$ data for $O(N^3)$ operations—while not actually realizing any of that. (Why?)

33.7.1 ▪ The Linpack benchmark and the TOP500

There are several informal ways of measuring just "how big" a computer is. The most popular is the TOP500 list, maintained at `http://www.top500.org/`, which records a computer's performance on the *Linpack benchmark* [17]. *Linpack* is a package for linear algebra operations, no longer in common use, since it has been superseded by *Lapack* for shared memory and *Scalapack* for distributed memory computers. The benchmark operation is the solution of a (square, nonsingular, dense) linear system through LU factorization with partial pivoting, with subsequent forward and backward solution.

The LU factorization operation is one that has great opportunity for cache reuse, since it is based on the matrix-matrix multiplication kernel. (Subsequently using the factorization to solve a linear system involves recursion and is therefore harder to optimize; however, it is of a lower order of complexity, so of lesser importance, and consequently not discussed in this book.) It also has the property that the amount of work outweighs the amount of memory traffic and network communication: $O(n^3)$ versus $O(n^2)$. As a result, the Linpack benchmark is likely to run at a substantial fraction of the peak speed of the machine. Another way of phrasing this is to say that the Linpack benchmark is a *CPU-bound* or *compute-bound* algorithm.

Typical efficiency figures are between 60 and 90 percent. However, it should be noted that many scientific codes do not feature the dense linear solution kernel, so the performance on this benchmark is not indicative of the performance on a typical code. Linear system solution through iterative methods, for instance, is much less efficient in a flops-per-second sense, being dominated by the bandwidth between CPU and memory.

We will next describe the most common implementation that actually attains high performance.

33.7.2 ▪ Optimized implementation

The matrix-matrix multiplication algorithm has three loops, each of which we can block (section 33.1), giving a six-way nested loop. Since there are no recurrences on the output elements, all resulting loop exchanges are legal. Combine this with the fact that the loop blocking introduces three blocking parameters, and you'll see that the number of potential implementations is enormous. Here we present the global reasoning that underlies the Goto implementation; for a detailed discussion see [30].

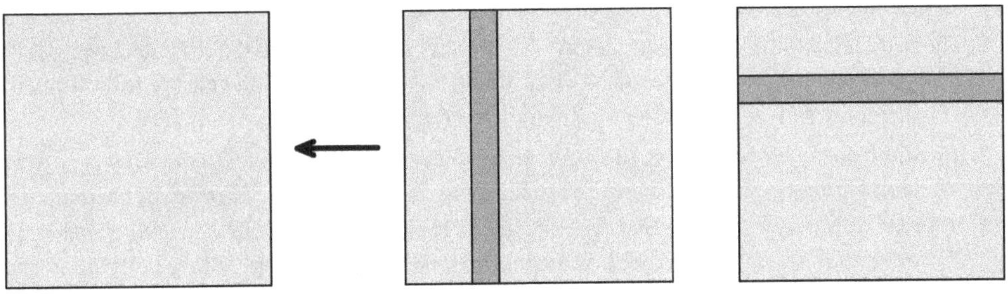

Figure 33.6. *Matrix-matrix multiplication as a sequence of low-rank updates*

We start by writing the product $C \leftarrow A \cdot B$ (or $C \leftarrow C + AB$ according to the BLAS standard) as a sequence of low-rank updates:

$$C_{**} += \sum_k A_{*k} B_{k*}.$$

See Figure 33.6. Next we derive the "block-panel" multiplication by multiplying a block of A by a "sliver" of B; see Figure 33.7. Finally, the inner algorithm accumulates a small row $C_{i,*}$,

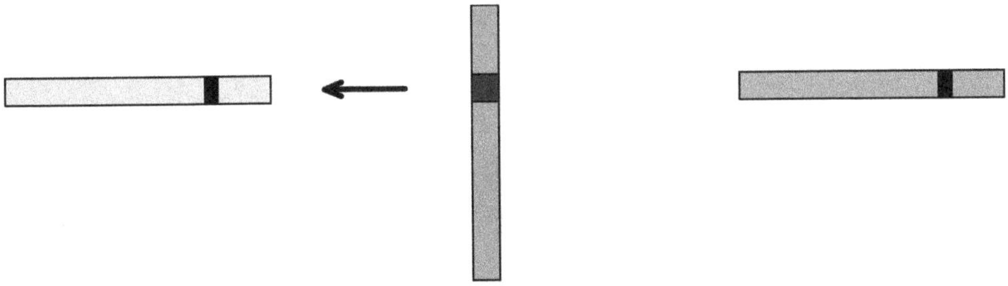

Figure 33.7. *The block-panel multiplication in the matrix-matrix algorithm*

typically of small size such as 4, by accumulating:

```
// compute C[i,*] :
for k:
   C[i,*] = A[i,k] * B[k,*]
```

See Figure 33.8. Now this algorithm is tuned.

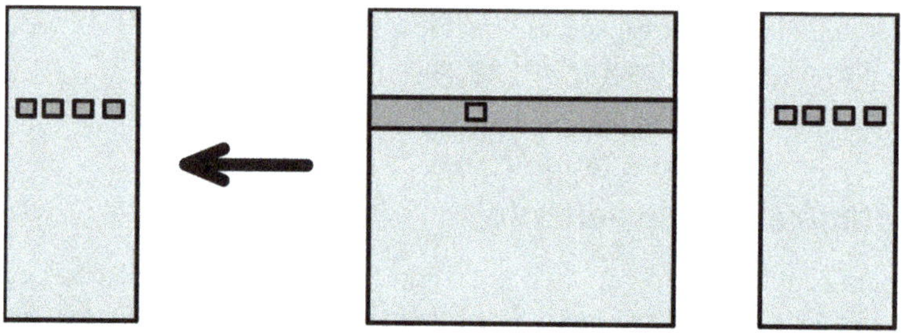

Figure 33.8. *The register-resident kernel of the matrix-matrix multiply*

- We need enough registers for `C[i,*]`, `A[i,k]`, and `B[k,*]`. On current processors that means that we accumulate four or eight elements of C.
- Those elements of C are accumulated, so they stay in register and the only data transfer is loading of the elements of A and B; there are no stores until the elements are fully formed!
- The elements `A[i,k]` and `B[k,*]` stream from L1.
- Since the same block of A is used for many successive slivers of B, we want it to stay resident; we choose the blocksize of A to let it stay in the L2 cache. Now we only stream B.
- In order to prevent TLB problems, A is stored by rows. If we start out with a matrix in (Fortran) *column-major* storage, this means we have to make a copy. Since copying is of a lower order of complexity, this cost is amortizable.

This algorithm is available in optimized libraries such as Intel's Math Kernel Library (MKL) [37], BLIS [52], and OpenBLas [45]. It can also be implemented in specialized hardware, as in the *Google TPU* [29], giving great energy efficiency.

33.8 ▪ Sparse matrix-vector product

In Chapter 15 we looked at two types of sparse matrices: stencil matrices, and general sparse matrices stored in Compressed Row Storage (CRS) format. We will now consider performance aspects of the general *sparse matrix-vector product*. (For a variety of reasons this operation is more common than the matrix-matrix product; sparse Gaussian elimination is an important matrix operation, but beyond the scope of this book.) We distinguish between shared and distributed memory cases.

33.8.1 ▪ Shared memory

With a sparse matrix in CRS format, the matrix-vector product $y \leftarrow Ax$ can be written as follows (but noting that Chapter 15 uses a slightly different implementation):

```
int element_counter{0};
for ( int row=0; row<m; ++row ) {
  double s{0};
  for ( int icol=0; icol<ncols[row]; ++icol ) {
    int col = cols[ colptr[row]+icol ];
    s += a[ element_counter++ ] * x[col];
  }
  y[row] = x;
}
```

Regarding parallelism we remark that the formulation given above is fully parallel in the components of the output vector, so simple schemes such as OpenMP loop parallelization (section 20.2) should work fine. This statement is no longer true if compressed column storage (CCS) or coordinate storage (COO) is used. Such implementations of sparse matrix storage require a substantial rewrite of the product routine to be executed in parallel.

For the data reuse, we observe that each element of y is written once, so caching is irrelevant. The same holds for the matrix A. However, both are accessed strictly sequentially, so at least cacheline utilization is perfect.

Data reuse of the input vector x is more tricky. Because of indirect addressing we have to load the array of column indices. Thus, for each multiplication and addition in the inner loop we need to load two doubles (one for the matrix and one for the input vector) and one integer, for the index. A further factor is that for general sparse matrices subsequent loads from the right-hand side need not be consecutive, so cacheline utilization can be poor.

The accumulator s will stay resident in register. Also, given enough elements per row, the load and store into y is of less relevance.

We conclude that the sparse matrix-vector product is largely bandwidth-bound, with at most some lower level cache reuse on the input vector. A more refined analysis for the case of stencil-based matrices can be found in section 32.5.

33.8.2 ▪ Distributed memory

Let us analyze the distributed memory parallel sparse matrix-vector product in some detail. We will assume that the matrix is distributed by block rows, where processor p owns (in the sense of computing the output there) the matrix rows with indices in some set I_p.

The line $y_i = y_i + a_{ij}x_j$, which in the dense case is executed for all j, and therefore induces an allgather (see section 22.3.4) of the right-hand side, now has to take into account that a_{ij} can be zero, so for some pairs $i \in I_p, j \notin I_p$ no communication will be needed. If both $i, j \in I_p$, we have a traditional single-processor product; the interesting case is $i \in I_p, j \notin I_p$, where x_j needs to be communicated to processor p from another processor.

Declaring for each $i \in I_p$ a sparsity pattern set

$$S_{p;i} = \{j \colon j \notin I_p, a_{ij} \neq 0\},$$

our multiplication instruction becomes

$$\begin{cases} y_i += a_{ij}\,\mathrm{local}(x_j) & \text{for } j \in I_p, a_{ij} \neq 0, \\ y_i += a_{ij}\,\mathrm{communicated}(x_j) & \text{for } j \in S_{p;i}. \end{cases}$$

If we want to avoid a flood of small messages, we combine all communication into a single message per processor. Defining

$$S_p = \cup_{i \in I_p} S_{p;i},$$

the algorithm now becomes

- collect all necessary off-processor elements x_j with $j \in S_p$ into one buffer;
- perform the matrix-vector product, reading all elements of x from local storage.

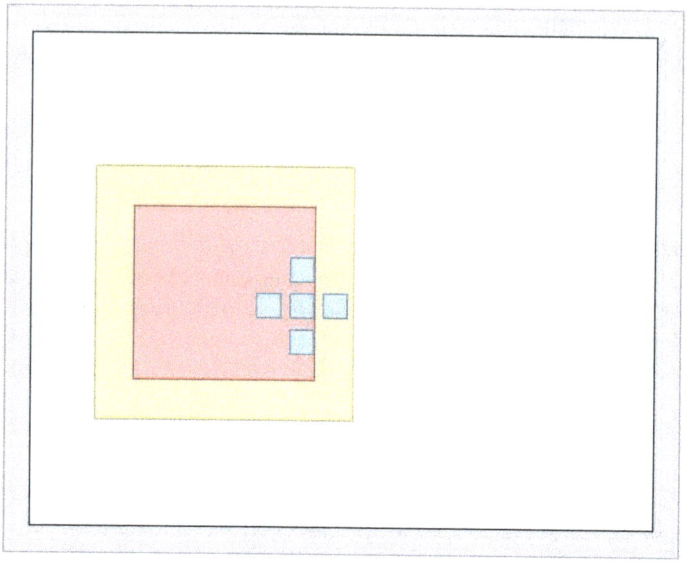

Figure 33.9. *The halo region of a processor, induced by a stencil*

33.8.2.1 ▪ Point-to-point messaging

Recall Figure 19.1, which illustrates a discretized boundary value problem on the simplest domain, a square, and let us now parallelize it. We do this by partitioning the domain; each processor gets the matrix rows corresponding to its subdomain. Figure 22.5 shows how this gives rise to connections between processors: the elements a_{ij} with $i \in I_p, j \notin I_p$ are now the "legs" of the stencil that reach beyond a processor boundary. The set S_p of all such j, defined above, is known as the *halo region* of a processor; see Figure 33.9.

Exercise 33.2. Show that a one-dimensional partitioning of the domain leads to a partitioning of the matrix into block rows with a contiguous block for each process. Show that a two-dimensional partitioning of the domain does not give this structure. You can do this in the abstract, or you can illustrate it: take a 4×4 domain (giving a matrix of size 16), and partition it over 4 processors. The one-dimensional domain partitioning corresponds to giving each processor one line out of the domain, while the two-dimensional partitioning gives each processor a 2×2 subdomain. Draw the matrices for these two cases.

One crucial observation about the parallel sparse matrix-vector product is that, for each processor, the number of other processors it is involved with is strictly limited. This has implications for the efficiency of the operation.

In the case of the dense matrix-vector product, partitioning the matrix over the processors by (block) rows does not lead to a scalable algorithm. In global terms we can explain this by the fact that, as the number of processors increases, the message size does not go down similarly to the work per processor. This argument is formalized in the HPC book [23, section 7.2.3].

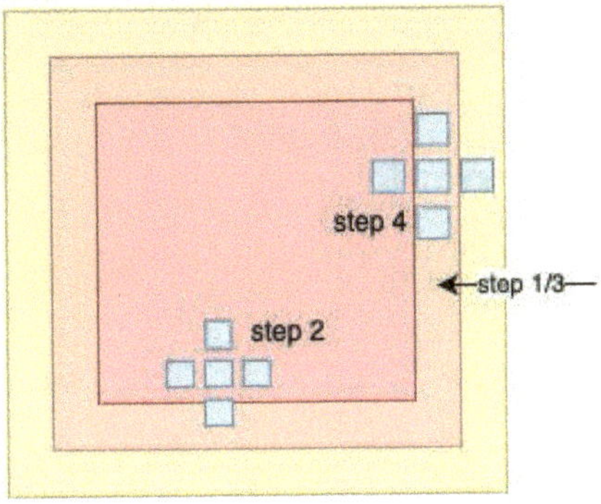

Figure 33.10. *Computation of the local domain, separated into interior and edges*

The observation that each processor communicates with just a few neighbors stays intact if we go beyond square domains to more complicated physical objects. If a processor receives a contiguous, more or less convex subdomain, the number of its neighbors will be limited. This implies that even in complicated problems each processor will only communicate with a small number of other processors. Compare this to the dense case where each processor had to receive data from *every* other processor. It is obvious that the sparse case is far more friendly to the interconnection network. (The fact that it also more common for large systems may influence the choice of network to install if you are about to buy a new parallel computer.)

33.8.2.2 ▪ Latency hiding

In the presentation above we left the scheme intact of separately gathering all neighbor information and performing the local product. This means that the latency of the communication will be an explicit component of the running time. This can be eliminated.

We can achieve *latency hiding* by adopting the following scheme:

1. start communicating halo points;
2. compute local points that do not depend on the halo;
3. wait for communication to conclude;
4. compute local points that depend on communicated halo points.

We make two observations about this scheme:

1. This uses MPI "nonblocking" operations; see section 22.6.3.
2. This considerably complicates the computation of the local domain, since we now separately compute the 2D interior and the four edges; see Figure 33.10.

Chapter 34

Profiling and tracing

Profiling is the act of finding overall statistics of a program run. As a first example, you could measure time; basic C++ native timers were discussed in Chapter 8. Here we go into more sophisticated profiling tools.

34.1 ▪ *gprof*

The profiler of the *GNU* compiler, *gprof*, requires recompilation and linking with an extra flag:

```
% gcc  -g -pg -c ./srcFile.c
% gcc  -g -pg -o MyProgram ./srcFile.o
```

The program is then run by itself,

```
% ./MyProgram
```

leaving behind a file *gmon.out*. This can be postprocessed and displayed:

```
% gprof    ./exeFile gmon.out > profile.txt
% gprof -l ./exeFile gmon.out > profile_line.txt
% gprof -A ./exeFile gmon.out > profile_annotated.txt
```

34.2 ▪ *perf*

Coming with most Unix distributions, *perf* does not require any instrumentation.

Profile generation is done by prefixing your command line with *perf record*. Various options exist, for instance, for methods of call graph generation:

```
perf record myprogram myoptions
perf record --call-graph fp myprogram myoptions
```

By default, event information is gathered into a file `perf.data`, but other names can be specified,

```
perf record -o myoutputfile myprogram myoptions
```

for a custom output file.

Postprocess and display:

```
perf report
perf report --demangle ## for C++
perf report -i myoutputfile
```

The display may be interactive. The following gives a pure ASCII display, limiting to events amounting to more than one percent, and printing out only the columns of percentage and routine name:

```
perf report --stdio \
    --percent-limit=1 \
    --fields=Overhead,Symbol
```

Example:

```
+   14.15%     4.07%  fsm.exe  fsm.exe              [.] std::vector<richdem::dephier::
     Depression<double>, std::allocator<richdem::dephier::Depression<double> > >::at
+    8.92%     4.58%  fsm.exe  fsm.exe              [.] std::vector<richdem::dephier::
     Depression<double>, std::allocator<richdem::dephier::Depression<double> > >::
     _M_range_check
```

This shows that 14% of the running time of the application is spent in indexing with `at`, and that more than half of that went into the range checking.

34.3 ▪ TAU

The TAU tool [50, 46] can do both tracing and profiling on distributed memory parallel codes. It has an instrumented mode, where the code is first instrumented in a source-to-source pass, and a noninstrumented mode that is only used for profiling.

We will not go into further detail on TAU in this book.

34.4 ▪ Other tools

There are other profiling and tracing tools. We mention *VTune* from Intel, and *MAP* from Arm, formerly Allinea. Both are commercial and very powerful.

Chapter 35
Floating point arithmetic

In the physical sciences, we usually work with real numbers, so it's convenient to pretend that computers can do this too. However, since numbers in a computer have only a finite number of bits, most real numbers cannot be represented exactly. In fact, even many fractions cannot be represented exactly, since they repeat; for instance, $1/3 = 0.333\ldots$, which is not representable in either decimal or binary.

In this chapter we discuss how numbers are realized in hardware, along with some of the implications of this for computing.

35.1 ▪ Representation of real numbers

Real numbers are stored using a scheme that is analogous to "scientific notation," where a number is represented as a *significand* and an *exponent*, for instance, $6.022 \cdot 10^{23}$, which has a significand `6022` with a *radix point* after the first digit, and an exponent `23`. This number stands for

$$6.022 \cdot 10^{23} = \left[6 \times 10^0 + 0 \times 10^{-1} + 2 \times 10^{-2} + 2 \times 10^{-3}\right] \cdot 10^{23}. \tag{35.1}$$

For a general approach, we introduce a *base* β, which is a small integer number, 10 in the preceding example, and 2 in computer numbers. With this, we write numbers as a sum of t terms:

$$\begin{aligned} x &= \pm 1 \times \left[d_1\beta^0 + d_2\beta^{-1} + d_3\beta^{-2} + \cdots + d_t\beta^{-t+1}b\right] \times \beta^e \\ &= \pm\Sigma_{i=1}^t d_i\beta^{1-i} \times \beta^e, \end{aligned} \tag{35.2}$$

where the components are

- the *sign bit*: a single bit storing whether the number is positive or negative;
- β is the base of the number system;
- $0 \le d_i \le \beta - 1$, the digits of the *mantissa* or *significand*—the location of the radix point (decimal point in decimal numbers) is implicitly assumed to be immediately following the first digit d_1;
- t is the length of the mantissa;
- $e \in [L, U]$ exponent; typically $L < 0 < U$ and $L \approx -U$.

Note that there is an explicit sign bit for the whole number, but the sign of the exponent is handled differently. For reasons of efficiency, e is not a signed number; instead it is considered as an unsigned number in *excess* of a certain minimum value. For instance, with 8 bits for the exponent we can represent the numbers $0 \cdots 256$, but with an excess of -127 this is interpreted as $-127 \cdots 128$. Additionally, the highest and lowest exponent values can be used to express special values such as infinity.

The general definition of floating point numbers, equation (35.2), leaves us with the problem that numbers can have more than one representation. For instance, $.5 \times 10^2 = .05 \times 10^3$. Since this would make computer arithmetic needlessly complicated, for instance, in testing equality of numbers, we use *normalized floating point numbers*. A nonzero number is normalized if its first digit is nonzero. This implies that the mantissa part is $1 \leq x_m < \beta$; in binary $1 \leq x_m < 2$.

A practical implication in the case of binary numbers is that the first digit is always 1, so we do not need to store it explicitly. This means that every normalized floating point number is of the form

$$1.d_1 d_2 \ldots d_t \times 2^e \tag{35.3}$$

and only the digits $d_1 d_2 \ldots d_t$ are stored.

Exercise 35.1. With quantities t, e, what is the smallest positive normalized number?

Unnormalized numbers do exist, but only for numbers smaller than the smallest positive normalized number. See section 35.2.4.3.

35.2 ▪ IEEE 754

Some decades ago, issues such as the length of the mantissa and the rounding behavior of operations could differ between computer manufacturers, and even between models from one manufacturer. This was obviously a bad situation from a point of portability of codes and reproducibility of results. The *IEEE 754* standard [35] codified all this in 1985, for instance, stipulating 24 and 53 bits (before normalization) for the mantissa in single and double precision arithmetic, using a storage sequence of sign bit, exponent, mantissa; see Table 35.1.

sign	exponent	mantissa	sign	exponent	mantissa
p	$e = e_1 \cdots e_8$	$s = s_1 \ldots s_{23}$	s	$e_1 \cdots e_{11}$	$s_1 \ldots s_{52}$
31	$30 \cdots 23$	$22 \cdots 0$	63	$62 \cdots 52$	$51 \cdots 0$
$\pm$	2^{e-127} (except $e = 0, 255$)	$2^{-s_1} + \cdots + 2^{-s_{23}}$	$\pm$	2^{e-1023} (except $e = 0, 2047$)	$2^{-s_1} + \cdots + 2^{-s_{52}}$

Table 35.1. *Single and double precision definition*

Remark. *The full name of the 754 standard is "IEEE Standard for Binary Floating-Point Arithmetic (ANSI/IEEE Std 754-1985)." It is also identical to IEC 559: "Binary Floating-Point Arithmetic for Microprocessor Systems," superseded by ISO/IEC/IEEE 60559:2011. IEEE 754 is a standard for binary arithmetic; there is a further standard,* IEEE 854, *that allows decimal arithmetic.*

The standard also declared the rounding behavior to be *correct rounding*: the result of an operation should be the rounded version of the exact result. See section 35.2.7.

exponent	numerical value	range
$(0\cdots0)=0$	$\pm 0.s_1\cdots s_{23}\times 2^{-126}$	$s=0\cdots01\Rightarrow 2^{-23}\cdot 2^{-126}=2^{-149}\approx 10^{-50}$
		$\cdots$
		$s=1\cdots11\Rightarrow (1-2^{-23})\cdot 2^{-126}$
$(0\cdots01)=1$	$\pm 1.s_1\cdots s_{23}\times 2^{-126}$	$s=0\cdots00\Rightarrow 1\cdot 2^{-126}\approx 10^{-37}$
$(0\cdots010)=2$	$\pm 1.s_1\cdots s_{23}\times 2^{-125}$	
	$\cdots$	
$(01111111)=127$	$\pm 1.s_1\cdots s_{23}\times 2^{0}$	$s=0\cdots00\Rightarrow 1\cdot 2^0=1$
		$\cdots$
		$s=0\cdots01\Rightarrow 1+2^{-23}\cdot 2^0=1+\epsilon$
		$\cdots$
		$s=1\cdots11\Rightarrow (2-2^{-23})\cdot 2^0=2-\epsilon$
$(10000000)=128$	$\pm 1.s_1\cdots s_{23}\times 2^{1}$	
	$\cdots$	
$(11111110)=254$	$\pm 1.s_1\cdots s_{23}\times 2^{127}$	
$(11111111)=255$	$s_1\cdots s_{23}=0\Rightarrow\pm\infty$ $s_1\cdots s_{23}\neq 0\Rightarrow NaN$	

Table 35.2. *Interpretation of single precision numbers depending on the exponent bit pattern*

35.2.1 ▪ Definition of the floating point formats

An inventory of the meaning of all bit patterns in *IEEE 754 single precision* is given in Table 35.2. Recall from section 35.1 above that for normalized numbers the first nonzero digit is a 1, which is not stored, so the bit pattern $d_1d_2\ldots d_t$ is interpreted as $1.d_1d_2\ldots d_t$.

The highest exponent is used to accommodate `Inf` and `Nan`; see section 35.2.5. The lowest exponent is used to accommodate unnormalized numbers; see section 35.2.4.3.

Exercise 35.2. Every programmer, at some point in their life, makes the mistake of storing a real number in an integer or the other way around. This can happen, for instance, if you call a function differently from how it was defined:

```
void a(float x) {....}
int main() {
  int i;
  .... a(i) ....
}
```

What happens when you print `x` in the function? Consider the bit pattern for a small integer, and use Table 35.2 to interpret it as a floating point number. Explain that it will be a subnormal number.

(This is one of those errors you won't forget after you make it. In the future, whenever you see a number on the order of 10^{-305} you'll recognize that you probably made this error.)

These days, almost all processors adhere to the IEEE 754 standard. Early generations of the *NVidia Tesla GPUs* were not standard-conforming in single precision. The justification for this was that single precision is more likely used for graphics, where exact compliance matters less.

For many scientific computations, double precision is necessary, since the precision of calculations gets worse with increasing problem size or runtime.

35.2.2 ▪ The "bfloat" format

IEEE 754-2008 has a definition for the *binary16* half precision format, which has a 5-bit exponent and 11-bit mantissa.

In *ML* it is more important to express the range of values than to be precise about the exact value. (This is the opposite of traditional scientific applications, where close values need to be resolved.) This has led to the definition of the *bfloat16* "brain float" format [7], which is a 16-bit floating point format. It uses 8 bits for the exponent and 7 bits for the mantissa. This means that it shares the same exponent range as the IEEE single precision format; see Figure 35.1.

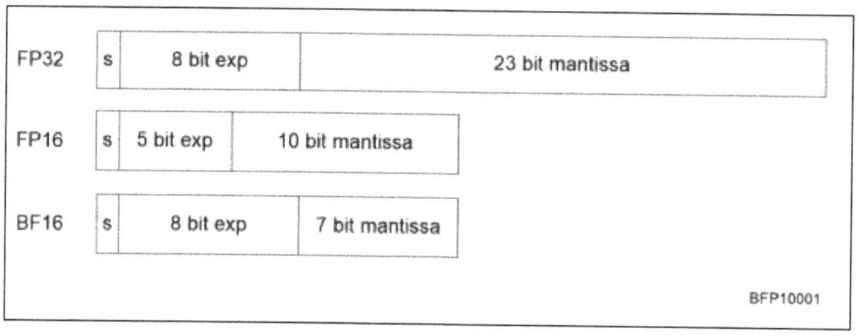

Figure 35.1. *Comparison of fp32, fp16, and bfloat16 formats. (Illustration from [8].)*

First of all, conversion between bfloat16 and fp32 is simple:

- Since bfloat16 and fp32 have the same structure in the first two bytes, a bfloat16 number can be derived from an fp32 number by truncating the third and fourth bytes. However, rounding may give better results in practice.
- Conversely, casting a bloat16 to fp32 only requires filling the final two bytes with zeros.

A second argument for using bfloat16 is that it effectively doubles the available bandwidth. Thus, we see proposals for using this format where bandwidth is a limiting factor, and converting to regular formats elsewhere.

35.2.3 ▪ Machine precision

If x is a number and $\tilde{x}$ its representation in the computer, we call $x - \tilde{x}$ the *representation error* or *absolute representation error*, and $\frac{x-\tilde{x}}{x}$ the *relative representation error*.

Often we are only interested in the order of magnitude of the representation error, and we will write $\tilde{x} = x(1+\epsilon)$, where $|\epsilon| \leq \beta^{-t}$. This maximum relative representation error is called the *machine precision*, or sometimes *machine epsilon*. Typical values are

$$\begin{cases} \epsilon \approx 10^{-7} & \text{32-bit single precision,} \\ \epsilon \approx 10^{-16} & \text{64-bit double precision.} \end{cases} \tag{35.4}$$

(After you have studied the section on the IEEE 754 standard, can you derive these values from the number of bits in the mantissa?)

Machine precision can be defined another way: ϵ is the smallest number that can be added to 1 so that $1 + \epsilon$ has a different representation than 1. A small example shows how aligning exponents can shift a too small operand so that it is effectively ignored in the addition operation:

$$\begin{array}{lll} & 1.0000 & \times 10^0 \\ + & 1.0000 & \times 10^{-5} \\ \hline \end{array} \Rightarrow \begin{array}{lll} & 1.0000 & \times 10^0 \\ + & 0.00001 & \times 10^0 \\ \hline = & 1.0000 & \times 10^0 \end{array} . \tag{35.5}$$

Yet another way of looking at this is to observe that, in the addition $x + y$, if the ratio of x and y is too large, the result will be identical to x.

The machine precision is the maximum attainable accuracy of computations: it does not make sense to ask for more than 6 or so digits of accuracy in single precision, or 15 in double.

Exercise 35.3. The number $e \approx 2.72$, the base for the natural logarithm, has various definitions. One of them is

$$e = \lim_{n \to \infty} (1 + 1/n)^n . \tag{35.6}$$

Write a single precision program that tries to compute e in this manner. (Do not use the `pow` function: code the power explicitly.) Evaluate the expression for an upper bound $n = 10^k$ for some k. (How far do you let k range?) Explain the output for large n. Comment on the behavior of the error.

Exercise 35.4. The exponential function e^x can be computed as

$$e = 1 + x + \frac{x^2}{2!} + \frac{x^3}{3!} + \cdots . \tag{35.7}$$

Code this and try it for some positive x, for instance, $x = 1, 3, 10, 50$. How many terms do you compute?

Now compute e^{-x} and from it e^x. Use, for instance, the same x values and number of iterations as for e^x.

What do you observe about the e^x versus e^{-x} computation? Explain.

Machine epsilon and other quantities can be found as

```
#include <limits>
std::numeric_limits<float>::epsilon();
std::numeric_limits<double>::epsilon();
```

See further section 2.2.1.

35.2.4 ▪ Overflow and underflow

Since we use only a finite number of bits to store floating point numbers, not all numbers can be represented. The ones that cannot be represented fall into two categories: those that are too large or too small (in some sense), and those that fall in the gaps.

The second category, where a computational result has to be rounded or truncated to be representable, is the basis of the field of roundoff error analysis. We will study this in some detail in section 35.3.

Numbers can be too large or too small in the following ways.

35.2.4.1 ▪ Overflow

The largest number we can store has every digit equal to β:

	unit	fractional			exponent
digit	$\beta - 1$	$\beta - 1$	$\cdots$	$\beta - 1$	
value	1	β^{-1}	$\cdots$	$\beta^{-(t-1)}$	U

(35.8)

which adds up to

$$(\beta - 1) \cdot 1 + (\beta - 1) \cdot \beta^{-1} + \cdots + (\beta - 1) \cdot \beta^{-(t-1)} = \beta - \beta^{-(t-1)}, \tag{35.9}$$

and the smallest number (that is, the most negative) is $-\left(\beta - \beta^{-(t-1)}\right)$; anything larger than the former or smaller than the latter causes a condition called *overflow*.

35.2.4.2 ▪ Underflow

The number closest to zero is $\beta^{-(t-1)} \cdot \beta^L$:

	unit	fractional			exponent
digit	0	0	$\cdots$	$0, \beta - 1$	$\emptyset$
value	0	0	$\cdots$	$0, \beta^{-(t-1)}$	L

(35.10)

A computation that has a result less than that (in absolute value) causes a condition called *underflow*.

The above "smallest" number cannot actually exist if we work with normalized numbers. Therefore, we also need to look at "gradual underflow."

35.2.4.3 ▪ Gradual underflow

The normalized number closest to zero is $1 \cdot \beta^L$:

	unit	fractional			exponent
digit	1	0	$\cdots$	0	$\emptyset$
value	1	0	$\cdots$	0	L

(35.11)

Trying to compute a number less than that in absolute value is sometimes handled by using *subnormal* (or *denormalized* or *unnormalized*) numbers, a process known as *gradual underflow*. In this case, a special value of the exponent indicates that the number is no longer normalized. In the case of IEEE standard arithmetic (see Table 35.2 for single precision) this is done through a zero exponent field.

However, this is typically tens or hundreds of times slower than computing with regular floating point numbers. Not all processors have hardware support for gradual underflow. Ones that do include the *IBM Power6* (and up), *NVidia Fermi* (and up), but processors can have their default set to apply *flush-to-zero*. Section 33.6 explores performance implications.

35.2.4.4 ▪ What happens with over/underflow?

The occurrence of overflow or underflow means that your computation will be "wrong" from that point on. Underflow will make the computation proceed with a zero where there should have been a nonzero; overflow is represented as `Inf`, short for "infinite."

Exercise 35.5. For real numbers x, y, the quantity $g = \sqrt{(x^2 + y^2)/2}$ satisfies

$$g \leq \max\{|x|, |y|\}, \tag{35.12}$$

so it is representable if x and y are. What can go wrong if you compute g using the above formula? Can you think of a better way?

Computing with `Inf` is possible to an extent: adding two of those quantities will again give `Inf`. However, subtracting them gives `NaN`; see the next section.

In none of these cases will the computation end: the processor will continue. However, you can query whether such an exception has occurred; see section 35.2.6.

Limits can be found through such functions as

```
#include <limits>
std::numeric_limits<double>::denorm_min();
std::numeric_limits<double>::min();
std::numeric_limits<double>::max();
```

See further section 2.2.1 for the `limits` header.

35.2.5 ▪ Floating point exceptions

The IEEE 754 standard has two special quantities: `Inf` for "infinity" and `NaN` for "not a number." Whereas Infinity is the result of overflow or dividing by zero, "Not a Number" is the result of, for instance, subtracting infinity from infinity.

To be precise, processors will represent as `NaN` ("not a number") the result of

- addition, `Inf` − `Inf`, but note that `Inf`+`Inf` gives `Inf`;
- multiplication, $0 \times$ `Inf`;
- division, $0/0$ or `Inf`/`Inf`;
- remainder, `Inf` rem x or x rem `Inf`;
- $\sqrt{x}$ for $x < 0$;
- comparison, $x < y$ or $x > y$ where any operand is `NaN`.

Since the processor can continue computing with such a number, it is referred to as a "quiet `NaN`." By contrast, some `NaN` quantities can cause the processor to generate an *interrupt* or *exception*. This is called a "signaling `NaN`."

If `NaN` appears in an expression, the whole expression will evaluate to that value. The rule for computing with `Inf` is a bit more complicated [28].

There are uses for a signaling `NaN`. You could, for instance, fill allocated memory with such a value, to indicate that it is uninitialized for the purposes of the computation. Any use of such a value is then a program error, and would cause an exception.

The *2008 revision* of IEEE 754 suggests using the most significant bit of a `NaN` as the `is_quiet` bit to distinguish between quiet and signaling `NaN`s.

Remark. *`NaN` and `Inf` do not always propagate:*

- *A finite number divided by `Inf` is zero;*
- *Various transcendental functions treat `Inf` correctly, such as* $\tan^{-1}(\text{Inf}) = \pi/2$.

The 2008 version of the standard treated the quiet `NaN` as "missing data," meaning that the minimum of 1 and a quiet `NaN` was 1. This led to min/max being nonassociative. This was fixed in the 2019 standard, where `NaN`s always propagate.

35.2.6 ▪ Handling of exceptions

The C/C++ languages allow access to floating point behavior through the `fenv.h` or `cfenv` header. This can be used to set rounding behavior, or to query *floating point exception*, such as overflow or divide by zero.

35.2.6.1 ▪ Testing

The header defines symbolic names for exceptions to be tested, such as `FE_DIVBYZERO`, `FE_OVERFLOW`, `FE_UNDERFLOW`. The actual testing is done through the function `fetestexcept`:

Code:

```
// fenv/divzero.cpp
float result = 1.f/zero;
cout << "result: " << result << '\n';
if (std::fetestexcept(FE_DIVBYZERO))
  std::cout << "division by zero reported\n";
else
  std::cout
    << "division by zero not reported\n";
```

Output:

```
result: inf
division by zero reported
```

35.2.6.2 ▪ Changing behavior

Another functionality offered by the header is to change rounding behavior, with values `FE_DOWNWARD`, `FE_TONEAREST`, `FE_TOWARDZERO`, `FE_UPWARD`:

Code:

```
// fenv/round.cpp
fesetround(FE_UPWARD);
float thirdup = one/3.f;
fesetround(FE_DOWNWARD);
float thirddn = one/3.f;
cout << "difference: "
     << thirdup-thirddn << '\n';
```

Output:

```
difference: 2.98023e-08
```

(Can you relate the output of this code to the value of machine epsilon?)

35.2.7 ▪ Correct rounding

The IEEE 754 standard does not only declare the way a floating point number is stored, it also gives a standard for the accuracy of operations such as addition, subtraction, multiplication, and division. The model for arithmetic in the standard is that of *correct rounding*: the result of an operation should be as if the following procedure is followed:

- The exact result of the operation is computed, whether this is representable or not.
- This result is then rounded to the nearest computer number.

In short: the representation of the result of an operation is the rounded exact result of that operation. Of course, after two operations it no longer needs to hold that the computed result is the exact rounded version of the exact result.

If this statement sounds trivial or self-evident, consider subtraction as an example. In a decimal number system with two digits in the mantissa we could have a computation:

$$\begin{aligned} 1.0 - 9.4 \cdot 10^{-1} = \\ 1.0 - 0.94 = 0.06 \\ = 0.6 \cdot 10^{-2}. \end{aligned} \tag{35.13}$$

Note that in an intermediate step the mantissa .094 appears, which has one more digit than the two we declared for our number system. The extra digit is called a *guard digit*. Without a guard digit, this operation would have proceeded as $1.0 - 9.4 \cdot 10^{-1}$, where $9.4 \cdot 10^{-1}$ would be normalized to 0.9, giving a final result of 0.1, which is almost double the correct result.

Exercise 35.6. Consider the computation $1.0 - 9.5 \cdot 10^{-1}$, and assume again that numbers are rounded to fit the 2-digit mantissa. Why is this computation in a way a lot worse than the example?

One guard digit is not enough to guarantee correct rounding. An analysis that we will not reproduce here shows that three extra bits are needed [27].

Remark. *The* 2008 *revision of the 754 standard declares that mathematical library functions should also be correctly rounded. However, not all compilers obey this.*

35.2.8 ▪ Subtraction and cancellation

Subtraction behaves very differently from addition. Whereas in addition errors are added, giving only a gradual increase of overall roundoff error, subtraction has the potential for greatly increased error in a single operation.

For example, consider subtraction with 3 digits to the mantissa: $1.24 - 1.23 = 0.01 \rightarrow 1.00 \cdot 10^{-2}$. While the result is exact, it has only one significant digit.[1] To see this, consider the case where the first operand 1.24 is actually the rounded result of a computation that should have resulted in 1.235:

$$\begin{array}{lllll} .5 \times 2.47 - 1.23 & = 1.235 - 1.23 & = 0.005 & = 5.0 \cdot 10^{-3} & \text{exact} \\ & \qquad\qquad\downarrow & & & \\ & = 1.24 - 1.23 & = 0.01 & = 1. \cdot 10^{-2} & \text{computed} \end{array} \tag{35.14}$$

[1]Normally, a number with 3 digits to the mantissa suggests an error corresponding to rounding or truncating the fourth digit. We say that such a number has 3 *significant digits*. In this case, the last two digits have no meaning, resulting from the normalization process.

Now, there is a 100% error, even though the relative error of the inputs was as small as could be expected. Clearly, subsequent operations involving the result of this subtraction will also be inaccurate. We conclude that subtracting almost equal numbers is a likely cause of numerical roundoff; see an example in section 35.3.3.

35.3 ▪ Why it is important to know this

35.3.1 ▪ Associativity

The implementation of floating point numbers implies that simple arithmetic operations such as adding or multiplying no longer are *associative*, the way they are in mathematics. That is,

$$(a+b)+c \neq a+(b+c).$$

Let's consider a simple example, showing how associativity is affected by the rounding behavior of floating point numbers. Let floating point numbers be stored as a single digit for the mantissa, one digit for the exponent, and one guard digit; now consider the computation of $4+6+7$. Evaluation left to right gives

$$\begin{array}{lll} (4\cdot 10^0 + 6\cdot 10^0) + 7\cdot 10^0 & \Rightarrow 10\cdot 10^0 + 7\cdot 10^0 & \text{addition} \\ & \Rightarrow 1\cdot 10^1 + 7\cdot 10^0 & \text{rounding} \\ & \Rightarrow 1.0\cdot 10^1 + 0.7\cdot 10^1 & \text{using guard digit} \\ & \Rightarrow 1.7\cdot 10^1 & \\ & \Rightarrow 2\cdot 10^1 & \text{rounding.} \end{array} \tag{35.15}$$

On the other hand, evaluation right to left gives

$$\begin{array}{lll} 4\cdot 10^0 + (6\cdot 10^0 + 7\cdot 10^0) & \Rightarrow 4\cdot 10^0 + 13\cdot 10^0 & \text{addition} \\ & \Rightarrow 4\cdot 10^0 + 1\cdot 10^1 & \text{rounding} \\ & \Rightarrow 0.4\cdot 10^1 + 1.0\cdot 10^1 & \text{using guard digit} \\ & \Rightarrow 1.4\cdot 10^1 & \\ & \Rightarrow 1\cdot 10^1 & \text{rounding.} \end{array} \tag{35.16}$$

The conclusion is that the sequence in which rounding and truncation is applied to intermediate results makes a difference.

Exercise 35.7. The above example used rounding. Can you come up with a similar example in an arithmetic system using truncation?

35.3.2 ▪ Associativity and parallelism

The lack of associativity has an interesting consequence for parallel computations: the way a computation is spread over parallel processors influences the result.

As a very simple example, consider computing the sum of four numbers $a+b+c+d$. On a single processor execution proceeds left to right, corresponding to the following associativity:

$$((a+b)+c)+d. \tag{35.17}$$

On the other hand, spreading this computation over two processors, where processor 0 has a, b and processor 1 has c, d, corresponds to

$$((a+b)+(c+d)). \tag{35.18}$$

Generalizing this, we see that reduction operations will most likely give a different result on different numbers of processors.

35.3.3 ▪ Practical example: The "abc" formula

As a practical example of cancellation, consider the quadratic equation $ax^2+bx+c=0$, which has solutions $x=\frac{-b\pm\sqrt{b^2-4ac}}{2a}$. Suppose $b>0$ and $b^2\gg 4ac$; then $\sqrt{b^2-4ac}\approx b$ and the "+" solution will be inaccurate. In this case it is better to compute $x_-=\frac{-b-\sqrt{b^2-4ac}}{2a}$ and use $x_+\cdot x_-=c/a$.

For an illustration, we consider the equation

$$f(x)=\epsilon x^2-(1+\epsilon^2)x+\epsilon,$$

which has, for ϵ small, the roots

$$x_+\approx\epsilon^{-1},\qquad x_-\approx\epsilon.$$

We have two problems here. First of all, for ϵ less than machine precision we have $b\approx 1$, $b^2-4ac=1$, and $x_-=0$, which means that this solution is totally wrong. Even if the *discriminant* $b^2-4ac>1$, we get problems with cancellation, and the function value is grossly inaccurate: for the textbook solution, $f(x_-)\approx\epsilon$, while for the solution without cancellation $f(x_-)\approx\epsilon^3$.

	textbook		accurate	
ϵ	x_-	$f(x_-)$	x_-	$f(x_-)$
10^{-3}	$1.000\cdot10^{-03}$	$-2.876\cdot10^{-14}$	$1.000\cdot10^{-03}$	$-2.168\cdot10^{-19}$
10^{-4}	$1.000\cdot10^{-04}$	$5.264\cdot10^{-14}$	$1.000\cdot10^{-04}$	0.000
10^{-5}	$1.000\cdot10^{-05}$	$-8.274\cdot10^{-13}$	$1.000\cdot10^{-05}$	$-1.694\cdot10^{-21}$
10^{-6}	$1.000\cdot10^{-06}$	$-3.339\cdot10^{-11}$	$1.000\cdot10^{-06}$	$-2.118\cdot10^{-22}$
10^{-7}	$9.992\cdot10^{-08}$	$7.993\cdot10^{-11}$	$1.000\cdot10^{-07}$	$1.323\cdot10^{-23}$
10^{-8}	$1.110\cdot10^{-08}$	$-1.102\cdot10^{-09}$	$1.000\cdot10^{-08}$	0.000
10^{-9}	0.000	$1.000\cdot10^{-09}$	$1.000\cdot10^{-09}$	$-2.068\cdot10^{-25}$
10^{-10}	0.000	$1.000\cdot10^{-10}$	$1.000\cdot10^{-10}$	0.000

(35.19)

Exercise 35.8. Write a program that computes the roots of the quadratic equation, both the "textbook" way and as described above.

- Let $b=-1$ and $a=-c$, and $4ac\downarrow 0$ by taking progressively smaller values for a and c.
- Print out the computed root, the root using the stable computation, and the value of $f(x)=ax^2+bx+c$ in the computed root.

Now suppose that you don't care much about the actual value of the root: you want to make sure the residual $f(x)$ is small in the computed root. Let x^* be the exact root; then

$$f(x^*+h)\approx f(x^*)+hf'(x^*)=hf'(x^*). \tag{35.20}$$

Now investigate separately the cases $a\downarrow 0, c=-1$ and $a=-1, c\downarrow 0$. Can you explain the difference?

Exercise 35.9. Consider the functions

$$\begin{cases} f(x) = \sqrt{x+1} - \sqrt{x}, \\ g(x) = 1/\big(\sqrt{x+1} + \sqrt{x}\big). \end{cases} \tag{35.21}$$

- Show that they are the same in exact arithmetic; however:
- Show that f can exhibit cancellation and that g has no such problem.
- Write code to show the difference between f and g. You may have to use large values for x.
- Analyze the cancellation in terms of x and machine precision. When are $\sqrt{x+1}$ and $\sqrt{x}$ less than ϵ apart? What happens then? (For a more refined analysis, when are they $\sqrt{\epsilon}$ apart, and how does that manifest itself?)
- The inverse function of $y = f(x)$ is

$$x = (y^2 - 1)^2/(4y^2). \tag{35.22}$$

  Add this to your code. Does this give any indication of the accuracy of the calculations?

Make sure to test your code in single and double precision. If you speak Python, try the `bigfloat` package.

35.4 ▪ Integers

In our processors we have hardware that is very good at dealing with (unsigned) bit strings, but for programming we want numbers that can be signed. The problem is then how to interpret bit strings as integral numbers, so that we can efficiently use our hardware to deal with both positive and negative numbers.

The solution commonly taken splits the integer range in two, with the lower half of numbers interpreted as nonnegative, and the higher half as negative.

The resulting scheme, which is the one that is used most commonly, is called *2's complement*. Using this scheme, the representation of integers is formally defined as follows.

Definition 35.1. *Let n be an integer; then the 2's complement "bit pattern" $\beta(n)$ is a nonnegative integer defined as follows:*

- *If $0 \le n \le 2^{31} - 1$, the normal bit pattern for n is used, that is,*

$$0 \le n \le 2^{31} - 1 \Rightarrow \beta(n) = n. \tag{35.23}$$

- *For $-2^{31} \le n \le -1$, n is represented by the bit pattern for $2^{32} - |n|$:*

$$-2^{31} \le n \le -1 \Rightarrow \beta(n) = 2^{32} - |n|. \tag{35.24}$$

We denote the inverse function that takes a bit pattern and interprets as integer with $\eta = \beta^{-1}$.

The following diagram shows the correspondence between bitstrings and their interpretation as 2's complement integer:

bitstring n	$00\cdots0$	...	$01\cdots1$	$10\cdots0$	...	$11\cdots1$
interpretation as unsigned int	0	...	$2^{31}-1$	2^{31}	...	$2^{32}-1$
interpretation $\beta(n)$ as 2's comp. integer	0	...	$2^{31}-1$	-2^{31}	...	-1

Some observations:

- There is no overlap between the bit patterns for positive and negative integers, in particular, there is only one pattern for zero.
- The positive numbers have a leading bit zero, the negative numbers have the leading bit set. This makes the leading bit act a little like a sign bit; however, you cannot make a number change sign by flipping this bit.
- If you have a positive number n, you get $-n$ by flipping all the bits and adding 1. (What is the inverse operation?)

Exercise 35.10. For the "naive" scheme and the 2's complement scheme for negative numbers, give pseudocode for the comparison test $m < n$, where m and n are integers. Be careful to distinguish between all cases of m, n positive, zero, or negative.

C++ implementation details of integers can be found in section 2.1.

Part VI

Software Carpentry

In this part we will look at some topics that can be described as "software carpentry." The term software carpentry is due to Greg Wilson (at the time of the University of Toronto) who wondered, "What should computer scientists teach to physical scientists and engineers?" It can roughly be described as the computing skills that scientists need to master to get more done in less time and with less pain.

Carpentry topics discussed here are the workings of the compiler (Chapter 36), the CMake build system (Chapter 37), and version control (Chapter 38). All of our presentation takes place in a Unix/Linux context. If you use an IDE such as *VSCode*, *CLion*, or *XCode*, these details may be hidden from you so they are not a daily concern. However, it is still good to be aware of how they are handled "under the hood."

Chapter 36

Compiling, linking, libraries

If you use an integrated development environment (IDE) for code development, building a program is a single press on a button. Behind the scenes, however, several steps are involved, and it useful to know what they are. This chapter goes into detail on compiling and linking, also touching on the related topic of libraries. The CMake utility for automating this process will be discussed in Chapter 37.

36.1 ▪ The steps of the compilation process

The compilation process involves more than merely invoking the compiler. For instance, your program likely contains `#include` statements, which are processed in a separate stage. Here is an outline of the steps, and we'll see them in more detail below.

Let's take a look at a simple "hello world" program. Rather than transforming your source in one fell swoop into an executable, the following steps happen:

1. The preprocessor generates a file `hello.i` where all includes are inlined and other macros expanded; see section 36.3 for the preprocessor. This file is usually immediately deleted: you need to supply a compiler flag for it to be left behind.
2. An *assembly listing* `hello.s` of your program is generated—again, to be immediately deleted after use. This is a sort of "readable machine language":

```
        .arch armv8-a
        .text
        .cstring
        .align  3
lC0:
        .ascii "hello world\0"
        .text
        .align  2
        .globl _main
_main:
LFB10:
        stp     x29, x30, [sp, -16]!
```

3. The main tangible result of the compilation is `hello.o`, the object file, containing actual machine language. The object file is not directly readable, but we will look at the `nm` tool in section 36.5.1.

4. Finally, the *linker* ties together the object file and system libraries into a self-contained executable or a library file. This will be discussed in section 36.5.

Remark. *Object files may be unreadable to human eyes, but their format is well-defined. The* ELF format *[25] is a standard for executables, object code, shared libraries, and core dumps that is widely used in Unix-like systems.*

36.2 ▪ Include and library paths

If your program uses libraries, whether system-installed or your own, you need to indicate the following:

1. The compiler needs to find the *header files*.
2. The linker needs to find the library file. In the C++ case of a *header-only library* this step is not needed.

These locations are indicated by command-line options:

```
// compile
gcc -c mysource.cpp -I${SOMELIB_INC_DIR}
// link
gcc -o myprogram mysource.o -L${SOMELIB_LIB_DIR} -lsomelib
```

The compile line has the `-I` option for "include" that specifies the location of the library header file. You can specify multiple include options. (Instead of listing these on the command line every time, you would of course put them in a makefile, or use CMake to generate such command lines.)

Correspondingly, the source has a line

```
#include <somelib.h>
```

or

```
#include <somelib/somelib.h>
```

The link line has the `-L` option for "library," which specifies the location of the actual library files, and the `-l` option for the library name. You can specify multiple library directories. The `-l` option is interpreted as follows: `-l somelib` makes the linker search for files

```
libsomelib.a
libsomelib.so
libsomelib.dylib
```

along the library paths.

Remark. *Starting with C++20, header files have been increasingly replaced by the* module *mechanism; see section 24.2.*

36.3 ▪ The C preprocessor

In this section we take a closer look at the C preprocessor (CPP). This program does a source-to-source translation on your program code, for instance, inlining include files. You can call this by the Unix command `cpp`, but usually it is implicitly called by the compiler.

36.3.1 ▪ Header includes

The #include directive causes the named file to be included. That file is in fact an ordinary text file, either part of your own sources, part of some library you are using, or a header that is stored somewhere in your system. As a result, your source file is transformed to another source file in a source-to-source translation stage, and only that second file is actually compiled by the compiler.

Normally, this intermediate file with all include files textually included is immediately destroyed again after the compilation, but in rare cases you may want to dump it for debugging. See your compiler documentation for how to generate this file.

Compiling the "hello world" program, the C preprocessor generates a text file where all preprocessor directives have been resolved, for instance, by textual inclusion of include files. In the case of the "hello world" program in C, that's the `stdlib.h` and `stdio.h` files. The preprocessor output file will look something like this:

```
# 0 "hello.c"
# 0 "<built-in>"
# 0 "<command-line>"
# 1 "hello.c"
# 12 "hello.c"
# 1 "/Library/Developer/CommandLineTools/SDKs/MacOSX13.sdk/usr/include/stdlib.h" 1 3 4
# 61 "/Library/Developer/CommandLineTools/SDKs/MacOSX13.sdk/usr/include/stdlib.h" 3 4
# 1 "/Library/Developer/CommandLineTools/SDKs/MacOSX13.sdk/usr/include/Availability.h" 1 3 4
```

etc.

36.3.2 ▪ Macros

Your code may occasionally have compile-time constants, such as the size of a `std::array`. If you want to change this value, do you have to edit and recompile your program? You can skip the edit stage by using a macro for the value,

```
std::array<int,N> fixed_array;
```

and have the value of `N` be defined on the compile line, using the `-D` flag:

```
icpc -c yourprogram.cpp -DN=100000
```

Now what if you want a default value in your source, but optionally redefine it in the compilation stage? You can solve this by testing for definition in the source with #ifndef: "if not defined":

```
#ifndef N
#define N 10000
#endif
```

See section 36.3.3.2 for more on "define" directives.

36.3.2.1 ▪ Parametrized macros

Instead of simple text substitution, you can have *parametrized preprocessor macros*. As an example, the following macro checks for return codes that require a routine to exit prematurely:

```
#define CHECK_FOR_ERROR(i) if (i!=0) return i
...
ierr = some_function(a,b,c); CHECK_FOR_ERROR(ierr);
ierr = more_function(d,e);   CHECK_FOR_ERROR(ierr);
```

You see that such parametrized macros look a little like function definitions, except that

- the parameters have no type: they are substituted textually;

- the macro substitution is not a scope, unless you explicitly surround the expansion text in curly braces;
- the whole definition has to fit on one line; you can escape the line end with a backslash if you are writing a long macro.

When you introduce parameters, it's a good idea to use lots of parentheses. The following definition is dangerous:

```
#define MULTIPLY(a,b) a*b
...
x = MULTIPLY(1+2,3+4);
```

This expands to

```
1+2*3+4
```

A better version uses parentheses:

```
#define MULTIPLY(a,b) ( (a)*(b) )
...
x = MULTIPLY(1+2,3+4);
```

Another popular use of macros is to simulate multidimensional indexing:

```
#define INDEX2D(i,j,n) (i)*(n)+j
...
double array[m*n];
for (int i=0; i<m; i++)
  for (int j=0; j<n; j++)
    array[ INDEX2D(i,j,n) ] = ...
```

(See section 19.3.2.)

Exercise 36.1. Write a macro that simulates 1-based indexing:

```
#define INDEX2D1BASED(i,j,n) /* your definition here */
...
double array[m*n];
for (int i=1; i<=m; i++)
  for (int j=n; j<=n; j++)
    array[ INDEX2D1BASED(i,j,n) ] = ...
```

36.3.3 ▪ Conditionals

There are two types of *preprocessor conditionals*: test for defined macros, and tests on a numeric expression. We start with a common idiom.

36.3.3.1 ▪ Disable a block of code

The #if macro tests on the nonzero value of its following expression. A common application is to temporarily remove code from compilation:

```
#if 0
  bunch of code that needs to
  be disabled
#endif
```

36.3.3.2 ▪ Check for defined macros

The #ifdef test tests for a macro being defined. Conversely, #ifndef tests for a macro not being defined. For instance,

```
#ifndef N
#define N 100
#endif
```

Why would a macro already be defined? Well, you can do that on the compile line:

```
icpc -c file.cc -DN=500
```

The C++23 standard introduced additionally #elifdef and #elifndef.

36.3.3.3 ▪ Numeric expression

You can also test on C-like expressions. The #if 0 idiom was actually a special case of this, since zero is interpreted as false.

Here are some examples in which macros are implicitly expanded:

```
#if VARIANT == 1
  some code
#elif CUDA_VERSION > 12000
  other code
#else
#error Invalid combination
#endif
```

Note the #error pragma, which is a good idea if you have many nested conditions.

36.3.4 ▪ More

36.3.4.1 ▪ Line and file macros

The CPP has built-in macros `__LINE__` / `__FILE__` that lend themselves to informative error reporting. The following macro not only checks on an error condition, but also reports where the error occurred:

```
#define CHECK_FOR_ERROR(ierr) \
  if (ierr!=0) { \
    printf("Error %d detected in line %d of file %s\n",\
           ierr,__LINE__,__FILE__); \
    return -1 ; }
```

See section 27.3.1 for a language-native alternative.

36.3.4.2 ▪ String concatenation

The preprocessor has a mechanism for string concatenation. You can use this to define variable names dynamically. This is not advisable, since it leads to hard-to-understand code.

36.4 ▪ Single file compilation

You can compile a single file:

- If it is self-contained, you can compile straight to the executable (see Figure 36.1):

  ```
  g++ -o myprogram myprogram.cpp
  ```

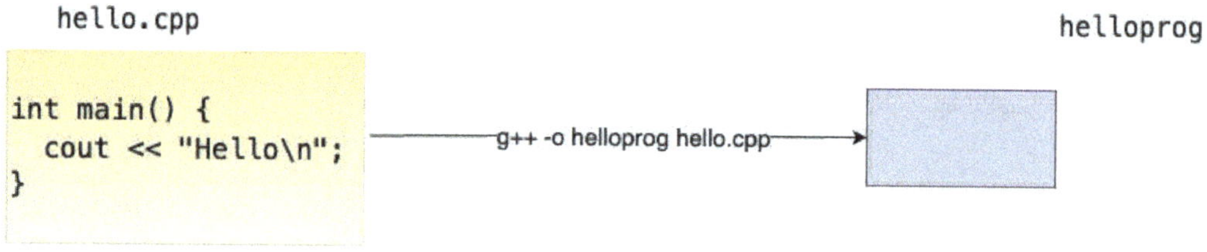

Figure 36.1. *Compiling a single file program*

- If it is one of many files, to be linked later (see section 36.5), you first compile to an object file,

  ```
  g++ -c myfunctions.cpp
  ```

  and link that later into an executable.

In these two commands you see the *command-line options* `-c` and `-o`. There are many more options, often compiler-dependent. At this point we only mention two generally available options:

- `-g`: This option is indispensable if you want to debug your program later in an interactive *debugger* such as `gdb`. Technically it adds the *symbol table* to the binary. Informally it means that the debugger can reconstruct the source code from the binary.
- `-O`, usually followed by a low number such as `-O0` or `-O2`: This indicates the *optimization level*, with `-O3` usually being the highest level. Increasing the optimization level can make your code faster, but there can be trade-offs. This is compiler- and application-dependent.

36.5 ▪ Separate compilation and linking

In this section we consider the *linker*: a program that is rarely invoked explicitly, but that is crucial for tying together the pieces of your executable.

Even for a single-source program the linker comes into action, to link the object file to the standard library; see section 36.6.5. However, we start with the more obvious case: a program consisting of multiple independently compiled source files. Here we have a main program, calling a function that is defined in another file. (We dispense with header files for this example.)

Main program:

```
// compilecxx/fooprog.cpp
extern void bar(string);

int main() {
  bar("hello world\n");
  return 0;
}
```

Subprogram:

```
// compilecxx/foosub.cpp
void bar( string s ) {
  cout << s;
}
```

As before, you can make the program with one command.

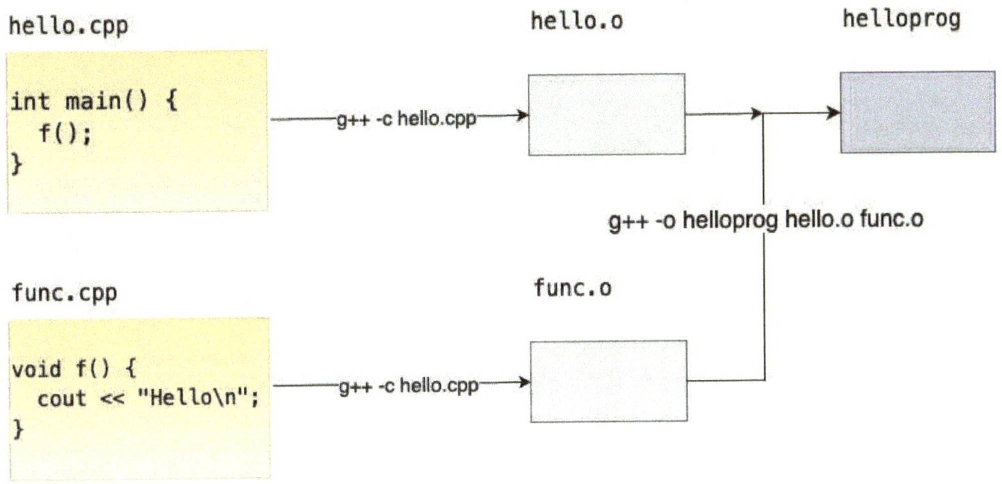

Figure 36.2. *Compiling a program from multiple source files*

Output
[code/compilecxx] makeoneprogram:

```
icpx -g -O2 -std=c++20  -Wl,-demangle -o oneprogram fooprog.cpp foosub.cpp
./oneprogram
hello world
```

However, you can also do it in steps, compiling each file separately and then linking them together. This is illustrated in Figure 36.2.

Output
[code/compilecxx] makeseparatecompilex:

```
icpx -g -O2 -std=c++20 -c fooprog.cpp
icpx -g -O2 -std=c++20 -c foosub.cpp
icpx -g -O2 -std=c++20 -Wl,-demangle -o fooprog fooprog.o foosub.o
./fooprog
hello world
```

In this example,

- the `-c` option on the first two lines tells the compiler to compile the source file, giving an *object file*;
- the third command then acts as the *linker*, tying together the object files into an executable;
- the `-Wl,-demangle` is a *linker option*: the prefix `-Wl` tells the compiler to pass `-demangle` to the linker; *demangling* is discussed in section 36.5.2.

36.5.1 ▪ Displaying linker symbols with `nm`

Most of a compiler-generated binary file consists of the instructions that you coded in C++, translated into machine language, which is much harder to understand. Fortunately, you don't need to look at machine language often. Often what interests you about object files is only knowing what functions are defined in it, and what functions are used in it.

For this, we use the `nm` command, which displays the *linker symbols* in a file. A linker symbol consists of a routine name, and extra information such as parameter types. Using the `nm` command to display a compiled C file will usually give straightforward information:

```
[c:264] nm foosub.o
0000000000000000 T _bar
                 U _printf
```

Lines with `T` indicate routines that are defined; lines with `U` indicate routines that are used but not defined in this file. In this case, `printf` is a standard library routine that will be supplied in the linker stage.

Among the other symbol types, `D` indicates a global or static variable in the initialized data section, while `B` is an uninitialized variable.

36.5.2 ▪ Name demangling in C++

With C++ the function names as rendered by `nm` will look a little strange because of *name mangling*. For instance, the function

```
void bar( string s ) {
  cout << s;
}
```

gives

```
[] nm foosub.o
0000000000000000 T __Z3barNSt7__cxx1112basic_stringIcSt11char_traitsIcESaIcEEE
                 U __ZNSt8ios_base4InitC1Ev
                 U __ZNSt8ios_base4InitD1Ev
                 U
    __ZSt16__ostream_insertIcSt11char_traitsIcEERSt13basic_ostreamIT_T0_ES6_PKS3_l
                 U __ZSt4cout
```

You sort of recognize the `bar` function in this. Add an option `nm -C` to get demangled names:

```
[scientific-computing-private/code/compilecxx 1354] [] nm -C foosub.o
0000000000000000 T bar(std::__cxx11::basic_string<char, std::char_traits<char>, std::
    allocator<char> >)
                 U std::ios_base::Init::Init()
                 U std::ios_base::Init::~Init()
                 U std::basic_ostream<char, std::char_traits<char> >& std::__ostream_insert
    <char, std::char_traits<char> >(std::basic_ostream<char, std::char_traits<char> >&,
    char const*, long)
                 U std::cout
```

Another possibility is to pipe the `nm` output through `c++filt`:

```
nm foosub.o | c++filt
```

You may also want to demangle names in linker errors, when your object files leave some references undefined. For this, add an option `-Wl,-demangle` to the link line:

```
Compile: g++ -g -O2 -std=c++17 -c undefined.cxx
Link line: g++ -Wl,-demangle -o undefined undefined.o
Undefined symbols for architecture arm64:
  "f(int, int)", referenced from:
      _main in undefined.o
ld: symbol(s) not found for architecture arm64
collect2: error: ld returned 1 exit status
```

The mangled names are available programmatically:

```
#include <typeinfo>
cout << typeid( &Myclass::method ).name() << '\n'
```

Demangling also has an API:

```
#include <cxxabi.h>
char* abi::__cxa_demangle
    ( const char* mangled, char* output, size_t* length,int status );
```

36.6 ▪ Libraries

If you have written some functions or classes and you want to share them with other people (perhaps by selling them), handing over individual object files is inconvenient. Instead, the solution is to combine them into a library. This section shows you the basic Unix mechanisms. You would typically use these in a Makefile; if you use CMake it's all done for you; see Chapter 37.

36.6.1 ▪ Static libraries

First we look at *static libraries*, for which the *archive utility* `ar` is used. A static library is linked into your executable, becoming part of it. This has the advantage that you can give such an executable to someone else, and it will immediately work. On the other hand, this may lead to large executables; you will learn about shared libraries next, which do not suffer from this problem.

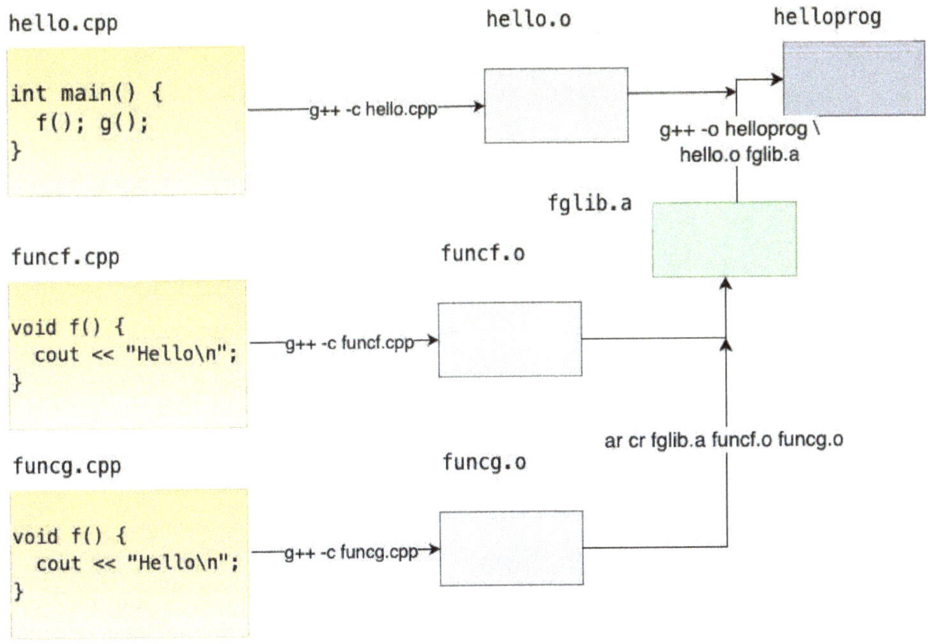

Figure 36.3. *Using a static library*

Consider a short example of using a library to build a program (Figure 36.3). We create a directory to contain your library, and create the library file there. The library can be linked into your executable by explicitly giving its name, or by specifying a library path:

Output
[code/compilecxx] staticprogram:

```
==== Use of static library ====

---- Build library:
for o in foosub.o ; do ar cr libs/libfoo.a ${o} ; done
---- Linking:
g++ -o staticprogram fooprog.o -Llibs -lfoo
---- Program:
-rwxr-xr-x  1 eijkhout  staff  52042 Oct 21 10:46 staticprogram

---- running:
hello world
---- done
```

The `nm` command tells you what's in the library, as for object files in section 36.5.1 above, but now it also tells you what object files are in the library.

We show this for C:

Code:

```
==== Making static library ====
for o in foosub.o ; do
  ar cr libs/libfoo.a ${o}
done
nm  libs/libfoo.a
```

Output
[code/compilec] staticlib:

```
foosub.o:
0000000000000000 T bar
0000000000000000 N .debug_info_seg
                 U printf
```

For C++ we show the output below where we note the `-C` flag for name *demangling*.

Code:

```
==== Making static library ====
for o in foosub.o ; do
  ar cr libs/libfoo.a ${o}
done
nm -C libs/libfoo.a
```

Output
[code/compilecxx] staticlib:

```
foosub.o:
                 U __cxa_atexit
0000000000000000 N .debug_info_seg
                 U __dso_handle
                 U __gxx_personality_v0
0000000000000010 t __sti__$E
0000000000000000 T bar(std::__cxx11::
      basic_string<char, [...]
0000000000000000 b _INTERNALaee936d8::std
      ::__ioinit
0000000000000000 W std::__cxx11::
      basic_string<char, [...]
[and more]
```

36.6.2 ▪ Shared libraries

Although they are somewhat more complicated to use, *shared libraries* have several advantages. For instance, since they are not linked into the executable but only loaded at runtime, they lead to (much) smaller executables. They are not created with `ar`, but through the compiler, typically by adding the flag `-shared`. For instance:

Output
[code/compilecxx] makedynamiclib:

```
%%%%
Demonstration: making shared library
%%%%
icpx -g -O2 -std=c++20  -Wl,-demangle -o libs/libfoo.so -shared foosub.o
```

Investigating the library with `nm`:

Output
[code/compilecxx] showdynamiclib:

```
%%%%
Contents of shared library (U/T lines only)
%%%%
0000000000001110 T bar(std::__cxx11::basic_string<char, std::char_traits<char>,
    std::allocator<char> >)
                 U std::basic_ostream<char, std::char_traits<char> >& std::
    __ostream_insert<char, std::char_traits<char> >(std::basic_ostream<char, std
    ::char_traits<char> >&, char const*, long)@GLIBCXX_3.4.9
                 U std::ios_base_library_init()@GLIBCXX_3.4.32
                 U std::cout@GLIBCXX_3.4
```

Remark. *If running* `nm` *on a* `libwhatever.so` *reports "no symbols," add the* `-D` *option.*

36.6.3 ▪ Finding libraries: Library path

Shared libraries are not actually linked into the executable; instead, the executable needs the information where the library is to be found at execution time. One way to do this is with `LD_LIBRARY_PATH`; see Figure 36.4.

36.6.4 ▪ Finding libraries: `rpath`

Another solution is to have the path be included in the executable through the `rpath` *linker option*:

```
%% g++ -o foo fooprog.o -L../lib -Wl,-rpath,'pwd'/../lib -lfoo
%% ./foo
hello world
```

The link line now contains the library path twice:

1. once with the `-L` directive so that the linker can resolve all references, and
2. once with the linker directive `-Wl,-rpath,'pwd'/../lib`, which stores the path into the executable so that it can be found at runtime.

Remark. *You may also come across a syntax with* `rpath=`,

```
g++ -o foo fooprog.o -L../lib -Wl,-rpath='pwd'/../lib -lfoo
```

but beware that that is a GNU extension.

Remark. *On* Apple OS Ventura *and later, the use of* `LD_LIBRARY_PATH` *is no longer supported for security reasons, so using the* `rpath` *is the only option.* Use the command `ldd` to get information about what shared libraries your executable uses. (On Mac OS X, use `otool -L` instead.)

36.6.5 ▪ Standard library

Certain functionality, such as I/O or file and process management, is used in all programming languages, but belongs more to the OS than to the language proper. That's why this has been

Output
[code/compile] dynamicprogram:

```
Linking to shared library

clang -o libs/libfoo.so -shared foosub.o
clang -o dynamicprogram fooprog.o -Llibs -lfoo
-rwxr-xr-x  1 eijkhout  staff  49720 Nov 28 12:00 dynamicprogram

.. note the size of the program

-rwxr-xr-x  1 eijkhout  staff  49720 Nov 28 12:00 dynamicprogram

.. note unresolved link to a library

otool -L dynamicprogram | grep libfoo
        libs/libfoo.so (compatibility version 0.0.0, current version 0.0.0)

.. running by itself:

clang -o libs/libfoo.so -shared foosub.o
clang -o dynamicprogram fooprog.o -Llibs -lfoo
-rwxr-xr-x  1 eijkhout  staff  49720 Nov 28 12:00 dynamicprogram
hello world

.. note resolved with LD_LIBRARY_PATH

LD_LIBRARY_PATH=${LD_LIBRARY_PATH}:./libs otool -L dynamicprogram | grep libfoo
        libs/libfoo.so (compatibility version 0.0.0, current version 0.0.0)

.. running with updated library path:

clang -o libs/libfoo.so -shared foosub.o
clang -o dynamicprogram fooprog.o -Llibs -lfoo
-rwxr-xr-x  1 eijkhout  staff  49720 Nov 28 12:00 dynamicprogram
LD_LIBRARY_PATH=${LD_LIBRARY_PATH}:./libs dynamicprogram
hello world
```

Figure 36.4. *Making and using a dynamic library*

bundled in a *standard library*, called `libstdc` or `libstdc++`. Error messages about the contents of this library typically refer to `GLIBC` or `GLIBCXX` with a version number.

Here we use `ldconfig` to find all known libraries, pick out the `libstdc++`, and then search for `LIBCXX` in it:

```
[] /sbin/ldconfig -p | grep stdc++
        libstdc++.so.6 (libc6,x86-64) => /lib64/libstdc++.so.6
        libstdc++.so.5 (libc6,x86-64) => /lib64/libstdc++.so.5
[] strings /lib64/libstdc++.so.6 | grep LIBCXX
GLIBCXX_3.4
GLIBCXX_3.4.1
   [...]
GLIBCXX_3.4.19
```

Sometimes functionality is requested from a later version than is present in your system. That usually means you have to update your compiler.

Chapter 37

The CMake ecosystem

CMake is a build system, that is, software that assists in building other software. It is the *de facto* standard for C++ packages; it is sometimes used for C packages, but there it has competition from *autotools*; and it can be used for several other languages.

The following is not an exhaustive treatment, but rather an introduction that should give you enough basic vocabulary to handle most common cases.

37.1 ▪ CMake workflow

CMake is a general build system that uses other systems such as *Make* as a backend. The following is a typical workflow:

1. The configuration stage. Here the `CMakeLists.txt` file is parsed, and a `build` directory populated. This typically looks like

   ```
   mkdir build
   cd build
   cmake <src_dir location>
   ```

2. The build stage. Here the installation-specific compilation in the build directory is performed. The build directory contains all temporaries, leaving the source directory untouched.

   With *Make* as the "generator" this would be

   ```
   cd build
   make
   ```

   but more generally

   ```
   cmake --build <build directory>
   ```

   Alternatively, you could use generators such as *ninja*, *Visual Studio*, or *XCode*:

   ```
   cmake -G ninja
   ```

3. The install stage. This can move binary files to a permanent location, such as putting library files in `/usr/lib`:

   ```
   make install
   ```

or

```
cmake --install <build directory>
```

However, the install location already has to be set in the configuration stage. We will see later in detail how this is done.

37.1.1 ▪ Directory structure

There are two approaches to locating the build directory, characterized as "in-source" and "out-of-source."

In the first approach, the build directory is created in the source tree, in which case the *CMake* command is

```
cmake ..
```

In the out-of-source approach the build directory is placed elsewhere, typically next to the source directory. In this case the CMake invocation becomes

```
cmake ../src_directory
```

The install directory can be anywhere. If no *prefix* is specified, installable files go to system locations such as `/usr/lib` and `/usr/include`. The explicit specification of a prefix directory is discussed below in section 37.2.1.

The resulting directory structures for in-source and out-of-source building are illustrated in Figure 37.1.

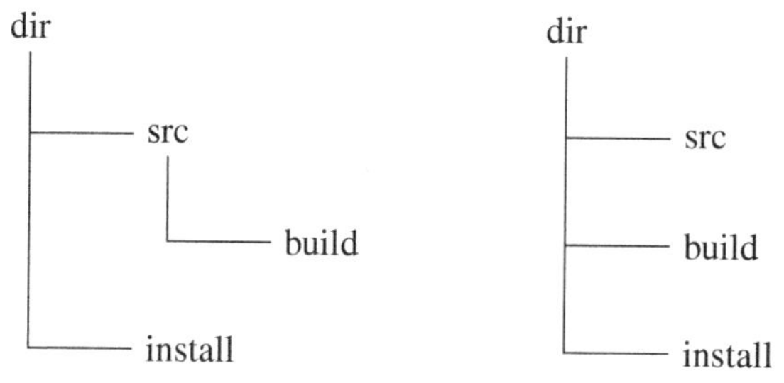

Figure 37.1. *In-source (left) and out-of-source (right) build schemes*

37.1.2 ▪ Target philosophy

Modern *CMake* works through declaring targets and their requirements. Targets are things that will be built, and requirements can be such things as

- source files,
- include paths and other paths,
- compiler and linker options.

There is a distinction between build requirements—the paths/files/options used during building—and usage requirements—the paths/files/options that need to be in force when your targets are being used.

For requirements during building:

```
target_some_requirement( <target> PRIVATE <requirements> )
```

Usage requirements:

```
target_some_requirement( <target> INTERFACE <requirements> )
```

Combined:

```
target_some_requirement( <target> PUBLIC <requirements> )
```

For future reference, requirements are specified with `target_include_directories`, `target_compile_definitions`, `target_compile_options`, `target_compile_features`, `target_sources`, `target_link_libraries`, `target_link_options`, `target_link_directories`. We will see some of those below.

37.1.3 ▪ Languages

CMake is largely aimed at C++, but it easily supports C as well. For *Fortran* support, first do

```
enable_language(Fortran)
```

Note the capitalization: this also holds for all variables such as `CMAKE_Fortran_COMPILER`.

Currently supported languages are `C`, `CXX`, `CSharp`, `CUDA`, `OBJC`, `OBJCXX`, `Fortran`, `HIP`, `ISPC`, `Swift`, and a couple of variants of `ASM`.

37.1.4 ▪ Script structure

Commands learned in this section	
`cmake_minimum_required`	declare minimum required version for this script
`project`	declare a name for this project

CMake is driven by the `CMakeLists.txt` file. This needs to be in the root directory of your project. (You can additionally have files by that name in subdirectories.)

Since *CMake* has changed quite a bit over the years, and is still evolving, it is a good idea to start each script with a declaration of the (minimum) required version:

```
cmake_minimum_required( VERSION 3.12 )
```

You can query the version of your *CMake* executable:

```
$ cmake --version
cmake version 3.19.2
```

You also need to declare a project name and version, which need not correspond to any file names:

```
project( myproject VERSION 1.0 )
```

37.2 ▪ Examples cases

37.2.1 ▪ Executable from sources

Commands learned in this section	
add_executable	declare an executable as target
target_sources	specify sources for a target
install	indicate location where to install this project
PROJECT_NAME	macro that expands to the project name

If you have a project that is supposed to deliver an executable, you declare it in your CMakeLists.txt:

```
add_executable( myprogram )
target_sources( myprogram PRIVATE program.cxx )
```

(Including sources directly in the add_executable statement is a deprecated practice.) Often, the name of the executable is the name of the project, so you'd use the automatically defined macro PROJECT_NAME:

```
add_executable( ${PROJECT_NAME} )
```

In order to move the executable to the install location, you need a clause:

```
install( TARGETS myprogram DESTINATION . )
```

Without the DESTINATION clause, a default bin directory will be created; specifying DESTINATION foo will put the target in a foo subdirectory of the installation directory. In addition to the TARGETS keyword, you can also specify DIRECTORY to install a whole directory into the prefix location. (In the figure on the right we have also indicated the build directory, containing generated temporaries. From now on we will not show the build directory.)

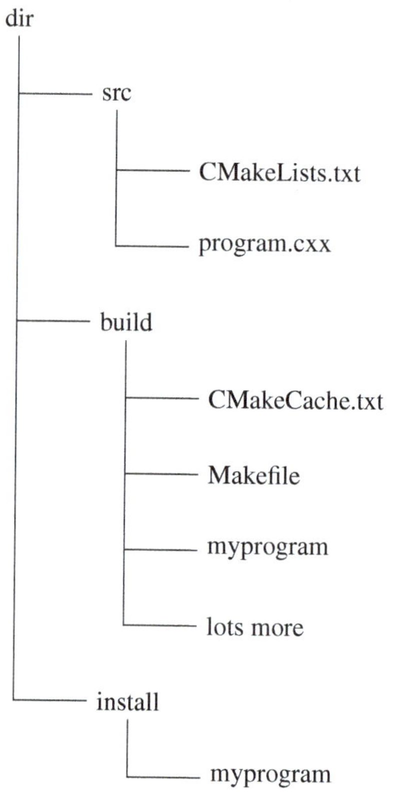

Here is the full CMakeLists.txt:

```
cmake_minimum_required( VERSION 3.13 )
project( singleprogram VERSION 1.0 )

add_executable( program )
target_sources( program PRIVATE program.cxx )
install( TARGETS program DESTINATION . )
```

37.2.2 ▪ Making libraries

Commands learned in this section	
target_include_directories	indicate location of include files
add_library	declare a library and its sources
target_link_libraries	indicate that the library belongs with an executable

37.2.2.1 ▪ Multiple files

If there is only one source file, the previous section is all you need. If there are multiple files, you could write

```
add_executable( program )
target_sources( program PRIVATE
    program.cxx aux.cxx aux.h )
```

You can also put the nonmain source files in a separate directory:

```
add_executable( program )
target_sources( program PRIVATE
    program.cxx lib/aux1.cxx lib/aux2.cxx lib/aux.h)
```

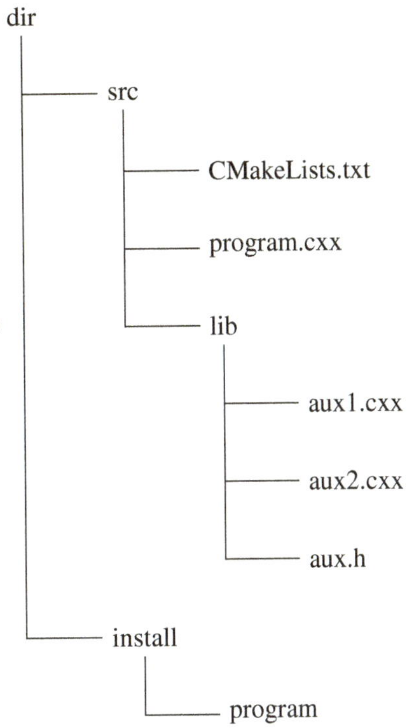

However, often you will build libraries. We start by making a `lib` directory and indicating that header files need to be found there when the program is compiled:

```
target_include_directories( program PRIVATE lib )
```

The actual library is declared with an `add_library` clause:

```
add_library( auxlib )
target_sources( auxlib PRIVATE
    lib/aux1.cxx lib/aux2.cxx lib/aux.h )
```

Next, you need to link that library into the program:

```
target_link_libraries( program PRIVATE auxlib )
```

The `PRIVATE` clause means that the library is only for purposes of building the executable. (Use `PUBLIC` to have the library be included in the installation; we will explore that in section 37.2.2.3.)

The full `CMakeLists.txt`:

```
cmake_minimum_required( VERSION 3.13 )
project( cmakeprogram VERSION 1.0 )

add_executable( program )
target_sources( program PRIVATE program.cxx )

add_library( auxlib STATIC )
target_include_directories( program PRIVATE lib )

target_link_libraries( program PRIVATE auxlib )
install( TARGETS program DESTINATION . )
```

Note that private shared libraries make no sense, as they will give runtime unresolved references.

37.2.2.2 ▪ Testing the generated makefiles

It is a feature of the Make utility that it will only recompile the strictly necessary files when a limited edit has been made. The makefiles generated by *CMake* behave accordingly. With the structure above, we first touch the `aux.cxx` file, which necessitates rebuilding the library:

```
----------------
touch a source file and make:
Consolidate compiler generated dependencies of target auxlib
[ 25%] Building CXX object CMakeFiles/auxlib.dir/aux.cxx.o
[ 50%] Linking CXX static library libauxlib.a
[ 50%] Built target auxlib
Consolidate compiler generated dependencies of target program
[ 75%] Linking CXX executable program
[100%] Built target program
```

On the other hand, if we edit a header file, the main program needs to be recompiled too:

```
----------------
touch a source file and make:
Consolidate compiler generated dependencies of target auxlib
[ 25%] Building CXX object CMakeFiles/auxlib.dir/aux.cxx.o
[ 50%] Linking CXX static library libauxlib.a
[ 50%] Built target auxlib
Consolidate compiler generated dependencies of target program
[ 75%] Linking CXX executable program
[100%] Built target program
```

37.2.2.3 ▪ Making a library for release

Commands learned in this section	
SHARED	indicated to make shared libraries

In order to create a library we use add_library and we link it into the target program with target_link_libraries.

By default the library is build as a static .a file, but adding

```
add_library( auxlib SHARED )
```

or adding a runtime flag

```
cmake -D BUILD_SHARED_LIBS=TRUE
```

changes that to a shared .so type. Related: the -fPIC compile option is set by CMAKE_POSITION_INDEPENDENT_CODE.

The full *CMake* file:

```
cmake_minimum_required( VERSION 3.13 )
project( cmakeprogram VERSION 1.0 )

add_executable( program )
target_sources( program PRIVATE program.cxx )

add_library( auxlib STATIC )
target_sources( auxlib PRIVATE lib/aux.cxx lib/aux.h )

target_link_libraries( program PUBLIC auxlib )
target_include_directories( program PRIVATE lib )

install( TARGETS program DESTINATION bin )
install( TARGETS auxlib DESTINATION lib )
install( FILES lib/aux.h DESTINATION include )
```

Note that we give a path to the library files. This is interpreted relative to the current directory, (as of CMake-3.13); this current directory is available explicitly as CMAKE_CURRENT_SOURCE_DIR.

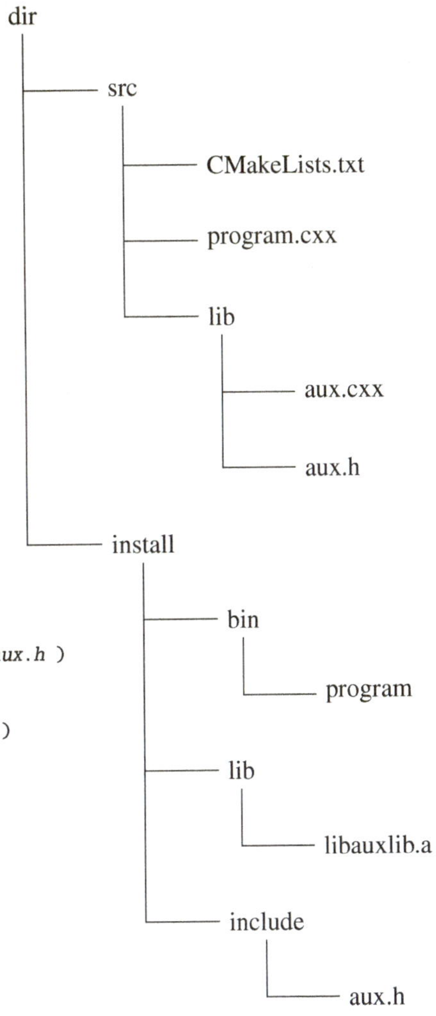

37.2.3 ▪ Using subdirectories during the build

Commands learned in this section	
target_include_directories	indicate include directories needed
target_sources	specify more sources for a target
CMAKE_CURRENT_SOURCE_DIR	variable that expands to the current directory
file	define single-name synonym for multiple files
GLOB	define single-name synonym for multiple files

Suppose you have a directory with header files, as in the diagram on the right. The main program would have

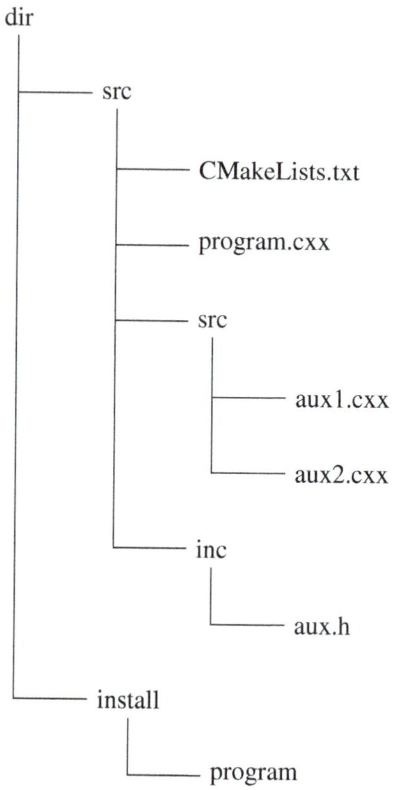


```
#include <iostream>
using namespace std;

#include "aux.h"

int main() {
  aux1();
  aux2();
  return 0;
}
```

and which is compiled as

```
g++ -c program.cxx -I./inc
```

To make sure the header file gets found during the build, you specify that include path with target_include_directories:

```
target_include_directories(
        program PRIVATE
        "${CMAKE_CURRENT_SOURCE_DIR}/inc" )
```

It is best to make such paths relative to CMAKE_CURRENT_SOURCE_DIR, or the source root CMAKE_SOURCE_DIR, or equivalently PROJECT_SOURCE_DIR

Usually, when you start making such a directory structure, you will also have sources in subdirectories. If you only need to compile them into the main executable, you could list them into a variable

```
set( SOURCES program.cxx src/aux1.cxx aux2.cxx )
```

and use that variable. However, this is deprecated practice; it is recommended to use target_sources:

```
target_sources( program PRIVATE src/aux1.cxx src/aux2.cxx )
```

Use of a wildcard is not trivial:

```
file( GLOB AUX_FILES "src/*.cxx" )
target_sources( program PRIVATE ${AUX_FILES} )
```

Complete *CMake* file:

```
cmake_minimum_required( VERSION 3.14 )
project( cmakeprogram VERSION 1.0 )

add_executable( program )
target_sources( program PRIVATE program.cxx )
## target_sources( program PRIVATE src/aux1.cxx src/aux2.cxx )
file( GLOB AUX_FILES "src/*.cxx" )
target_sources( program PRIVATE ${AUX_FILES} )
target_include_directories(
        program PRIVATE
        "${CMAKE_CURRENT_SOURCE_DIR}/inc" )

install( TARGETS program DESTINATION . )
```

37.2.4 ▪ Recursive building; *rpath*

Commands learned in this section	
`add_subdirectory`	declare a subdirectory where CMake needs to be run
`CMAKE_CURRENT_SOURCE_DIR`	directory where this command is evaluated
`CMAKE_CURRENT_BINARY_DIR`	
`LIBRARY_OUTPUT_PATH`	
`FILES_MATCHING PATTERN`	wildcard indicator

If your sources are spread over multiple directories, it is a good idea to invoke CMake recursively in each. For this there needs to be a `CMakeLists.txt` file in each directory, and you need to declare the existence of those directories. Let's start with the obvious choice of putting library files in a `lib` directory with `add_subdirectory`:

```
add_subdirectory( lib )
```

For instance, a library directory would have a `CMakeLists.txt` file:

```
cmake_minimum_required( VERSION 3.14 )
project( auxlib )

add_library( auxlib SHARED )
target_sources( auxlib PRIVATE aux.cxx aux.h )
target_include_directories(
    auxlib PUBLIC "${CMAKE_CURRENT_SOURCE_DIR}" )
install( TARGETS auxlib DESTINATION lib )
install( FILES aux.h DESTINATION include )
```

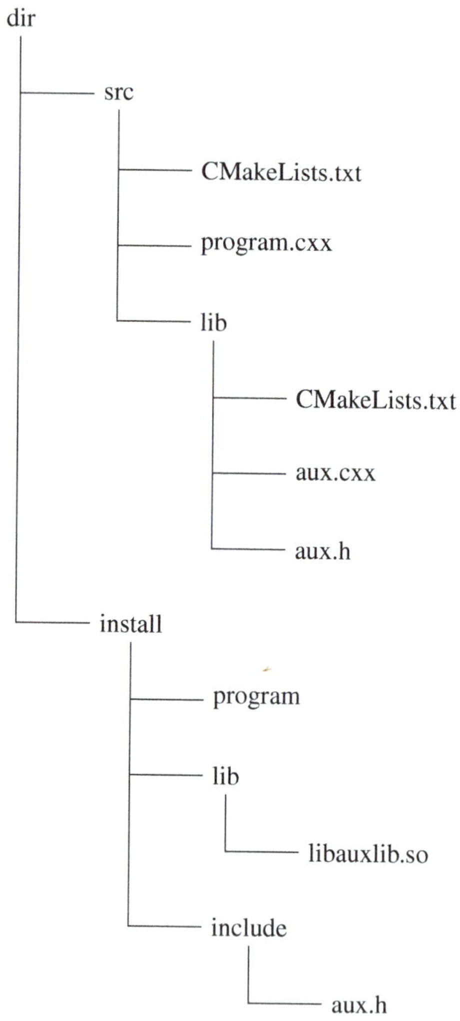

to build the library file from the sources indicated, and to install it in a `lib` subdirectory. We also add a clause to install the header files in an include directory:

```
install( FILES aux.h DESTINATION include )
```

For installing multiple files, use

```
install(DIRECTORY ${CMAKE_CURRENT_BINARY_DIR}
    DESTINATION ${LIBRARY_OUTPUT_PATH}
    FILES_MATCHING PATTERN "*.h")
```

One problem is to tell the executable where to find the library. For this we use the *rpath* mechanism. (See section 36.6.4.) By default, *CMake* sets it so that the executable in the build location can find the library. If you use a nontrivial install prefix, the following lines work:

```
set( CMAKE_INSTALL_RPATH "${CMAKE_INSTALL_PREFIX}/lib" )
set( CMAKE_INSTALL_RPATH_USE_LINK_PATH TRUE )
```

Note that these have to be specified before the target.

The whole file:

```
cmake_minimum_required( VERSION 3.14 )
project( cmakeprogram VERSION 1.0 )

set( CMAKE_INSTALL_RPATH "${CMAKE_INSTALL_PREFIX}/lib" )
set( CMAKE_INSTALL_RPATH_USE_LINK_PATH TRUE )

add_executable( program )
target_sources( program PRIVATE program.cxx )
add_subdirectory( lib )
target_include_directories(
        auxlib PUBLIC "${CMAKE_CURRECT_SOURCE_DIR}" )
target_link_libraries(
        program PUBLIC auxlib )

install( TARGETS program DESTINATION . )
```

37.2.5 ▪ Programs that use other libraries

So far we have discussed executables and libraries that can be used by themselves. What if your build result needs external libraries? We will discuss how to find those libraries in section 37.3; here we point out their use.

The issue is that these libraries need to be findable when someone uses your binary. There are two strategies:

- make sure they have been added to the `LD_LIBRARY_PATH`;
- have the *linker* add their location through the `rpath` mechanism to the binary itself. This second option is in fact the only one on recent versions of *Apple Mac OS* because of "system integrity protection."

As an example, assume your binary needs the `Catch2` and `fmtlib` libraries. You would then, in addition to the `target_link_directories` specification, have

```
set_target_properties(
        ${PROGRAM_NAME} PROPERTIES
        BUILD_RPATH    "${CATCH2_LIBRARY_DIRS};${FMTLIB_LIBRARY_DIRS}"
        INSTALL_RPATH "${CATCH2_LIBRARY_DIRS};${FMTLIB_LIBRARY_DIRS}"
    )
```

Note that multiple paths are separated by semicolons.

37.2.6 ▪ Header-only libraries

A library is declared as header-only by the `INTERFACE` keyword:

```
add_library( header_only_lib INTERFACE )
```

37.3 ▪ Finding and using external packages

If your program depends on other libraries, there is a variety of ways to let *CMake* find them.

37.3.1 ▪ CMake command-line options

You can indicate the location of your external library explicitly on the command line.

```
cmake -D OTHERLIB_INC_DIR=/some/where/include
      -D OTHERLIB_LIB_DIR=/somewhere/lib
```

Example *CMake* file:

```
cmake_minimum_required( VERSION 3.13 )
project( pkgconfiglib VERSION 1.0 )

# with environment variables
# set( AUX_INCLUDE_DIR $ENV{TACC_AUX_INC} )
# set( AUX_LIBRARY_DIR $ENV{TACC_AUX_LIB} )

# with cmake -D options
option( AUX_INCLUDE_DIR "include dir for auxlib" )
option( AUX_LIBRARY_DIR   "lib dir for auxlib" )

add_executable( program )
target_sources( program PRIVATE program.cxx )
target_include_directories(
        program PUBLIC
        ${AUX_INCLUDE_DIR} )
target_link_libraries( program PUBLIC auxlib )
target_link_directories(
        program PUBLIC
        ${AUX_LIBRARY_DIR} )
install( TARGETS program DESTINATION . )
```

37.3.2 ▪ Package finding through "*find_library*" and "*find_package*"

Commands learned in this section	
find_library	find a library with a FOOConfig.cmake file
CMAKE_PREFIX_PATH	used for finding FOOConfig.cmake files
find_package	find a library with a FindFOO module
CMAKE_MODULE_PATH	location for FindFOO modules

The find_package command looks for files with a name FindXXX.cmake, which are searched for on the CMAKE_MODULE_PATH. Unfortunately, the working of find_package depends somewhat on the specific package. It is common for packages to set a variable FooFound that you can test:

```
find_package( Foo )
if ( FooFound )
    # do something
else()
    # throw an error
endif()
```

The find_package can take an extra parameter, with values REQUIRED for required packages, and QUIET for packages that are optional. In the latter case you can test for them and take alternative action.

Some libraries come with a FOOConfig.cmake file, which is searched for on the CMAKE_PREFIX_PATH through find_library. You typically set this variable to the root of the package installation, and CMake will find the directory of the .cmake file.

You can test the variables set:

```
find_library( FOOLIB foo )
if (FOOLIB)
  target_link_libraries( myapp PRIVATE ${FOOLIB} )
else()
  # throw an error
endif()
```

As an example, the *range-v3* library can be discovered with

```
find_package( range-v3 REQUIRED )
target_link_libraries( ${PROGRAM_NAME} PUBLIC range-v3::range-v3 )
```

37.3.3 ▪ Use of other packages through "*pkgconfig*"

These days, many packages support the `pkgconfig` mechanism.

1. Suppose you have a library `mylib`, installed in `/opt/local/mylib`.
2. If `mylib` supports `pkgconfig`, there is most likely a path `/opt/local/mylib/lib/pkgconfig`, containing a file `mylib.pc`.
3. Add the path that contains the `.pc` file to the `PKG_CONFIG_PATH` environment variable.

CMake is now able to find `mylib`:

```
find_package( PkgConfig REQUIRED )
pkg_check_modules( MYLIBRARY REQUIRED mylib )
```

This defines the variables

```
MYLIBRARY_INCLUDE_DIRS
MYLIBRARY_LIBRARY_DIRS
MYLIBRARY_LIBRARIES
```

which you can then use in the `target_include_directories`, `target_link_directories`, `target_link_libraries` commands.

37.3.4 ▪ Writing your own *pkgconfig*

We extend the configuration of section 37.2.4 to generate a `.pc` file.

First of all we need a template for the `.pc` file:

```
prefix="@CMAKE_INSTALL_PREFIX@"
exec_prefix="${prefix}"
libdir="${prefix}/lib"
includedir="${prefix}/include"

Name: @PROJECT_NAME@
Description: @CMAKE_PROJECT_DESCRIPTION@
Version: @PROJECT_VERSION@
Cflags: -I${includedir}
Libs: -L${libdir} -l@libtarget@
```

Here the @-signs delimit CMake macros that will be substituted when the `.pc` file is generated; dollar-sign macros go into the file unchanged.

Generating the file is done by the following lines in the CMake configuration:

```
set( libtarget auxlib )
configure_file(
    ${CMAKE_CURRENT_SOURCE_DIR}/${PROJECT_NAME}.pc.in
    ${CMAKE_CURRENT_BINARY_DIR}/${PROJECT_NAME}.pc
    @ONLY
)
install(
    FILES ${CMAKE_CURRENT_BINARY_DIR}/${PROJECT_NAME}.pc
    DESTINATION share/pkgconfig
)
```

37.3.5 ▪ Fetch content

Sometimes the easiest way to use a library in your project is to let CMake download and install it, right in your project. This is done through the `FetchContent` module. You declare what library to use with `FetchContent_Declare`, and effect its installation with `FetchContent_MakeAvailable`. This then gives you targets (for which see the library documentation) that you can use.

Example:

```
cmake_minimum_required( VERSION 3.20 )
project( program VERSION 1.0)

include( FetchContent )
FetchContent_Declare(
    fmtlib
    GIT_REPOSITORY https://github.com/fmtlib/fmt.git
    )
FetchContent_MakeAvailable( fmtlib )

add_executable( program program.cxx )
target_link_libraries( program PRIVATE fmt::fmt )

install( TARGETS program DESTINATION . )
```

The main advantage of this is that it avoids all complications with separate installation, and having to set paths. The disadvantage is that this increases disk usage (suppose you have a few dozen small programs that all use the same auxiliary library) and build time. Also, it's harder to customize the build of that library.

For flexibility, you could first test if the package is discoverable, and only fetch otherwise:

```
cmake_minimum_required( VERSION 3.20 )
project( program VERSION 1.0 )

find_package( fmt QUIET )
if( fmt_FOUND )
    message( STATUS "Found installation of fmtlib" )
else()
    message( STATUS "Installing fmtlib for you" )
    include( FetchContent )
    FetchContent_Declare(
        fmtlib
        GIT_REPOSITORY https://github.com/fmtlib/fmt.git
        )
    FetchContent_MakeAvailable( fmtlib )
endif()

add_executable( program program.cxx )
target_link_libraries( program PRIVATE fmt::fmt )

install( TARGETS program DESTINATION . )
```

37.4 ▪ Customizing the compilation process

Commands learned in this section	
add_compile_options	global compiler options
target_compile_features	compiler-independent specification of compile flags
target_compile_definitions	preprocessor flags

37.4.1 ▪ Customizing the compiler and compiler flags

It's probably a good idea to tell *CMake* explicitly what compiler you are using, otherwise it may find some default GCC version that came with your system. Use the variables CMAKE_CXX_COMPILER , CMAKE_C_COMPILER, CMAKE_Fortran_COMPILER, CMAKE_LINKER.

Alternatively, set environment variables CC, CXX, FC by the explicit paths of the compilers. For example, for Intel compilers:

```
export CC='which icx'
export CXX='which icpx'
export FC='which ifx'
```

For flags, set the variable CMAKE_CXX_FLAGS or CMAKE_C_FLAGS or CMAKE_Fortran_FLAGS; also CMAKE_LINKER_FLAGS and CMAKE_EXE_LINKER_FLAGS (but see section 37.2.4 for the popular rpath options).

37.4.2 ▪ Global and target flags

Most of the time, compile options should be associated with a target. For instance, some file could need a higher or lower optimization level, or a specific C++ standard. In that case, use target_compile_features.

Certain options may need to be global, in which case you use add_compile_options. Example:

```
if (MVSC)
    add_compile_options(/W3 /WX)
else()
    add_compile_options(-W -Wall -Werror)
endif()
```

System-specific options can be set by interrogating the CMAKE_SYSTEM_NAME variable:

```
if ( CMAKE_SYSTEM_NAME STREQUAL "WIN32" )
  target_compile_options( myapp PRIVATE /W4 )
elseif ( CMAKE_SYSTEM_NAME STREQUAL "Darwin" )
  target_compile_options( myapp PRIVATE -Wall -Wextra -Wpedantic )
endif()
```

37.4.2.1 ▪ Universal flags

Certain flags have a universal meaning, but compiler-dependent realization. For instance, to specify the C++ standard:

```
target_compile_features( mydemo PRIVATE cxx_std_17 )
```

Alternatively, you can set this from the command line:

```
cmake -D CMAKE_CXX_STANDARD=20
```

The variable `CMAKE_CXX_COMPILE_FEATURES` contains the list of all features you can set.

Optimization flags can be set by specifying the `CMAKE_BUILD_TYPE`:

- `Debug` corresponds to the `-g` flag;
- `Release` corresponds to `-O3 -DNDEBUG`;
- `MinSizeRel` corresponds to `-Os -DNDEBUG`
- `RelWithDebInfo` corresponds to `-O2 -g -DNDEBUG`.

This variable will often be set from the command line:

```
cmake .. -DCMAKE_BUILD_TYPE=Release
```

but you can also

```
set( CMAKE_BUILD_TYPE RelWithDebInfo )
```

Unfortunately, this seems to be the only way to influence optimization flags, other than explicitly setting compiler flags.

37.4.3 ▪ Macro definitions

CMake can provide macro definitions,

```
target_compile_definitions
  ( programname PUBLIC
    HAVE_HELLO_LIB=1 )
```

and your source could test these:

```
#ifdef HAVE_HELLO_LIB
#include "hello.h"
#endif
```

37.5 ▪ CMake scripting

Commands learned in this section	
`option`	query a command-line option
`message`	trace message during CMake-ing
`set`	set the value of a variable
`CMAKE_SYSTEM_NAME`	variable containing the operating system name
`STREQUAL`	string comparison operator

The `CMakeLists.txt` file is a script, though it doesn't much look like it:

- Instructions consist of a command, followed by a parenthesized list of arguments.
- (All arguments are strings: there are no numbers.)
- Each command needs to start on a new line, but otherwise white space and line breaks are ignored.

Comments start with a hash character.

37.5.1 ▪ Messages, errors, and tracing

The `message` command can be used to write output to the console. This command has two arguments:

```
message( STATUS "We are rolling!")
```

Instead of `STATUS` you can specify other logging levels (this parameter is actually called "mode" in the documentation); for instance, running

```
cmake --log-level=NOTICE
```

will display only messages of "notice" status or higher. The possibilities here are `FATAL_ERROR`, `SEND_ERROR`, `WARNING`, `AUTHOR_WARNING`, `DEPRECATION`, `NOTICE`, `STATUS`, `VERBOSE`, `DEBUG`, `TRACE`.

The `NOTICE`, `VERBOSE`, `DEBUG`, `TRACE` options were added in CMake-3.15.

For a complete trace of everything *CMake* does, use the command-line option `--trace`.

You can get a verbose make file by using the option

```
-D CMAKE_VERBOSE_MAKEFILE=ON
```

on the *CMake* invocation. You still need `make V=1`.

37.5.2 ▪ Variables

Variables are set with `set`, or can be given on the command line,

```
cmake -D MYVAR=myvalue
```

where the space after `-D` is optional.

Using the variable by itself gives the value, except in strings, where a shell-like notation is needed:

```
set(SOME_ERROR "An error has occurred")
message(STATUS "${SOME_ERROR}")
set(MY_VARIABLE "This is a variable")
message(STATUS "Variable MY_VARIABLE has value ${MY_VARIABLE}")
```

Variables can also be queried by the *CMake* script using the `option` command:

```
option( SOME_FLAG "A flag that has some function" defaultvalue )
```

Some variables are set by other commands. For instance, the `project` command sets `PROJECT_NAME` and `PROJECT_VERSION`.

37.5.2.1 ▪ Environment variables

Environment variables can be queried with the `ENV` command:

```
set( MYDIR $ENV{MYDIR} )
```

37.5.3 ▪ Control structures

37.5.3.1 ▪ Conditionals

There is a variety of conditionals, testing string equality, string matching, variable definedness, etc. Some examples:

```
if( NOT DEFINED SOMEVAR )
  message( FATAL_ERROR "\nYou need to set the SOMEVAR on the commandline\n" )
endif()
```

```
if ( MYVAR MATCHES "value$" )
    message( NOTICE "Variable ended in 'value'" )
elseif( stuff )
    message( stuff )
else()
    message( NOTICE "Variable was otherwise" )
endif()
```

37.5.3.2 ▪ Looping

CMake has looping constructs: first of all while loops and for loops over lists of strings.

```
while( myvalue LESS 50 )
    message( stuff )
endwhile()
```

```
foreach ( var IN ITEMS item1 item2 item3 )
  ## something with ${var}
endforeach()
foreach ( var IN LISTS list1 list2 list3 )
  ## something with ${var}
endforeach()
```

Numeric loops use the RANGE keyword. A range has inclusive bounds, with lower bound zero, and stride one by default:

```
foreach ( idx RANGE 10 )
foreach ( idx RANGE 5 10 )
foreach ( idx RANGE 5 10 2 )
endforeach()
```

Chapter 38

Source code management with *git*

In this tutorial you will learn `git`, the currently most popular *version control* (also *source code control* or *revision control*) system. Other similar systems are *Mercurial* and *Microsoft Sharepoint*. Earlier systems were *SCCS*, *CVS*, *Subversion*, and *Bitkeeper*.

Version control is a system that tracks the history of a software project, by recording the successive versions of the files of the project. These versions are recorded in a *repository*, either on the machine you are working on or remotely.

This has many practical advantages:

- It becomes possible to undo changes.
- Sharing a repository with another developer makes collaboration possible, including multiple edits on the same file.
- A repository records the history of the project.
- You can have multiple versions of the project, for instance, for exploring new features, or for customization for certain users.

The use of a version control system is industry standard practice, and `git` is by far the most popular system these days.

38.1 ▪ Concepts and overview

Older systems were based on having one *central repository* that all developers coordinated with. These days a setup is popular where each developer (or a small group) has a *local repository*, which gets synchronized to a *remote repository*. In so-called *distributed version control* systems there can even be multiple remote repositories to synchronize with.

It is possible to track the changes of a single file, but often it makes sense to bundle a group of changes together in a *commit*. That also makes it easy to roll back such a group of changes.

If a project is in a state that constitutes some sort of a milestone, it is possible to attach a *tag*, or mark the state as a *release*.

Modern version control systems allow you to have multiple *branch*es, even in the same local repository. This way you can have a main branch for the release version of the project, and one or more development branches for exploring new features. These branches can be merged when you're satisfied that a new feature has been sufficiently tested.

38.2 ▪ Create and populate a repository

In this section you will create a repository and make a local copy to work on. You can create a repository two different ways:

1. Create the remote repository and do a clone.
2. Create the repository locally, and then connect it to a remote; this is more work.

38.2.1 ▪ Create a repository by cloning

The easiest way to start a new repository is to use a website such as *github.com* or *gitlab.com*, create the repository there, and then clone it to your local machine. Syntax:

```
git clone URL [ localname ]
```

This gives you a directory with the contents of the repository. If you leave out the local name, the directory will have the name of the repository:

```
Cmd >> git clone https://github.com/TACC/empty.git
    ↪empty
Out >>
Cloning into 'empty'...
warning: You appear to have cloned an empty
    ↪repository.
Cmd >> cd empty
Cmd >> ls -a
Out >>
.
..
.git
Cmd >> git status
Out >>
On branch main
No commits yet
nothing to commit (create/copy files and use "git
    ↪add" to track)
```

Clone an empty repository and check that it is indeed empty.

As you see, even an empty repository contains a directory *.git*. This contains bookkeeping information about your repository; you will hardly ever look into it.

38.2.2 ▪ Create a repository locally

You can also create a directory for your repository, and connect it to a remote site later. For this you do `git init` in the directory that is either empty or already contains the material that you want to add later. Here, we start with an empty directory:

```
Cmd >> mkdir newrepo
Cmd >> cd newrepo
Cmd >> git init
Out >>
Initialized empty Git repository in
    ↪/users/demo/git/newrepo/.git/
Cmd >> ls -a
Out >>
.
..
.git
Cmd >> git status
Out >>
On branch master
No commits yet
nothing to commit (create/copy files and use "git
    ↪add" to track)
```

Create a directory, and make it into a repository.

The disadvantage of this method over cloning an empty repo is that you now have to connect your directory to a remote repository. See section 38.5.

38.2.3 ▪ Main versus master

It used to be that the default branch (we haven't discussed branches yet; see below) was called "master." In a shift of terminology, the preferred name is now "main." Sites such as *GitHub* and *GitLab* may already create this name by default; the `git` version 2.51.0 software still uses "master" but has an option for other names.

Renaming a branch is possible. You can use `git status` to see what branch you are on.

```
Cmd >> git status
Out >>
On branch master
No commits yet
nothing to commit (create/copy files and use "git
    ↪add" to track)
```

See what the main branch is.

Move the current branch:

```
Cmd >> git branch -m main
Cmd >> git status
Out >>
On branch main
No commits yet
nothing to commit (create/copy files and use "git
    ↪add" to track)
```

Rename the branch.

For good measure, check the name again with `git status`.

```
Cmd >> git branch -m main
Cmd >> git status
Out >>
On branch main
No commits yet
nothing to commit (create/copy files and use "git
    ↪add" to track)
```

Check branch names.

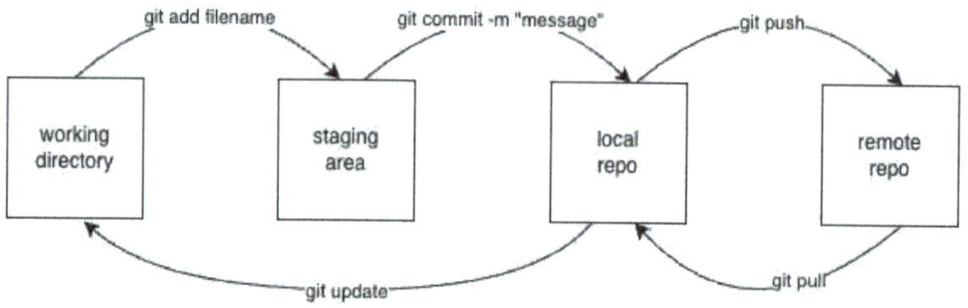

Figure 38.1. *git workflow of adding (top arrows) and pulling (bottom)*

38.3 ▪ Adding and changing files

38.3.1 ▪ Creating a new file

If you create a file it does not automatically become part of your repository. This takes a sequence of steps. If you create a new file, and you run `git status`, you'll see that the file is listed as "untracked."

```
Cmd >> echo foo > firstfile
Cmd >> git status
Out >>
On branch main
No commits yet
Untracked files:
(use "git add <file>..." to include in what will be
    ↪committed)
firstfile
nothing added to commit but untracked files present
    ↪(use "git add" to track)
```

Create a file with the usual tools such as an editor. Here we use *echo* as a shortcut. The file will initially be untracked.

You need to `git add` on your file to tell `git` that the file belongs to the repository. (You can add a single file, or use a wildcard to add multiple.) However, this does not actually add the file: it moves it to the *staging area* (see Figure 38.1). The status now says that it is a change to be committed:

```
Cmd >> git add firstfile
Cmd >> git status
Out >>
On branch main
No commits yet
Changes to be committed:
(use "git rm --cached <file>..." to unstage)
new file:   firstfile
```

Add the file to the local repository.

Use `git commit` to add these changes to the repository. It is easiest to supply a short description with the `-m` option; without this option `git` will open an editor (to be precise, the value of the variable `EDITOR`) for you to type one:

```
Cmd >> git commit -m "adding first file"
Out >>
[main (root-commit) f968ac6] adding first file
1 file changed, 1 insertion(+)
create mode 100644 firstfile
Cmd >> git status
Out >>
On branch main
nothing to commit, working tree clean
```

Commit these changes.

38.3.2 ▪ Changes to a file in the repository

Let us investigate the process of adding changes to a file to the repository:

```
Cmd >> echo bar >> firstfile
Cmd >> cat firstfile
Out >>
foo
bar
Cmd >> git status
Out >>
On branch main
Changes not staged for commit:
(use "git add <file>..." to update what will be
    ↪committed)
(use "git restore <file>..." to discard changes in
    ↪working directory)
modified:   firstfile
no changes added to commit (use "git add" and/or "git
    ↪commit -a")
```

Make changes to a file that is tracked. You would typically use an editor, but we use *echo* to append.

If you need to check what changes you have made, `git diff` on that file will tell you differences between the edited, but not yet added or committed, file and the previous commit version:

```
Cmd >> git diff firstfile
Out >>
diff --git a/firstfile b/firstfile
index 257cc56..3bd1f0e 100644
--- a/firstfile
+++ b/firstfile
@@ -1 +1,2 @@
foo
+bar
```

See what the changes are compared to the previously committed version.

You now need to repeat `git add` and `git commit` on that file:

```
Cmd >> git add firstfile
Cmd >> git commit -m "changes to first file"
Out >>
[main b1edf77] changes to first file
1 file changed, 1 insertion(+)
Cmd >> git status
Out >>
On branch main
nothing to commit, working tree clean
```

Commit the changes to the local repo.

If you have edited multiple files you can specify those with a wildcard. You can also specify to add all updated files:

```
git add -u :. ## updated, already added files in the current directory
git add -u :. ## updated, already added files in the whole repository
```

The changes are now in your local repo; you need to `git push` to update the upstream repo; see section 38.5.

Doing `git log` will give you the history of the repository, listing the commit numbers and the messages that you entered on those commits.

```
Cmd >> git log
Out >>
commit b1edf778c17b7c7e6cb1a8ac73fa9b61464eba14
Author: Victor Eijkhout <eijkhout@tacc.utexas.edu>
Date:   Sat Jan 29 14:14:40 2022 -0600
changes to first file
commit f968ac6c05dd877db84705a4dcdadbc0bed2c535
Author: Victor Eijkhout <eijkhout@tacc.utexas.edu>
Date:   Sat Jan 29 14:14:39 2022 -0600
adding first file
```

Get the log of all commits so far.

38.4 ▪ Undoing changes

There are various levels of undo, depending on whether you have added or committed those changes.

38.4.1 ▪ Undo uncommitted change

Scenario: you have edited a file that is in the repo, you want to undo that change, and you have not yet committed the change:

First of all, do `git diff` to confirm:

```
Cmd >> echo bar >> firstfile
Cmd >> cat firstfile
Out >>
foo
bar
bar
Cmd >> git status
Out >>
On branch main
Changes not staged for commit:
(use "git add <file>..." to update what will be
    ↪committed)
(use "git restore <file>..." to discard changes in
    ↪working directory)
modified:   firstfile
no changes added to commit (use "git add" and/or "git
    ↪commit -a")
Cmd >> git diff firstfile
Out >>
diff --git a/firstfile b/firstfile
index 3bd1f0e..58ba28e 100644
--- a/firstfile
+++ b/firstfile
@@ -1,2 +1,3 @@
foo
bar
+bar
```

Make regrettable changes.

Doing git checkout on that file gets the last committed version and puts it back in your working directory:

```
Cmd >> git checkout firstfile
Out >>
Updated 1 path from the index
Cmd >> cat firstfile
Out >>
foo
bar
Cmd >> git status
Out >>
On branch main
nothing to commit, working tree clean
```

Restore previously committed version.

38.4.2 ▪ Restore a file from a previous commit

A more complicated scenario is where you have committed the change. Then you need to find the commit ID.

You can use git log to get the IDs of all commits. This is useful if you want to roll back to pretty far in the past. However, if you only want to roll back the last commit, use git show HEAD to get a description of just that last commit:

```
Cmd >> git log
Out >>
commit e411fad261fd82eb93c328c44978699e946abc0d
Author: Victor Eijkhout <eijkhout@tacc.utexas.edu>
Date:   Sat Jan 29 14:14:42 2022 -0600
changes to first file
commit 63d6ad16beb4e2d12574fb238c29e8ba11fc6732
Author: Victor Eijkhout <eijkhout@tacc.utexas.edu>
Date:   Sat Jan 29 14:14:41 2022 -0600
adding first file
Cmd >> git show HEAD
Out >>
commit e411fad261fd82eb93c328c44978699e946abc0d
Author: Victor Eijkhout <eijkhout@tacc.utexas.edu>
Date:   Sat Jan 29 14:14:42 2022 -0600
changes to first file
diff --git a/firstfile b/firstfile
index 257cc56..3bd1f0e 100644
--- a/firstfile
+++ b/firstfile
@@ -1 +1,2 @@
foo
+bar
```

Find the commit ID that you want to roll back.

Now do:

```
git checkout sdf234987238947 -- myfile myotherfile
```

38.4.3 ▪ Undo a commit

As above, find the commit number.

Then do `git revert sdlksdfkl2343` (with the right ID). This will normally open an editor for you to leave comments; you can prevent this with the `--no-edit` option:

```
Cmd >> git revert $commit --no-edit
Out >>
[main 3dca724] Revert "changes to first file"
Date: Sat Jan 29 14:14:42 2022 -0600
1 file changed, 1 deletion(-)
```

Use "git revert" to roll back.

This will restore the file to its state before the last add and commit, and it will in general leave the repository back in the state it was in before that commit:

```
Cmd >> cat firstfile
Out >>
foo
Cmd >> git status
Out >>
On branch main
nothing to commit, working tree clean
```

See that we have indeed undone the commit.

However, the log will show that you have reverted a certain commit:

```
Cmd >> git log
Out >>
commit 3dca724a1902e8a5e3dba007c325542c6753a424
Author: Victor Eijkhout <eijkhout@tacc.utexas.edu>
Date:   Sat Jan 29 14:14:42 2022 -0600
Revert "changes to first file"

This reverts commit
    ↪e411fad261fd82eb93c328c44978699e946abc0d.
commit e411fad261fd82eb93c328c44978699e946abc0d
Author: Victor Eijkhout <eijkhout@tacc.utexas.edu>
Date:   Sat Jan 29 14:14:42 2022 -0600
changes to first file
commit 63d6ad16beb4e2d12574fb238c29e8ba11fc6732
Author: Victor Eijkhout <eijkhout@tacc.utexas.edu>
Date:   Sat Jan 29 14:14:41 2022 -0600
adding first file
```

But there will be an entry in the log.

The `git reset` command can also be used for various types of undo.

38.5 ▪ Remote repositories and collaboration

The repository where you have been adding files and changes with `git commit` is the *local repository* (see Figure 38.1). This is great for tracking changes, and reverting them when needed, but a major reason for using source code control is collaboration with others. For this you need a *remote repository*. This involves a set of commands:

```
git remote [ other keywords ] [ arguments ]
```

Suppose you have some changes, added to the local repository with `git add` and `git commit`:

```
Cmd >> git add newfile && git commit -m "adding first
    ↪file"
Out >>
[main 8ce1de4] adding first file
1 file changed, 1 insertion(+)
create mode 100644 newfile
```

Committed changes.

If the repository was created with git init, suppose you need to connect it to some remote repository with

```
git remote add servername url
```

Often, the remote name is *origin* by convention, so you often see

```
git remote add origin url
```

If you want to see what your remote is, do

```
git remote -v
```

```
Cmd >> git remote add mainserver
    ↪git@github.com:TACC/tinker.git
Cmd >> git remote -v
Out >>
mainserver      git@github.com:TACC/tinker.git (fetch)
mainserver      git@github.com:TACC/tinker.git (push)
```

Connect local repo to a remote one.

Finally, you can git push committed changes to this remote. *git* doesn't just push everything here: since you can have multiple branches locally, and multiple *upstreams* remotely, you initially specify both:

```
git push -u servername branchname
```

```
Cmd >> git push -u mainserver main
Out >>
To github.com:TACC/tinker.git
8333bc1..8ce1de4  main -> main
Branch 'main' set up to track remote branch 'main'
    ↪from 'mainserver'.
```

Push changes.

After this, git push suffices.

38.5.1 ▪ Changing the transport

You may have made your clone with

```
git clone https://....
```

but when you git push for the first time you get some permission-related errors.

Do

```
git remote -v
# output: origin  https://username@github.org/username/reponame.git
# where you replace ''username'' with your own GitHub name
git remote set-url origin git@github.org:username/reponame.git
```

38.5.2 ▪ Collaboration on the same repository

Let's see how changes from one clone of a repository can propagate to another clone. This can be because more than one person is working on a project, or because one person is working from more than one machine.

We make one local repository in directory *person1*:

```
Cmd >> git clone git@github.com:TACC/tinker.git
    ↪person1
Out >>
Cloning into 'person1'...
```

Person 1 makes a clone.

Create another clone in *person2*. Normally the cloned repositories would be two user accounts, or the accounts of one user on two machines:

```
Cmd >> git clone git@github.com:TACC/tinker.git
    ↪person2
Out >>
Cloning into 'person2'...
```

Person 2 makes a clone.

Now the first user creates a file, adds, commits, and pushes it. (This of course requires an upstream to be set, but since we did a `git clone`, this is automatically done.)

```
Cmd >> ( cd person1 && echo 123 >> p1 && git add p1
    ↪&& git commit -m "add p1" && git push )
Out >>
[main 6f6b126] add p1
1 file changed, 1 insertion(+)
create mode 100644 p1
To github.com:TACC/tinker.git
8863559..6f6b126  main -> main
```

Person 1 adds a file and pushes it.

The second user now does

```
git pull
```

to get these changes. Again, because we create the local repository by `git clone` it is clear where the pull is coming from. The pull message will tell us what new files are created, or how many other files were changed:

```
Cmd >> ( cd person2 && git pull )
Out >>
From github.com:TACC/tinker
8863559..6f6b126  main       -> origin/main
Updating 8863559..6f6b126
Fast-forward
p1 | 1 +
1 file changed, 1 insertion(+)
create mode 100644 p1
```

Person 2 pulls, getting the new file.

38.5.3 ▪ Merging changes

If you work with someone else, or even if you work solo on a project, but from more than one machine, it may happen that there will be multiple changes on a single file. That is, two local repositories have changes committed and are now pushing to the same remote.

In the following script we start with the same situation of the previous example, where we have two local repositories, as a stand-in for two users, or two different machines.

We have a file of four lines:

```
Cmd >> cat person1/fourlines
Out >>
1
2
3
4
```

We have a four-line file.

The first user makes an edit on the first line; we confirm the state of the file:

```
Cmd >> ( cd person1 && sed -i -e '1s/1/one/'
    ↪fourlines && cat fourlines )
Out >>
one
2
3
4
```

Person 1 makes a change.

This user pushes the change:

```
Cmd >> ( cd person1 && git add fourlines && git
    ↪commit -m "edit line one" && git push )
Out >>
[main 6767e3f] edit line one
1 file changed, 1 insertion(+), 1 deletion(-)
To github.com:TACC/tinker.git
fdd70b7..6767e3f  main -> main
```

Person 1 pushes the change.

The other user also makes a change, but on line 4, so that there is no conflict:

```
Cmd >> ( cd person2 && sed -i -e '4s/4/four/'
    ↪fourlines && cat fourlines )
Out >>
1
2
3
four
```

Person 2 makes a different change to the same file.

This change is added with `git add` and `git commit`, but we proceed more cautiously in pushing: first we pull any changes made by others with

```
git pull --no-edit
git push
```

```
Cmd >> ( cd person2 && git add fourlines && git
    ↪commit -m "edit line four" && git pull
    ↪--no-edit && git push )
Out >>
[main 27fb2b2] edit line four
1 file changed, 1 insertion(+), 1 deletion(-)
From github.com:TACC/tinker
fdd70b7..6767e3f  main       -> origin/main
Auto-merging fourlines
Merge made by the 'recursive' strategy.
fourlines | 2 +-
1 file changed, 1 insertion(+), 1 deletion(-)
To github.com:TACC/tinker.git
6767e3f..62bd424  main -> main
```

This change does not conflict; we can pull/push.

Now if the first user does a pull, they see all the merged changes:

```
Cmd >> ( cd person1 && git pull && cat fourlines )
Out >>
From github.com:TACC/tinker
6767e3f..62bd424  main       -> origin/main
Updating 6767e3f..62bd424
Fast-forward
fourlines | 2 +-
1 file changed, 1 insertion(+), 1 deletion(-)
one
2
3
four
```

Person 1 pulls to get all the changes.

38.5.4 ▪ Conflicting changes

There can be various reasons for `git` to report a conflict:

- You are trying to pull changes from another developer, but you have changes yourself that you haven't yet committed. If you don't want to commit your changes (maybe you're still busy editing) you can use `git stash` to set your edits aside. You can later retrieve them with `git stash pop`, or decide to forget all about them with `git stash drop`.
- There is a conflict between your changes and those you are trying to pull from another developer, or from yourself on another machine. This is the case we will look at here.
- Very similarly, there can also be conflicts between two branches you try to merge. We will look at that in section 38.6.1.

As before, we have directories *person1* and *person2* containing independent clones of a repository. We have a file four lines long, but contrary to above, we now make edits that are too close together for `git`'s auto-merge to deal with them.

```
Cmd >> cat person1/fourlines
Out >>
1
2
3
4
```

The original file.

Now developer 1 makes a change on line 1:

```
Cmd >> ( cd person1 && sed -i -e '1s/1/one/'
     ↪fourlines && git add fourlines && git commit
     ↪-m "edit line one" && git push )
Out >>
[main a10216d] edit line one
1 file changed, 1 insertion(+), 1 deletion(-)
To github.com:TACC/tinker.git
4955e50..a10216d  main -> main
```

With apologies for some scripting trickery, we use an edit by `sed`, changing `1` on line 1 to `one`. We add, commit, and push this change.

In the meantime, developer 2 makes another change, to the original file. This change can be added and committed to the local repository without any problem:

```
Cmd >> ( cd person2 && sed -i -e '2s/2/two/'
    ↪fourlines && cat fourlines  && git add
    ↪fourlines && git commit -m "edit line two" )
Out >>
1
two
3
4
[main c9b6ded] edit line two
1 file changed, 1 insertion(+), 1 deletion(-)
```

Change the `2` on line two to `two`. We add and commit this to the local repository.

However, if we try to `git push` this change to the remote repository, we get an error that the remote is ahead of the local repository. So we first pull the state of the remote repository. In the previous section this led to an automatic merge; not so here.

```
Cmd >> ( cd person2 && git pull --no-edit || echo )
Out >>
From github.com:TACC/tinker
4955e50..a10216d  main       -> origin/main
Auto-merging fourlines
CONFLICT (content): Merge conflict in fourlines
Automatic merge failed; fix conflicts and then commit
    ↪the result.
```

The `git pull` call results in a message that the automatic merge failed, indicating what file was the problem.

You can now edit the file by hand, or by using some merge tool:

```
Cmd >> ( cd person2 && cat fourlines )
Out >>
<<<<<<< HEAD
1
two
=======
one
2
>>>>>>> a10216da358649df80aaaeb94f1ceef909c2ed83
3
4
```

In between the chevron'ed lines you first get the `HEAD`, that is, the local state, followed by the pulled remote state. Edit this file, commit the merged file, and push.

38.5.5 ▪ Pull requests

The previous sections described collaboration on a repository that you have write permission for. For large projects you may not have this: the owner of the project may want a safer mechanism where you submit changes for approval in the form of a *pull request*, and they will do the merge of your changes into the repository.

This involves the following steps:

1. make a *fork* of the repository;
2. clone this fork;
3. make a branch with your changes;
4. make a pull request.

It is possible to do this whole workflow from the command line, but sites such as *GitHub* and *GitLab* make this far easier.

38.6 ▪ Branching

With a *branch* you can keep a completely separate version of all the files in your project.

Initially we have a file on the `main` branch:

```
Cmd >> cat firstfile
Out >>
foo
Cmd >> git status
Out >>
On branch main
nothing to commit, working tree clean
```

We have a file, committed and all.

We create a new branch, named `dev`, and check it out:

```
git branch dev
git checkout dev
```

This initially has the same content:

```
Cmd >> git branch dev && git branch -a
Out >>
dev
* main
Cmd >> git checkout dev && git branch -a
Out >>
Switched to branch 'dev'
* dev
main
```

Make a development branch.

We make changes, and commit them to the current branch:

```
Cmd >> cat firstfile
Out >>
foo
Cmd >> echo bar > firstfile && cat firstfile
Out >>
bar
Cmd >> git status
Out >>
On branch dev
Changes not staged for commit:
(use "git add <file>..." to update what will be
    ↪committed)
(use "git restore <file>..." to discard changes in
    ↪working directory)
modified:   firstfile
no changes added to commit (use "git add" and/or "git
    ↪commit -a")
Cmd >> git add firstfile && git commit -m "dev
    ↪changes"
Out >>
[dev b07cd2e] dev changes
1 file changed, 1 insertion(+), 1 deletion(-)
```

Make changes and commit them to the `dev` branch.

If we switch back to the *main* branch, everything is as before when we made the *dev* branch:

```
Cmd >> git checkout main && cat firstfile && git
    ↪status
Out >>
Switched to branch 'main'
foo
On branch main
nothing to commit, working tree clean
```

The other branch is still unchanged.

The first time you try to push a new branch you need to establish it upstream:

```
git push --set-upstream origin mynewbranch
```

We can inspect differences between branches with

```
git diff branch1 branch2
```

```
Cmd >> git diff main dev
Out >>
diff --git a/firstfile b/firstfile
index 257cc56..5716ca5 100644
--- a/firstfile
+++ b/firstfile
@@ -1 +1 @@
-foo
+bar
```

We can check differences between branches.

38.6.1 ▪ Branch merging

One of the points of having branches is to merge them after you have done some development in one branch.

We start with the four-line file from before:

```
Cmd >> cat fourlines
Out >>
1
2
3
4
Cmd >> git status
Out >>
On branch main
nothing to commit, working tree clean
```

The main branch is up-to-date.

Also as before, we have a *dev* branch that contains these contents.

We switch back to the *main* branch and make a change. This will not be visible in the *dev* branch:

```
Cmd >> git checkout main
Out >>
Switched to branch 'main'
Cmd >> sed -i -e '1s/1/one/' fourlines && cat
    ↪fourlines
Out >>
one
2
3
4
Cmd >> git add fourlines && git commit -m "edit line
    ↪1"
Out >>
[main c51d4ff] edit line 1
1 file changed, 1 insertion(+), 1 deletion(-)
```

On line 1, change 1 to *one*.

We switch to the *dev* branch and make another file. The change in the main branch is indeed not here:

```
Cmd >> git checkout dev
Out >>
Switched to branch 'dev'
Cmd >> sed -i -e '4s/4/four/' fourlines && cat
    ↪fourlines
Out >>
1
2
3
four
Cmd >> git add fourlines && git commit -m "edit line
    ↪4"
Out >>
[dev dbb0c03] edit line 4
1 file changed, 1 insertion(+), 1 deletion(-)
```

On line 4, change 4 to *four*. This change is far enough away from the other change that there should be no conflict.

Switching back to the *main* branch, we use

```
git merge dev
```

to merge the *dev* changes into *main*.

```
Cmd >> git checkout main
Out >>
Switched to branch 'main'
Cmd >> git merge dev
Out >>
Auto-merging fourlines
Merge made by the 'recursive' strategy.
fourlines | 2 +-
1 file changed, 1 insertion(+), 1 deletion(-)
Cmd >> cat fourlines
Out >>
one
2
3
four
```

Merge the *dev* branch into the main one with `git merge`. Note the "auto-merge" message, and confirm that both changes to the file are there.

If two developers make changes on the same line, or on adjacent lines, *git* will not be able to merge and you have to edit the file as in section 38.5.4.

38.7 ▪ Releases

At a certain point in your development process you may want to mark the current state of the repository as "finished." You can do this by

1. attaching `tag` to the state of the repository, or
2. creating an `archive`: a released version that has the repo information stripped.

38.7.1 ▪ Tags

A tag is a marked state of the repository. There are two types of tags:

1. light-weight tags are no more than a synonym for a commit:

   ```
   git tag v0.09
   ```

2. annotated tags, which carry an information message:

   ```
   git tag -a v0.1 "base classes finished"
   ```

You list all tags with `git tag`, you get information on a tag with `git show v0.1`, and you push a tag to a remote server with

```
git push origin v0.1
```

You can retrieve the tagged state of the repository with

```
git checkout v0.1
```

but beware that changes you now make cannot be pushed to anything: this is a "detached HEAD" state. If you want to fix bugs in a tagged state, you can create a branch based on the tag:

```
git checkout -b version0.2 v0.1
```

Remark. *Hosting sites such as* GitHub *make tagged releases easy through a web interface.*

38.7.2 ▪ Archives, releases

If you want to make a released version of your software, that can be downloaded and does not rely on the `git` software, use the `archive` command:

```
git archive master --format=tgz --prefix=MyProject-v1 -o MyProject-v1.tgz
```

Part VII

Exercises and projects

Chapter 39

Infectious disease simulation

In recent years, the spread of infectious diseases has been a hot topic. First there was the anti-vaccination movement, and then people had to deal with the outbreak of the coronavirus, for which initially no vaccine even existed. Apart from any sociological angle, this issue can be tackled by any number of sciences. In this project we will model how fast a disease spreads through a partly vaccinated population, depending on various parameters. The approach taken here is one of explicitly modeling a population through its members, rather than taking a statistical approach.

This section contains a sequence of exercises that builds up to a somewhat realistic simulation of infectious disease propagation.

39.1 ▪ Model design

It is possible to model disease propagation statistically, but here we will build an explicit simulation: we will maintain an explicit description of all the people in the population, and track for each of them their status.

We will use a simple model where a person can be

- sick: when they are sick, they can infect other people;
- susceptible: they are healthy, but can be infected;
- recovered: they have been sick, but no longer carry the disease, and cannot be infected for a second time;
- vaccinated: they are healthy, do not carry the disease, and cannot be infected.

In more complicated models a person could be infectious during only part of their illness, or there could be secondary infections with other diseases, etc. We keep it simple here: any sick person can infect others while they are sick.

In the exercises below we will gradually develop a model of how the disease spreads from an initial source of infection. The program will then track the population from day to day, running indefinitely until none of the population is sick. Since there is no re-infection, the run will always end. Later we will add mutation to the model, which can extend the duration of the epidemic.

39.1.1 ▪ Other ways of modeling

Instead of capturing every single person in code, a "contact network" model, it is possible to use an ODE approach to disease modeling. You would then model the percentage of infected persons by a single scalar, and derive relations for that and other scalars [3, 39].

This is known as a "compartmental model," where each of the three SIR states, susceptible, infected, removed, is a compartment: a section of the population. Both the contact network and the compartmental model capture part of the truth. In fact, they can be combined. We can consider a country as a set of cities, where people travel between any pair of cities. We then use a compartmental model inside a city, and a contact network between cities.

In this project we will only use the network model.

39.2 ▪ Coding

The following sections are a step-by-step development of the code for this project. Later we will discuss running this code as a scientific experiment.

Remark. *In various places you need a random number generator. It is preferred that you use the C++ native one, rather than one from the C language.*

39.2.1 ▪ Person basics

The most basic component of a disease simulation is to infect a person with a disease, and see the time development of that infection. Thus you need a person class and a disease class.

Before you start coding, ask yourself what behaviors these classes need to support.

- Person. The basic methods for a person are
  1. get infected;
  2. get vaccinated; and
  3. progress by one day.

  Furthermore you may want to query what the state of the person is: are they healthy, sick, recovered?
- Disease. For now, a disease itself doesn't do much. (Later in the project you may want it to have a method `mutate`.) However, you may want to query certain properties:
  1. chance of transmission; and
  2. number of days a person stays sick when infected.

A test for a single person could have output along the following lines:

```
On day 10, Joe is susceptible
On day 11, Joe is susceptible
On day 12, Joe is susceptible
On day 13, Joe is susceptible
On day 14, Joe is sick (5 days to go)
On day 15, Joe is sick (4 days to go)
On day 16, Joe is sick (3 days to go)
On day 17, Joe is sick (2 days to go)
On day 18, Joe is sick (1 days to go)
On day 19, Joe is recovered
```

Exercise 39.1. Write a `Person` class with the following methods:

- `status_string()` : returns a description of the person's state as a `string`;
- `one_more_day()` : update the person's status to the next day;
- `infect(s)` : infect a person with a disease, where the disease object

  ```
  Disease s(n);
  ```

  is specified to run for n days.

Your main program could, for instance, look like

```
// infect/person.cpp
for ( int step = 1; ; ++step ) {

  joe.one_more_day();
  /* ... */
  cout << "On day " << step << ", Joe is "
       << joe.status_string() << '\n';
  if (joe.is_recovered())
    break;
}
```

where the infection part has been left out.

Your main concern is how to model the internal state of a person. This is actually two separate issues:

1. the state, and
2. if sick, how many days to go to recover.

You can find a way to implement this with a single integer, but it's better to use two. Also, write enough support methods such as the `is_recovered` test.

39.2.1.1 ▪ Person tests

It is easy to write code that seems to do the right thing, but does not behave correctly in all cases. So it is a good idea to subject your code to some systematic tests.

Make sure your `Person` objects pass these tests:

- After being infected with a 100% transmittable disease, they should register as sick.
- If they are vaccinated or recovered, and they come in contact with such a disease, they stay in their original state.
- If a disease has a transmission chance of 50%, and a number of people come into contact with it, about half of them should get sick. This test may be a little tricky to write.

Can you use the *Catch2* unit testing framework? See Chapter 26.

39.2.2 ▪ Interaction

Next we model interactions between people: one person is healthy, another is infected, and when the two come into contact the disease may be transferred.

```
// infect/interaction.cpp
Person infected,healthy;
infected.infect(flu);
/* ... */
  healthy.touch(infected);
```

The disease has a certain probability of being transferred, so you need to specify that probability. You could let the declaration be

```
Disease flu( 5, 0.3 );
```

where the first parameter is the number of days an infection lasts, and the second the transfer probability.

Exercise 39.2. Add a transmission probability to the `Disease` class, and add a `touch` method to the `Person` class. Design and run some tests.

Exercise 39.3. Bonus: can you get the following disease specification to work?

```
// infect/interaction.cpp
Disease flu;
flu.duration() = 20;
flu.transfer_probability() = p;
```

Why could you consider this better than the earlier suggested syntax?

39.2.2.1 ▪ Interaction tests

Adapt the above tests, but now a person comes in contact with an infected person, rather than directly with a disease.

39.2.3 ▪ Population

Next we need a `Population` class, where a population contains a `vector` consisting of `Person` objects. Initially we only infect one person, and there is no transmission of the disease.

The `Population` class should at least have the following methods:

- `random_infection` to start out with an infected segment of the population;
- `random_vaccination` to start out with a number of vaccinated individuals.
- counting functions `count_infected` and `count_vaccinated`.

To run a realistic simulation you also need a `one_more_day` method that takes the population through a day. This is the heart of your code, and we will develop this gradually in the next section.

39.2.3.1 ▪ Population tests

Most population testing will be done in the following section. For now, make sure you pass the following test:

- With a vaccination percentage of 100%, everyone should indeed be vaccinated.

39.3 ▪ Epidemic simulation

To simulate the spread of a disease through the population, we need an update method that progresses the population through one day:

- sick people come into contact with a number of other members of the populace; and

- everyone gets one day older, meaning mostly that sick people get one day closer to recovery.

We develop this in a couple of steps.

39.3.1 ▪ No contact

At first assume that people have no contact, so the disease ends with the people it starts with.

The trace output should look something like

```
Size of
population?
In step   1 #sick:    1 :  ? ? ? ? ? ? ? ? ? ? + ? ? ? ? ? ? ? ? ? ?
In step   2 #sick:    1 :  ? ? ? ? ? ? ? ? ? ? + ? ? ? ? ? ? ? ? ? ?
In step   3 #sick:    1 :  ? ? ? ? ? ? ? ? ? ? + ? ? ? ? ? ? ? ? ? ?
In step   4 #sick:    1 :  ? ? ? ? ? ? ? ? ? ? + ? ? ? ? ? ? ? ? ? ?
In step   5 #sick:    1 :  ? ? ? ? ? ? ? ? ? ? + ? ? ? ? ? ? ? ? ? ?
In step   6 #sick:    0 :  ? ? ? ? ? ? ? ? ? ? - ? ? ? ? ? ? ? ? ? ?
Disease ran its course by step 6
```

Remark. *Such a display is good for a sanity check on your program behavior. If you include such displays in your writeup, make sure to use a monospace font, and don't use a population size that needs line wrapping. In further testing, you should use large populations, but do not include these displays.*

Exercise 39.4. Program a population without infection.

- Write the `Population` class. The constructor takes the number of people:

  ```
  Population population(npeople);
  ```

- Write a method that infects a number of random people:

  ```
  // infect/pandemic.cpp
  population.random_infection(fever,initial_infect);
  ```

- Write a method `count_infected` that counts how many people are infected.
- Write a `one_more_day` method that updates all persons in the population.
- Loop the `one_more_day` method until no people are infected: the `Population::one_more_day` method should apply `Person::one_more_day` to all people in the population.

Write a routine that displays the state of the population, using, for instance, ? for susceptible, + for infected, - for recovered.

39.3.1.1 ▪ Tests

Test that for the duration of the disease, the number of infected people stays constant, and that the sum of healthy and infected people stays equal to the population size.

39.3.2 ▪ Contagion

This past exercise was too simplistic: the original patient zero was the only one who ever got sick. Now let's incorporate contagion, and investigate the spread of the disease from a single infected person.

We start with a very simple model of infection.

Exercise 39.5. Write a simulation where in each step the direct neighbors of an infected person can now get sick themselves.

Run a number of simulations with population sizes and contagion probabilities. Are there cases where people escape getting sick?

39.3.2.1 ▪ Tests

Do some sanity tests:

- If one person is infected with a disease with $p = 1$, the next day there should be three people sick, unless the infected person is the first or last, in which case there are two.
- If person 0 is infected, and $p = 1$, the simulation should run for a number of days equal to the size of the population.
- What does the previous case look like if $p = 0.5$?

39.3.3 ▪ Vaccination

Exercise 39.6. Incorporate vaccination: read another number representing the percentage of people who have been vaccinated. Choose those members of the population randomly.

Describe the effect of vaccinated people on the spread of the disease. Why is this model unrealistic?

39.3.4 ▪ Spreading

To make the simulation more realistic, we let every sick person come into contact with a fixed number of random people every day. This gives us more or less the *SIR model* [41].

Set the number of people that a person comes into contact with, per day, to 6 or so. (You can also let this be an upper bound for a random value, but that does not essentially change the simulation.) You have already programmed the probability that a person who comes into contact with an infected person gets sick themselves. Again start the simulation with a single infected person.

Exercise 39.7. Code the random interactions. Now run a number of simulations varying

- the percentage of people vaccinated, and
- the chance the disease is transmitted on contact.

Record how long the disease runs through the population. With a fixed number of contacts and probability of transmission, how is this number a function of the percentage that is vaccinated?

Report this function as a table or graph. Make sure you have enough data points for a meaningful conclusion. Use a realistic population size. You can also do multiple runs and report the average, to even out the effect of the random number generator.

Exercise 39.8. Investigate the matter of "herd immunity": if enough people are vaccinated, then some people who are not vaccinated will still never get sick. Let's say you want to have the probability of being not vaccinated, yet never getting sick, to be over 95 percent. Investigate the percentage of vaccination that is needed for this as a function of the contagiousness of the disease.

As in the previous exercise, make sure your dataset is large enough.

Remark. *The screen output you used above is good for sanity checks on small problems. However, for realistic simulations you have to think what a realistic population size is. If your university campus is a population where random people are likely to meet each other, what would be a population size to model that? How about the city where you live?*

Likewise, if you test different vaccination rates, what granularity do you use? With increases of 5 or 10 percent you can print all results to your screen, but you may miss things. Don't be afraid to generate a large amount of data and feed them directly to a graphing program.

39.3.4.1 ▪ Sanity tests

As your model gets more realistic it becomes harder to test it fully, if only because of the use of random numbers. Still ...

- With zero vaccination, the disease should run for some logarithm of the size of the population.
- With hundred percent vaccination, apart from one sick person, the disease will run for as long as that person is sick.

39.3.5 ▪ Mutation

The COVID years have shown how important mutations of an original virus can be. Next, you can include mutation in your project. We model this as follows:

- Every so many transmissions, a virus will mutate into a new variant.
- A person who has recovered from one variant is still susceptible to other variants.
- For simplicity assume that each variant leaves a person sick the same number of days, and
- vaccination is all-or-nothing: one vaccine is enough to protect against all variants.
- On the other hand, having recovered from one variant is not protection against others.

Implementationwise, we model this as follows. First of all, we need a `Disease` class, so that we can infect a person with an explicit virus;

```
// infect/infect_lib.hpp
void touch( const Person&,long int ps=0 );
void infect( const Disease& );
```

A `Disease` object now carries the information such as the chance of transmission, or how long a person stays under the weather. Modeling mutation is a little tricky. You could do it as follows:

- There are a global `variants` counter for new virus variants, and a global `transmissions` counter.
- Every time a person infects another, the newly infected person gets a new `Disease` object, with the current variant, and the transmissions counter is updated.
- There is a parameter that determines after how many transmissions the disease mutates. If there is a mutation, the global `variants` counter is updated, and from that point on, every infection is with the new variant. (Note: this is not very realistic. You are free to come up with a better model.)

- Each `Person` object has a vector of variants that they are recovered from; recovery from one variant only makes them immune from that specific variant, not from others.

Exercise 39.9. Add mutation to your model. Experiment with the mutation rate: as the mutation rate increases, the disease should stay in the population longer. Does the relation with vaccination rate that you observed before change?

39.3.5.1 ▪ Tests

Implement some sanity tests.

Suppose a person never recovers from a disease (can you think of examples?). The number of mutations should increase roughly exponentially (why isn't the rate actually exponential?); test this.

39.3.6 ▪ Diseases without vaccine: Ebola and COVID-19

This section is optional, for bonus points.

The project so far applies to diseases for which a vaccine is available, such as MMR for measles, mumps, and rubella. The analysis becomes different if no vaccine exists, such as is the case for *Ebola*, and for *COVID-19* when it first emerged.

Instead, you need to incorporate "social distancing" into your code: during a pandemic, people do not get in touch with random others anymore, but only those in a very limited social circle. Design a model distance function, and explore various settings.

The difference between Ebola and COVID-19 is how long an infection can go unnoticed: the *incubation period*. With Ebola, infection is almost immediately apparent, so such people are removed from the general population and treated in a hospital. For COVID-19, a person can be infected, and infect others, for a number of days before symptoms appear and they are sequestered from the population.

Add this parameter to your simulation and explore the behavior of the disease as a function of it.

39.4 ▪ Ethics

The subject of infectious diseases and vaccination is full of ethical questions. The main one is, *The chances of something happening to me are very small, so why shouldn't I bend the rules a little?* This reasoning is most often applied to vaccination, where people for some reason or another refuse to get vaccinated.

Explore this question and others you may come up with: it is clear that everyone bending the rules will have disastrous consequences, but what if only a few people did this?

39.5 ▪ Parallelism

The main computation in your code is the update of the population. Argue that this is a fully parallel operation. Use OpenMP to make the loop indeed parallel, and test the speedup you get.

Can you also express this as a range algorithm? Again test the speedup you get. On high core counts you may need to figure out the equivalent of `OMP_PROC_BIND=true`. This depends on how your compiler has implemented the parallel range algorithm.

39.6 ▪ Bonus: Testing

Read [20]. Can you test the hypothesis of that article?

39.7 ▪ Bonus: Mathematical analysis

The SIR model can also be modeled through coupled difference or differential equations.

1. The number S_i of susceptible people at time i decreases by a fraction

   $$S_{i+1} = S_i(1 - \lambda_i \, dt),$$

   where λ_i is the product of the number of infected people and a constant that reflects the number of meetings and the infectiousness of the disease. We write

   $$S_{i+1} = S_i(1 - \lambda I_i \, dt).$$

2. The number of infected people similarly increases by $\lambda S_i I_i$, but it also decreases by people recovering (or dying):

   $$I_{i+1} = I_i(1 + \lambda S_i \, dt - \gamma \, dt).$$

3. Finally, the number of "removed" people equals that last term:

   $$R_{i+1} = R_i(1 + \gamma I_i).$$

Exercise 39.10. Code this scheme. What is the effect of varying dt?

Exercise 39.11. For the disease to become an epidemic, the number of newly infected has to be larger than the number of recovered. That is,

$$\lambda S_i I_i - \gamma I_i > 0 \Leftrightarrow S_i > \gamma / \lambda.$$

Can you observe this in your simulations?

The parameter γ has a simple interpretation. Suppose that a person stays ill for δ days before recovering. If I_t is relatively stable, that means every day the same number of people get infected as recover, and therefore a $1/\delta$ fraction of people recover each day. Thus, γ is the reciprocal of the duration of the infection in a given person.

39.8 ▪ Project writeup and submission

39.8.1 ▪ Program files

In the course of this project you have written more than one main program, but some code is shared between the multiple programs. Organize your code with one file for each main program, and a single library file with the class methods.

You can do this two ways:

1. You make a library file, say `infect_lib.cc`, and your main programs each have a line

   ```
   #include "infect_lib.cc"
   ```

   This is not the best solution, but it is acceptable for now.

2. The better solution requires you to use *separate compilation* for building the program, and you need a *header* file. You would now have `infect_lib.cc`, which is compiled separately, and `infect_lib.h`, which is included in both the library file and the main program:

   ```
   #include "infect_lib.h"
   ```

   See section 24.1 for more information.

Submit all source files with instructions on how to build all the main programs. You can put these instructions in a file with a descriptive name such as `README` or `INSTALL`, or you can use a *makefile*.

39.8.2 ▪ Writeup

In the writeup, describe the "experiments" you have performed and the conclusions you draw from them. The exercises above give you a number of questions to address.

For each main program, include some sample output, but note that this is no substitute for writing out your conclusions in full sentences.

The exercises in section 39.3.4 ask you to explore the program behavior as a function of one or more parameters. Include a table to report on the behavior you found. You can use MATLAB or Matplotlib in Python (or even Excel) to plot your data, but that is not required.

Chapter 40

Google PageRank

40.1 ▪ Basic ideas

We are going to simulate the internet. In particular, we are going to simulate the *Google PageRank* algorithm by which *Google* determines the importance of webpages.

Let's start with some basic classes:

- A `Page` contains some information such as its title and a global numbering in Google's datacenter. It also contains a collection of links.
- We represent a link with a pointer to a `Page`. Conceivably we could have a `Link` class, containing further information such as probability of being clicked, or number of times clicked, but for now a pointer will do.
- Ultimately we want to have a class `Web` which contains a number of pages and their links. The web object will ultimately also contain information such as relative importance of the pages.

This application is a natural one for using pointers. When you click on a link on a webpage you go from looking at one page in your browser to looking at another. You could implement this by having a pointer to a page, and clicking updates the value of this pointer.

Exercise 40.1. Make a class `Page` which initially just contains the name of the page. Write a method to display the page. Since we will be using pointers quite a bit, let this be the intended code for testing:

```
// google/web2.cpp
auto homepage = make_shared<Page>("My Home Page");
cout << "Homepage has no links yet:" << '\n';
cout << homepage->as_string() << '\n';
```

Next, add links to the page. A link is a pointer to another page, and since there can be any number of them, you will need a `vector` of them. Write a method `click` that follows the link. Intended code:

```
// google/web2.cpp
auto utexas = make_shared<Page>("University Home Page");
homepage->add_link(utexas);
```

```
auto searchpage = make_shared<Page>("google");
homepage->add_link(searchpage);
cout << homepage->as_string() << '\n';
```

Exercise 40.2. Add some more links to your homepage. Write a method `random_click` for the `Page` class. Intended code:

```
// google/web2.cpp
for (int iclick=0; iclick<20; ++iclick) {
  auto newpage = homepage->random_click();
  cout << "To: " << newpage->as_string() << '\n';
}
```

How do you handle the case of a page without links?

40.2 ▪ Clicking around

Exercise 40.3. Now make a class `Web` which foremost contains a bunch (technically, a `vector`) of pages—or rather, of pointers to pages. Since we don't want to build a whole internet by hand, let's have a method `create_random_links` which makes a random number of links to random pages. Intended code:

```
// google/web2.cpp
Web internet(netsize);
internet.create_random_links(avglinks);
```

Now we can start our simulation. Write a method `Web::random_walk` that takes a page, and the length of the walk, and simulates the result of randomly clicking that many times on the current page (current page, not the starting page).

Let's start working towards PageRank. First we see if there are pages that are more popular than others. You can do that by starting a random walk once on each page. Or maybe a couple of times.

Exercise 40.4. Apart from the size of your internet, what other design parameters are there for your tests? Can you give a back-of-the-envelope estimation of their effect?

Exercise 40.5. Your first simulation is to start on each page a number of times, and count where that lands you. Intended code:

```
// google/web2.cpp
  vector<int> landing_counts(internet.number_of_pages(),0);
  for ( auto page : internet.all_pages() ) {
    for (int iwalk=0; iwalk<5; ++iwalk) {
      auto endpage = internet.random_walk(page,2*avglinks,tracing);
      landing_counts.at(endpage->global_ID())++;
    }
  }
```

Display the results and analyze. You may find that you finish on certain pages too many times. What's happening? Fix that.

40.3 ▪ Graph algorithms

There are many algorithms that rely on gradually traversing the web. For instance, any graph can be *connected*. You test that by doing the following:

- Take an arbitrary vertex v. Make a "reachable set" $R \leftarrow \{v\}$.
- Now see where you can get from your reachable set:

$$\forall_{v \in V} \forall_{w \text{ neighbor of } v} : R \leftarrow R \cup \{w\}.$$

- Repeat the previous step until R does not change anymore.

After this algorithm concludes, is R equal to your set of vertices? If so, your graph is called (fully) connected. If not, your graph has multiple *connected components*.

Exercise 40.6. Code the above algorithm, keeping track of how many steps it takes to reach each vertex w. This is the *single source shortest path* algorithm (for unweighted graphs).

The *diameter* is defined as the maximal shortest path. Code this.

40.4 ▪ Page ranking

The PageRank algorithm now asks, if you keep clicking randomly, what is the distribution of how likely you are to wind up on a certain page. The way we calculate that is with a probability distribution: we assign a probability to each page so that the sum of all probabilities is one. We start with a random distribution:

Code:

```
// google/web2.cpp
ProbabilityDistribution
  random_state(internet.number_of_pages());
random_state.set_random();
cout << "Initial distribution: " <<
    ↪random_state.as_string() << '\n';
```

Output:

```
Initial distribution: 0:0.00,
    ↪1:0.02, 2:0.07, 3:0.05,
    ↪4:0.06, 5:0.08, 6:0.04,
    ↪7:0.04, 8:0.04, 9:0.01,
    ↪10:0.07, 11:0.05,
    ↪12:0.01, 13:0.04,
    ↪14:0.08, 15:0.06,
    ↪16:0.10, 17:0.06,
    ↪18:0.11, 19:0.01,
```

Exercise 40.7. Implement a class `ProbabilityDistribution`, which stores a vector of floating point numbers. Write methods for

- accessing a specific element;
- setting the whole distribution to random; and
- normalizing so that the sum of the probabilities is 1;
- a method rendering the distribution as string could be useful too.

Next we need a method that, given a probability distribution, gives you the new distribution corresponding to performing a single click. (This is related to *Markov chains*; see the HPC book [23, section 10.2.1].)

Exercise 40.8. Write the method

```
ProbabilityDistribution Web::globalclick
    ( ProbabilityDistribution currentstate );
```

Test it by

- starting with a distribution that is nonzero in exactly one page;
- printing the new distribution corresponding to one click;
- doing this for several pages and inspecting the result visually.

Then start with a random distribution and run a couple of iterations. How fast does the process converge? Compare the result to the random walk exercise above.

Exercise 40.9. In the random walk exercise you had to deal with the fact that some pages have no outgoing links. In that case you transitioned to a random page. That mechanism is lacking in the `globalclick` method. Figure out a way to incorporate this.

Let's simulate some simple "search engine optimization" trick.

Exercise 40.10. Add a page that you will artificially make look important: add a number of pages that all link to this page, but no one links to them. (Because of the random clicking, they will still sometimes be reached.)

Compute the rank of the artificially hyped page. Did you manage to trick Google into ranking this page high? How many links did you have to add?

Sample output with in the second case 50 fake pages pointing to the final page:

```
Internet has 5000 pages
Top score: 109:0.0013, 3179:0.0012, 4655:0.0010, 3465:0.0009, 4298:0.0008
With fake pages:
Internet has 5051 pages
Top score: 109:0.0013, 3179:0.0012, 4655:0.0010, 5050:0.0010, 4298:0.0008
Hyped page scores at 4
```

40.5 ▪ Graphs and linear algebra

The probability distribution is essentially a vector. You can also represent the web as a matrix W with $w_{ij} = 1$ if page i links to page j. (For details see the HPC book [23, section 25.5].) How can you interpret the `globalclick` method in these terms?

Exercise 40.11. Add the matrix representation of the `Web` object and reimplement the `globalclick` method. Test for correctness.

Do a timing comparison.

The iteration you did above to find a stable probability distribution corresponds to the "power method" in linear algebra. Look up the Perron–Frobenius theory and see what it implies for page ranking.

40.6 ▪ Parallelism

Explore the OpenMP library (Chapter 20) to parallelize the various algorithms you have developed in this project.

Argue that a CRS sparse matrix representation is easy to parallelize. How is that for the more direct implementation of a graph as a linked structure?

Chapter 41

Redistricting

In this project you can explore "gerrymandering," the strategic drawing of districts to give a minority population a majority of districts.[2]

41.1 ▪ Basic concepts

We are dealing with the following concepts:

- A state is divided into census districts, which are given. Based on census data (income, ethnicity, median age) one can usually make a good guess as to the overall voting in such a district.
- There is a predetermined number of congressional districts, each of which consists of census districts. A congressional district is not a random collection: the census districts have to be contiguous.
- Every couple of years, to account for changing populations, the district boundaries are redrawn. This is known as redistricting.

There is considerable freedom in how redistricting is done: by shifting the boundaries of the (congressional) districts it is possible to give a population that is in the overall minority a majority of districts. This is known as *gerrymandering* [48].

For background reading, see `https://redistrictingonline.org/`.

To do a small-scale computer simulation of gerrymandering, we make some simplifying assumptions:

- First of all, we dispense with census district: we assume that a district consists directly of voters, and that we know their affiliation. In practice one relies on proxy measures (such as income and education level) to predict affiliation.
- Next, we assume a one-dimensional state. This is enough to construct examples that bring out the essence of the problem:

  Consider a state of five voters, and we designate their votes as `AAABB`. Assigning them to three (contiguous) districts can be done as `AAA|B|B`, which has one "A" district and two "B" districts.

[2]This project is obviously based on the North American political system. Hopefully the explanations here are clear enough. Please contact the author if you know of other countries that have a similar system.

- We also allow districts to be any positive size, as long as the number of districts is fixed.

41.2 ▪ Basic functions

41.2.1 ▪ Voters

We dispense with census districts, expressing everything in terms of voters, for which we assume a known voting behavior. Hence, we need a `Voter` class, which will record the voter ID and party affiliation. We assume two parties and leave an option for being undecided.

Exercise 41.1. Implement a `Voter` class. You could, for instance, let ± 1 stand for `A/B`, and 0 for undecided.

// gerry/linear.cpp
```
cout << "Voter 5 is positive:" << '\n';
Voter nr5(5,+1);
cout << nr5.print() << '\n';
```

// gerry/linear.cpp
```
cout << "Voter 6 is negative:" << '\n';
Voter nr6(6,-1);
cout << nr6.print() << '\n';
```

// gerry/linear.cpp
```
cout << "Voter 7 is weird:" << '\n';
Voter nr7(7,3);
cout << nr7.print() << '\n';
```

41.2.2 ▪ Populations

Exercise 41.2. Implement a `District` class that models a group of voters.

- You probably want to create a district out of a single voter, or a vector of them. Having a constructor that accepts a string representation would be nice too.
- Write methods `majority` to give the exact majority or minority, and `lean` that evaluates whether the district overall counts as A party or B party.
- Write a `sub` method to creates subsets:

```
District District::sub(int first,int last);
```

- For debugging and reporting, it may be a good idea to have a method

```
string District::print();
```

Code:

```
// gerry/linear.cpp
   cout << "Making district with one B voter"
        << '\n';
   Voter nr5(5,+1);
   District nine( nr5 );
   cout << ".. size: " << nine.size() << '\n';
   cout << ".. lean: " << nine.lean() << '\n';
   /* ... */
   cout << "Making district ABA" << '\n';
   District nine( vector<Voter>
                  { {1,-1},{2,+1},{3,-1} } );
   cout << ".. size: " << nine.size() << '\n';
   cout << ".. lean: " << nine.lean() << '\n';
```

Output:

```
Making district with one B voter
.. size: 1
.. lean: 1

Making district ABA
.. size: 3
.. lean: -1
```

Exercise 41.3. Implement a `Population` class that will initially model a whole state.

Code:

```
// gerry/linear.cpp
string pns( "-++--" );
Population some(pns);
cout << "Population from string "
     << pns << '\n';
cout << ".. size: " << some.size() << '\n';
cout << ".. lean: " << some.lean() << '\n';
Population group=some.sub(1,3);
cout << "sub population 1--3" << '\n';
cout << ".. size: " << group.size() << '\n';
cout << ".. lean: " << group.lean() << '\n';
```

Output:

```
Population from string -++--
.. size: 5
.. lean: -1
sub population 1--3
.. size: 2
.. lean: 1
```

In addition to an explicit creation, also write a constructor that specifies how many people and what the majority is:

```
// gerry/linear.cpp
Population( int population_size,int majority,bool trace=false )
```

Use a random number generator to achieve precisely the indicated majority.

41.2.3 ▪ Districting

The next level of complication is to have a set of districts. Since we will be creating this incrementally, we need some methods for extending it.

Exercise 41.4. Write a class `Districting` that stores a `vector` of `District` objects. Write `size` and `lean` methods:

Code:

```
// gerry/linear.cpp
cout << "Making single voter population B" <<
    ↪'\n';
Population people( vector<Voter>{ Voter(0,+1) } );
cout << ".. size: " << people.size() << '\n';
cout << ".. lean: " << people.lean() << '\n';

Districting gerry;
cout << "Start with empty districting:" << '\n';
cout << ".. number of districts: "
     << gerry.size() << '\n';
```

Output:

```
Making single voter population B
.. size: 1
.. lean: 1
Start with empty districting:
.. number of districts: 0
```

Exercise 41.5. Write methods to extend a `Districting`:

```
// gerry/linear.cpp
cout << "Add one B voter:" << '\n';
gerry = gerry.extend_with_new_district( people.at(0) );
cout << ".. number of districts: " << gerry.size() << '\n';
cout << ".. lean: " << gerry.lean() << '\n';
cout << "add A A:" << '\n';
gerry = gerry.extend_last_district( Voter(1,-1) );
gerry = gerry.extend_last_district( Voter(2,-1) );
cout << ".. number of districts: " << gerry.size() << '\n';
cout << ".. lean: " << gerry.lean() << '\n';

cout << "Add two B districts:" << '\n';
gerry = gerry.extend_with_new_district( Voter(3,+1) );
gerry = gerry.extend_with_new_district( Voter(4,+1) );
cout << ".. number of districts: " << gerry.size() << '\n';
cout << ".. lean: " << gerry.lean() << '\n';
```

41.3 ▪ Strategy

Now we need a method for districting a population:

```
Districting Population::minority_rules( int ndistricts );
```

Rather than generating all possible partitions of the population, we take an incremental approach (this is related to the solution strategy called *dynamic programming*):

- The basic question is to divide a population optimally over n districts.
- We do this recursively by first solving a division of a subpopulation over $n-1$ districts.
- Then we extend that with the remaining population as one district.

This means that you need to consider all the ways of having the "remaining" population into one district, and that means that you will have a loop over all ways of splitting the population, outside of your recursion; see Figure 41.1.

- For all $p = 0, \ldots n-1$ consider splitting the state into $0, \ldots, p-1$ and $p, \ldots, n-1$.
- Use the best districting of the first group, and make the last group into a single district.
- Keep the districting that gives the strongest minority rule, over all values of p.

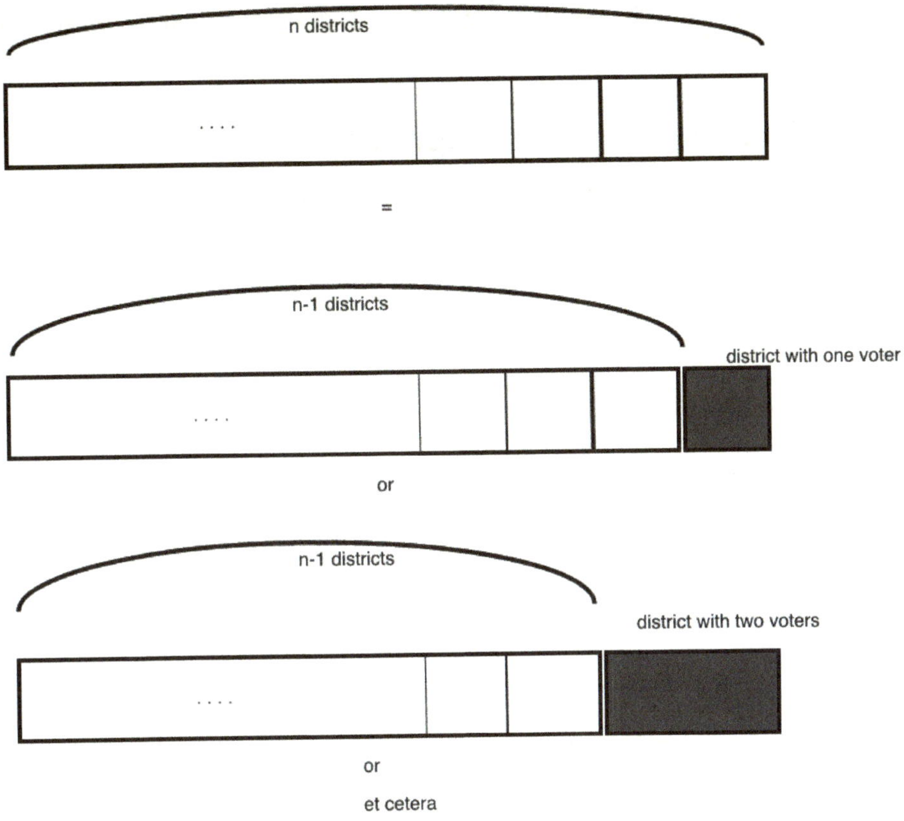

Figure 41.1. *Multiple ways of splitting a population*

You can now realize the above simple example:

AAABB => AAA|B|B

Exercise 41.6. Implement the above scheme:

Code:

```
// gerry/linear.cpp
Population five("+++--");
cout << "Redistricting population: " << '\n'
     << five.print() << '\n';
cout << ".. majority rule: "
     << five.rule() << '\n';
int ndistricts{3};
auto gerry = five.minority_rules(ndistricts);
cout << gerry.print() << '\n';
cout << ".. minority rule: "
     << gerry.rule() << '\n';
```

Output:

```
Redistricting population:
[0:+,1:+,2:+,3:-,4:-,]
.. majority rule: 1
[3[0:+,1:+,2:+,],[3:-,],[4:-,],]
.. minority rule: -1
```

Note: the range for p given above is not quite correct: for instance, the initial part of the population needs to be big enough to accommodate $n-1$ voters.

Exercise 41.7. Test multiple population sizes; how much majority can you give party B while still giving party A a majority?

41.4 ▪ Efficiency: Dynamic programming

If you think about the algorithm you just implemented, you may notice that the districtings of the initial parts get recomputed quite a bit. A strategy for optimizing for this is called *memoization*.

Exercise 41.8. Improve your implementation by storing and reusing results for the initial subpopulations.

In a way, we solved the program backward: we looked at making a district out of the last so-many voters, and then recursively solved a smaller problem for the first however-many voters. But in that process, we decided what is the best way to assign districts to the first one voter, first two, first three, etc. Actually, for more than one voter, say five voters, we found the result on the best attainable minority rule assigning these five voters to one, two, three, four districts.

The process of computing the "best" districting forward is known as *dynamic programming*. The fundamental assumption here is that you can use intermediate results and extend them, without having to reconsider the earlier problems.

Consider, for instance, that you've considered districting ten voters over up to five districts. Now the majority for eleven voters and five districts is the minimum of

- ten voters and five districts, and the new voter is added to the last district; or
- ten voters and four districts, and the new voter becomes a new district.

Exercise 41.9. Code a dynamic programming solution to the redistricting problem.

41.5 ▪ Extensions

The project so far has several simplifying assumptions:

- Congressional districts need to be approximately the same size. Can you put a limit on the ratio between sizes? Can the minority still gain a majority?

Exercise 41.10. The biggest assumption is of course that we considered a one-dimensional state. With two dimensions you have more degrees of freedom of shaping the districts. Implement a two-dimensional scheme; use a completely square state, where the census districts form a regular grid. Limit the shape of the congressional districts to be convex.

The *efficiency gap* is a measure of how "fair" a districting of a state is.

Exercise 41.11. Look up the definition of efficiency gap (and "wasted votes") and implement it in your code.

41.6 ▪ Parallelism

Your redistricting code does not feature any long loops with independent iterations, so you cannot use an `omp parallel for` directive. However, where you take a minimum over two splittings you can process these in parallel. Implement this with the OpenMP tasking mechanism.

41.7 ▪ Ethics

The activity of redistricting was intended to give people a fair representation. In its degenerate form of gerrymandering this concept of fairness is violated because the explicit goal is to give the minority a majority of votes. Explore ways that this unfairness can be undone.

In your explorations above, the only characteristic of a voter was their preference for party A or B. However, in practice voters can be considered part of communities. The Voting Rights Act is concerned about "minority vote dilution." Can you show examples that a color-blind districting would affect some communities negatively?

Chapter 42

Amazon delivery truck scheduling

This chapter contains a sequence of exercises that builds up to a simulation of delivery truck scheduling.

42.1 ▪ Problem statement

Scheduling the route of a delivery truck is a well-studied problem. For instance, minimizing the total distance that the truck has to travel corresponds to the *Traveling Salesman Problem (TSP)*. However, in the case of *Amazon delivery truck* scheduling the problem has some new aspects:

- A customer is promised a window of days when delivery can take place. Thus, the truck can split the list of places into sublists, with a shorter total distance than going through the list in one sweep.
- Except that *Amazon Prime* customers need their deliveries guaranteed the next day.

42.2 ▪ Coding up the basics

Before we try finding the best route, let's put the basics in place to have any sort of route at all.

42.2.1 ▪ Address list

You probably need a class `Address` that describes the location of a house where a delivery has to be made.

- For simplicity, let give a house (i, j) coordinates.
- We probably need a `distance` function between two addresses. We can either assume that we can travel in a straight line between two houses, or that the city is built on a grid, and you can apply the so-called *Manhattan distance*.
- The address may also require a field recording the last possible delivery date.

Exercise 42.1. Code a class `Address` with the above functionality, and test it:

Code:

```
// amazon/route.cpp
    Address one(1.,1.),
      two(2.,2.);
    cerr << "Distance: "
         << one.distance(two)
         << '\n';
```

Output:

```
Distance: 1.41421
```

Next we need a class `AddressList` that contains a list of addresses.

Exercise 42.2. Implement a class `AddressList`; it probably needs the following methods:

- `add_address` for constructing the list;
- `length` to give the distance one has to travel to visit all addresses in order;
- `index_closest_to` that gives you the address on the list closest to another address, presumably not on the list.

You have options here:

- Do you let your `AddressList` actually contain a `vector<Address>` or do you let it inherit from that container? See section 14.2.
- Another approach is to use a linked list. This has certain advantages; see section 42.6.

Write your code sufficiently abstract that you can accommodate these options.

42.2.2 ▪ Add a depot

Next, we model the fact that the route needs to start and end at the depot, which we put arbitrarily at coordinates $(0, 0)$. We could construct an `AddressList` that has the depot as first and last element, but that may run into problems:

- If we reorder the list to minimize the driving distance, the first and last elements may not stay in place.
- We may want elements of a list to be unique: having an address twice means two deliveries at the same address, so the `add_address` method would check that an address is not already in the list.

We can solve this by making a class `Route`, which inherits from `AddressList`, but the methods of which leave the first and last elements of the list in place.

42.2.3 ▪ Greedy construction of a route

Next we need to construct a route. Rather than solving the full Traveling Salesman Problem (TSP), we start by employing a *greedy search* strategy:

> Given a point, find the next point by some local optimality test, such as shortest distance. Never look back to revisit the route you have constructed so far.

Such a strategy is likely to give an improvement, but most likely will not give the optimal route.

Let's write a method

```
Route::Route greedy_route();
```

that constructs a new address list, containing the same addresses, but arranged to give a shorter length to travel.

Exercise 42.3. Write the `greedy_route` method for the `AddressList` class.

1. Assume that the route starts at the depot, which is located at $(0,0)$. Then incrementally construct a new list by
2. maintaining an `Address` variable `we_are_here` of the current location;
3. repeatedly finding the address closest to `we_are_here`.

Extend this to a method for the `Route` class by working on the subvector that does not contain the final element.

Test it on this example:

Code:

```
// amazon/route.cpp
Route deliveries;
deliveries.add_address( Address(0,5) );
deliveries.add_address( Address(5,0) );
deliveries.add_address( Address(5,5) );
cerr << "Travel in order: "
     << deliveries.length() << '\n';
assert( deliveries.size()==5 );
auto route = deliveries.greedy_route();
assert( route.size()==5 );
auto len = route.length();
cerr << "Square route:\n "
     << route.as_string()
     << "\n has length " << len << '\n';
```

Output:

```
Travel in order: 24.1421
Square route:  (0,0) (0,5) (5,5)
     ↪(5,0) (0,0)
 has length 20
```

Reorganizing a list can be done in a number of ways:

- First of all, you can try to make the changes in place. This runs into the objection that maybe you want to save the original list; also, while swapping two elements can be done with the `insert` and `erase` methods, more complicated operations are tricky.
- Alternatively, you can incrementally construct a new list. Now the main problem is to keep track of which elements of the original have been processed. You could do this by giving each address a boolean field `done`, but you could also make a copy of the input list, and remove the elements that have been processed. For this, study the `erase` method for `vector` objects.

42.3 ▪ Optimizing the route

The above suggestion of each time finding the closest address is known as a *greedy search* strategy. It does not give you the optimal solution of the TSP. Finding the optimal solution of the TSP is hard to program—you could do it recursively—and takes a lot of time as the number of addresses grows. In fact, the TSP is probably the most famous of the class of *NP-hard* problems, which are generally believed to have a running time that grows faster than polynomial in the problem size.

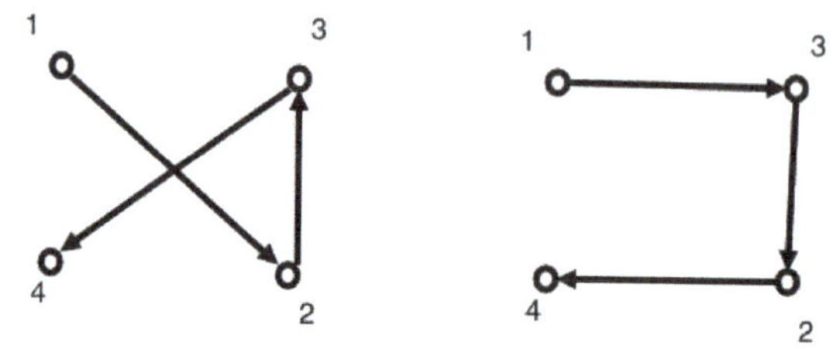

Figure 42.1. *Illustration of the "Opt2" idea of reversing part of a path*

However, you can approximate the solution heuristically. One method, the Kernighan–Lin algorithm [49], is based on the *Opt2* idea: if you have a path that "crosses itself," you can make it shorter by reversing part of it. Figure 42.1 shows that the path 1 – 2 – 3 – 4 can be made shorter by reversing part of it, giving 1 – 3 – 2 – 4. Since recognizing where a path crosses itself can be hard, or even impossible for graphs that don't have Cartesian coordinates associated, we adopt a scheme where we try all possible reversals:

```
for all nodes m<n on the path [1..N]:
  make a new route from
    [1..m-1] + [m--n].reversed + [n+1..N]
  if the new route is shorter, keep it
```

Exercise 42.4. Code the Opt2 heuristic: write a method to reverse part of the route, and write the loop that tries this with multiple starting and ending points. Try it out on some simple test cases to convince you that your code works as intended.

Let's explore issues of complexity. (For an introduction to complexity calculations, see the HPC book [23, section 20].) The TSP is one of a class of *NP complete* problems, which very informally means that there is no better solution than trying out all possibilities.

Exercise 42.5. What is the runtime complexity of the heuristic solution using Opt2? What would the runtime complexity be of finding the best solution by considering all possibilities? Make a very rough estimation of runtimes of the two strategies on some problem sizes: $N = 10, 100, 1000, \ldots$.

Exercise 42.6. (Optional) Reversing sublists is an important operation on your data structure. How many operations does that take? Explore implementing your `AddressList` not as a `vector` but as a `std::list`: a linked list. What is the complexity of reversing a sublist now? Do timing measurements bear this out?

Exercise 42.7. Earlier you had programmed the greedy heuristic. Compare the improvement you get from the Opt2 heuristic, starting both with the given list of addresses, and with a greedy traversal of it.

For realism, how many addresses do you put on your route? How many deliveries would a delivery driver make on a typical day?

42.4 ▪ Multiple trucks

If we introduce multiple delivery trucks, we get the "Multiple Traveling Salesman Problem" [6]. With this we can module both the cases of multiple trucks being out on delivery on the same day, or one truck spreading deliveries over multiple days. For now we don't distinguish between the two.

The first question is how to divide up the addresses:

1. We could split the list in two, using some geometric test. This is a good model for the case where multiple trucks are out on the same day. However, if we use this as a model for the same truck being out on multiple days, we are missing the fact that new addresses can be added on the first day, messing up the neatly separated routes.

2. Thus it may in fact be reasonable to assume that all trucks get an essentially random list of addresses.

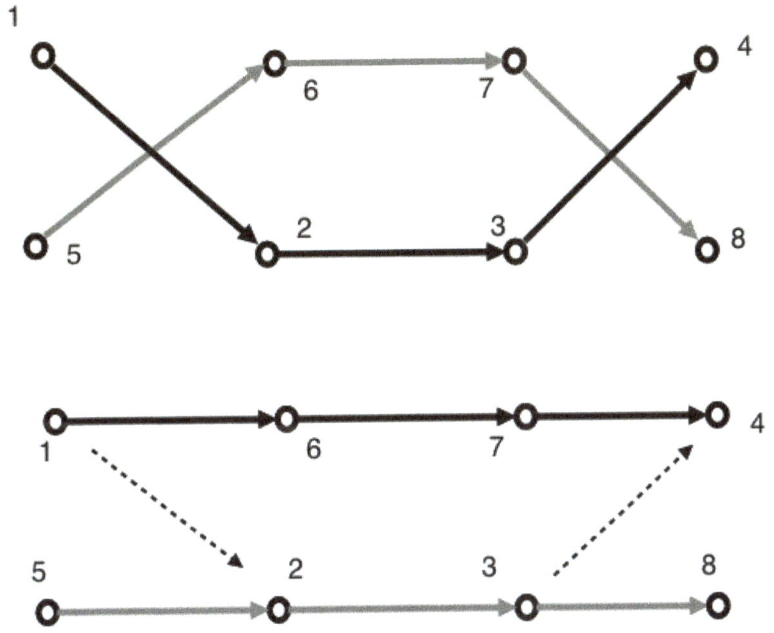

Figure 42.2. *Extending the 'Opt2' idea to multiple paths*

Can we extend the Opt2 heuristic to the case of multiple paths? For inspiration take a look at Figure 42.2: instead of modifying one path, we could switch bits out between one path and another. When you write the code, take into account that the other path may be running backwards! This means that based on split points in the first and second paths you now have four resulting modified paths to consider.

Exercise 42.8. Write a function that optimizes two paths simultaneously using the multipath version of the Opt2 heuristic. For a test case, see Figure 42.3.

You have quite a bit of freedom here:

- the start points of the two segments should be chosen independently;

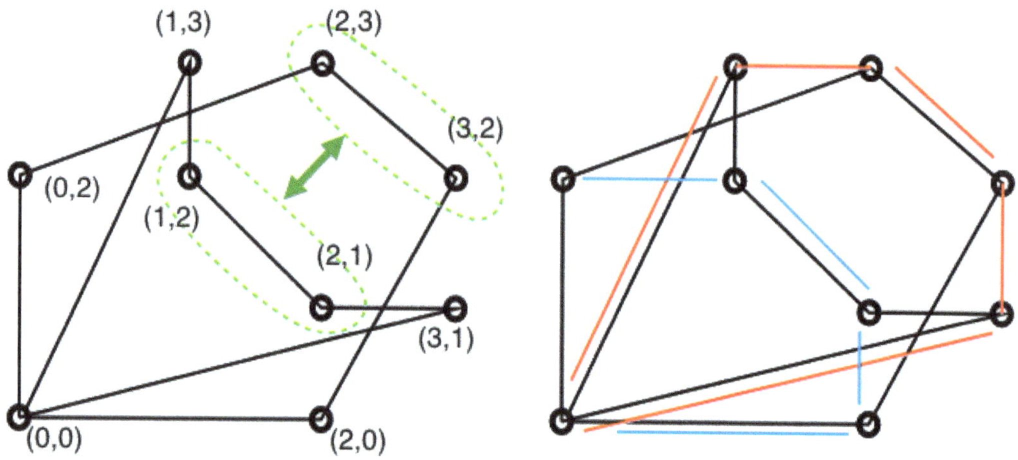

Figure 42.3. *Multiple paths test case*

- the lengths can be chosen independently, but need not be; and finally
- each segment can be reversed.

More flexibility also means a longer runtime of your program. Does it pay off? Do some tests and report results.

Based on the above description there will be a lot of code duplication. Make sure to introduce functions and methods for various operations.

42.5 ▪ Amazon Prime

In section 42.4 you made the assumption that it doesn't matter on what day a package is delivered. This changes with *Amazon Prime*, where a package has to be delivered guaranteed on the next day.

Exercise 42.9. Explore a scenario where there are two trucks, and each has a number of addresses that cannot be exchanged with the other route. How much longer is the total distance? Experiment with the ratio of Prime to non-Prime addresses.

42.6 ▪ Dynamicism

So far we have assumed that the list of addresses to be delivered to is given. This is of course not true: new deliveries will need to be scheduled continuously.

Exercise 42.10. Implement a scenario where every day a random number of new deliveries is added to the list. Explore strategies and design choices.

42.7 ▪ Parallelism

In this project you implemented two algorithms: the greedy strategy, and the Opt2 heuristic. The latter is the easier to parallelize: the Opt2 code explores many possibilities of where to exchange route segments. Implement this with the OpenMP tasking mechanism; see section 20.8.2.

The greedy strategy is harder to parallelize. Can you come up with a strategy that is parallel, but may not give quite the same result?

42.8 ▪ Ethics

People sometimes criticize Amazon's labor policies, including those regarding its drivers. Can you make any observations from your simulations in this respect?

Chapter 43

High performance linear algebra

Linear algebra is fundamental to much of computational science. Applications involving PDEs come down to solving large systems of linear equation; solid state physics involves large eigenvalue systems. But even outside of engineering applications linear algebra is important: the major computational part of deep learning networks involves matrix-matrix multiplications.

Linear algebra operations such as the matrix-matrix product are easy to code in a naive way. However, this does not lead to high performance. In these exercises you will explore the basics of a strategy for high performance.

Remark. *The algorithm you will develop in this project is an example of* cache-oblivious programming; *see section 33.4. While this gives considerably higher performance than the naive algorithm, for the highest performance a more sophisticated approach is needed, which involves considerable tuning, as well as a little* assembly coding *[30].*

43.1 ▪ Mathematical preliminaries

The matrix-matrix product $C \leftarrow A \cdot B$ is defined as

$$\forall_{ij}\colon c_{ij} \leftarrow \sum_k a_{ik} b_{kj}.$$

Straightforward code for this would be

```
for (i=0; i<a.m; i++)
  for (j=0; j<b.n; j++)
    s = 0;
    for (k=0; k<a.n; k++)
      s += a[i,k] * b[k,j];
    c[i,j] = s;
```

However, this is not the only way to code this operation. The loops can be permuted, giving a total of six implementations.

Exercise 43.1. Code one of the permuted algorithms and test its correctness. If the reference algorithm above can be said to be "inner-product based," how would you describe your variant?

Yet another implementation is based on a block partitioning. Let A, B, C be split on 2×2 block form:

$$A = \begin{pmatrix} A_{11} & A_{12} \\ A_{21} & A_{22} \end{pmatrix}, \qquad B = \begin{pmatrix} B_{11} & B_{12} \\ B_{21} & B_{22} \end{pmatrix}, \qquad C = \begin{pmatrix} C_{11} & C_{12} \\ C_{21} & C_{22} \end{pmatrix}.$$

Then

$$\begin{aligned} C_{11} &= A_{11}B_{11} + A_{12}B_{21}, \\ C_{12} &= A_{11}B_{12} + A_{12}B_{22}, \\ C_{21} &= A_{21}B_{11} + A_{22}B_{21}, \\ C_{22} &= A_{21}B_{12} + A_{22}B_{22}. \end{aligned} \tag{43.1}$$

Convince yourself that this actually computes the same product $C = A \cdot B$. For more on block algorithms, see the HPC book [23, section 5.3.6].

Exercise 43.2. Write a matrix class with a multiplication routine:

```
Matrix Matrix::MatMult( Matrix other );
```

First implement a traditional matrix-matrix multiplication, then make it recursive. For the recursive algorithm you need to implement submatrix handling: you need to extract submatrices, and write a submatrix back into the surrounding matrix.

Note: this copying is not efficient. Later you will see a better strategy.

43.2 ▪ Matrix storage

The simplest way to store an $M \times N$ matrix is as an array of length MN. Inside this array we can decide to store the rows end-to-end, or the columns. While this decision is obviously of practical importance for a library, from a point of performance it makes no difference.

Remark. *Historically, linear algebra software such as the BLAS has used columnwise storage, meaning that the location of an element (i, j) is computed as $i + j \cdot M$ (we will use zero-based indexing throughout this project, both for code and mathematical expressions). The reason for this stems from the origins of the BLAS in the Fortran language, which uses column-major ordering of array elements. On the other hand, C-style arrays (such as `x[5][6]`) in the C/C++ languages have row-major ordering, where element (i, j) is stored in location $j + i \cdot N$.*

Above, you saw the idea of block algorithms, which requires taking submatrices. For efficiency, we don't want to copy elements into a new array, so we want the submatrix to correspond to a subarray.

Now we have a problem: only a submatrix that consists of a sequence of columns is contiguous. The formula $i + j \cdot M$ for location of element (i, j) is no longer correct if the matrix is a subblock of a larger matrix.

For this reason, linear algebra software describes a submatrix by three parameters M, N, LDA, where "LDA" stands for "leading dimension of A" (see BLAS [40] and Lapack [2]). This is illustrated in Figure 43.1.

Exercise 43.3. In terms of M, N, LDA, what is the location of the (i, j) element?

Implementationwise we also have a problem. If we use `std::vector` for storage, it is not possible to take subarrays, since C++ insists that a vector has its own storage. The solution is to use `span`; see section 4.1.

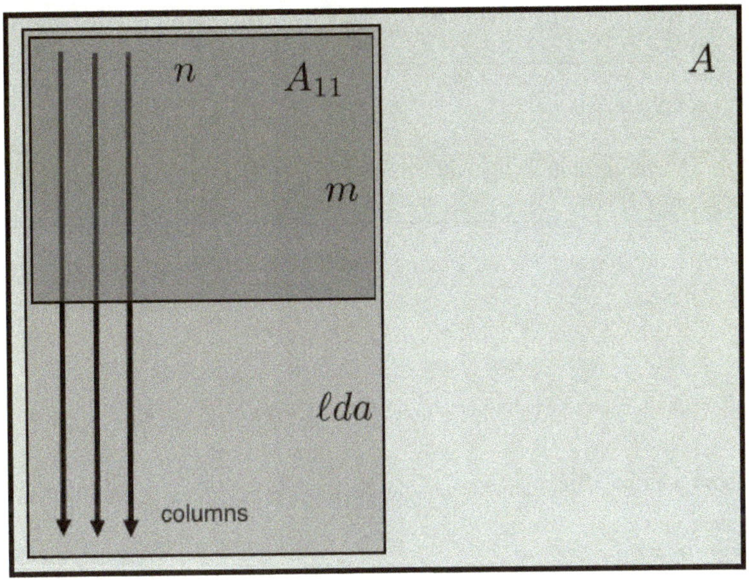

Figure 43.1. *Submatrix out of a matrix, with M, N, LDA of the submatrix indicated*

Now we have different types of matrices: top level matrices that store a `vector<double>`, and submatrices that store a `span<double>`. It could be done using `std::variant` (section 11.3), but let's not.

Instead, let's adopt the following idiom, where we create a vector at the top level, and then create matrices from its memory:

```
// gemm/lapack_alloc.cpp
// example values for M,LDA,N
M = 2; LDA = M+2; N = 3;
// create a vector to contain the data
vector<double> one_data(LDA*N,1.);
// create a matrix using the vector data
Matrix one(M,LDA,N,one_data.data());
```

Now all types of matrices are created from a `double*`. (If you have not previously programmed in C, you need to get used to the `double*` mechanism. See section 4.3.)

Exercise 43.4. Start implementing the `Matrix` class with a constructor

```
Matrix::Matrix(int m,int lda,int n,double *data)
```

and private data members:

```
// gemm/lapack_alloc.cpp
private:
  int m,n,lda;
  span<double> data;
```

Write a method

```
double& Matrix::at(int i,int j);
```

that you can use as a safe way of accessing elements.

Exercise 43.5. Alternatively, do the above exercise using the C++23 mdspan and C++26 submdspan constructs.

Let's start with simple operations.

Exercise 43.6. Write a method for adding matrices. Test it on matrices that have the same M, N, but different LDA.

Use of the at method is great for debugging, but it is not efficient. Use the preprocessor to introduce alternatives,

```
#ifdef DEBUG
  c.at(i,j) += a.at(i,k) * b.at(k,j)
#else
  cdata[ /* expression with i,j */ ] += adata[ ... ] * bdata[ ... ]
#endif
```

where you access the data directly with

```
// gemm/lapack_alloc.cpp
auto get_double_data() {
  double *adata;
  adata = data.data();
  return adata;
};
```

Exercise 43.7. Implement this. Use the #define preprocessor directive for the optimized indexing expression. (See section 36.3.2.1.)

43.2.1 ▪ Submatrices

Next we need to support constructing actual submatrices. Since we will mostly aim for decomposition in 2×2 block form, it is enough to write four methods. This can actually be done two different ways:

```
Matrix Left(int j);
Matrix Right(int j);
Matrix Top(int i);
Matrix Bot(int i);
```

```
Matrix TopLeft(int i,int j);
Matrix TopRight(int i,int j);
Matrix BotLeft(int i,int j);
Matrix BotRight(int i,int j);
```

where, for instance, `Left(5)` gives the columns with $j < 5$, or `BotRight(5,6)` gives the bottom right block starting at $5, 6$.

Exercise 43.8. Implement these methods and test them. Are you using span or mdspan / submdspan?

43.3 ▪ Multiplication

You can now write a first multiplication routine, for instance, with a prototype

```
void Matrix::MatMult( Matrix& other,Matrix& out );
```

Alternatively, you could write

```
Matrix Matrix::MatMult( Matrix& other );
```

but we want to keep the amount of creation/destruction of objects to a minimum.

43.3.1 ▪ One level of blocking

Next, write

```
void Matrix::BlockedMatMult( Matrix& other,Matrix& out );
```

which uses the 2×2 form above.

43.3.2 ▪ Recursive blocking

The final step is to make the blocking recursive.

Exercise 43.9.

- Write a method

```
void RecursiveMatMult( Matrix& other,Matrix& out );
```

which executes the 2×2 block product, using again `RecursiveMatMult` for the blocks.

- When the block is small enough, use the regular `MatMult` product.

43.4 ▪ Performance issues

If you experiment a little with the cutoff between the regular and recursive matrix-matrix product, you see that you can get a good factor of performance improvement. Why is this?

The matrix-matrix product is a basic operation in scientific computations, and much effort has been put into optimizing it. One interesting fact is that it is just about the most optimizable operation under the sun. The reason for this is, in a nutshell, that it involves $O(N^3)$ operations on $O(N^2)$ data. This means that, in principle, each element fetched will be used multiple times, thereby overcoming the *memory bottleneck*.

Exercise 43.10. Make sure that your code has timers; see Chapter 8. Can you see a performance difference between the naive code and your optimized code? What is the peak speed of your processor, and how close are you getting to it? Is this number dependent on the size of your matrix?

To understand performance issues relating to hardware, you need to do some reading; see sections 31.2 and 33.1.

Exercise 43.11. Argue that the naive matrix-matrix product implementation is unlikely actually to reuse data.

Explain why the recursive strategy does lead to data reuse.

Above, you set a cutoff point for when to switch from the recursive to the regular product.

Exercise 43.12. Argue that continuing to recurse will not have much benefit once the product is contained in the cache. What are the cache sizes of your processor?

Do experiments with various cutoff points. Can you relate this to the cache sizes?

43.5 ▪ Parallelism

The four clauses of equation (43.1) target independent areas in the C matrix, so they could be executed in parallel on any processor that has at least four cores.

Use the "task" mechanism of the OpenMP library (Chapter 20) to parallelize the `BlockedMatMult`.

43.6 ▪ Bonus: Optimal performance

The final question is: how close are you getting to the best possible speed? Unfortunately you are still a way off. You can explore that as follows.

Your computer is likely to have an optimized implementation, accessible through

```
#include <cblas.h>

cblas_dgemm
  ( CblasColMajor, CblasNoTrans, CblasNoTrans,
    m,other.n,n, alpha,adata,lda,
    bdata,other.lda,
    beta,cdata,out.lda);
```

which computes $C \leftarrow \alpha A \cdot B + \beta C$.

Exercise 43.13. Use another CPP conditional to implement `MatMult` through a call to `cblas_dgemm`. What performance do you now get?

You see that your recursive implementation is faster than the naive one, but not nearly as fast as the CBlas one. This is because

- the CBlas implementation is probably based on an entirely different strategy [30], and
- it probably involves a certain amount of assembly coding.

Chapter 44
The great garbage patch

This chapter contains a sequence of exercises that builds up to a *cellular automaton* simulation of turtles in the ocean, garbage that is deadly to them, and ships that clean it up. To read more about this, see `https://theoceancleanup.com/`.

Thanks to Ernesto Lima of TACC for the idea and initial code of this exercise.

44.1 ▪ Problem and model solution

There is lots of plastic floating around in the ocean, and that is harmful to fish and turtles and cetaceans. Here you get to model the interaction between

- plastic, randomly located;
- turtles that swim about; they breed slowly, and they die from ingesting plastic;
- ships that sweep the ocean to remove plastic debris.

The simulation method we use is that of a *cellular automaton*:

- we have a grid of cells;
- each cell has a "state" associated with it, namely, it can contain a ship, a turtle, or plastic, or be empty; and
- on each next time step, the state of a cell is a simple function of the states of that cell and its immediate neighbors.

The purpose of this exercise is to simulate a number of time steps and explore the interaction between parameters: what amount of garbage will cause turtles to die out? how many ships are enough to protect the turtles?

44.2 ▪ Program design

The basic idea is to have an `ocean` object that is populated with turtles, trash, and ships. Your simulation will let the ocean undergo a number of time steps:

```
for (int t=0; t<time_steps; t++)
  ocean.update();
```

Ultimately your purpose is to investigate the development of the turtle population: is it stable? does it die out?

While you can make a "hackish" solution to this problem, partly you will be judged on your use of modern/clean C++ programming techniques. A number of suggestions are made below.

44.2.1 ▪ Grid update

Here is a point to be aware of. Can you see what's wrong with doing an update entirely in place as follows?

```
for ( i )
  for ( j )
    cell(i,j) = f( cell(i,j), .... other cells ... );
```

44.3 ▪ Testing

It can be complicated to test this program for correctness. The best you can do is to try out a number of scenarios. For that it's best to make your program input flexible: use the `cxxopts` package [13], and drive your program from a shell script.

Here is a list of things you can test:

1. Start with only a number of ships; after 1000 time steps check that you still have the same number.
2. Likewise with turtles; if they don't breed and don't die, check that their number stays constant.
3. With only ships and trash, does it all get swept?
4. With only turtles and trash, do they all die off?

It is harder to test that your turtles and ships don't "teleport" around, but only move to contiguous cells. For that, use visual inspection.

44.3.1 ▪ Animated graphics

The output of this program is a prime candidate for visualization. In fact, some tests ("make sure that turtles don't teleport") are hard to do other than by looking at the output. Start by making an ASCII rendering of the ocean grid, as in Figure 44.1. Then animate your drawing as explained in section 5.4.

In each time step you would

1. send the cursor to the home position, by this magic output:

   ```
   // turtles/pacific.cpp
   #include <cstdio>
       /* ... */
       // ESC [ i ; j H
       printf( "%c[0;0H",(char)27);
   ```

2. display your grid as in Figure 44.1;
3. sleep for a fraction of a second.

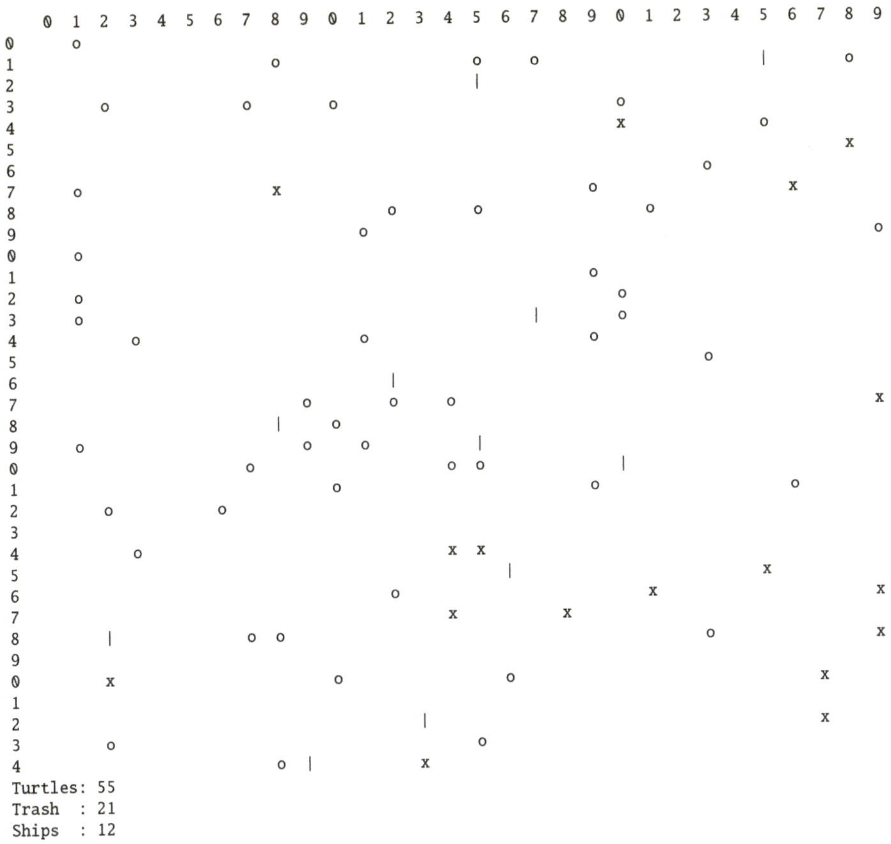

Figure 44.1. *ASCII art printout of a time step*

44.4 ▪ Modern programming techniques

44.4.1 ▪ Object-oriented programming

While there is only one ocean in your simulation, you should still make an `ocean` class, rather than having a global array object. All functions are then methods of the single object you create of that class.

44.4.2 ▪ Data structure

We lose very little generality by ignoring the depth of the ocean and the shape of coastlines, and model the ocean as a 2D grid.

If you write an indexing function `cell(i,j)` you can make your code largely independent of the actual data structure chosen. Argue why `vector<vector<int>>` is not the best storage:

1. What do you use instead?
2. When you have a working code, can you show by timing that your choice is indeed superior?

44.4.3 ▪ Cell types

Having "magic numbers" in your code ($0 =$ empty, $1 =$ turtle, etc.) is not elegant. Make an `enum` or `enum class` (see section 2.5) so that you have names for what's in your cells:

```
// turtles/pacific.cpp
cell(i,j) = occupy::turtle;
```

If you want to print out your ocean, it might be nice if you can directly format your cells:

```
// turtles/pacific.cpp
for (int i=0; i<iSize; ++i) {
  print( "{} ",i%10 );
  for (int j=0; j<jSize; ++j) {
    print( "{:>3}",cell(i,j) );
  }
  print("\n");
}
```

44.4.4 ▪ Ranging over the ocean

It is easy enough to write a loop as

```
for (int i=0; i<iSize; i++)
  for (int j=0; j<jSize; j++)
    ... cell(i,j) ...
```

However, it may not be a good idea to always sweep over your domain so orderly. Can you implement the following?

```
for ( auto [i,j] : permuted_indices() ) {
    ... cell(i,j) ...
```

See section 11.5 about *structured binding*.

Likewise, if you need to count how many pieces of trash there are around a turtle, can you get the following code to work?

```
// turtles/pacific.cpp
int count_around( int ic,int jc,occupy typ ) const {
  int count=0;
  for ( auto [i,j] : neighbors(ic,jc) ) {
    if (cell(i,j) == typ)
      ++count;
  }
  return count;
};
```

44.4.5 ▪ Random numbers

For the random movement of ships and turtles you need a random number generator. Do not use the old C generator, but the new `random` one; see Chapter 9.

Try to find a solution so that you use exactly one generator for all places where you need random numbers. Hint: make the generator `static` in your class.

44.5 ▪ Parallelism

The main computation in your code is the update of the ocean. Argue that this is a fully parallel operation. Use OpenMP to make the loop indeed parallel, and test the speedup you get.

Can you also express this as a range algorithm? Again test the speedup you get. On high core counts you may need to figure out the equivalent of `OMP_PROC_BIND=true`. This depends on how your compiler has implemented the parallel range algorithm.

44.6 ▪ Explorations

Instead of having the ships move randomly, can you give them a preferential direction to the closest garbage patch? Does this improve the health of the turtle population?

Can you account for the relative size of ships and turtles by having a ship occupy a 2×2 block in your grid?

So far you have let trash stay in place. What if there are ocean currents? Can you make the trash "sticky" so that trash particles start moving as a patch if they touch?

Turtles eat sardines. (No they don't.) What happens to the sardine population if turtles die out? Can you come up with parameter values that correspond to a stable ecology or a destabilized one?

44.6.1 ▪ Code efficiency

Investigate whether your implementation of the `enum` in section 44.4.3 has any effect on timing. Parse the fine print of section 2.5.

You may remark that ranging over a largely empty ocean can be pretty inefficient. You could contemplate keeping an "active list" of where the turtles, etc., are located, and only looping over that. How would you implement that? Do you expect to see a difference in timing? Do you actually?

How is runtime affected by choosing a vector-of-vectors implementation for the ocean? (See section 44.4.2.)

Chapter 45

Graph algorithms

In this project you will explore some common graph algorithms and their various possible implementations. The main theme here will be that the common textbook exposition of algorithms is not necessarily the best way to phrase them computationally.

As background knowledge for this project, you are encouraged to read the HPC book [23, Chapter 10]; for an elementary tutorial on graphs, see [23, Chapter 25].

45.1 ▪ Traditional algorithms

We first implement the "textbook" formulations of two *single source shortest path (SSSP)* algorithms: on unweighted and then on weighted graphs. In the next section we will then consider formulations that are in terms of linear algebra.

In order to develop the implementations, we start with some necessary preliminaries.

45.1.1 ▪ Code preliminaries

45.1.1.1 ▪ Adjacency graph

We need a class `Dag` for a directed acyclic graph (DAG):

```
// tree/dijkstra1.cpp
class Dag {
private:
  vector<vector<int>> dag;
public:
  // Make Dag of 'n' nodes, no edges for now.
  Dag( int n )
    : dag( vector<vector<int>>(n) ) {};
```

It's probably a good idea to have a function

```
// tree/dijkstra1.cpp
const auto& neighbors( int i ) const { return dag.at(i); };
```

that, given a node, returns a list of the neighbors of that node.

Exercise 45.1. Finish the `Dag` class. In particular, add a method to generate example graphs. Write a method that gives a textual rendering of the graph.

45.1.1.2 ▪ Node sets

The classic formulation of SSSP algorithms, such as the *Dijkstra shortest path algorithm* (see the HPC book [23, section 10.1.3]) uses sets of nodes that are gradually built up or depleted.

You could implement that as a vector,

```
vector< int > set_of_nodes(nnodes);
for ( int inode=0; inode<nnodes; inode++)
  // mark inode as distance unknown:
  set_of_nodes.at(inode) = inf;
```

where you use some convention, such as negative distance, to indicate that a node has been removed from the set.

However, C++ has an actual `set` container with methods for adding an element, finding it, and removing it; see section 4.4.2. This makes for a more direct expression of our algorithms. In our case, we'd need a set of int/int or int/float pairs for the node number and edge weight, depending on the graph algorithm. (It is also possible to use a `map`, using an `int` as lookup key, and `int` or `float` as values.)

For the unweighted graph we only need a set of finished nodes, and we insert node 0 as our starting point:

```
// tree/queuelevel.cpp
using node_info = std::pair<unsigned,unsigned>;
std::set< node_info > distances;
distances.insert( {0,0} );
```

For Dijkstra's algorithm we need both a set of finished nodes and nodes that we are still working on. We again set the starting node, and we set the distance for all unprocessed nodes to infinity:

```
// tree/queuedijkstra.cpp
const unsigned inf = std::numeric_limits<unsigned>::max();
using node_info = std::pair<unsigned,unsigned>;
std::set< node_info > distances,to_be_done;

to_be_done.insert( {0,0} );
for (unsigned n=1; n<graph_size; ++n)
  to_be_done.insert( {n,inf} );
```

(Why do we need that second set here, while it was not necessary for the unweighted graph case?)

Exercise 45.2. Write a code fragment that tests if a node is in the `distances` set.

- You can of course write a loop for this. In that case know that iterating over a set gives you the key/value pairs. Use *structured bindings*; see section 11.5.
- But it's better to use an "algorithm," in the technical sense of "algorithms built into the standard library." In this case, `find`.
- … except that with `find` you have to search for an exact key/value pair, and here you want to search: "is this node in the `distances` set with whatever value." Use the `find_if` algorithm; see section 4.4.2.

45.1.2 ▪ Level set algorithm

We start with a simple algorithm: the SSSP algorithm in an unweighted graph; see the HPC book [23, section 10.1.1] for details. Equivalently, we find level sets in the graph.

For unweighted graphs, the distance algorithm is fairly simple. Inductively:

- assume that we have a set of nodes reachable in at most n steps;
- then their neighbors (that are not yet in this set) can be reached in $n + 1$ steps.

The algorithm outline is

```
// tree/queuelevel.cpp
for (;;) {
  if (distances.size()==graph_size) break;
  /*
  * Loop over all nodes that are already done
  */
  for ( auto [node,level] : distances ) {
    /*
   * set neighbors of the node to have distance 'level + 1'
   */
    const auto& nbors = graph.neighbors(node);
    for ( auto n : nbors ) {
      /*
     * See if 'n' has a known distance,
     * if not, add to 'distances' with level+1
     */
  /* ... */
        {
          cout << "node " << n << " level " << level+1 << '\n';
          distances.insert( {n,level+1} );
        }
```

Exercise 45.3. Finish the program that computes the single source shortest path (SSSP) algorithm and test it.

This code has an obvious inefficiency: for each level we iterate through all finished nodes, even if all their neighbors may already have been processed.

Exercise 45.4. Maintain a set of "current level" nodes, and only investigate these to find the next level. Time the two variants on some large graphs.

45.1.3 ▪ Dijkstra's algorithm

In Dijkstra's algorithm we maintain both a set of nodes for which the shortest distance has been found, and one for which we are still determining the shortest distance. Note: a tentative shortest distance for a node may be updated several times, since there may be multiple paths to that node. The "shortest" path in terms of weights may not be the shortest in number of edges traversed!

The main loop now looks something like

```
// tree/queuedijkstra.cpp
for (;;) {
  if (to_be_done.size()==0) break;
  /*
  * Find the node with least distance
  */
```

```
  /* ... */
  cout << "min: " << nclose << " @ " << dclose << '\n';
  /*
 * Move that node to done,
 */
  to_be_done.erase(closest_node);
  distances.insert( *closest_node );
  /*
 * set neighbors of nclose to have that distance + 1
 */
  const auto& nbors = graph.neighbors(nclose);
  for ( auto n : nbors ) {
    // find 'n' in distances
  /* ... */
      {
        /*
     * if 'n' does not have known distance,
     * find where it occurs in 'to_be_done' and update
     */
  /* ... */
        to_be_done.erase( cfind );
        to_be_done.insert( {n,dclose+1} );
  /* ... */
}
```

(Note that we erase a record in the `to_be_done` set, and then reinsert the same key with a new value. We could have done a simple update if we had used a `map` instead of a `set`.)

The various places where you find nodes in the finished/unfinished sets are up to you to implement. You can use simple loops, or use `find_if` to find the elements matching the node numbers.

Exercise 45.5. Fill in the details of the above outline to realize Dijkstra's algorithm.

45.2 ▪ Linear algebra formulation

In this part of the project you will explore how much you make graph algorithms look like linear algebra.

45.2.1 ▪ Code preliminaries

45.2.1.1 ▪ Data structures

You need a matrix and a vector. The vector is easy:

```
// tree/graphmvpdijkstra.cpp
class Vector {
private:
  vector<vectorvalue> values;
public:
  Vector( int n )
    : values( n,infinite ) {};
```

For the matrix, use initially a dense matrix:

```
// tree/graphmvpdijkstra.cpp
class AdjacencyMatrix {
private:
  vector<vector<matrixvalue>> adjacency;
```

```
public:
  AdjacencyMatrix(int n)
    : adjacency( vector<vector<matrixvalue>>
                 ( n,vector<matrixvalue>(n,empty) ) ) {
  };
```

However, later we will optimize that.

Remark. *In general it's not a good idea to store a matrix as a vector-of-vectors (see section 14.1.1), but in this case we need to be able to return a matrix row, so it is convenient. Optionally you can explore the use of* `mdspan`*; see section 4.1.2.*

45.2.1.2 ▪ Matrix vector multiply

Let's write a routine

```
Vector AdjacencyMatrix::leftmultiply( const Vector& left );
```

This is the simplest solution, but not necessarily the most efficient one, as it creates a new vector object for each matrix-vector multiply.

As explained in the theory background (HPC book [23, section 10.2]) graph algorithms can be formulated as matrix-vector multiplications with unusual add/multiply operations. Thus, the core of the multiplication routine could look like

// tree/graphmvp.cpp
```
  for ( int row=0; row<n; ++row ) {
    for ( int col=0; col<n; ++col) {
      result[col] = add( result[col], mult( left[row],adjacency[row][col] ) );
    }
  }
```

45.2.2 ▪ Unweighted graphs

Exercise 45.6. Implement the `add/mult` routines to make the SSSP algorithm on unweighted graphs work.

45.2.3 ▪ Dijkstra's algorithm

As an example, consider the following adjacency matrix:

```
.  1 . .  5
. .  1 . .
. . .  1 .
. . . .  1
 1 . . . .
```

The shortest distance $0 \to 4$ is 4, but in the first step a larger distance of 5 is discovered. Your algorithm should show an output similar to this for the successive updates to the known shortest distances:

```
Input :  0 . . . .
step 0:  0 1 . . 5
step 1:  0 1 2 . 5
step 2:  0 1 2 3 5
step 3:  0 1 2 3 4
```

Exercise 45.7. Implement new versions of the `add/mult` routines to make the matrix-vector multiplication correspond to Dijkstra's algorithm for Single Source Shortest Path (SSSP) on weighted graphs.

45.2.4 ▪ Sparse matrices

The matrix data structure described above can be made more compact by storing only nonzero elements. Implement this.

45.3 ▪ Parallelism

Explore the OpenMP library (Chapter 20) to parallelize the various algorithms you have developed in this project.

Argue that a CRS sparse matrix representation is easy to parallelize. Realize this with OpenMP and measure speedup.

How hard is it to parallelize the implementation of a graphs as node sets, as you started this project? In this case the level sets are key to parallel processing. However, on any but very large graphs you may not see much speedup.

45.4 ▪ Further explorations

How elegant can you make your code through operator overloading?

Can you code the all-pairs shortest path algorithm?

Can you extend the SSSP algorithm to also generate the actual paths?

45.5 ▪ Tests and reporting

You now have two completely different implementations of some graph algorithms. Generate some large matrices and time the algorithms.

Discuss your findings, paying attention to the amount of work performed and amount of memory needed.

Bibliography

[1] E. Anderson, Z. Bai, C. Bischof, J. Demmel, J. Dongarra, J. Du Croz, A. Greenbaum, S. Hammarling, A. McKenney, S. Ostrouchov, and D. Sorensen. *LAPACK Users' Guide, Second Edition.* SIAM, Philadelphia, PA, 1995. (Cited on p. 158)

[2] E. Anderson, Z. Bai, C. Bischof, J. Demmel, J. Dongarra, J. Du Croz, A. Greenbaum, S. Hammarling, A. McKenney, and D. Sorensen. LAPACK: A portable linear algebra library for high-performance computers. In *Proceedings Supercomputing '90*, pages 2–11. IEEE Computer Society Press, Los Alamitos, California, 1990. (Cited on p. 438)

[3] Roy M. Anderson and Robert M. May. Population biology of infectious diseases: Part I. *Nature*, 280:361–367, 1979. `https://doi.org/10.1038/280361a0`. (Cited on p. 406)

[4] Satish Balay, William D. Gropp, Lois Curfman McInnes, and Barry F. Smith. Efficient management of parallelism in object oriented numerical software libraries. In E. Arge, A. M. Bruaset, and H. P. Langtangen, editors, *Modern Software Tools in Scientific Computing*, pages 163–202. Birkhäuser Press, 1997. (Cited on pp. 63, 158)

[5] Satish Balay, William D. Gropp, Lois Curfman McInnes, and Barry F. Smith. PETSc webpage. `http://www.mcs.anl.gov/petsc`, 2011. (Cited on p. 63)

[6] Tolga Bektas. The multiple traveling salesman problem: An overview of formulations and solution procedures. *Omega*, 34(3):209–219, 2006. (Cited on p. 433)

[7] bfloat16 floating point format. `https://en.wikipedia.org/wiki/Bfloat16_floating-point_format`. (Cited on p. 340)

[8] bfloat16 hardware numerics definition. `https://software.intel.com/sites/default/files/managed/40/8b/bf16-hardware-numerics-definition-white-paper.pdf`. Document Number: 338302-001US. Intel Corporation, 2018. (Cited on p. 340)

[9] Paolo Bientinesi, John A. Gunnels, Margaret E. Myers, Enrique S. Quintana-Ortí, and Robert A. van de Geijn. The science of deriving dense linear algebra algorithms. *ACM Trans. Math. Softw.*, 30(1):1–26, 2005. (Cited on p. 247)

[10] Alfredo Buttari, Victor Eijkhout, Julien Langou, and Salvatore Filippone. Performance optimization and modeling of blocked sparse kernels. *Int. J. High Perf. Comput. Appl.*, 21:467–484, 2007. (Cited on p. 317)

[11] Yaeyoung Choi, Jack J. Dongarra, Roldan Pozo, and David W. Walker. Scalapack: A scalable linear algebra library for distributed memory concurrent computers. In *Proceedings of the Fourth Symposium on the Frontiers of Massively Parallel Computation (Frontiers '92), McLean, Virginia, Oct. 19–21, 1992*, pages 120–127, IEEE, 1992. (Cited on p. 158)

[12] C++ core guidelines. `https://isocpp.github.io/CppCoreGuidelines/CppCoreGuidelines`. (Cited on pp. 20, 33, 34, 43, 110, 133, 234, 236, 242)

[13] cxxopts. `https://github.com/jarro2783/cxxopts`. (Cited on p. 444)

[14] M. J. Daydé and I. S. Duff. Use of level 3 BLAS in LU factorization in a multiprocessing environment on three vector multiprocessors: The ALLIANT FX/80, the CRAY-2, and the IBM 3090 VF. Technical Report RAL-90-083, November 1990. (Cited on p. 158)

[15] Adrien Devresse, Nicolas Cornu, Luc Grosheintz-Laval, Omar Awile, Tom de Geus, Fernando Pereira, Matthias Wolf, and HighFive Contributors. Highfive - header-only C++ HDF5 interface, February 2024. (Cited on p. 290)

[16] Edsger Dijkstra. The humble programmer. *Commun. ACM*, 15(10):859–866. `https://doi.org/10.1145/355604.361591`. (Cited on p. 229)

[17] J. J. Dongarra. The LINPACK benchmark: An explanation. In *Proceedings of the 1st International Conference on SuperComputing*, pages 456–474. Springer-Verlag, Berlin, 1988. (Cited on p. 328)

[18] Jack J. Dongarra, Jeremy Du Croz, Sven Hammarling, and Iain Duff. A set of level 3 basic linear algebra subprograms. *ACM Trans. Math. Softw.*, 16(1):1–17, March 1990. (Cited on p. 158)

[19] Jack J. Dongarra, Jeremy Du Croz, Sven Hammarling, and Richard J. Hanson. An extended set of FORTRAN basic linear algebra subprograms. *ACM Trans. Math. Softw.*, 14(1):1–17, March 1988. (Cited on p. 158)

[20] David Donoho, Mahsa Lotfi, and Batu Ozturkler. The mathematics of mass testing for COVID-19, 2020. `https://www.siam.org/publications/siam-news/articles/the-mathematics-of-mass-testing-for-covid-19`. (Cited on p. 413)

[21] Iain S. Duff, Michael A. Heroux, and Roldan Pozo. An overview of the sparse basic linear algebra subprograms: The new standard from the BLAS technical forum. *ACM Trans. Math. Softw.*, 28(2):239–267, 2002. (Cited on p. 158)

[22] Victor Eijkhout. Parallel programming in MPI and OpenMP. `http://theartofhpc.com/pcse.html`. (Cited on p. 175)

[23] Victor Eijkhout. The science of computing. `http://theartofhpc.com/istc.html`. (Cited on pp. 153, 165, 175, 189, 199, 213, 332, 417, 418, 432, 438, 449, 450, 451, 453)

[24] S. C. Eisenstat and H. F. Walker. Choosing the forcing terms in an inexact Newton method. *SIAM J. Sci. Comput.*, 17:16–32, 1996. (Cited on p. 167)

[25] Executable and linkable format. `https://en.wikipedia.org/wiki/Executable_and_Linkable_Format`. (Cited on p. 356)

[26] K. Gallivan, W. Jalby, and U. Meier. The use of BLAS3 in linear algebra on a parallel processor with a hierarchical memory. *SIAM J. Sci. Stat. Comput.*, 8(6):1079–1084, 1987. (Cited on p. 158)

[27] D. Goldberg. Computer arithmetic. Appendix in [33]. (Cited on p. 345)

[28] David Goldberg. What every computer scientist should know about floating-point arithmetic. *Computing Surveys*, 23(1):5–48, 1991. (Cited on p. 343)

[29] Google Cloud TPUs. `https://cloud.google.com/tpu/`. (Cited on p. 330)

[30] Kazushige Goto and Robert A. van de Geijn. Anatomy of high-performance matrix multiplication. *ACM Trans. Math. Softw.*, 34(3):1–25, 2008. (Cited on pp. 329, 437, 442)

[31] William Gropp, Thomas Sterling, and Ewing Lusk. *Beowulf Cluster Computing with Linux, 2nd Edition.* MIT Press, 2003. (Cited on p. 212)

[32] GSL: Guideline support library. `https://github.com/microsoft/GSL`. (Cited on p. 232)

[33] John L. Hennessy and David A. Patterson. *Computer Architecture. A Quantitative Approach, 3rd Edition.* Morgan Kaufman Publishers, 2002. (Cited on p. 456)

[34] David S. Hollman, Bryce Adelstein Lelbach, H. Carter Edwards, Mark Hoemmen, Daniel Sunderland, and Christian R. Trott. mdspan in c++: A case study in the integration of performance portable features into international language standards. In *2019 IEEE/ACM International Workshop on Performance, Portability and Productivity in HPC (P3HPC)*, pages 60–70. IEEE, 2019. (Cited on p. 37)

[35] IEEE 754-2019 standard for floating-point arithmetic. In *IEEE Std 754-2019 (Revision of IEEE 754-2008)*, pages 1–84. IEEE, 2019. (Cited on p. 338)

[36] Intel ISPC user's guide. `https://ispc.github.io/ispc.html`. (Cited on p. 176)

[37] Intel oneAPI Math Kernel Library. `https://www.intel.com/content/www/us/en/developer/tools/oneapi/onemkl.html`. (Cited on p. 330)

[38] L. V. Kantorovich and G. P. Akilov. *Functional Analysis in Normed Spaces*. Pergamon Press, 1964. (Cited on p. 167)

[39] Kermack-McKendrick Model. https://mathworld.wolfram.com/Kermack-McKendrickModel.html. (Cited on p. 406)

[40] C. L. Lawson, R. J. Hanson, D. R. Kincaid, and F. T. Krogh. Basic linear algebra subprograms for Fortran usage. *ACM Trans. Math. Softw.*, 5(3):308–323, 1979. (Cited on pp. 158, 438)

[41] Mathematical modelling of infectious diseases. `https://en.wikipedia.org/wiki/Epidemic_model`. (Cited on p. 410)

[42] MPI forum: MPI documents. `https://www.mpi-forum.org/docs/`. (Cited on p. 211)

[43] MPL: A C++17 message passing library based on MPI. `https://github.com/rabauke/mpl`. (Cited on pp. 211, 225)

[44] Kunle Olukotun, Basem A. Nayfeh, Lance Hammond, Ken Wilson, and Kunyung Chang. The case for a single-chip multiprocessor. *SIGOPS Oper. Syst. Rev.*, 30(5):2–11, 1996. (Cited on p. 309)

[45] OpenBLAS. `https://github.com/OpenMathLib/OpenBLAS`. (Cited on p. 330)

[46] Performance Research Lab. TAU - tuning and analysis utilities. `https://www.cs.uoregon.edu/research/tau/home.php`. (Cited on p. 336)

[47] M. Pharr and W.R. Mark. ispc: A SPMD compiler for high-performance CPU programming. In *Innovative Parallel Computing (InPar), 2012*, pages 1–13, 2012. (Cited on p. 176)

[48] RedistrictingOnline.org. `https://redistrictingonline.org/`. (Cited on p. 421)

[49] S. Lin and B. Kernighan. An effective heuristic algorithm for the traveling salesman problem. *Operations Research*, 21:498–516, 1973. (Cited on p. 432)

[50] S. Shende and A. D. Malony. The tau parallel performance system. *International Journal of High Performance Computing Applications*, 20:287–331, 2006. (Cited on p. 336)

[51] SYCL specification. `https://registry.khronos.org/SYCL/`. (Cited on p. 205)

[52] Field G. Van Zee and Robert A. van de Geijn. BLIS: A framework for rapidly instantiating BLAS functionality. *ACM Trans. Math. Softw.*, 41(3):14:1–14:33, June 2015. (Cited on p. 330)

[53] VT100 user guide. `https://vt100.net/docs/vt100-ug/chapter3.html`. (Cited on p. 54)

[54] R. Vuduc, J. Demmel, and K. Yelikk. OSKI: A library of automatically tuned sparse matrix kernels. *Journal of Physics: Conference Series*, 16(1):521–530, 2005. (Cited on p. 317)

[55] Samuel Williams, Andrew Waterman, and David Patterson. Roofline: An insightful visual performance model for multicore architectures. *Commun. ACM*, 52:65–76, 2009. (Cited on p. 314)

[56] Wm. A. Wulf and Sally A. McKee. Hitting the memory wall: Implications of the obvious. *SIGARCH Comput. Archit. News*, 23(1):20–24, 1995. (Cited on p. 299)

Index

Index of C++ Keywords